The Power of Ideology

Since the Roman Empire, leaders have used ideology to organize the masses and instill amongst them a common consciousness, and equally to conquer, assimilate, or repel alternative ideologies. Ideology has been used to help create, safeguard, expand, or tear down political communities, states, empires, and regional or world systems. This book explores the multiple effects that competing ideologies have had on the world system for the past one thousand seven hundred years. The author examines the nature and content of Christianity, Islam, Confucianism, Protestantism, secularism, balance-of-power doctrine, nationalism, imperialism, anti-imperialist nationalism, liberalism, communism, fascism, Nazism, ethno-nationalism, and transnational radical Islamism; alongside the effects their originators sought to craft and the consequences they generated.

This book argues that for centuries world actors have aspired to propagate through the world arena a structure of meaning that reflected their own system of beliefs, values, and ideas. This would effectively promote and protect their material interests, and—believing their system to be superior to all others—they felt morally obliged to spread it. Radical transnational Islamism, Hybel argues, is driven by the same set of goals. This book will be of interest to students and scholars of international politics, international relations theory, history, and political philosophy.

Alex Roberto Hybel is the Susan Eckert Lynch Professor of Government at Connecticut College, USA. His most recent publications include *The Bush Administrations and Saddam Hussein: Deciding on Conflict*, and *Made by the USA: The International System*.

Routledge Advances in International Relations and Global Politics

The Power of Ideology

From the Roman Empire to Al-Qaeda

Alex Roberto Hybel

Routledge
Taylor & Francis Group

LONDON AND NEW YORK

First published 2010
by Routledge
2 Park Square, Milton Park, Abingdon, Oxon, OX14 4RN

Simultaneously published in the USA and Canada
by Routledge
711 Third Avenue, New York, NY 10017

Routledge is an imprint of the Taylor & Francis Group, an informa business

First issued in paperback 2012

© 2010 Alex Roberto Hybel

Typeset in Times New Roman by
Taylor & Francis Books

British Library Cataloguing in Publication Data
A catalogue record for this book is available from the British Library

Library of Congress Cataloging in Publication Data
Hybel, Alex Roberto.
   The power of ideology : from the Roman Empire to Al-Qaeda / Alex
Roberto Hybel.
      p. cm. – (Routledge advances in international relations and global
   politics ; 73)
   Includes bibliographical references and index.
   1. Political science–History. 2. Ideology–History. I. Title.
   JA83.H93 2009
   320.5–dc22   2008049958

ISBN13: 978-0-415-48534-0 (hbk)
ISBN13: 978-0-203-87706-7 (ebk)
ISBN13: 978-0-415-5046-5 (pbk)

Contents

Acknowledgments

I started researching and writing this book during the fall of 2002 in Japan, and completed the revisions in June of 2008 in China. I researched and wrote other portions of the manuscript in the USA and Spain. For the opportunity to conduct my work in four very different countries, I am grateful to Connecticut College; the Fulbright Foundation; Sophia University in Tokyo, Japan; the International University Studies in Seville, Spain; the General Archives of the Indies, also in Seville, Spain; and the Hopkins-Nanjing Center, in Nanjing, China.

Several individuals merit special acknowledgments for their help. As I have for nearly two decades, I remain grateful to Susan Eckert Lynch for her generous support. Three of my former students, Vasilena Ivanova, Inez Chesire Schanker, and Sheri Martin, provided extensive and valuable research material as my assistants during critical stages of the research; Vasilena in the USA, Inez in Spain, and Sheri in China. A great deal of what I have learned about Japan and its international role during the twentieth century I owe to Professors Alexis Dudden and Angus Lockyer. Dr. Daniel Garcia Contreros and Dr. Jose Carlos Janes Sanchez pointed me in the right direction while researching in Seville, Spain. The American Co-Director of the Hopkins-Nanjing Center, Jan Kiely, and Professor Hua Tao played the same role while I was completing the manuscript in Nanjing, China. A few years ago, Robert Gay encouraged me to present some of my still raw ideas to members of the Toors Cummings Center for International Studies and Liberal Arts. Discussions with him, and our colleague Professor Yibing Huang, convinced me that the task I had initiated was worthwhile concluding.

Throughout the years, many of my students read portions of my work. Several forwarded constructive comments. Justin Kaufman's, Katherine Conway's, Aaron Cantrell's, Priscilla Tan's, and Sheri Martin's insightful critiques forced me to reassess and alter some of my initial arguments. The discerning, and sometimes highly critical, observations provided by Routledge's three anonymous readers induced me to expand, re-examine, and change parts of my theoretical construct and historical analysis. My mother-in-law, Barbara Peurifoy, once again edited and re-edited the manuscript countless times. Sharon Moody helped me uncover formatting mistakes, and put together the final copies.

Friends and family make the lonely task of writing a lengthy and compli-
cated book bearable. Alexis Dudden, Robert Gay, Candace Howes, Lee Hisle,
Julie Worthen, Lee Higdon, Jose Carlos Janes Sanchez, Maribel Amarillo,
Fred Paxton, Sylvia Malizia, Jan and Susan Lindberg, Mary Devins, Tristan
Borer, John Nugent, Yibing Huang, and Erika and Jaimie Groves, merit
special thanks.

Ultimately, however, it would have been nearly impossible to finish this book
without the love, understanding, and companionship of my wife Jan, and our
two daughters, Sabrina and Gabriela. I dedicate the book to the three of them.

Stonington, Connecticut

Introduction

Between then and now—ideology's journey

"[T]he highest ideals which motivate us the most can only ever take effect in conflict with other ideals which are just as sacred to other people as ours are to us."[1]

The argument

Politics is about interests; but interests are rooted in values, beliefs, and ideas.[2] Ideology, which operates as the means to express them, plays multiple roles. Its initial one is to define the interests a group, a social class, a state, or an empire strives to create, guard, and promote.[3] To become viable, the ideology offers an explanation and an evaluation of political, economic, and social conditions; provides its holders a compass that helps orient them and develop a sense of identity; and tenders a prescription for political, economic, or social action.[4]

For more than two millennia, leaders have used ideology to organize the masses and instill among them a common consciousness; and to conquer, assimilate, or repel alternative ideologies. A common goal of powerful agents is to achieve ideological hegemony. Ideological hegemony is realized when subordinate groups accept as their own the values, beliefs, and ideas of the leading group, and when such an entity rarely has to rely on force or the threat of force to guard its position of privilege. However, when an aspiring hegemon strives to achieve ideological dominance, social groups unwilling to accept its dictates often create and propagate counter-ideologies.

In this book I present three arguments. I begin with the contention that throughout history, political leaders have used ideology to: i) create a political community; ii) transform a political community into an agent in the form of an empire or state; iii) protect or augment the power of an empire or state; iv) free a political community from an empire or state in order to establish a separate state; v) create and protect a regional or world system; vi) destroy an existing regional or world system and replace it with a new one; or vii) validate the use of violence to realize any of the aforesaid goals. I then postulate that major changes in the world arena have ensued when agents with conflicting ideologies confronted one another, when one or more agents strove to impose

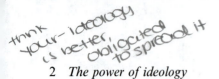
think your ideology is better, obligated to spread it

on a regional or world system their own ideologies, or when an agent's drive to create a hegemonic ideology helped induce one or more counter-ideologies. I close with the proposition that today's world system owes its existence, albeit indirectly and partially, to Confucianism; that the major thrust to impose on the world arena a particular system of beliefs, values, and ideas was initiated by Spain's monarchy in the early sixteenth century; and that though in subsequent centuries Britain and the USA relied on ideologies that differed substantially from Spain's, their intent did not. Spain, Britain, and the USA each aspired to propagate throughout the world arena a structure of meaning that reflected each of their own system of beliefs, values, and ideas. Each actor's action was driven by two interrelated ideas. Each calculated that a world system dominated by its own structure of beliefs, values, and ideas would help protect and promote its material interests. And each was convinced that because its system of beliefs, values, and ideas was vastly superior to that of others, it had a moral obligation to spread it.

World politics, constructivism, and ideology — a theoretical construct

The traditional approach to theorizing is built on the assumptions that there are regularities in the social world that can be uncovered; that the regularities can be discovered by using methodologies similar to those applied to the physical sciences; that facts and values are different; that theories are neutral about values; and that the soundness of theories can be established by focusing on facts. Neorealists have relied on the above suppositions to construct their arguments. K. Waltz has built a theory of international politics on the notion that the structure of the international system is defined by its anarchic ordering principle and the distribution of the material capabilities of its most powerful states.[5] "The structure of the system," he writes, "changes with changes in the distribution of capabilities across the system's units. And changes in structure change expectations about how the units of the system will behave and about the outcomes their interactions will produce."[6] The theory, as outlined, is designed to explain the effects generated by different types of structures on the interactions of their social actors in different moments in history. Neoliberals have posited a theory that partially competes with Neorealism. R. Keohane concurs with much of Waltz's theory but modifies it by adding that international institutions created by the system's actors constrain activities and reshape their expectations, interests, and power. Institutions assume the role of mediators, and as such they help moderate the level of competitiveness that typically arises in an anarchical international system.[7]

Because challenges to the traditional approach have taken different forms, no single rubric can capture their complete scope. Still, for present purposes I will place them, as suggested by other analysts, under the heading of "critical approaches."[8] Despite their differences, critical analysts share four intellectual orientations.[9] First, they question attempts by traditionalists to formulate objective, empirically verifiable truths. Second, instead of depending solely on the scientific method for the generation of knowledge, they advocate reliance on a plurality of approaches. Third, they view actors not as rational beings but as socially constructed identities, and contend that identities help shape interests and actions. And fourth, in addition to denying the possibility of developing value-neutral theories, they advocate the creation of theories designed to expose and dissolve the structures of domination.

The debates between traditionalists and their critics, and internally amongst critics of the traditionalist perspective, have been both intensive and extensive, but lately an alternative school of thought has gained preeminence. Generally referred to as the constructivist perspective, it has attempted to bridge some of the differences in the intellectual debate. As explained by C. Reus-Smit, the constructivist approach relies on three core arguments. It asserts that material structures do not exist independently of the identities of the social actors interpreting them; that the identities of social actors shape their interests, preferences, and actions; and that social actors and normative structures are reciprocally formed. In the words of two noted scholars: "All institutions have a structural dimension made up of one or more international relations or constitutive principles that generates socially empowered and interested state agents as a function of their respective occupancy of the positions defined by those principles."[10]

each molds the other

In short, according to constructivism, the structure of meaning takes its form through time as the system's leading actors legitimize it. A legitimized structure of meaning helps define the social identities of actors, which in turn help shape their interests and actions. Thus, the relationship between the international system's structure of meaning and the identities, interests, and actions of social actors is not unidirectional. Just as the international system's structure affects the identities, interests, and actions of social actors, they, in turn, mold the international system's structure of meaning.[11]

Though the approach I rely on throughout this study does not fit neatly in any one camp, it favors constructivism. First, I concur with those who contend that the world system is, and has always been, in a state of anarchy. So far this is a fact, not a questionable assumption. No one has yet to demonstrate that there has ever been an institution with the formal and legitimate authority to rule the world system. From this statement one ought not to infer that I assume that the world system is in a permanent state of disorder. As numerous scholars have attested, order can exist in a world system that lacks a formal and legitimate government. Second, though I acknowledge the contingent nature of knowledge, I also believe that criteria are needed to differentiate credible from far-fetched explanations of the political realm. Hence, I accept the positivists' assertion that the best one can hope for is to build theories that stand the test of time through failed falsification attempts. Third, I side with those who argue that despite the fact that the world system of today is not the world system of yesteryears, certain forms of behavior persist. It is for the analyst to uncover what has and has not changed. Fourth, while I recognize that the scientific method is the most rigorous approach to the generation of knowledge, I share the belief adhered to by many historical sociologists that the world system is too complex to be encapsulated by a very small number of factors. The analysis I present here is eclectic, and as I strive to posit a few theoretical arguments, I depend on the wisdom of a broad range of historians, anthropologists, sociologists, economists, political theorists, and political scientists. Fifth, I have not conceived the arguments that follow with the intent of reifying and legitimizing some existing order, or exposing and dissolving structures of domination. If either purpose is inferred, it is solely the result of the reader's imagination. As an analyst, I reserve the right to remain emotionally and ethically unattached, and to be inspired solely by questions that intrigue me. And sixth, like historical sociologists and social constructivists, I view actors as agents with socially constructed identities, and argue that their identities help shape interests and actions. Moreover, I second the constructivists' claim that the identities of social actors, along with their interests and actions, shape the world system's structure of meaning and it, in turn, helps shape the identities of the social actors.[12]

If one endorses the last contention, it is logical to ask: what concept does one use to represent a world system's structure of meaning, the socially constructed identities of its actors, and the relationship between the two? Based on Max Weber's assertion that humans "are cultural beings with the capacity and will to take a deliberate attitude toward the world and to lend it significance,"[13] constructivists contend that actions initiated by world agents are culturally constituted. Anchored in this general affirmation and the claim that culture refers to the cumulative deposit of knowledge that has been socially transmitted, constructivists posit a set of interrelated arguments. By acting on the basis of shared knowledge and expectations, actors reaffirm in certain cases, and reproduce in other instances, knowledge and expectations. Under particular conditions, the reaffirmation and reproduction of knowledge and expectations can transform the structure of the world system by altering its culture. This transformation can, in turn, change the culture of other agents in the system and, consequently, their future actions.[14]

To validate his constructivist approach and exhibit some of Neorealism's limitations, Alexander Wendt uses culture to explain transformations undergone by the structure of the international system and the effects they have had in the way states have interacted.[15] Neorealism's shortcomings, argues Wendt, are caused by its assumptions that the structure of the international system is defined solely by its material capabilities and that it has never had an agent acknowledged by its members to possess the authority, legitimacy, and power to rule it. By emphasizing only those two conditions, Neorealists overlook that since the Treaty of Westphalia the structure of the international system has undergone two measurable cultural alterations. These changes modified the structure of the international system, which in turn affected state interactions. Prior to the seventeenth century, international actors lived in "a Hobbesian culture," where the logic of anarchy was "kill or be killed" and agents were constantly preparing for war or were at war. This logic, continues Wendt, began to change after 1648. "The kill or be killed logic of the Hobbesian state of nature," began to be "replaced by the live and let live logic of the Lockean anarchical society." Under the previous logic, actors viewed one another as enemies; under the new culture they began to regard each other as rivals. This distinction is critical. Rivals, unlike enemies, acknowledge the significance of sovereignty. Sovereignty, in the Lockean culture, is viewed as a right. Each actor has the right to some property. This means that sovereignty is more than material property; it also stands for a set of shared ideas and expectations about how they should treat and interact with one another. The effect of this change, continues Wendt, has been significant. Under the new international culture the death rate of states became almost nil; small states prospered; inter-state war became rare and normally limited; and territorial boundaries were "hardened."[16] During the twentieth century, particularly after the end of the Second World War, the structure of the international system, at least in the North Atlantic region, started to be replaced by what Wendt calls a "Kantian culture." This new culture is dominated by two norms: non-violence and team-play. Its effect has been noteworthy. Since late 1945, states in the North Atlantic region have consistently operated as a "security team" and have not resorted to violence to address their differences.[17]

Though sympathetic to Wendt's contention that culture matters, I am not persuaded that it helps us explain some of the critical changes experienced by the world system and the effects the transformations had on its structure of meaning and on the relationships between its members. A brief analysis of three historical trends should help explain my misgivings.

Following Napoleon's ascension to power in the late eighteenth century, France launched a series of invasions, most of which were designed to enlarge its territorial capacity. Political scientists generally concur that Europe's central leaders gathered at the Congress of Vienna in 1815 to reaffirm the concept of sovereignty and to try to prevent, via the shared adoption of a balance-of-power doctrine, attempts to replicate Napoleon's behavior. What political scientists often overlook is that amongst those who sought to endorse the concept of sovereignty were leaders who feared that emerging nationalist sentiments could lead to the disintegration of their empires and the formation of new nation-states. As subsequent developments would demonstrate, particularly after 1848, their apprehension was justified.[18]

This case highlights a couple of potential challenges to Wendt's argument. To start with, it casts doubt on the relevance of Lockean culture during the period of transition between the eighteenth and nineteenth centuries by demonstrating that Napoleon was not willing to conform to it. One could try to refute this objection with two counter-arguments. First, one might rely on Kenneth Waltz's claim that system theory is designed to explain not the foreign policy action of any one agent but the overall interaction that takes place between them. The problem with this refutation is that it discounts the very important role individual agents are assumed to play in creating the culture that characterizes the structure of the world system. A substantially more effective way of dismissing the challenge is by noting that what guided the response of those actors who allied against Napoleon was their commitment to defend the Lockean culture.

Wendt's argument does not fare as well when the focus switches to the inability of an agent to protect itself from internal groups that question its legitimacy. During part of the nineteenth century and early years of the twentieth century, nationalist groups within the Austrian and Ottoman Empires sought to create their own independent sovereign states. Their actions reflected a contradiction that cannot be captured by culture alone, for it was spawned by the concurrent beliefs of distinct national groups that it was their right to question the legitimacy of well-established sovereign agents and create their own separate sovereign nation-states. The culture of sovereignty, in other words, functioned as a force that generated at the same time opposition and aspiration when it encountered nationalism. This objection cannot be set aside with the claim that in every international system each sovereign agent is assumed to be a unitary actor. In the nineteenth century, not every actor possessed the power and authority to act as a unitary entity. By discarding this fact, the analyst purges a critical source of tension that could help explicate changes in the system's structure of capabilities and of meaning during that period.

The second case refers to the way the Lockean culture was spread throughout the international system. Wendt concedes that Europe's leading actors unintentionally spread the culture throughout the globe via colonialism. The problem is that by focusing on culture—or, more specifically, on the Lockean culture—Wendt seems to think that the contradictions spawned by the spread of the Lockean culture via colonialism do not weaken his overall argument. I will address the issue in a later chapter; for the time being, I will simply summarize my concerns. First, it is important to emphasize that during the nineteenth century the Lockean culture might have sought to define the structure of meaning of Europe and parts of the Western Hemisphere, but not of the international system. From Europe's perspective, sovereignty and legitimacy were concepts that did not apply to Africa and a great number of Asian actors. A perusal of Article 22 of the Covenant of the League Nations shows that even after the end of the First World War the West, with Japan's participation, continued to dictate which entities should be extended the right to become sovereign agents and which ones would remain as mandates, that is, actors that would require external supervision or control because they were insufficiently "civilized."[19] Second, an analysis of the ideas relied on by several European agents, the USA, and Japan to design, justify, and promote their imperialist and colonialist policies reveal the growth of a structure of meaning more complex and rich than the one envisioned by Wendt. Imperialism and colonialism did more than export a Lockean culture; they also engendered anti-imperialism, anti-colonialism, and nationalism. As the latter ideas gained currency, they redefined the Lockean culture, and thus the world system's structure of meaning. More than a century ago, nationalism was not embedded in the Lockean culture; today, it nearly is. In yesteryears anti-imperialist sentiment helped defined the Lockean culture only when targets of imperialism were Western entities; today the attitude is directed toward all actors.

The third case is both similar to, and different from, the first one. Germany, Italy, and Japan went to war, in part, to augment their territorial power by violating the sovereignty of other actors. Their actions, just like Napoleon's more than a century earlier, challenged the legitimacy of the Lockean culture. More importantly, the leaders of Germany, Italy, and Japan constructed their imperialist policies on the idea that as members of superior civilizations it was their right to impose their will on others. This belief ran contrary to the idea that informed the Lockean culture, which according to Wendt was, and continues to be, guided by the assumption that though agents will sometimes use violence to settle disputes, they will do so within "live and let live" limits.[20]

My intent here is not to discredit the significance of culture. My single objective has been to contend that culture, as a definer of the international system's structure of meaning, has limited explanatory value. Its principal shortcoming is that it fails to capture tensions that might arise within the same culture or by forces that challenge it. By failing to expose tensions within and outside the culture, new and old, advocates of culture as a critical dimension of international politics unintentionally brush aside its dynamic nature. This particular shortcoming becomes more evident when one asks: what factor or set of factors spawned the two changes in the culture of meaning identified by Wendt? Though Wendt emphasizes the need to explain changes, his analytical perspective cannot help explain why the world system's structure of meaning changed and is presently undergoing a new transformation.[21]

I concur with Constructivists that material and ideational forces define the world system, that its structure of meaning has changed through the centuries, and that this change might have affected the behavior of states. The focus of my analysis, however, is not only on how different structures of meaning have affected the behavior of world's actors, but also on how agents sought to create structures of meaning for a political community, an empire, a state, a regional system, and a world system. More to the point, my investigation is built on the contention that in order to comprehend the effect a world system's structure of meaning has on the actions of agents, it is first necessary to understand who were the actors that strove to build it, and what structure of meaning they designed for their own political community, empire, or state. Stated in the context of an example, one cannot explicate the world system's structure of meaning during the Cold War era and its effects without first delineating the competing structures of meaning its chief actors, the USA and the Soviet Union, sought to impose on the world system.

For centuries, ideas have been used to bring together different groups in order to create an agent that stands as a unit in a regional or world system. Many of today's states became states through the infusion of nationalism. As Waltz notes, "the growth of nationalism is synonymous with the integration of the masses into a common political form."[22] Scores of entities that became states first had to free themselves from states or empires that claimed the right to rule them. To achieve this end, their leaders relied on nationalism to create lucid categories, discourses, and symbols that could connect discrete social networks into a single category.[23] To rephrase Fiona Adamson's commentary regarding the emergence of the Algerian state, in a great number of contemporary cases, before there was a state, there was a movement bounded by a nationalist ideology.[24] Political leaders have also used nationalism to avert the breakup of empires or states, but not always effectively. France's leaders, in their efforts to retain control of Algeria, relied on French nationalism to convey the sentiment that "Algerians" were French, thus no different from those who resided in continental France.

Nationalism, however, is not the only idea political leaders have brought into play to create states or empires, or protect them. In the fourth century, Constantine drew on Christianity to try to prevent the demise of the Roman Empire. Several centuries later, Muslim leaders counted on Islamic beliefs, values, and ideas to help conceive one of history's largest empires. The aspirations of political leaders, moreover, have sometimes transcended the boundaries of states and empires. On more than one occasion, they aimed to infuse the domain of their regional system, or the world system itself, with ideas that personified their own state or empire. In the mid-sixteenth century, the king of Spain relied on Christianity to colonize large parts of the southern half of the Western Hemisphere, and tried to create a world system imbued with its values. He did not succeed, but his failure did not dissuade others from pursuing the same goals, albeit guided by different beliefs, values, and ideas. Few cases epitomize better this development than Britain's actions during the nineteenth century, and those initiated by the USA and the Soviet Union during the Cold War era. Each agent's leading goal was to impose on the world system a structure of meaning that reflected its leading beliefs, values, and ideas.

Multiple political beliefs, values, and ideas have inhabited the world arena at any one time, but few have had appreciable effects on the actions of states or empires, or the structure of a regional or world system. Those agents whose beliefs, values, and ideas have had measurable effects, moreover, often have inadvertently persuaded other agents to advocate contending beliefs, values, and ideas. For example, though at the end of the First World War liberalism and communism were still nascent doctrines, their rapid growth and dispersion throughout the world system helped strengthen fascism and Nazism. For the next twenty years, representatives of each doctrine struggled to determine which state would create the world system's structure of meaning. Victory by the USA and the Soviet Union did not bring the battle to an end; it merely narrowed the sets of beliefs, values, and ideas competing for prominence in the world system. Nor did the end of the Cold War give way to the unobstructed spread of liberalism throughout the world system. By the year 2008, many actors vied, if not for the privilege to be the sole definer of the world system's structure of meaning, at least for the right to prevent the USA from imposing its beliefs, values, and ideas on them. Some of those actors strove to revive old values, beliefs, and ideas; others advocated new ones.

Ideology has earned a place amongst the most controversial terms in contemporary political science. Ever since Napoleon Bonaparte, after his short-lived love affair with the ideologues, acerbically renounced ideology, the word acquired certain derogatory connotation, tinges of which have persisted until today. It is commonly assumed that as a concept, ideology has a modern origin. It is viewed as "the product of the social, political, and intellectual upheavals that accompanied the Industrial Revolution: the spread of democratic ideals, the politics of mass movements, the idea that, since we have made the world, we can also remake it."[25] As the reader will have surmised from my discourse so far, I outright reject this contention. I acknowledge that ideology's conceptualization is modern; its use, however, is not.

My theoretical framework takes some of its clues from M. Mann, A. Gramsci, and M. Rejai's works. It is built on the contention that though power and ideology are distinct concepts, in the political arena they are tightly interconnected. Humans, as Mann notes, do not seek power for the sake of being powerful. Power materializes when an agent tries to fulfill a need. Power in general refers to the "ability to pursue and attain goals through mastery of one's environment." Social power is a narrower concept; it represents the "mastery of other people." Social power can be differentiated according to its extensive or intensive reach. Extensive power denotes the capacity to organize large groups of people over a very large region with the purpose of either generating a modicum of cooperation or minimizing conflict. Intensive power, in turn, stands for the "ability to organize tightly and command a high level of mobilization or commitment from the participants, whether the area and numbers covered are great or small."[26]

Power has multiple resources; most international relations scholars, however, have focused on its material elements. Power-based theories designed by Realists, Neorealists, and orthodox Marxists consider almost exclusively the role of coercion and force as the base of control and domination. Gramsci's analysis of ideology enables us to challenge this narrow perspective.[27] In the 1930s, Gramsci sought to explain why capitalism had continued to thrive in the bourgeois democracies of the West. He identified two different forms of political control: domination and ideological hegemony. Domination, he argued, refers to the use of physical coercion. However, no regime, regardless of how strong it is, can constantly depend on its material capabilities to sustain itself. To perpetuate its control, the regime had to infuse on its subjects its own system of beliefs, values, and ideas. In time, the system of beliefs, values, and ideas is so internalized by the regime's subjects that they view the philosophy, culture, and morality of the ruling class as the natural order of things.[28] Mann concurs with the general tone of Gramsci's work, and goes beyond.

According to Mann, power can be divided into four resources: ideological, economic, military, and organizational. "The struggle to control ideological, economic, military, and political organizations provides the central drama of social development."[29] He relies on three related arguments to delineate the nature of ideological power. First, to understand and act upon the world, humans must impose on the sense perceptions of others, concepts and categories of meaning. Any agent who monopolizes the right to conceptualize meaning possesses power. Second, in order to sustain cooperation, humans must have norms; they must know how they should act morally in their relations to one another. Historically, religions have been the principal carrier of shared normative understandings. Gramsci concurs. He refers to religions as organic ideologies. They function as the backbone of society in that they "organize human masses, and create the terrain on which men move, acquire consciousness of their position, struggle, etc."[30] Third, groups that monopolize meaning, norms, and aesthetic and ritual practices, possess considerable extensive and intensive power.[31] In short, control "of an ideology that combines meanings, values, norms, aesthetics, and rituals brings general social power."[32]

At this stage it would be justifiable to conceptualize the term ideology. Readers who have long adhered to Realism or Neorealism's central tenets, however, may still be disinclined to accept ideology's relevance in "real-life" world politics. It behooves me, thus, to address in a summary form some of the concerns raised by representatives of both schools. The chapters that follow should, I hope, address in greater detail whatever trepidations they might still have.

During much of the Cold War, Realists, and subsequently Neorealists, argued that the leaders of the Soviet Union did not believe in Marxist–Leninist ideology. They generally contended that the pressures of the anarchic system forced the Soviet Union, just like the USA, to strive for security above all other objectives.[33] N. Gould-Davies refutes their argument by noting that new sources, never intended for public scrutiny, demonstrate that Soviet officials took ideology very seriously. Though his disclosure is helpful, of much greater value, at least for present purposes, is his step-by-step challenge to claims by Realists that an agent's ideology has little impact on its actions. In a detailed analysis he identifies several ways in which analysts misconstrue the role of ideology. For the sake of brevity, I will identify them and add a short explanation.

A state guided by ideology need not have, as often assumed, a fixed, unalterable, master plan. To identify a specific set of goals is very different from claiming complete knowledge about how to achieve them. Ideologues do not discard the significance of uncertainty. Though they may want to execute a particular plan, many of them are cognizant that if they hope to succeed in an uncertain world they must be flexible. Not all ideologues need to be incessantly aggressive; sometimes they can cooperate with their adversaries. Despite the fact that at some point ideologues must ask whether their willingness to compromise and cooperate with adversaries indicates that their original ideology no longer defines their goals, such a conclusion cannot be inferred without a thorough analysis through time of many policy steps. One would have great difficulty proving that Moscow's collaboration with Washington during the Second World War was indicative that the Soviets had abandoned Marxist–Leninist ideology. During that period the domestic political, economic, and social structure of the Soviet Union remained unchanged. The same claim cannot be made about China's commitment to communist ideology following Mao Zedong's death. Though China's political, economic, and social structures have not changed at the same pace, the three are dramatically different from what they were thirty years ago. Its regime's willingness to adopt a quasi-open market economy and allow the swelling of class inequality discredits any attempt on its part to claim that its actions are driven by the same ideology that guided it during Mao's era. Lastly, it is a fallacy to argue that ideology and security are mutually exclusive and, thus, that they function as alternative terms of explanation. The security of the USA is tightly related not just to the material conditions of the state and its people, but also to the beliefs, values, and ideas that have defined them for more than two centuries. It may be possible to argue that, faced with the certainty of complete annihilation by the Soviet Union, the leaders and people of the USA would have agreed some thirty years ago to adopt the beliefs, values, and ideas that typified communism. But that extreme case does not undermine the contention that the security of the USA is related to its ideology.[34]

Conceptualizations of ideology are abundant. Instead of conducting an extensive evaluation of alternative characterizations, I will discuss Rejai's. His description and classification capture ideology's central objectives and components. According to Rejai, a good conceptualization of ideology must be neutral rather than critical, sufficiently precise but not overly restrictive, and operational. Ideology, he explained, covers five dimensions: the cognitive, the affective, the evaluative, the programmatic, and the social base.[35] The cognitive dimension refers to the way ideology perceives the social and the political environment. Each world view is composed of facts and fiction, knowledge and belief. The basic distinction between knowledge and belief is that the first one is subject to the rules of logic and can be tested, while beliefs are notions about society and politics that are accepted without specific and testable empirical evidence. Each ideology, moreover, relies on myths and distorts reality. As Karl Marx and Frederick Engels wrote in *The German Ideology*, "in all ideologies men and their circumstances appear upside down as in a *camera obscura*."[36] Karl Mannheim presented a related argument in his *Ideology and Utopia* when he proposed that each ideology is made up of

"more or less conscious disguises of the real nature of a situation." And in
Power and Society, Harold Lasswell and Abraham Kaplan made a similar
point when they referred to ideology as "the political myth" created in order
"to preserve the social structure."[37] The communication of ideology and its
myth or myths is achieved through simplification. Simplification, in turn, is
attained through the use of both linguistic and non-linguistic symbols that
"capture in economical fashion large expanses of meanings and communicate
these meanings in an instantaneous fashion."[38]

Each ideology has an emotive dimension—it appeals to sentiments and
strives to elicit an emotional response from its followers. As explained by D.
Bell, "what gives ideology its force is its passion ... in fact, the most important, latent, function of ideology is to tap emotion."[39] To contend that each
ideology has an emotive element is not to argue that reason is totally absent
from all ideologies. The balance between reason and emotion can vary from
one ideology to another. Some ideologies are more prone than others to
accept information that disputes its beliefs; such variance is in part determined by the centrality of the beliefs.

The evaluative dimension refers to ideology's normative functions. Every
ideology both denounces an existing social and political condition, and
advances an alternative set of norms. Whether an ideology is designed to
protect or transform an existing social and political order, it attempts to
evoke a sense of rage, injustice, and moral protest against its counterpart. The
attack is typically presented as a justified response to the presumed lack of
morality on the part of the intended target. The normative propositions are
generally disguised as factual statements and always directed towards the
creation of a better social and political order. All ideologies are action oriented. To a greater or lesser degree, depending on the ideology's level of flexibility, they all demand consistency between principles and behavior. The
fourth dimension—that is, the programmatic dimension—focuses on how
each ideology strives to translate values into active commitments. Each
ideology sets forth, implicitly or explicitly, a hierarchy of values and objectives, and each sometimes includes statements of priorities identifying
immediate, intermediate, and ultimate goals.[40]

Lastly, with regard to the social-base dimension, each ideology is associated
with a social group, class, collectivity, or nation; it must have some type of
mass appeal. An ideology's rationale, goals, and objectives are presented to a
social group, class, collectivity, or nation in a relatively simple and under-
standable way for the purpose of drawing out from it a commitment to
action. Mobilization demands organization, which is generated by an elite.
The ideology of the elite is always more sophisticated than the ideology of the
masses. The elite are more effective at articulating the ideology's belief system
than the masses, because they have a deeper and more coherent understanding of its structures of meaning. The extent to which the elite can use
ideology to manipulate and control the masses is partly dependent on the
ideology's degree of openness and flexibility.[41]

Based on the above five dimensions, Rejai conceptualized the term as follows:

> Political ideology is an emotion-laden, myth-saturated, action-related system of beliefs and values about people and society, legitimacy and authority, that is acquired to a large extent as a matter of faith and habit. The myths and values of ideology are communicated through symbols in a simplified, economical, and efficient manner. Ideological beliefs are more or less coherent, more or less articulate, more or less open to new evidence and information. Ideologies have a high potential for mass mobilization, manipulation, and control; in that sense, they are mobilized belief systems.[42]

Ideologies perform six functions for individuals, groups, or governments. First, they set forth standards of behavior by providing rationales for deeds, giving order to surrounding life, and explaining the world's ambiguities. Second, they give individuals identity and a sense of belonging. Third, they bring solidarity and cohesion to society. Fourth, they generate optimism. Fifth, they enable the manipulation and control of the masses. And finally, they help protect, challenge, or, occasionally, destroy an existing political system.[43]

The above arguments about, and descriptions of, ideology can be linked as follows. Self-interest, to paraphrase Max Weber, is common to all ages and thus requires no explanation. Throughout history, however, self-interest took different forms, and the changes were cultivated by different beliefs, values, and moral standards. In each instance, as explained by Gramsci, a particular social group created within itself one or more strata of intellectuals who gave it homogeneity and an awareness of its own function in the political, economic, and social fields. Typically, the social group used ideology to organize the masses and instill among them a common consciousness, and to conquer, assimilate, or repel any alternative ideology. The end goal of every major social set was to achieve ideological hegemony. Ideological hegemony was realized when subordinate groups accepted as their own the moral, political, and cultural values of the leading group, and when such a group seldom had to rely on force to guard its place of privilege. As noted by L. Althusser, historically, ideology was used to create, solidify, and protect a system of social dominance. It was, and continues to be, the skeleton of every social order, and it is unlikely to disappear.

Theoretical–historical abstract

For much of the past two millennia, the most common political community has been the empire. Historically, the birth and expansion of an empire was spawned by the power aspirations of its leaders and the need to curb the risks and uncertainty produced by the environment of the greater region. The shared reasoning was that the augmentation of territory would bring about an increase in power, which in turn would yield a less chaotic and unstable regional milieu. Leaders of empires recognized early on that the recurring use of military or economic coercion to protect their realms and to regulate the activities of their respective inhabitants was costly. As a result, they concluded that they could achieve both goals via the propagation of a common set of values and attitudes, and by the establishment of comprehensive rules of behavior.

Religion was one of the first non-material means brought into play by leaders to help create, protect, and enlarge empires.[44] Leaders relied on religion to identify things that were essentially wrong and inadequate about human existence, and on its myths and simplifications to analyze the causes of social problems. They used religion to organize the masses, to instill among them a common consciousness and a rationale for being, and to provide solutions.[45] Religion was Christianity's first design, but leaders of the Roman Empire in the fourth century amplified its reach by also making it a political ideology. Islam, on the other hand, was instituted as both a religion and a political tool. With Islam functioning as both a religious precept and an ideological tool, Muslims changed a non-Islamic community into an Islamic one, and then transformed it into an Islamic Empire.[46] Muslims were amongst the first to demonstrate that an empire's power reach is measured not just by overt material acts of control, but also "by the degree to which the values, attitudes and institutions of the expansionist nation infiltrate and overcome those of the recipient one."[47]

The clash between Christianity and Islam spawned, intermittently, highly destructive wars for more than a thousand years. The apogees of these struggles were the Christian crusades. Then, in the fifteenth century, leaders at opposite ends of the globe used ideology to narrow and broaden their political horizons. Their incongruous actions helped transform the nature and structure of the modern world system. After the 1430s, China's leaders solidified their Confucian conviction that trade and travel to distant lands were objectionable traits. Their system of beliefs, values, and ideas helped bring to an end the maritime adventures the empire had launched at the start of the century, and reduced measurably its naval capacity. Unbeknownst to China's leaders, their actions inadvertently transferred the power to transform the world system to some of their European counterparts. Unobstructed by an empire noticeably stronger than theirs, Spain, Britain, and to a lesser extent Portugal and the Dutch Republics, became the leading creators and propagators of ideas that eventually would help convert a political community into an empire; create a new political community; alter a political community's political, economic, and social structure; develop regional and global systems; and justify war.

Throughout different parts of the Americas, Spain's monarchs fell back on Catholic precepts to rationalize their imperial behavior, whereas Britain relied on newly invented Protestant norms to justify its own colonial acts. In the late eighteenth century, political leaders in Britain's American colonies sought to create a new sovereign state based on the then unique ideals of freedom and equality. During the following century, Mexico and the newly liberated states in Central and South America tried, with limited success, to appropriate many of the values and beliefs fueled by the American and French revolutions to structure their own political regimes. On the other side of the Atlantic, through much of Europe, political leaders aroused nationalist sentiments to break up empires and create new sovereign nation-states, or to shape separate kingdoms that shared a common nationality into a nation-state. Simultaneously, many of them used a mixture of Christianity and nationalism to encourage and justify the transformation of Africa and parts of South and Southeast Asia into colonies.

Nationalism and balance-of-power doctrine clashed in 1914 and brought about the First World War. Twenty years after the "war to end all wars" had ended, another catastrophic war erupted. The Second World War was more than a global struggle between powerful entities, each striving to guard or enlarge its own sphere of dominance. It was also a struggle between actors with incongruous ideologies, each determined to shield and expand the reach of its own state's system of beliefs, values, and ideas. The defeat of fascism and Nazism in 1945 did not engender a less ideological world arena. The Cold War that followed became a competition between two actors with clashing ideologies, each determined to impose on the international system its own unique structure of meaning. During that same period, a less-observed struggle proceeded throughout most of Africa and parts of South and Southeast Asia. One colony after another resorted to nationalism to unchain itself from its colonial ruler and create its own state. In many of those cases, the joy produced by the recently gained independence soon gave way to the sorrow engendered by the emergence of ethnicity as an ideological tool.

At the end of the Cold War many influential figures predicted that the USA would be able to propagate its market-democracy ideology unendingly and with little opposition throughout the world system. Violent events soon forced them to concede their mistake. A wide range of nationalist, ethnic, and religious fundamentalist groups sought to ensure, in many cases with the aid of force, that their own claims would be heeded. By the start of the twenty-first century it had become evident that the USA's efforts to create a world according to its ideological tenets would not go unchallenged and would be costly. Whether its endeavor will pay off in the long run remains unclear.

The interaction between ideology and politics that has ensued in the world arena since the early decades of the fourth century can be captured in the form of propositions.

The construction and protection of a political community, be it in the form of a state, an empire, or a non-state actor, necessitates the creation, propagation, and enforcement of rules designed to control the behavior of the members of the community. The values, beliefs, and ideas embedded in the ideology of the leaders of the political community shape its rules of behavior.

Syria
rebels vs. gov't
different ideas

A state's rules of behavior sometimes engender deep dissatisfaction among some of its citizens. Any effort by a group of citizens to break away from, restructure, or destroy the state is headed by the creation and diffusion of an ideology that tries to draw mass support within, and sometimes outside, the state, and that mirrors the values and beliefs of the leaders of the insurgent group.

An empire's rules of behavior eventually generate intense discontent among some of its members. Any attempt by one or more actors to break away from, restructure, or destroy the empire is preceded by the conceptualization and dissemination of an ideology that tries to attract mass support within, and sometimes outside, the empire, and that reflects the values, beliefs, and ideas of the leaders of the discordant group.

The construction and protection of a regional or world system necessitates the creation, propagation, and enforcement of rules designed to direct the interaction between the system's independent political communities. The values, beliefs, and ideas embedded in the ideology of the leaders of the regional world system shape its rules of behavior.

Any attempt on the part of two or more powerful actors with contradictory and conflicting ideologies to create a regional or world system that reflects their distinct values, beliefs, and ideas eventually generates tensions that could result in a major war.

Every regional or world system demarcated by rules of behavior embedded in the ideology of its most powerful actor or actors in due course experiences challenges from disgruntled members. The restructuring or destruction of the system is preceded by the conceptualization and dissemination of an ideology that reflects the values and beliefs of the leading insurgent political community or communities, and by the gathering of support from other political communities.

Structure of the book

A comprehensive analysis of the multiple effects of ideology on world politics is beyond the scope of this study. To conduct such an analysis, I would have to reach far into the first millennium before the Common Era for it was during that period that ideological power resources developed considerably.[48] My analytical objective is both different and narrower. It is driven, in part, by the wish to bring to light the sources of the ideological structure that define, and contradictions that affect, today's world system. Chapter 1 begins with a probe of the Roman and Islamic Empires, and the religions they relied on, respectively—Christianity and Islam—to further their political interests. The analysis is accompanied by an examination of the effects their rivalry had on their own regional system in the seventh and eighth centuries.[49] It continues with an investigation of the rise and demise of the Frankish Empire in Western Europe, and the way the events helped strengthen feudalism and enabled the Christian church to use Christianity as an ideology to pursue its political objectives. Because ideology served as a driving force in other regions besides Europe and the Middle East, the last section focuses on Confucianism, its effects on China's actions in the world arena at the start of the fifteenth century, and the indirect impact of China's decision on the world system's structure of meaning.

Chapter 2 discusses the ideological contradictions that ensued during the fifteenth, sixteenth, and seventeenth centuries. Spain's triumph over Islam toward the end of the fifteenth century rejuvenated Christianity's original imperialist undertone and served as a rationale, not for the maritime voyages that led members of the Iberian peninsula to the "new world," but for the way they justified their actions and administered the lands they stumbled onto and the people who inhabited them. During this period, the Dutch members of Spain's European dominion sought to free themselves from their foreign rulers, inspired by the belief that to prosper commercially their intensely independent provinces had to be united by social discipline and religious toleration. Devotion to this belief system helped the Dutch gain the status of a major power during the seventeenth century. A third critical actor was the Ottoman Empire. By the start of the fifteenth century, the Ottomans had gained control of much of the Balkan Peninsula. The territories and the very institutions of the empire they created were, in a sense, successors to the Byzantine Empire. This time, however, the new empire, despite its willingness to accept the practice of different cultures and traditions, rooted its legitimacy in Islam.[50] Islam's principal political role was to provide unity and strength to a very large empire.[51] Though not adverse to jihad, its leaders relied on it only if they felt the world of Islam was threatened. In time, the West learned to accept this new reality, and both sides became amenable to averting conflict via accommodation.[52]

During this period, the manifestation of secular realism and the fragmentation of Christianity throughout other parts of Europe helped bring feudalism to an end, facilitated the development of the idea that states are sovereign entities, and spawned a new ideology—reason of state. What is more, Spain's transatlantic success did not go unnoticed throughout Europe. By the end of the seventeenth century, English colonists had occupied other parts of the Americas.[53] Though England's material intent differed little from Spain's, the kind of Christianity it relied on to justify its actions did.

Chapter 3 explains how the ideologies that became part of the political arena during the 1750–1871 period materialized, and how they affected the world system and its actors. Given that the period was remarkably complex, the chapter shifts directions a number of times. It begins with an analysis of the ideology that motivated the inhabitants of the English–American colonies to gain independence and the measures they took to attain it. The chapter then alters course in order to focus on the decision by Europe's leading actors after the French Revolution and the end of the Napoleonic wars to adopt a balance-of-power doctrine, the steady rise of nationalism throughout Europe, and the strain on the European system spawned by the confrontation between these two ideologies. Though the stress induced by the simultaneous presence of both belief systems continued to grow steadily, the chapter switches direction once again in order to scrutinize another very important development. The third section discusses Britain's drive during the nineteenth century to create a world economic system and become its hegemon, and the ideology that defined its actions. Europe was not the only region experiencing substantial changes during the nineteenth century. The next-to-last section focuses on the divergent transformations the Americas underwent as the century aged, and the ideologies adhered to by its leading actors. The chapter closes with an overall assessment of the material and ideological tensions afflicting the world system at the beginning of the 1870s.

Chapter 4 is divided into three parts. The first section resumes the analysis of the contradictions and tensions generated by Europe's adherence to the balance-of-power ideology and nationalism throughout the post-1871 period. It addresses the way the clash between the two ideologies eventually spawned a world conflict that brought to an end the Austrian and the Ottoman Empires, and disrupted Germany's continental aspirations. Special attention is given to the failed effort on the part of the leaders of the Ottoman Empire to counter the forces of nationalism with a renewed emphasis on Islamism. The second section explores the imperialist and nationalist methods and ideologies employed by Europe's central actors, along with the USA and Japan, to enlarge their military power and economic gains throughout parts of Latin America, Asia, and Africa.

Imperialism involuntarily set in motion nationalist anti-colonial ideologies among those who had become its victims.[54] The third section of Chapter 4 discusses the initial attempts by four different targets of imperialism to combat it with their own home-brewed nationalism. The chapter closes with an assessment of the 1920s world system and a summary of the tensions that hampered it. The conclusion serves as a gateway to the next chapter.

It is not uncommon for political scientists and historians to view the period between 1919 and the early 1990s as two distinct periods, with 1945 functioning as the dividing point. Chapter 5 views the period between 1919 and the early 1990s as a continuous ideological struggle. The chapter takes its clues from Isaiah Berlin's declaration that one of the outstanding characteristics of the twentieth century has been the "great ideological storms that... altered the lives of virtually all mankind."[55] In the 1930s, the Soviet Union was the principal advocate of communism, the USA was the chief proponent of free-market democracy, Japan adhered to fascism, and Germany was guided by Nazi precepts.[56] During the Second World War, the leading voices of the first two ideologies joined forces to battle and defeat the adherents of the last two. With the war behind them, the USA and the Soviet Union rapidly ignored their earlier alliance and competed with one another for political and ideological dominance of the world system. Some forty-five years later, communism endured Nazism's and fascism's earlier fate. Chapter 5 discusses the structures of meaning that gave rise to the four ideologies, the circumstances that helped foment the enmity between the advocates of each ideology, the conditions that spawned the defeat of Nazism, fascism, and communism, and the transformations the world system underwent as the rivalry between the entities ensued. Since advocates of Realism and Neorealism are likely to question the idea of viewing the 1919–early 1990s period as anextended ideological struggle, the chapter also counters some of their objections.

Chapter 6 is divided into four sections. With no one else to challenge the USA's hegemonic status at the end of the Cold War, Washington launched a campaign designed to impose its beliefs, values, and principles on the entire world system. The first section of the chapter discusses the nature of Washington's ideological drive. In its fervor to spread its vision worldwide, Washington failed to consider that there might still exist ideological incongruities lingering from the previous era, and that its decrees and actions might generate ideological counteractions from disgruntled actors. Throughout the 1950s, 1960s, and parts of the 1970s, Africans relied on anti-colonial nationalism to free themselves from Western domination. Shortly after the European powers had departed, Africans replaced their control with a very narrow form of self-identity—ethnicity. The increased focus on ethnicity gave way to the creation and development of weak and volatile African states. The second section examines these developments.

The third section of Chapter 6 concentrates on attempts by different sets of actors to offset the USA's doctrinarian measures with their own distinct ideological articulations. It is divided into two parts. The first part analyzes the steady increase in popularity of leftist populism throughout parts of Latin America as an antidote to Washington's neoliberal policies. The emergence of a Latin American populist counterforce undermined, at least temporarily, Washington's master plan to redesign the region's beliefs, values, and principles and, thus, its policies. The second part of the third section examines the rise of radical Islamic fundamentalism and the shift in strategy its leaders designed and advocated in the 1990s and the first decade of the twenty-first century.

The world system of the early twenty-first century is much more complex than many scholars had predicted it would be. Certainly the USA remains the world system's leading actor, and its capability to project its ideology is still unmatched, but the challenges it faces are considerable. The last section of Chapter 6 closes with a discussion of the problems the USA will encounter in the near future.

Chapter 7 revisits the various arguments postulated throughout the book. A summary re-examination of the various chapters reaffirms the contention that to understand changes in the structure of the world system, it is imperative to expose the nature of the ideologies that drove the actions of a variety of actors and the tensions that competing systems of beliefs and values generated within political entities, states, empires, and regional and international systems. The chapter closes with an appraisal of the perils engendered by the failure to study ideologies that may seem at first glance irrelevant to the challenges afflicting the globe.

1 Political ideology in late antiquity and the Middle Ages

He who fights so the word of God may prevail is on the path of God.[1]

Introduction

Probably no leader in antiquity captured the relationship between ideology and foreign policy more eloquently than Pericles in the funeral oration he delivered at the burial of the first Athenian soldiers killed in the war between Athens and Sparta. According to Pericles, the Athenian soldiers who died perished to defend a political ideal, a democratic way of life. My interest, however, is not motivated by the desire to locate the period when a set of political leaders first used ideology as a foreign policy instrument. As already noted, one of my intellectual aims is to bring to light the sources of the ideological structures that define, and contradictions that affect, today's world system. My objectives in this chapter are to explain: i) the transformation of religion into political ideology; ii) the way leaders first used religious-based ideologies either to help prevent the demise of an empire or create a new one; and iii) how a political ideology helped prevent the leaders of an empire from expanding its power far beyond their regional base.

Christianity as a political force

Distinct political communities populated the globe during the first millennium CE. The largest ones, structured in the form of empires, extended from Rome through Persia and the Kushan Empire to China.[2] Two of them, the Roman and Sassanid Empires, interacted within the context of a regional system of their own creation. By the middle of the seventh century the system's structure had been altered by the rise of Islam.

Wealth during Antiquity and the Middle Ages was relatively static. Agriculture and the exploitation of peasant slaves were the means empires commonly relied on to expand their material goods. In turn, both elements depended on the amount of territory and the number of trade routes empires controlled.[3] The relationships were relatively simple—the greater the size of an empire's territory and the more major trade routes it controlled, the greater its taxable income and power.[4] It was no coincidence that the Roman and Sassanid Empires emerged at the crossroads of trade and commerce in the eastern Mediterranean.

By the third century, pressures from inside and outside the Roman Empire had transformed it, in the words of one of its own historians, from a "kingdom of gold into one of iron and rust."[5] During that period, Rome was compelled to maintain a large military presence along the frontiers of the Rhine and Danube regions to prevent invasions from "barbarians," and along its eastern flank to offset attempts by the Parthian Empire to widen its power. Rome's problems took a turn for the worse around the middle of the century, when the Persian Sassanids launched raids that reached deep into Roman provinces.[6] It was also around this time that the Goths, along with the Franks and the Alemanni, overran the empire's northern and western borders.[7]

The unrelenting military challenges undermined the empire's economy and destabilized its social order. They affected the economic system in two distinct ways. As the wars on the different fronts gained momentum, so did inflation. With inflation came the need to raise the soldiers' pay. Faced with an enlarged imperial budget, the emperors were forced to set up new taxes. The wars, moreover, had a direct effect on the empire's agricultural system. In dire need of soldiers, the empire had no choice but to recruit workers from large farms. With a sizeable portion of the labor force reduced, the number of independent family farms declined and agricultural output plummeted.[8] The burdens generated by the external threats destabilized the social order in two other ways. At the top of the power pyramid, assassination often became the instrument of choice for the removal of emperors.[9] Commoners, in turn, took to piracy and theft. No less challenging was the drive to create a social structure that impaired the ability by members of one class to ascend to the next one.

Diocletian became the empire's new leader in 284. Convinced that no single individual could "simultaneously direct wars, fight all the battles, govern the Empire, and watch out for usurpers," he created a tetrarchy.[10] He relinquished part of his authority to a joint Augustus, appointed two subordinate Caesars, and divided the empire into four prefectures and twelve dioceses.[11] The tetrarchy did not generate internal harmony. Subsequent to the retirement of Diocletian and his co-emperors, two major struggles erupted in the Roman Empire. The East and the West battled each other to decide which one would govern the entire empire, while two leaders in the West fought one another for the right to rule the region. By 312 Constantine had became the sole emperor in the West. He and Licinius, who had assumed control of the East the year before, temporarily put their differences aside and agreed to acknowledge each other's authority. Their fragile accord, however, was soon fractured by a rapidly emerging religion—Christianity.

Christianity materialized in Palestine. The first Jews to become Christians claimed that Jesus of Nazareth was the "messiah," was divine, and had been prophesied in scripture.[12] Through Christianity they sought to extend authoritative answers to the religious yearnings of the time, describe ways of attaining unending life in the company of the divine, and offer a societal structure that would help its members achieve salvation. In a short time the new belief spread throughout the Jewish communities of Syria and Asia Minor and to other parts of the Roman Empire. The poor and uneducated in the cities became Christianity's first members. Their interest in creating a sense of community soon resonated with the viewpoints and wants of a wide range of people. A few members of the aristocracy became attracted to the idea that by becoming a Christian, a person was stepping up from a bewildered and immature stage of moral and intellectual development into the heart of Greek–Roman civilization. Women, in particular, treasured the notion that in Christ there was neither male nor female and that men cared for their wives as Christ cherished the church.[13]

As their numbers increased, so did their need for creating an organized religious structure. Members of congregations in different cities rapidly began to elect their own overseers—*episkopoi* (bishops)—to lead them in worship and manage their funds. In due course the elected bishops broadened their own authorities. They established a nearly monarchical organization and asserted that they inherited their powers directly from those extended by Jesus to his original disciples. With their new status, the bishops sought to prevent doctrinal and sectarian divisions, keep internal discipline, and limit encroachment by the civilian government. They further enhanced their influence via the formation of councils. The councils were established for the purpose of bringing together bishops from different cities and regions in order to address problems and determine orthodox opinion.[14]

By the time Constantine had become emperor, Christianity was no longer a sect disconnected from the Roman world. Christianity's strength, nonetheless, varied significantly from one part of the empire to another. It was a struggling religion in North Africa and Western Europe, while in the eastern section of the empire it had gained considerable strength, and its leaders and members were beginning to think about the idea of establishing one Great Church with a single rule of faith.[15]

The fate of Christianity took a major turn in 312, when Constantine, who had worshiped Sol Invictus (the Syrian sun god that had been brought to Rome some sixty-five years earlier), attributed his military and political success to the Christian god, and became its avid promoter.[16] Hopeful that by decriminalizing Christianity he would be able to purge some of the ills afflicting the empire and generate greater internal unity, Constantine, and his counterpart in the eastern section, Licinius, formulated the *Edict of Milan*.

> I, Constantine Augustus, and I, Licinius Augustus, met happily in Milan, and in the course of our discussions in all matters relating to public well-being and security, we thought it right that our very first ordinances would benefit the majority of our people, should concern the respect due to the divinity, that is to say that Christians should be given full liberty to

follow the religion of their choice ... [W]e should embark upon this policy of not refusing to anyone the opportunity of devoting himself either to the cult of Christians or to whatever religion he feels is most suited to him ... [17]

Immediately thereafter, Constantine began to sponsor the building of churches, gave the bishop of Rome property to construct a new cathedral, and exempted the clergy from taxation, military service, and forced labor.

Relations between Constantine and Licinius remained stable for several years. Both emperors reached an "entente cordiale," with each addressing matters within his own sphere of influence and consulting the other when the problem affected both parties.[18] During this period, however, Licinius began to have second thoughts about their accord. Fearful that the *Edict of Milan* and Constantine's policies were undermining his own power and authority in the East, Licinius expelled Christians and executed several bishops. Constantine retaliated, and by 324 his forces had defeated Licinius's army and had gained control of the densely Christianized territories of Asia Minor.[19]

To contend that Constantine used Christianity to try to generate unity within the empire is not to argue that Christians were united, that he moved forcefully and rapidly to propagate Christianity throughout the domain, and that he succeeded in bringing together the realm. By the time Constantine defeated Licinius, Christians were already deeply divided on a number of issues. One of the most important ones was theological. Arius, a priest in Alexandria, engendered a major dispute when he claimed that though Jesus, as the son of God, was superior to other humans, his divinity did not equal God's. According to Socrates Scholasticus, Arius presented the following argument: "If the Father begot the Son, he [who] was begotten had a beginning of existence: hence it is clear that there was when the Son was not."[20] Jesus, explained Arius, derived his divinity through the full obedience of his Father's will. Alexander, Arius's bishop in Alexandria, immediately ordered his subordinate to stop voicing such an opinion. Arius rebuffed the demand and soon gained the backing of other bishops. Dissatisfied with the dispute, Constantine called for the convocation of the Church's first ecumenical council. At a gathering in Nicaea in 325, he asked the bishops to determine whether Jesus was one with God. Though unable to fully comprehend their rationale for concluding that the two were one, Constantine welcomed the accord.

Despite the agreement and his continuing belief that he could use Christianity as a means to unify the empire, Constantine recognized that it would be unwise to try to accelerate the conversion process.[21] Of special concern to Constantine and the Christian bishops was the role of the aristocracy. Both understood that the legitimization of Christianity depended heavily on whether the aristocracy adopted it as its religion. Aristocrats, who viewed serving in public office as their right and responsibility, had had a similar attitude toward priesthood and the performance of pagan rites. "The incentives for aristocrats to hold public priesthoods [had been] similar to those for holding public office; both sorts of position allowed aristocrats to play an important role in the state and thereby to gain the public approval they coveted."[22] This meant that Constantine, his successors, and the bishops had to convert pagan aristocrats with a great deal of patience, and convince them that affiliation with the Christian church would secure and augment their status.[23]

By the same token, as Christians endeavored to convert pagan aristocrats, they had no choice but to moderate certain original Christian values. Conscious that the adage "it is easier for a camel to pass through the eye of a needle than for a rich man to go to heaven" would not sit well with most aristocrats, bishops fashioned an immunity clause. Men of great wealth, they averred, could avoid condemnation so long as they put some of their own material resources to good Christian use.[24] Likewise, nobility, a concept greatly valued by aristocrats and associated with family pedigree, significant achievements, and cultural superiority, stood in stark contrast with the Christian version. But rather than rebuking the aristocrats' conceptualization, Christians broadened the formulation of nobility and identified piety as its most important value.[25]

The next major move to establish Christianity as the empire's sole religion started in the 380s, when Theodosius, who ruled the eastern part of the empire, made Easter and Christmas legal holidays; declared the doctrine of the Trinity the empire's official religion; banned non-religious public and private activities on Sundays; ordered that all heretics be considered demented and insane and the places they met not be recognized as churches; and instructed that Jews be prohibited from proselytizing Christians, marrying them, being in the army, and holding state office.[26] These steps eventually began to yield some of the goals sought by the rulers of the Roman Empire. By the middle of the fifth century, non-Christians had been outlawed and Christianity had become a critical instrument of the imperial goal: "one God, one empire, one religion."

Reliance on Christianity as a political tool did not avert the empire's demise. As the reach of Christianity expanded, albeit not as a unified ideology, the entity within which the development occurred experienced severe losses. Subjected to challenges emanating from the west, the north, and the east, the empire's ability to protect itself had diminished steadily since the first century. For a while, only outlying provinces fell to barbarian invaders. In the fifth century, however, Rome itself became the target of repeated attacks, and by the start of the sixth century the Roman Empire was no longer Roman. The Ostrogoths dominated Italy, the Franks held sway over northern Gaul, the Burgundies ruled Provence, the Visigoths reigned over southern Gaul and Spain, the Vandals ran northern Africa and the western Mediterranean, and the Angles and Saxons presided over England.

With the downfall of its western part, the Roman Empire became the Byzantine Empire. With its power center located in Constantinople, the leaders of the abridged empire faced two challenges. In the West, the belief that they had to reunite the empire remained alive. Around the middle of the sixth century, Justinian launched a series of expeditions designed to regain control over parts of the western section. His success was brief. In the East, leaders of the Byzantine Empire had no choice but to cope with the threat of an old rival—the Sassanid Empire.

Around 250 BCE, on the high plateau of Iran, the nomadic Parthians, under their chieftain Arsaces, launched a successful revolt against Greek rule and established an independent dynasty. Eventually the Parthians managed both to consolidate their control over the region and to transform the dynasty into an empire that, in time, became a dangerous rival to Rome. The fate of the Parthian Empire took a radical turn in 226 CE, when Ardashir deposed its overlord. Ardashir, who had succeeded his father Papak, who in turn was a son of a Persian priest named Sassan, inaugurated the Sassanid Empire. He replaced the Parthians' feudal system with a highly centralized administration, and reintroduced Zoroastrianism in order to establish a religious kingship and regulate social and political life. Ardashir's son, Shapur, assumed power in 244 and by 259 had defeated the Roman armies thrice. He solidified the religious nature of the Sassanid Empire by holding spiritual, along with political and social, leadership and by granting the aristocracy the highest ranks in the priesthood.[27]

Zoroastrianism is attributed to the prophet Zoroaster. Sedentary communities in northern Iran may have been among the first to practice Zoroastrianism during the fifth and sixth centuries. It was not a monotheistic religion. Ahuramazdah (sovereign knowledge) was considered the leading god. Six assistant deities, who represented the personal aspects of Ahuramazdah, surrounded him. Ahuramazdah and his six attending gods were believed to be in a permanent state of war with evil spirits led by Ahriman. Humans took sides in the struggle; the side they chose was determined by the kind of person they were.

As the power of the Sassanid Empire rose, so did the intensity of its rivalry with the Byzantine Empire. The enmity reached its peak when Justinian tried to regain control of northern Africa and the western area of the Roman Empire in the 550s. During this period, the Sassanid Empire's new leader, Khosrau I, invaded Syria and captured Antioch on the eastern Mediterranean Sea. His son Khosrau II followed in his father's steps. He took over Jerusalem, overpowered Egypt and Anatolia, and set up camp next to Constantinople. That was as far as he went. Mindful that the wars had enfeebled their respective empires, and with neither side being able to eradicate the power of the other, the leaders of the two empires negotiated a peace agreement during the early years of the seventh century. But by then it was too late. A new actor, with a markedly more encompassing and grounded religious identity, was ready to spring into action and overpower both.[28]

A question often posed is whether Christianity contributed to the demise of the Roman Empire. It is generally agreed that Christianity did not help unify the empire. A religion that lacks internal coherence and is acutely divided theologically is unlikely to fuse any entity that is already burdened by deep cleavages. Scholars, however, are not of one mind regarding whether Christianity actually helped spawn the fall of the Roman Empire.

E. Gibbon argued that it did. The rapid ascension of Christianity and the spread of monasticism meant that a "large portion of public and private wealth was consecrated to the specious demands of charity and devotion; and the soldiers' pay was lavished on the useless multitudes of both sexes, who could only plead the merits of abstinence and chastity." A. H. M. Jones forwarded a similar argument when he wrote: "The Christian church imposed a new class of idle mouths on the resources of the empire ... a large number lived on the alms of the peasantry, and as time went on more and more monasteries acquired landed endowments which enabled their inmates to devote themselves entirely to their spiritual duties."[29] J. Herrin, B. Ward-Perkins, M. Grant, and M. Doyle question Gibbons's and Jones's line of reasoning. Herrin notes that private donations, not imperial resources, "began to account for much of the income of monasteries, individual churches, and holy shrines, initiating a process of transformation, which would completely alter the ancient system of charity." Ward-Perkins posits that Rome's success or failure was determined by the economic welfare of its taxpayers. Grant allows for the possibility that Christianization might have accelerated the empire's fall, but emphasizes that a number of other factors played markedly more important roles. Doyle notes that although both western and eastern parts of the empire experienced the same pressures and the same demands on the political mobilization of resources, the West fell sooner because it possessed fewer free-floating and easy-to-mobilize resources than the East.[30]

A mixture of some of the above arguments may help craft a more persuasive explanation. Constantine's attempt to use Christianity to unify and avert the fall of the empire indicates that he was aware of the internal and external dangers afflicting it. His decision, however, came too late. The economic wealth and military power of the western part of the empire were already so depleted that even a solidly unified Christian religion would have not been compelling enough to generate the common front required to avert its demise. Evidence such as the speed with which the Germanic tribes breached the Rhine frontier, sacked Rome, crossed the Pyrenees, and entered Spain in the first two decades of the fifth century, and the domination after 476 of Italy, Gaul, and Spain, respectively, by the Ostrogoths, the Franks, and the Visigoths, help support this contention. Of equivalent consequence is the fact that while the western part of the empire failed to withstand the pressure emanating from its external rivals, the eastern section endured its own external challenges well into the second millennium. The greater success by the Byzantine Empire can be attributed to its ability to attain a balance between the wealth it generated and the costs it was forced to absorb to defend itself. This balance was brought about by the empire's capability to protect valuable trade routes, along with its decisions to withdraw from the western areas that were difficult to defend and to fuse its power in its eastern provinces at a lesser cost.[31] In due course, however, the equilibrium proved to be unsustainable. During the reign of Basil II (976–1025), his forces spawned a series of victories that stretched the empire's frontiers close to where they had been when Rome's power had been at its peak. By the start of the new millennium the Byzantine Empire had committed the same error the Roman Empire had made. At the pinnacle of its affluence and power, the Byzantine Empire was dangerously overstretched.[32] But it was also during this period that Christianity, under the patriarchy of Constantinople, became a critical player in the political and public arenas.

A précis is in order at this juncture. According to M. Cranston, though ideologies and religions are sometimes thought to belong to the same logical category, the differences between the two are sometimes more important than the similarities. A religious theory of reality, he adds, is constructed in terms of the divine order and rarely focuses on the real world alone. "A religion may present a vision of a just society, but it cannot easily have a practical political program. The emphasis on religion is on faith and worship; its appeal is to inwardness and its aim the redemption and purification of the human spirit." Ideology, on the other hand, posits an explanatory theory about human experience and the external world; sets out a program of social and political organization; proposes that the realization of the program will entail struggle; strives to persuade and recruit loyal adherents, and demands that they be committed; and tries to appeal to a large group.[33]

My intent is not to contend that religion and ideology belong to the same "logical" category. Instead, it is to argue that though religion is generally constructed in terms of a "divine order," with an emphasis on faith and worship for the purpose of purifying the human spirit, throughout history it has not been uncommon for political, along with ecclesiastic, leaders to impose on it a political program designed to transform the political, economic, and social structure of society.

Christianity, though not born as a religion, became a religion first and then a political ideology. It became a political tool when Constantine, with extensive backing from ecclesiastic leaders, promulgated its acceptance within the Roman Empire.[34] His objective was political. Fearful that his empire was disintegrating, he viewed Christianity as the instrument that might help stop or revert the process. As time went by, he and succeeding emperors, with the backing of Christian bishops, sought to broaden Christianity's terrestrial scope.[35] As an ideology, it did not bring about the unification of the Roman Empire. It fell short as an instrument of power because it had matured slowly, and by the time it became an acceptable practice the empire had materially overextended itself. Christianity's restricted political authority, moreover, limited its appeal as a means to advocate and justify the empire's expansion by way of territorial conquests. In time this constraint would fade away, and eventually it would be used principally to validate taking arms against an emerging, and very powerful, group of heretics—Muslims.

The birth and development of a political religion

Islam had an inauspicious beginning during the second decade of the seventh century. Muhammad, its creator, first preached it in Mecca, his birthplace. The city, located in western Arabia, was an important trade route between the Mediterranean world to the west and the Asian world to the east, and was dominated by one of the most powerful tribes in the region, the Quraysh. After claiming that he had received revelations from the angel Gabriel, who recited the words of God to him regularly, Muhammad put forward a series of pronouncements.[36] He relied on earlier religious traditions to delineate the proper forms of political, economic, and social conduct. His declarations focused simultaneously on relationships between God and the believer, and between the believer and the rest of mankind.[37] Of great import to the materialization of the Islamic state were the idea of a unique, unified, and independent community; the concept of an absolute higher authority; and the belief that authority had to be centralized within the community.[38]

Muhammad's summons to a life of virtue, his assurance that the pure would be rewarded after death with everlasting joy, his call for the creation of a unified and separate Islamic community, and his appeal to the citizens of Mecca to cease the worship of idols, did not sit well with the city's merchant aristocracy. Fearful that his actions would undermine their legitimacy and power, they took aggressive steps against him. Unable to curb the challenge from Mecca's leaders, Muhammad and his followers moved to Yathrib (later known as Al-Madina), a small town more than two hundred miles north of Mecca. At his new post, Muhammad built a political, military, and religious base. He exercised religious and spiritual authority over Yathrib, served as its civilian ruler, and mounted an operation designed to gain control of Mecca.

After an eight-year struggle with Mecca's leaders, Muhammad and his followers conquered the city and compelled its citizens to renounce the worship of idols and accept Islam.[39] By the time Muhammad died in 632, his power extended over much of Arabia's western region and most of its central and southern parts. As the Apostle of God, he "brought and taught a religious revelation ... [A]s the head of the Muslim *Umma* [community], he promulgated laws, dispensed justice, collected taxes, conducted diplomacy, made war, and made peace. The *Umma*, which began as a community, had become a state. It would soon become an empire."[40]

Immediately after his death, Muhammad's followers faced two choices: form a single polity under one leader or break into separate communities, each under a different ruler. Their decision to remain a single society and to name Muhammad's father-in-law, Abu Bakr, the first caliph helped determine Islam's destiny.[41] In what it is referred to as the Apostasy Wars, armed groups of believers then marched against Arabia's main centers of power and rapidly gained control of the entire peninsula. Umar ibn al-Khattab succeeded Abu Bakr, and Uthman ibn Affar followed in the steps of the second caliph.[42] Under their leadership, Arab Muslims created a new empire in the

Near East. From the Byzantine Empire they took Palestine, Syria, northern Mesopotamia, Armenia, southern Anatolia, and Egypt; and from the Sassanid Empire they seized southern Iraq, Khuzestan, Azerbaijan, and Iran. Their actions brought about the demise of the Sassanid Empire. By 712, the Islamic Empire had also absorbed Spain in the west and Sind in northeast India.

During the first one hundred and twenty years following its birth, Islam experienced two major challenges. Differences regarding succession and the nature of Islamic authority emerged in 656. Members of the Hashim clan contended that Muhammad's cousin and son-in-law, Ali, should assume the role of imam and that his descendants should follow in his steps. Members of the Umayyad clan opposed the idea. After a five-year struggle, the two sides agreed to recognize Mu'waiyah, a member of the Umayyad clan, as the next caliph. His ascension marked the beginning of the Umayyad caliphate.[43]

The second major struggle ensued nearly a century later. Islam rejected the establishment of privileged orders, except for those who accepted Islam over those who did not. The caliph's function was to serve Islam, and he derived his authority from the free consent of Muslims. By the middle of the eighth century, an increasing number of half-Arab and non-Arab Muslim subjects of the Islamic Empire began to argue that the leaders were guiding it in the wrong direction. Their contention was that instead of advancing Islam, the caliphs were serving the needs of special-interest groups, and were using methods similar to those employed by the leaders of previous empires. In 747, a Persian slave who for thirty years had been denouncing Umayyad rule and calling on members of the Abbasid clan to take over, launched a revolt in the eastern part of Iran.[44] After a three-year struggle, the Abbasid caliphate replaced the Umayyad caliphate.[45]

The change in caliphate did not moderate the empire's territorial expansion. The new rulers' first major symbolic act was to transfer the empire's center of power from Damascus, where the Umayyads had ruled for a century, to a city located on the west bank of the Tigris, at the intersection of major trade routes—Baghdad. From this time forth, the power and authority of the Persians spread steadily throughout the empire. Conscious that they ruled over a vast and diverse area and lacked the support of an established system, they relied on the intrinsic value of Islam as a belief system to create a relatively coherent empire.[46]

By the start of the tenth century, however, the Islamic Empire had lost much of its internal unity. The division that had emerged shortly after Muhammad's death, but that seemed resolved in 661 when the Hashim and Umayyad clans agreed on Mu'awiyah as the new caliph, eventually spread throughout the entire empire. The two clans that had brought about the rapid expansion of the empire, the Umayyad and Abbasid, were Sunnis. Their authority continued to be contested by those who remained committed to the belief that the descendants of Ali and Muhammad's daughter Fatima were the rightful caliphs—the Shiites. The second source of the emerging disunity was related to the functions the empire's central figures had carried out since its inception.

Muhammad's early successors played dual roles—they were proclaimed *caliph*, "Deputy of the Prophet of God," and *amir al-muminin*, "Commander of the Faithful."[47] By the start of the tenth century, the same person no longer carried out both functions. By then, independent amirs, who nominally acknowledged the Abbasid suzerainty, were ruling the provinces of Spain, North Africa, and Egypt. Eager to assert the primacy of the military commander in Baghdad over the provincial leaders, the governor of Iraq was given the title of *amir al-umara*, "Commander of Commanders."[48] But this action did not translate into an increase in his power and authority. Initially, rulers of the provinces were willing to recognize him as the representative of Islam's religious unity and formal head of the state, but it was not long before they began to call themselves caliphs.[49] These two conditions symbolized the end of the Islamic Empire and the start of a more pluralistic, but markedly less powerful, political entity, more appropriately referred to as "commonwealth."[50]

Islam versus Christianity

By the time Baghdad recognized that it could no longer retain its grip over its distant provinces, western Europe had already undergone a major transformation. A series of rival kingdoms emerged from the ruins of the Roman provincial administration in the northern portions of Gaul in the fifth century. In due time, the members of the Frankish Empire relied on their military might and Christianity to expand their power measurably and forge a common identity amongst the inhabitants of the various regions they dominated.[51] Much of this power, however, was dissipated once again in the middle of the sixth century, when Frankish kings began to reward their supporters and the Church with estates and revenues. With wealth and power somewhat equalized, the competition for supremacy between various families regained intensity. No one proved to be more committed and more effective at enlarging its domain than the Carolingian family.

Fearful that Islam would become unstoppable unless a counterattack was mounted, the Bishop of Rome called on the Carolingians to assume this responsibility. By 759, Pepin the Short had expelled the Muslims from Narbonne and pushed them as far south as the Pyrenees.[52] Close to twenty years later, Pepin's son, Charlemagne, with encouragement from Pope Adrian I, led his troops deep into Spain and defeated the amir of Córdoba. Though ultimately Charlemagne was forced to pull back, he established a buffer zone between Muslim Spain and the Frankish lands, and imposed Christian hegemony on the inhabitants of the area.[53]

The interaction between Rome and Charlemagne during this period raised several questions regarding the relationship between politics and religion. Pope Leo III's coronation of Charlemagne as emperor in 800 led many within and outside the Church to ask: if the pope derived his authority from God, from whom did the emperor obtain his own authority? Did he receive it from the pope as claimed by the pope, or from God as proposed by the emperor?[54]

At the peak of its power some ten centuries earlier, the western part of the Roman Empire had been an autonomous political system capable of controlling from its center vast conquered areas and their inhabitants. Its demise forced local leaders to find alternative means of protection. To generate a foundation that would enable him to protect, and often enlarge, his kingdom, each king gave part of his own land in the form of a fief to a lord who, in turn, agreed to help defend the kingdom and provide a specified number of soldiers. The fief-holder, depending on how much land the king had granted him, either exerted direct control over the land under his dominion or subdivided it into fiefs amongst his own loyal men in return for their services.[55]

Though this arrangement brought about a modicum of order and retained its presence in western Europe through several centuries, its base was frail. Nobles, and sometimes kings, could be both lord and vassal. This arrangement often lured them to engage in private warfare and to offer their services to monarchs outside their realm in order to enlarge their personal fiefs. Chaos and a power vacuum soon resulted. The Church, which also controlled fiefs, capitalized on the state of affairs to enlarge its authority.

The Church's strategy evolved gradually. In its early days, it recognized and accepted the duality of power, chiefly because it had no choice. Concerning heavenly matters, the Church claimed that it had the authority to act as the leading voice; concerning terrestrial issues, it grudgingly accepted that the emperor's judgment assumed precedence over any other opinion. Aurelius Augustinus (354–430) proposed that the Church's authority was superior to that of the monarch. In *De civitate Dei* (The City of God), he noted that all creation was divided into *civitas Dei* and *civitas terrena*. "Mankind is divided into two sorts: such as live according to man, and such as live according to God. These we mystically call the 'two cities' or societies, the one predestined to reign eternally with God, the other condemned to perpetual torment with Satan." Because the Church derived its power directly from God and thus acted as the sole representative of *civitas Dei*, the monarch, as the agent of *civitas terrena*, had to subordinate his power to the former.

Augustinus's argument did not fall on deaf ears. In a letter to Emperor Anastasius in 494, Pope Gelasius I proposed that the world was ruled by "the consecrated authority of bishops and the royal power. Of these, the responsibility of the priests is more weighty insofar as they will answer for the kings of men themselves at the divine judgment." He added that in "the order of religion, in matters concerning the reception and right administration of heavenly sacraments, you ought to submit yourself rather than rule, and that in these matters you should depend on their judgment rather than seek to bend them to your will."[56] Still, though the "Gelasian doctrine" generated major debates as to who had authority over whom on spiritual and terrestrial issues, it was not until the eleventh century that the Church began to appropriate some of the monarch's power regarding secular concerns. Feudalism supplied the opportunity and rationale.

With feudalism came an increase in violence throughout western Europe. The clergy was amongst those who became recurring targets of violence.[57] To protect themselves and their property, the clergy enacted edicts that deemed sacrilegious any act initiated against either. At a council convoked in 975, Guy of Anjou, bishop of Le Puy, threatened the attending warriors and peasants with excommunication unless they took a peace oath. Inspired by the meeting's success, he organized other councils. In 989, the participants at the Council of Charoux enacted a series of canons that stated that anyone who attacked the "holy church," took as "booty sheep, asses, cows ... ," robbed, seized or struck a "priest, or a deacon, or any man of the clergy ... who is not bearing arms ... but who is simply going about his business ... and after examination by his own bishop, that person is found guilty of any crime, then he is found guilty of sacrilege, and if he furthermore does not come forward to make satisfaction, let him then be held to be excluded from the holy church of God."[58] Other councils followed, and new resolutions amplifying the reach of the previous canons were adopted. By the time the Council of Narbonne had finished its meeting in 1054, its members had limited the lawful use of arms to only eighty days a year and ruled that no Christian could spill the blood of another Christian.[59]

The Church's decision to engage in peacekeeping was still not designed to undermine the monarch's role. The ecclesiastics understood that they could not enforce their canons unless powerful secular monarchs and lords were willing to help them. But just as the peace movement led by the Church acted as a stabilizing force in a world that had become chaotic because of its feudal structure, it also became an agent of change. By erecting a series of barriers designed to curtail violence, the peace councils conferred upon the Church the "authority to determine who could employ arms, for what purpose, on whose command, against whom, and when."[60]

To validate and gain support for its decision to widen its terrestrial function, the Church had to elicit a rationale for war and identify an enemy of Christianity. The principal intent of the Church's "just war" doctrine was to regulate warfare and confine violence. To be just, war had to be conducted by a legitimate civil authority, within the limits of law, and its purpose had to be the recovery of real property or incorporeal rights. Monks and priests were not permitted to participate in war, and those who exercised violence had to possess the right disposition of heart. A holy Christian war, moreover, was an act to be waged for the goals or ideals of Christianity on the authority of its religious leader. Accordingly, while the doctrine of "'just war" set a wide range of restrictions on fighting, including participation in war by clerics, the doctrine of "holy war" eliminated most of them.[61]

Despite the fact that the Church did not develop the theological foundation of the doctrine of holy war until the end of the eleventh century, many of its members were already familiar with the idea.[62] Ambrose, the bishop of

Milan, was amongst its early proponents. He remarked in the fourth century that violence against Jews and heretics was justified because it reflected "the judgment of God" and the carriers of the act were protected by "the shield of faith." Later, in the sixth century, Gregory I claimed that the use of force was defensible if it was employed to propagate the faith. Neither, however, was successful at convincing Christian leaders to bestow primacy on the holy war doctrine.[63]

With the Peace of God movement embedded in the system, it was up to Pope Gregory VII and other reformers to posit the idea that war could be used as a means to serve the Church. Gregory VII did not forward a systematic rationale for warfare in the name of the Church. Nonetheless, time and again he claimed that military service for the papacy was an obligation for kings, princes, and soldiers. They were vassals to the prince of the apostles, and fighting for St. Peter was a manifestation of their faith. Responsibility for advancing a systematic and juridical justification rested on the shoulders of Gregorian bishops. Anselm of Lucca delineated the conditions under which those who ministered "with warlike arms" would "please God." Bernard of Angers seconded Anselm's reasoning by asserting that striking down and killing the "Antichrists" was "pleasing in the eyes of God." And Bonizo of Sutri laid down a code of moral action that avowed that if Christians fought "heretical novelties" according to their social status, God would be pleased.[64]

But who would be the "heretical novelties"? Humans have always needed a reference point to define and differentiate themselves from others. As they invest themselves with attractive qualities, they often impose on "others" objectionable characteristics. By the end of the eleventh century, Muslims, in the eyes of Christians, had become the "Antichrist." This transformation did not come about accidentally or surreptitiously.

From the moment Islam took root and expanded into an empire, Christians recognized that it would pose a challenge. Prior to the late eleventh century, however, most Christians viewed Muslims as just another barbarian group. They looked at the wars against Muslims chiefly as secular wars, not particularly different from those they fought against other foreign peoples.[65] The tenor of their opinion began to change after Muslims had defeated the Byzantine Empire's army at Manzikert in 1071. Following the event, its emperor, Alexius, requested assistance from Rome. It would be more than two decades, however, before Rome would manage to generate a strong anti-Muslim fervor among Christians.

At the Council of Clermont held in 1095, Pope Urban II sought to persuade Christians that instead of engaging in immoral and divisive wars against each other, they had to redirect their energies in a just war against non-Christians. He stated:

> You have thus far waged unjust wars at one time or another; you have brandished mad weapons to your mutual destruction, for no other reason

than covetousness and pride, as a result of which you have deserved
eternal death and sure damnation. We now hold out to you wars which
contain the glorious reward of martyrdom, which will retain that title of
praise for now and forever.[66]

The lands occupied by Muslims, he explained, were the grounds sanctified by
Jesus with his birth, physical presence, life among men, and death and resur-
rection. Turks have "seized more and more of the lands of the Christians,
have already defeated them in seven times as many battles, killed or captured
many people, have destroyed churches, and have devastated the kingdom of
God." By taking over such lands, Muslims were engaged in a sacrilegious
act.[67] Moreover, because Muslims did not have faith—that is, Christian
faith—reaching a negotiated compromise with them was unacceptable. The
only alternative left to the crusaders was to kill them. In order to "cleanse the
Holy City and the glory of the Sepulcher," the crusaders had to take arms
against the "pagan others," "the social antichrist," those who had "polluted
with their filthiness" the holy places.[68]

Eight crusades followed Urban II's entreaty to march towards Jerusalem
"for the remission of [their] sins,"[69] with the time span extending well into the
thirteenth century.[70] Though each crusade had its own particular rationale,
they all evolved from the same ideological framework. They sprang from the
beliefs that the crusades were authorized and supported by God, that parti-
cipating in them was a form of religious devotion, and that by becoming
crusaders the laity became more Christian.[71] In a short time, crusading
became much more than a religious act. It involved military activity in which
mysticism coexisted with political, economic, and social interests. "It expressed communal as well as individual attitudes to fundamental practical and
ideological issues: faith; self-esteem; religious and social control; honour;
pride; material and spiritual greed; the self-image of a civilization."[72]

By the start of the twelfth century, leaders of the Church were claiming that
the authority of the pope was superior to that of emperors. In a series of
pronouncements, known as the *Dictatus Papae*, Gregory VII declared that:

> [T]he Roman Pontiff alone is rightly to be called universal ...
> [F]or him alone it is lawful to enact new laws according to the
> needs of the time, to assemble together new congregations, to
> make an abbey of a canonry; and ... to divide a rich bishopric
> and unite the poor ones ...
> [T]he Pope is the only one whose feet are to be kissed by all
> Princes ...
> [H]e may depose emperors.
> [H]e may transfer bishops, if necessary, from one See to
> Another ...
> [H]e himself may be judged by no one ...

[T]he Roman Church has never erred, nor ever, by the witness
of Scripture, shall err to all eternity. [73]

The Church tested the worthiness of its pronouncement upon learning that
the second crusade had failed to prevent the king of Egypt and Syria from
regaining control of Jerusalem. Bernard of Clairvaux, Christendom's most
powerful monastic leader, urged Pope Eugenius III to order the mounting of
a third crusade. "[T]he power of others," argued Bernard, "is bound by defi-
nite limits"; the pope's power, on the other hand, "extends over those who
have received power over others."[74] Pope Innocent III continued the effort to
strengthen the papacy's terrestrial power. In addition to declaring that the
pope was set "between God and man, lower than God but higher than man,
who judges all and is judged by no one,"[75] he created a Church bureaucracy
with the financial resources equal to those of other powerful monarchs, and
named himself Constantinople's patriarch after soldiers of the fourth crusade
had occupied it in 1204.

A dysfunctional Western system

After two centuries of crusading and attempting to dictate terrestrial politics,
the Church began to experience a major challenge to its authority. Troubled
by the exorbitant costs generated by its political involvement, Christian secular leaders started to challenge the pope's temporal authority and belief that
Christian mores should be taken into account when formulating decisions
that affected the interests of their empires and principalities.

Divided into principalities, with each one guided by a prince determined to
guard his own privileges and authority, the Holy Roman Empire, no matter
how hard it tried, failed to regain its lost aura. To the east, a different type of
challenge encumbered the Byzantine Empire. By the start of the tenth century, the Islamic Empire had split into several independent regions. Military
autocrats, backed by their own personal troops, became the new rulers. This
change undermined the power and authority of the caliphs. During the next
two centuries, the empire absorbed a wave of attacks from both the west and
the east. The forces of Christendom moved back into both Spain and Sicily
and subsequently reached the near east. Despite the substantial threat generated by Christian forces, their overall effect on the Islamic Empire was substantially less pronounced than the one exacted by the nomadic people from
the depths of Asia.

Between the end of the twelfth century and the beginning of the next one,
Temuchin, the son of a poor noble, unified the disparate Mongol tribes that
lived in the outer reaches of the Gobi Desert. Temuchin was named Genghis
Khan ("Universal Ruler") in 1206. Shortly afterward, the new Mongol leader,
supported by a highly effective and mobile small army, forced into submission
southern Siberia and northern China.[76] By the middle of the thirteenth century, Mongols controlled an empire that extended from Poland to Siberia and

from Moscow to parts of the Middle East. Even so, they did not attempt to impose their values on their subjects. In China, Kublai Khan, a grandson of Genghis Khan, relocated the capital from Mongolia to Beijing and took on the Chinese dynastic name Yuan. More importantly, rather than imposing his nation's lifestyle, social structure, and religion on the Chinese, he adopted their ways of thinking, and their political theories and structures.

Mongols practiced a similar form of imperialism in the Middle East. Shortly after storming, looting, and burning Baghdad, and killing its leader and family, they sought to instill a new sense of political stability; promoted the reconstruction of town life, industry, and trade; and instead of trying to eradicate Islam they converted to it. By this time, however, the caliphate was no longer a powerful institution. It had been supplanted by the sultanate, which, in addition to becoming the real organ of political and military power, granted itself the religious privileges previously reserved to the caliphs.[77]

Competition between Iran, Turkey, and Egypt soon followed. Iran fell under the dominion of Mongol khans, while Turkish Muslims who had been heavily influenced by the Mongols ruled Turkey. Though Egypt also came under Turkish dominion, its sultans had been able to ward off the Mongol invasion. A series of internal crises in both Iran and Egypt, and the retreat of Mongols from Anatolia into Iran, freed Turks to fill the power vacuum that materialized. In 1281, Osman emerged as Anatolia's new leader. He and his two successors, guided by a powerful sense of religious mission and the claim that they were waging Holy War against non-Muslims, moved aggressively against the Byzantine Empire.[78] By the end of the fourteenth century they had succeeded in bringing under their control much of the Balkan Peninsula. The transformation carried remarkable real and symbolic value. The leaders of the new empire, despite their readiness to tolerate the practice of distinct cultures and traditions, strove to root its legitimacy in a non-Christian "universal" belief—the faith of Islam.[79] Islam "provided the unity that made a large-scale political community both possible and militarily powerful."[80] This conversion, combined with the fall of the last Islamic state in Iberia, shifted the ideological clash "from the southwestern to the southeastern European world."[81] The change did not signal that the Ottoman leaders were prepared to engage in "incessant warfare to expand the abode of Islam." or that the West was in constant fear of such a development. Jihad, as defined by most canonical sources, is to be initiated "when the world of Islam or the peace of the umma is threatened." In time, the West accepted this reality and both sides were often able to avert conflict via accommodation.[82]

The end of the crusades, the collapse of the Byzantine Empire, and the dawn of the Ottoman Empire paved the way for the emergence of new tensions in the world arena. To understand the nature and content of the strains that were about to emerge between the fifteenth and seventeenth centuries, however, it is first necessary to examine the steps taken by an empire that could have altered the course of history but chose, at the peak of its power, to retreat from the world arena.

The Chinese Empire and Confucianism

Confucius, born in 551 BCE, was one among many thinkers who tried to find a solution to the climate of violence and competition and the breakdown of the social and moral order that burdened China. He did not start with the idea of creating a new way of thinking. He proposed that existing problems could be eliminated by the promotion of earlier values—principles that emphasized humaneness, morality, and propriety. After his death in 479 BCE, several schools of thought emerged, but none had a substantial effect on China's political, economic, and social structure until the establishment of the Tang Dynasty in 618.

During the Tang Dynasty's reign, its emperors and their advisors sought to incorporate the canon of Confucian classics as the basis for the civil service examinations. Commitment to Confucianism remained strong during the Mongols' domination of China. Still, Confucianism's most notable period was yet to materialize. Political conditions in China in the fourteenth century inspired members of the Chinese elite to posit syncretist ideas, initially to protect their shared heritage and afterward to battle the occupiers. Claiming that Confucianism, Buddhism, and Daoism shared a common origin and complemented one another, they stressed that a system of social ethics was necessary to ensure the proper functioning of the state and society. One of the most important groups was the "White Lotus Society." Originating in the twelfth century, it combined elements from the Manichean and Maitreyan Buddhist doctrines. The central tenet of Manichean teaching was that the forces of good and evil struggled for mastery of the world. Maitreyan doctrine, which goes back to early Buddhism in India, had by the thirteenth century added to its teaching in China the claim that Maitreya was the Buddha who would descend from "the realm of wonderful joy" to relieve humankind's suffering before his actual arrival. Drawing from these ideas, leading teachers of the "White Lotus Society" propagated the view that the disorder into which China had been plunged demonstrated that Maitreya would soon arrive. They also produced a coherent ideology to recruit followers, form rebel armies with a common purpose, and establish civil governing.

In the 1330s, groups of rebel soldiers named the "Red Turbans" emerged. For an extended period the leaders of different Red Turban groups focused on promoting their own immediate interests rather than working together for a common cause. The division began to fade away when sectarian revolts prompted extensive rebellions throughout China in 1351. A year later, a young Buddhist novice named Zhu Yuanzhang joined a Red Turban rebel group and in a short time was commanding a force that numbered between twenty thousand and thirty thousand men. Within a ten-year period, leaders of other regions joined him. His military campaign against the Yuan Dynasty came to fruition in 1368, when his forces took over Dadu (present-day Beijing) and ousted the Mongols from China. The victory led to the birth of the

Ming Dynasty and an increased interest in Confucianism as a guide to political behavior.[83] Determined to abide by the Confucian belief that engaging in trade was far beneath an emperor's dignity and that doing so might provoke the wrath of heaven, Zhu Yuanzhang returned China's economy to its agricultural roots.[84] After some eight years, his government had reclaimed more than 8.8 million hectares of land, built and repaired over forty thousand water reservoirs, and planted some one billion trees. Zhu Yuanzhang's death in 1398 instigated a power struggle that ended in 1402, when his son, the Prince of Yan, gained control of the empire. His ascension to power spawned the "second foundation" of the Ming Dynasty. By 1410, Zhu Di (Cheng Zu was his eventual posthumous temple name) had cast away his father's belief, advocated by Confucian advisors, that China's prosperity rested in agriculture. His motto became: "Let there be mutual trade at the frontier barriers in order to supply the country's need and to encourage distant peoples to come."[85] With the new maxim as his guiding principle, Zhu Di launched the creation of one of the greatest seaports of his time, the Gangtan port in the southern Fujian province, and ordered Zheng He, a eunuch, to command the ships that would take representatives of the Chinese Empire to distant places.[86] Admiral Zheng He led seven missions, each one lasting two to three years, with the first one beginning in 1405 and the last one ending in 1433. His travels took him to Indonesia, India, the Persian Gulf, the Red Sea, and far down Africa's eastern coast. The fleets were immense. The largest of the ships reached four hundred and forty feet in length and carried nine masts. During his first trip he had under his authority a total of three hundred and seventeen ships, sixty-two of which were of the four hundred and forty foot category, and between twenty thousand and thirty thousand men.[87] Zhu Di's maritime expeditions were not motivated by a desire to expand the empire, impose China's system of beliefs, values, and ideas on other societies, or develop a better understanding of other parts of the world. During his trips, Zheng He did not add a single square mile of territory to the Chinese empire, nor did he make any claims for territory or suzerainty. The expeditions were mounted for the purpose of encouraging trade with China and exposing its superior civilization. With Zheng He playing the role of diplomat, visiting foreign rulers, expressing China's peaceful intentions, and bequeathing extravagant gifts, Zhu Di strove to demonstrate that no other society matched China's.[88] Zhu Di's death in 1424 intensified the debate within the imperial court as to whether it was appropriate for China to engage in mammoth naval voyages. From the moment the maritime expeditions began in 1405, the court's conservative Confucian faction argued that it was wrong to engage in anything so ignoble as trade and interaction with coarse barbarians. Despite the fact that Zhu Di did not undertake the voyages to conquer new lands for China, Confucian scholars repeatedly declared that superior men concerned themselves with justice, avoided almost all forms of competition, and did not seek what was distant or absent. They emphasized that Confucius had insisted that the task of good government was not to promote the accumulation of private wealth but to bring back the past and safeguard it.[89] The new emperor did not ignore the concerns of his Confucian advisors. He accepted their contention that moderation and agriculture were the basis of good government policy. Upon ascending to the throne on September 7, 1424, Zhu Di's son, Zhu Gaozhi, issued his first edict: "All voyages of the treasure ships are to be stopped. All ships moored at Taicang [near the mouth of the Yangzi River] are ordered back to Nanjing and all goods on the ships are to be turned over to the Department of Internal Affairs and stored." The "operative Confucian principle at work," under Zhu Gaozhi, "was that land is the basis of the empire's prosperity. The security of the empire lay within the Great Wall, not on the sea."[90] Zhu Gaozhi, who was greatly admired by his Confucian advisors for his benevolence and willingness to trust them, died in 1425. Zhu Zhanji, Zhu Di's grandson, became China's new leader. Like his predecessor, he remained attentive to the advice offered by his Confucian counselors. But it was also during Zhu Zhanji's rule that eunuch participation in government affairs intensified, and so did the internal struggle for the emperor's attention.[91] By 1430, it seemed as though the eunuchs had gained the upper hand. Concerned about China's loss of influence in the regional system, the emperor promised to restore its reputation abroad. Following the death of the most vocal opponent of overseas expeditions, Zhu Zhanji ordered the release of an edict that stated:

> The new reign of Xuande has commenced, and everything shall begin anew. [But] distant lands beyond the seas have not yet been informed. I send eunuchs Zheng He and Wang Jinghong with this imperial order to instruct these countries to follow the way of Heaven with reverence and to watch over their people so that all might enjoy the good fortune and lasting peace.

The fleet left January 12, 1432.[92] The seventh voyage, which lasted until July 1433, was Zheng He's last trip. He died at the age of sixty-two somewhere in the Indian Ocean as the ships were sailing back to China. Strikingly more significant was that the seventh voyage marked the end of the empire's sea expeditions, though China's maritime power was at this point unmatched both in the region and worldwide.[93] After ceasing the voyages, subsequent emperors redirected China's resources to strengthening the government and defending it from the Mongols' continued attempts to regain some of their lost power. To ensure that the empire would not launch a new series of expeditions, they banned the construction of large seagoing ships and passed edicts prohibiting long-distance maritime voyages. By the start of the sixteenth century, the Ming dynasty had made it a capital offense to construct ships of more than two masts. A quarter of a century later, it approved an edict ordering the destruction of all oceangoing ships and the arrest of merchants who sailed them. And by the middle of the same century, it had made it a crime to go to sea in a multimasted ship.[94] Why did China terminate the voyages? Was it because its leaders feared that distant travels would undermine China's capability to protect itself against the Mongol menace? Was it because in the 1430s China was facing a fiscal crisis that made it very difficult to pay for the costly ventures? Or was it because the emperor, though he had the final word as to which policy to adopt, came under intense pressure from Confucian advisors who argued that it was imperative to focus on the mainland and to disregard seafaring and overseas trade?

At first light the reader may be inclined to conclude that it is not possible to choose among the above three explanations but that jointly they may help explain China's decision to terminate its maritime adventures. This study disputes such a contention. As is argued below, an analysis that relies on a comparative perspective reveals a distinct, and markedly more parsimonious, explanation. However, because such a comparison requires a thorough discussion of a case depicted in the next chapter, for the moment the argument will simply be presented in a summary form. In the 1430s and 1440s, China's leaders faced opportunities and challenges quite similar to those encountered by Isabella and Ferdinand of Spain at the start of the sixteenth century. Like the Chinese a century earlier in their struggle against the Mongols, after a prolonged and costly war, the Spaniards managed to evict from the Iberian Peninsula the Muslim. The defeat of the Muslim did not mark the end of the Islamic Empire; it would remain a formidable adversary, and a possible threat to the Iberian Peninsula, for numerous years. Moreover, though jointly Isabella and Ferdinand had created a powerful kingdom, they still faced substantial threats from other European entities; and just like their Chinese counterparts, the Spanish monarchs were deeply concerned about the state of their treasury.

None of these challenges inhibited Isabella and Ferdinand. Impressed by the wealth their explorers had uncovered in the Americas, they were convinced that such new riches, along with the conquered territories, would help transform Spain into Europe's most powerful empire. Furthermore, swayed by the belief that as leaders of a superior civilization they had an ethical obligation to propagate Christianity, the Spanish monarchs wholeheartedly supported the extended maritime voyages. China on the other hand, did not venture into distant territories for the purpose of conquering or colonizing territories. Although equally convinced that its civilization was vastly superior to the societies its navigators encountered in their seven voyages, China never sought to persuade or force them to adopt its ways. Its leaders remained affixed to the Confucian belief system that their empire was a self-contained civilization, that trade with far-away foreign entities was an ignoble act, and that its well-being could not be improved by the wealth others might possess. One must conclude, thus, that though China and Spain encountered similar opportunities and obstacles, the difference in their responses can be partly attributed to their ideological disparity.

The political consequences of three ideologies: Christianity, Islam, and Confucianism

An empire's ability to avert or delay its downfall is in part a function of its capacity to contend with internal divisions and external threats, and to recognize that it cannot continue the drive to increase its power when the costs of further expansion begin to outweigh its benefits. By the fifth century the Roman Empire was no longer able to stand as a single entity. With the western part of the empire overrun by barbarian invaders, the Byzantine Empire was forced to cope with internal divisions and to impede attempts by the Sassanid Empire to enlarge its own dominion. Although hampered by multiple threats, the leaders of the Byzantine Empires did not stop seeking new glories. During the first half of the sixth century, Justinian, as emperor of the Byzantine Empire, sought to regain some of its lost territory, extinguish polytheism and heresy, and Christianize non-Christians. By so doing, however, he irreversibly weakened the power and authority of his empire.[95] The Sassanid Empire pursued a parallel policy. Eventually, exhausted by their conflicting imperial drives, the Byzantine and Sassanid Empires were compelled to agree, reluctantly, not to further undermine each other's pre-eminence. It did not take them long to break the accord; but by then it mattered little. Both became victims of a political community that owed its birth and development as an empire to a new religion—Islam.[96]

Islam's rapid emergence in the seventh century was facilitated not just by the presence of a power vacuum generated by the costly and exhausting rivalry between neighboring empires, but also by the ability of its advocates to create a political, economic, and social community. Though Muhammad and his successors faced substantial opposition as they sought to impose Islam on their immediate political adversaries, the resistance they encountered was markedly weaker than that met by Christians in the Roman and Byzantine Empires. Advocates of Islam were in a position of dominance from almost the moment they sought to propagate it, while promoters of Christianity struggled for centuries to make it the Roman and Byzantine Empires' prevailing ideology.[97]

Feudalism provided the Church the political vacuum it needed to anchor its political authority in one of Europe's principal areas. With the demise of the western part of the Roman Empire and the emergence of competing centers of power, the Church recognized it could exploit the existing condition in order to multiply its power. Determined to protect its institutional integrity and legitimacy, Church authorities issued a series of edicts that declared sacrilegious any action against its members and property. Emboldened by its success and by the continued absence of a united secular political front, the Church broadened its aspirations.

To monopolize norms is a route to power.[98] The Church identified itself as the sole entity with the authority and power to dictate how people should act morally and ethically toward one another and toward non-Christians. Based on the assertion that it possessed ultimate political authority, superior to that of secular kings and emperors, it claimed the sole right to design and interpret Christians norms, to use them to unify Christians, to order Christians to stop fighting one another, and to justify the ordering of crusades against non-Christian agents.

The crusades did not generate the results intended by its early advocates. The acute human and material costs inflicted by the military campaigns, along with the Church's ongoing attempts to enlarge the size of its territorial and material dominions, encouraged secular monarchs to try to re-appropriate from the papacy the power they claimed was rightfully theirs.

The contest for power between lay and ecclesiastical leaders ensued in a changing regional system. Caught between the ideological aspirations of Rome and Islam, the Byzantine Empire, after a brief revival, was torn by both and became a meager shadow of its magnificent past. Concomitantly, customary human greed undermined Arab Muslims' grip over the Islamic Empire. Its unwieldy size spawned disunity, which led to the establishment of independent regional entities controlled by military despots. With Islam still operating as their driving ideology, Turks soon became the principal military figures. After a relatively brief but fierce encounter with Mongols, Turks solidified their power by moving aggressively against the Byzantine Empire. Their triumphs marked the dawn of a different Islamic realm—the Ottoman Empire.

History rarely provides unmistakable markers that enable political analysts to claim the end of an era and the beginning of a new one. Unbeknownst to most political leaders and analysts of the fifteenth century, China's decision in the 1430s to stop its maritime voyages paved the way for a new epoch. As an empire poised to become the world's leading power, China had a population twice as large as Europe's, soil that produced all the substance needed by its inhabitants, an administration led by highly qualified bureaucrats, technology greatly admired by foreign visitors, an iron industry vastly superior to Britain's, and an armada that surpassed by a substantial margin the might of any European navy. But then China's leaders paid heed to Confucianism and turned their backs on the world. In so doing, they stopped their empire from becoming the world's hegemon, and made it possible for others to place their imprint on the course of world history.

In sum, Christianity, Islam, and Confucianism came into being in incongruent ways, evolved differently, had dissimilar effects, and experienced unlike fates. And yet all three were defined by the same set of dimensions and performed the same type of functions. As political ideologies, Christianity, Islam, and Confucianism each contained a cognitive, an affective, an evaluative, a programmatic, and a social-based dimension.

Christianity evolved into a religion and in time was embraced as a political ideology, albeit a divided one, for the purpose of averting the collapse of a decaying empire. Though Christianity failed to achieve its originally assigned political goal, eventually it transcended its originators' expectations. Opportunities emerged with the demise of a portion of the original empire in which Christianity took root. Without an emperor to curb its authority, and with kings and princes competing with one another in a feudal system, the Christian church bestowed upon itself the secular power and legitimacy to dictate the circumstances under which war could be used as a political tool. The crusades became the end product of this process, and Christianity became its justification—its political ideology. Ultimately, the ideological drive that spawned the crusades did not engender greater power for the Christian church. Averse to continuing to absorb the sizeable costs elicited by the religious military expeditions, the Christian secular leaders curtailed the terrestrial powers of the Church. However, their actions, as will be explained in the next chapter, did not lessen the power of Christianity as a structure of meaning.

Islam traveled a less cumbersome path. From its inception, it was created as a medium designed to engender unity between the social, economic, and political life, and the afterlife. Its emergence as a religion corresponded with its materialization as a political ideology. With few major material barriers obstructing its early evolution, Islam spread rapidly and helped create an empire. In due course, the Islamic Empire also would be undermined by its own success. Burdened by its leaders' inability to monitor and rule their vast realm, and unable to create a political ideology bound by a single, coherent voice, the empire gave way to the establishment of a commonwealth with multiple centers of political and religious power. Still, though by the fifteenth century the Islamic Empire had become the Ottoman Empire, its political essence remained Islam.

Confucianism's travails were of a nature highly distinct from those just recapped. With a birth predating both Christianity and Islam, Confucianism's role as a decisive political ideology was of limited consequence outside the Chinese Empire until the early stages of the fifteenth century. It was then, with a technology and material capacity vastly superior to those of other empires, that the leaders of the Chinese Empire sought political guidance in Confucianism and concluded that expanding its domain beyond its immediate region was a disreputable goal. Their decision eventually extended the West and its leaders the opportunity to shape the material and normative structure of the world system.

2 Beginnings and restructuring

The intermingling of religion and politics between the sixteenth and eighteenth centuries in Europe and the Americas

Introduction

The period between the start of the sixteenth century and the middle of the eighteenth century was marked by momentous ideological changes in the world arena. European actors aspiring to enlarge their power used Christianity to legitimize their conquests of distant lands and validate their attempts to change the belief systems of their new subjects. The Christian norms the conquerors relied on varied. The Spaniards depended on Catholicism to alter the existence of the inhabitants in the central and southern section of the Western Hemisphere (including Mexico), while the British used Protestantism to transform the lives of their northern counterparts. The actions of both actors and Portugal, along with the religions they exported, enlarged the world system measurably and transferred to it new structures of meaning. During this same period, several other changes came about. In Western Europe, Christianity's radical transformation helped engender costly religious wars. After a lengthy struggle, leaders agreed to tolerate each other's right to dictate which religion their countries would practice. Leaders, however, remained committed to using religion as the means to propagate their chosen system of beliefs, values, and ideas amongst their subjects. Their decision was based not on a renewed commitment to moral values, but on the belief that by using religion as a means to dictate how people should act morally in their relations with each other, they would protect their power. These changes set the foundation upon which the modern sovereign state would grow, and helped restructure Europe's regional system. As these changes were taking place, a nearby but different type of actor was experiencing a reversal of fortune. In Europe's eastern section, the leaders of the Ottoman Empire strove to further integrate it. As the successor to Byzantium, the Ottoman Empire, though still strong, was unable to match the political, bureaucratic, economic, and technological developments originated by its western rivals. Islam, the political religion that centuries earlier had helped give rise to the Islamic Empire and give it its unique structure of meaning, had lost much of its energy. Consequently, the empire began to endure the slow but steady crumbling of its power. This chapter describes these distinct occurrences, the ideological impetus that guided, accompanied, or resulted from them, and their effects on distinct entities, the regional system encompassed by Europe's leading actors and the Ottoman Empire, and the world system.

The old mixed with the new

The arrival of the Spaniards and the Portuguese in the New World in the late fifteenth century and early sixteenth century stimulated the second biggest population shift of modern times and paved the way for the creation of a new world system.[1] The population transfer was accompanied by a radical change in the world system's structure of meaning.

By the end of the thirteenth century, the Emirate of Granada in southern Spain was all that remained of Hispanic Islam. The frontiers between Moors and Spaniards lingered in a fluid and confused state for more than two hundred years. During this period, neither war nor peace defined the relationships between the bordering populations. The obstacles to a solution favorable to the Spaniards began to crumble in the late 1460s, when Isabella, half sister of the king of Castile, married Ferdinand, heir to the Aragonese throne. The married couple became the rulers of almost two-thirds of the peninsula's land and population after the death of Castile's king in 1474.[2]

With a substantial portion of Spain's territory still controlled by Moors, and with one of Europe's largest Jewish communities, Isabella and Ferdinand became determined to transform their kingdoms into true Christian kingdoms.[3] With assistance from the Portuguese, they launched the drive to expel Moors from Granada.[4] After a ten-year struggle, they succeeded. The victory had a monumental effect. As a historian noted in 1492: "[T]his is the end of the calamities of Spain. This is the term of the happiness of this barbarous people [Muslims], which, as they say, came from Mauritania some 800 years ago and inflicted its cruel and arrogant oppression on conquered Spain."[5] With the peninsula free of Moors, Isabella and Ferdinand concentrated their efforts on their second target—the "infidel" Jews.

In the summer of 1478, the two monarchs summoned a council to prepare a program designed to reform the Church in Spain. From early on, attendees launched a series of accusations against Jews who, in an attempt to avert violence and discrimination, had converted to Christianity. The "new" Christians, claimed council members, were reverting to the Jewish faith. This act threatened the fabric of Castilian society and its regime. Shortly thereafter, Pope Sixtus IV issued a bull authorizing the start of inquisitions in Seville.[6] In 1492, Isabella and Ferdinand released two edicts. The decrees stated that those who had not been baptized as Christians by the end of July would have to leave the kingdoms of Castile and Aragon, and would not be allowed to return. The implementations of diktats brought about the disintegration of what had been the largest Jewish community in Europe.[7]

With Castile and Aragon free of "infidels," the two monarchs pressed on. Determined to transform Spain into a geopolitical concept, they sought to revive Castile's economy, which had lost nearly two-thirds of its tax revenue since the beginning of the century. In addition to allowing municipal governments to employ craft guilds that benefited from wage, price, and production controls, they promoted the export of products that Castile could produce at competitive prices, and they introduced mercantilist measures that prohibited the export of gold and the import of commodities that might compete with national industry and agriculture.[8] As these measures were being implemented, the two monarchs wondered whether their attempts would be enough to outpace the benefits generated by Portugal's latest maritime victories.

Portugal in the fifteenth century was a weak European actor. With a very small and poor population, the monarchy had searched for access to overseas commodities to sell to wealthier entities throughout Europe.[9] During that period, it took over the uninhabited Madeira archipelago, began to colonize the Cape Verde islands, reached the Gulf of Guinea and created the settlement of Elmina, and rounded the tip of Africa. As the expeditions were being carried out, Christopher Columbus approached representatives of Portugal's king with a unique proposal. As an alternative to reaching Asia, Columbus proposed a westward course to Cipango (Japan) and Cathay (China) based on the estimation that the distance separating Europe from East Asia was two thousand four hundred nautical miles.[10] In 1492, shortly after the fall of Granada, Isabella and Ferdinand agreed to finance three-quarters of the costs of the expeditions. During the next twelve years Columbus completed four trips. By his last trip, many other adventurers had already explored much of the American Atlantic coast between Trinidad and the Amazon. Other triumphs followed shortly. Vastly superior military and maritime technology, the effective use of horses, and a range of endemic diseases previously unknown in the Americas facilitated the swift victories of the invaders.[11]

To help enlarge their kingdoms' material power, Isabella and Ferdinand relied once again on Christianity. Their success against the Moors had convinced them that they had been expressly chosen by God to spread Christianity. This conviction was strengthened by Pope Alexander VI, who, following the eviction of Moors from Granada and the inquisition against Jews, conferred on the royal couple the title "Catholic Kings." In praise for their commitment he released a bull that stated: "Among other works well-pleasing to the Devine Majesty and other things desirable to our heart, certainly the most outstanding is that the Catholic Faith and Christian Religion especially in our times is being exalted and spread everywhere and the salvation of souls subdued and brought under that faith."[12] As Francisco López de Gómara would note half a century later, "The Conquest of the Indies began when that of the Moors was over, for the Spanish have always fought against the infidels."[13]

Alexander VI's formal statement elicited an ethical dilemma. During the crusades and throughout the struggle against the Moors' occupation of Spain, the Church claimed that the wars were justified because they were against infidels who had wrongfully occupied Christ's land or had taken over territory (Spain) inhabited by Christians. To engage in war, the war had to be just; and for the war to be just, infidels had to act against Christians first. Equally as important, all through the crusades the Church's contention had been that because Muslims did not have Christian faith, reaching a negotiated compromise with them was unacceptable. The only alternative left to the crusaders was to kill the "infidels." By the start of the sixteenth century the Spaniards had modified both standards. They designed the justification during the conquering and colonization of the Canary archipelago in the 1470s.

Since none of the inhabitants of the Canary archipelago had ever attempted to take over the "Holy Land" or any territory occupied by Christians, to claim a just title to it the Spanish queen asserted that the extension of the faith principle justified wars against non-Christians and seizure of their territory. The logic was that it was just for Spaniards to rely on war because it was unlawful for the natives of the Canary archipelago to resist carriers of Christianity.[14] During the conquering of the archipelago, the Spaniards also had to resolve how they would treat its inhabitants. They designed three arguments. First, they argued that it was the responsibility of the conquerors to convert the natives to the Holy Christian Faith. Second, they concluded that the subjugated inhabitants had to be compelled to work in services assigned to them by the conquerors at just wages. And third, they proposed that those who accepted Christian dominion and its faith had to be accepted as Castilian subjects and, thus, were entitled to full possession of liberty and property.[15]

Isabella placed great value on the three principles. In 1503 she instructed the first governor of Española that:

> [W]e desire that the Indians be converted to our Holy Catholic Faith and their souls be saved and because this is the greatest benefit that we can desire for them, for this end it is necessary that they be instructed in the things of our faith, in order that they will come to a knowledge of it and you will take much care that this is accomplished.

She added, "Because for mining gold and performing other works which we have ordered done, it will be necessary to make use of the service of the Indians, compelling them to work in things of our service, paying to each one a wage which appears just." She also ordered that towns "be established in which the Indians can live together, as do persons who live in these our Kingdoms."[16]

The conquering and colonization of the American southern continent continued at a fervent pace for the next forty years. In the 1550s Charles V, who had become king of Spain in 1516 and emperor of the Holy Roman Empire and king of Austria in 1519, abdicated in favor of his son Philip II. By then, it was not uncommon for Charles V's advisors and myth creators to claim that

God had granted him the "Empire, kingdoms, dominions, and lordships, and universal monarchy of all, and by His hand will be guided."[17] In 1556, however, the Austrian branch of the Habsburg family assumed control of its patrimonies in eastern Europe, while Philip II remained head of the Spanish Empire and of Franche-Compté, the Netherlands, and the Italian possessions of Aragon. By the time Philip II had replaced his father, the Crown of Castile had divided its extensive American dominion into the Viceroyalty of New Spain and the Viceroyalty of Peru. A few principles defined the relationship between the Crown and its American viceroyalties. First, the viceroyalties belonged exclusively to the Crown, not to Spain. The Castilian crown possessed full sovereignty over them and had complete rights over all their offices and properties. Second, the Crown's just right over the viceroyalties was a consequence of its obligation to evangelize the Native Americans, as dictated by Pope Alexander VI's bull.[18] To facilitate evangelization, Castile and the Church established the clerical estate, a fully designed ecclesiastical organization with the same status as the clergy of metropolitan Spain.[19] They also agreed on the subordination of the Church to the Crown except on matters of dogma and the maintenance of religious discipline.[20] Third, in order to mobilize Native American labor systematically and legally, the Crown authorized the creation of *encomiendas*. With the *encomienda*, the Crown granted a person or corporation the right to collect stipulated dues and services from the inhabitants of towns, villages, and other populated places in a particular region for a specified period.[21]

The power of the Castilian kingdom continued to increase until the 1570s. Treasures from the Americas continued to fill up the royal reserves and private coffers. Still influenced by his father's vision, Philip II and his people looked forward to an age when there would be "but one shepherd and one flock in the world," and "one monarch, one empire, and one sword."[22] But that day would never arrive, not for Castile or for the Church. By the end of the sixteenth century Castile could not produce enough grain to feed its own inhabitants, its textile and shipbuilding industries were faltering, and its American trade and silver extraction were declining. To make matters worse, around the turn of the century Castile was struck by a plague that killed vast numbers of people. New epidemics and famines would continue to batter various Spanish kingdoms through much of the seventeenth century.[23] Castile's ill fortune materialized as Europe underwent a twofold ideological transformation.

Europe's religious–ideological transformation

Introduction

As Spain and Portugal were changing the political, economic, and social landscape of America, Europe's non-Iberian environment was undergoing its own makeover. Two distinct voices gave birth to a new set of ideas. In parts of continental Europe outside the Iberian Peninsula, an increasing number of merchants, philosophers, artists, and members of the clergy had been focusing less on God and more on man's human potentials. From them emerged voices that, without rebuffing God, elevated "reason of state" to a higher status. They started to assert, but seldom acknowledged openly, what had been the common practice of monarchs, kings, and princes—the primacy of self-interest over morality in the policy-making process. A second group retained its focus on God but questioned the Church's traditional role. This group, with its roots in Germany and German-speaking Switzerland, called for major reformations within the Church. In its challenge, its members stressed that the Church had undercut its spiritual authority due to its widespread corrupt activities, and that to attain salvation an individual did not need the Church to act as an intermediary. By the 1570s, seven out of ten subjects of the Holy Roman Empire were Protestants. In time, these two occurrences helped alter the nature and structure of Europe's political system.

From God to "reason of state"

In northern Italy, at the beginning of the 1400s, merchants took advantage of their location to establish commercial networks across Europe. Aware that in order to increase trade and ensure its safe passage they would need to design treaties between city-states, merchants met regularly at fairs and markets.[24] The growth of commerce was accompanied by the development of an elite that "saw business facts in a different light and from a different angle; a class, in short, that was in business." In time, the mental habits of the new elite, along with the public and private lives they lived, reached other classes and influenced all fields of human thought and action.[25] With this new interest came the development of a liberal spirit of inquiry—the belief that men should depend less on Church doctrine to address a wide array of issues. Men, not God, became the new measure of things in Renaissance Italy.[26] The consequences of this transformation were multiple and often interrelated.

With emphasis redirected to men, there arose an increased interest in the individual as hero, and in the concept of *virtu*. A Renaissance gentleman was an individual who, aided by an understanding of classical culture, developed both the skill and determination to mold his own destiny. The individual could project the combination of both qualities in war, diplomacy, literature, and the arts. The effects of this form of thinking in the political arena were substantial, and no one depicted the emerging political vision better than Niccolo Machiavelli.

Influenced by classical authors, Machiavelli posited a simple, practical, political theory.[27] He built his argument on the notions that history is taught by example, that power is a critical transformer of behavior, that men can be the authors of their own destiny and rarely engage in good acts unless necessary, and that rulers act solely for the purpose of serving their own political interests. He emphasized that a leader's self-interests, not morality, must always determine the state's political concerns, and that the uses of force, along with a deep understanding of the art of war, almost invariably bring about political success.[28] A prince, he wrote, should have:

> no other aim or thought, nor take up any other thing for his study, but war and its organization and discipline ... [I]t is of such virtue that it not only maintains those who are born princes, but often enables men of private fortune to attain to that rank ... The chief cause of the loss of states, is the contempt of this art, and the way to acquire them is to be well versed in the same.[29]

Machiavelli's argument was not unique. In response to those who claimed that he was proposing a new code of ethics for princes, he remarked that he was merely describing something already well known by successful rulers— that in order to protect the state the prince was often obliged "to act against faith, against charity, against humanity, and against religion."[30] His recipe for effective political behavior proved to be so cogent that in time it became a "grammar of power, not only for the 16th century, but for the ages that have followed."[31] Machiavelli's political precept, however, would not attain the status of political ideology until the Treaty of Westphalia in 1648, when those who asserted that religion was not a sufficient justification for war finally won widespread support.

A Christian house divided

Europe was in a state of limbo in the early 1400s. The Hundred Years War (1337–1453) between England and France, England's recurring wars with the Scots, and the constant battles between the princes of Germany's separate domains fostered fragmentation and produced power vacuums throughout major parts of Europe. The tension generated by these discords was compounded by the papacy's sustained, but unsuccessful, attempts to supersede the monarch's temporal authority, and its failure to curb corruption and incompetence within the Church.

In the early 1300s, ecclesiastical law decreed that a king could not tax the clergy without papal permission. At war with one another and in need of funds to finance their military campaigns, Philip IV and Edward I, as the respective leaders of the French monarchy and the English kingdom, challenged the decree. After failing to convince both monarchs to resolve their differences peacefully, and learning that the French ruler had proclaimed that in his kingdom temporal rule belonged entirely to him, Boniface VIII responded with a rebuke and a threat. Philip IV's assertion, stated the spiritual monarch, represented a terrible abuse of secular powers and he, as the pope, would excommunicate any prelate or ecclesiastical person who paid kings without his authorization. This was not the only dispute affecting the relationship between Philip IV and Boniface VIII. During that same period, the French monarch accused a bishop of committing treason and ordered his arrest. Dismayed by what he believed to be a major encroachment on his authority, Boniface VIII wrote to Philip IV: "[L]et no one persuade you, dearest son, that you have no superior or that you are not subject to the head of the ecclesiastical hierarchy. For he is a fool who thinks, and whoever affirms it pertinaciously is convicted as an unbeliever and is outside the fold of the good shepherd."[32] Angered by the admonition, the French monarch imprisoned the pope.[33] Boniface VIII's successor, Clement V, the first of a line of French popes who would reside in Avignon instead of Rome, came under Philip IV's control almost immediately. Shortly after assuming his new office, Clement V published a bull acknowledging the king's right both to tax the clergy and to put on trial and imprison any French clergy accused of treason, blasphemy, and heresy.

The power shift did not run its course with the end of the struggle between Philip IV and Boniface VIII. As monarchs strove to assert their temporal authority throughout Europe, a different type of unease began to surface. By the fall of Constantinople in the mid-fifteenth century, the fear that good actions in themselves could not help men and women achieve salvation had spread widely among members of the clergy. Good deeds, they argued, were praiseworthy only if God, who controlled human affairs as sternly as an absolute ruler, decreed so.[34] Many of these clergyman also expressed great discontent with the behavior of their own peers. Abbot Johannes Trithemius of Sponheim, for instance, criticized his monks for ignoring their vows of poverty and chastity. The bishop of Torcello, in turn, noted that the "morals of the clergy are corrupt; they have become an offense to the laity." Pope Leo, as he assessed the behavior of the clergy in France, observed in 1516 that the "lack of rule in the monasteries in France and the immodest life of the monks have come to such a pitch that neither kings, princes, nor the faithful have any respect for them." But even popes and those who served him directly were severely criticized. During that same period, Machiavelli charged that there could be no greater demonstration of papal "decadency than the fact that the nearer people are to the Roman Church, the head of their religion, the less religious they are."[35]

The spark that ignited the revolt against the Church was the sale of indulgences. In the fifteenth century, it was not uncommon to believe that sinning was permissible so long as one possessed the means to buy indulgences. Eager to augment revenues, Pope Sixtus IV proclaimed in 1476 that indulgences also applied to the dead residing temporarily in purgatory. The new proclamation enticed relatives of departed souls to buy papal grants to shorten their stay in purgatory. Impressed by the success of the campaign, the ruler of the Vatican announced in 1517 that in order to rebuild St. Peter's basilica he would grant donors "complete absolution and remissions of all" past sins and "preferential treatment" for future sins. By then, the acquisition of indulgences had become such a common practice that the dean of St. Paul's Cathedral,

John Colet, openly admitted that the commercialization of indulgences had transformed the Church into a "money machine."[36]

It was during this period that Martin Luther, a monk who had been appointed professor of philosophy at Wittenberg by the ruler of Saxony, was approached by a group of men asking him to assess the authenticity of papal indulgences they had received from Johann Tetzel, a friar acting as an agent of the archbishop of Mains. After being denounced by Tetzel for his repudiation of the indulgences' authenticity, Luther issued a postulate titled "Disputation for the Clarification of the Power of Indulgences." In it, he noted that the selling of pardons made light of sin because it degraded the contrition. In a letter to Rome, Luther argued that the pope lacked the authority to free unrepentant souls from purgatory and asked, with a touch of sarcasm: "Why does not the pope empty purgatory for the sake of holy love and of the dire need of the souls that are there, if he redeems a ... number of souls for the sake of miserable money with which to build a church?"[37]

By 1520, Luther had published several critiques of the Church's doctrine. In them he asserted that an individual's salvation did not depend on engaging in good works or on indulgences granted by the church that forgave individuals for their sins. To the question "by what means a man becomes justified, free, and a true Christian" Luther stated that "none among outward things, under whatever name they may be reckoned, has any influence in producing Christian righteousness or liberty, nor, on the other hand, unrighteousness or slavery." Faith alone, he claimed, enables man to be justified and free. He also noted that the Holy Scripture made no distinction between the laity and priests, and that the differentiation had led to the creation of a system that had become terribly corrupt.

> This bad system has now issued in such a pompous display of power and such a terrible tyranny that no earthly government can be compared to it, as if the laity were something else than Christian ... [W]e have become the slaves of the vilest men on earth, who abuse our misery to all the disgraceful and ignominious purposes of their own will.[38]

The papal monarchy immediately condemned Luther's declarations, demanded that his writings be burned, and asked him to repudiate his work and rejoin the faith. Undaunted, he refused to acquiesce.

As the struggle between Martin Luther and the Church ensued, different forms of Protestantism emerged throughout parts of Europe. Though not of one mind, the promoters of Protestantism shared a set of principles. They rejected papal authority; condemned the clergy; replaced Latin with native languages; and abandoned celibacy, worshiping of the Virgin and saints, and pilgrimages.[39] In an attempt to avert further losses, the papacy convened the Council of Trent in 1545, 1551, and 1562, and ordered the design of a more enlightened doctrine. In response, the council proposed that the Church stop selling indulgences, condemn clerical abuses, demand that bishops reside in the regions they presided over, prohibit the vending of Church offices, build a seminary in every diocese, and mount an educational offensive designed to promote orthodoxy among the laity. The reforms had their intended effect. Between 1570 and 1650, Protestantism throughout the European continent diminished from forty percent to twenty percent, but at a considerable human cost.[40]

England, France, Spain, Germany, and the Netherlands were amongst the first European entities to absorb the destruction brought about by the fissure between Catholics and Protestants. In the mid-1520s, England's ruler, Henry VIII, asked the pope to annul his marriage to Catherine of Aragon so that he could marry Anne Boleyn. When the pope refused, the king demanded that Parliament pass a law stipulating that he was the head of the English church and that the clergy served under his control. In spite of the changes brought about by the passage of the *Submission of the Clergy* law in 1533, England did not renounce Catholicism immediately. The first significant modification took place when Elizabeth I, who had assumed the throne in 1558, tried to balance the demands from both the Protestants and the Catholics. She sought to appease both sides by retaining several elements of Catholicism while strengthening the foundations of Protestantism.

Her compromise did not sit well with several of Europe's most powerful leaders. The pope excommunicated Elizabeth. During this time, Mary, Queen of Scots, determined to revive Catholicism in England, lent support to those plotting Elizabeth's assassination. Upon learning of Mary's actions, Elizabeth brought her to trial and condemned her to death. It was the king of Spain, Phillip II, however, who would ultimately take the most drastic step. With encouragement from the pope, he ordered his armada to invade England in 1588. Elizabeth's fleet, with backing from the kings of France and the Netherlands, had little trouble routing the would-be invaders.

England's two temporary allies underwent their own religious turmoil during this period. Between 1562 and 1598, France experienced a series of religious wars between Catholics and Protestants. Convinced that France would not have peace until he found a solution that addressed the needs and interests of moderate Protestants and Catholics, Henry IV produced the Edict of Nantes in 1598. Though by then the French monarch had become a Catholic, with the edict he granted Protestants the right to occupy public office, assemble, worship openly, and attend schools and universities.

The challenges faced by the Holy Roman Empire during this period were substantially more complex. Attempts by the Church and the ruler of the empire, Charles V, to persuade Luther to recant the arguments he had presented did not produce the desired results. Instead, they helped foster a stronger anti-Rome sentiment amongst Germans. Urged by Luther to confiscate church lands and property and redistribute them, state leaders within the empire did exactly that and, in the process, became strong advocates of his new religious doctrine. The divide took a turn to the worse in 1530. That year, at Augsburg, the papists released a *Confutation of the Protestant*

Confession of Faith. At its core, the document demanded that Protestants return to the Catholic faith immediately. The Protestants responded with their own formulation of Protestantism—the *Confession of Augsburg*—and creation of the League of Schmalkalden. Pressing threats mounted by the Ottoman Turks forced Charles V to tolerate the alliance formed by the German Protestant princes. Thus, by the early 1540s all of central and northern Germany had become Protestant, with only Austria, Bavaria, and the ecclesiastical principalities along the Rhine refusing to abandon the original doctrine.

Luther's death in 1546, and the relative but temporary absence of foreign challenges, enabled Charles V to try to regenerate religious orthodoxy in the Holy Roman Empire. With financial support from Pope Paul III, Charles V mounted a military campaign against the leaders of the Schmalkald League. Victory followed soon, but not for long. Fearful that Charles V would use his newly gained power against France, Henry II put aside his Catholic beliefs and extended his support to the German Protestants. The struggle continued until 1552, when Charles V, aware that his hope of unifying the Holy Roman Empire under a single religion would not be realized, assented to many of his enemies' demands. The settlement reached in 1555 at Augsburg granted recognition to Lutheranism and Roman Catholicism in Germany. It also extended to the ruler of each state the right to decide which religion would be practiced within his domain, as well as the right to force subjects unwilling to accept his faith to move to another state with their property.[41] The agreement also stipulated that courts would settle religious disputes.

The Augsburg Agreement remained the base of an unstable religious peace until 1618, when conflict re-emerged. What started as a religious struggle soon became a power contest embroiling German princes and neighboring actors, each one striving to control as much German territory as possible or to prevent their adversaries from expanding their territorial power.[42] Ultimately, intervention in the war by France and Sweden forced the emperor of the Holy Roman Empire to seek a peace settlement. By then, the emperor's control over the German territorial rulers had been almost nullified.[43] The peace of 1648 brought about major territorial changes and altered the power distribution in Europe measurably; with respect to religious matters, however, it did little more than reconfirm the agreements reached at Augsburg in 1555.[44]

The Reformation reinforced Germany's particularist tradition. The Holy Roman Empire had been an empire in name but not in fact since 1356.[45] For some three centuries, the empire had encompassed some three hundred entities of different sizes, but none was massively large. At the head it had an emperor, who in turn presided over kings, princes, dukes, and high-ranking Church officials, each determined to protect and enlarge, whenever possible, its territorial authority and power. Following the agreement, whether Protestant or Catholic, German leaders became more powerful and determined to protect their respective independent interests. Protestants benefited by taking over lands that had been owned by the Roman Catholic Church, while Catholic leaders gained greater access to church resources within their territories so as to be able to resist Protestantism. The incompatible drives made it nearly impossible for the leader of the empire to build the type of centralized state other powerful entities throughout Europe were erecting. Though the failure cannot be attributed solely to the division that emerged within the Christian church, the rift served well those who valued protecting their immediate interests more than creating a unified entity.

The Netherlands faced its own unique set of challenges. The relationship between the Dutch and the leaders of the Habsburg Empire had become acrimonious by the middle of the sixteenth century. As one of the nodal points of European trade since the eleventh century, the Dutch, with the aid of a remarkable entrepreneurial spirit, had engendered noticeable wealth. To control and defend the very large empire, Charles V had imposed a substantial portion of that responsibility on the seventeen provinces that made up the Netherlands.[46] During that same period, he sought to establish a hierarchically structured, centralized administration designed both to build defenses against floods and to reclaim land from the sea in order to create cultivable acreage, which would then be used to feed the region's rapidly growing population. Local communities objected. The decision by the monarch, they claimed, was an arrogation of local privileges, one that he imposed solely for the purpose of enlarging his own coffers.[47]

The religious divide that had taken hold over much of Europe further aggravated the relationship between the monarch and his Dutch subjects. Based on the sixteenth-century axiom that a political entity could not survive without a unified religion, Charles V resorted to severe measures to suppress the reformations advocated by Protestants and to restore the authority of the Roman Church.[48] His son, Philip II, exacerbated matters when he gained permission from Rome to create new bishoprics in 1559.[49] The Calvinists, though a minority, responded with outrage to what they considered an infringement on each province's right to be in charge of its own religious institutions, and to develop to the best of its abilities its trade and financial capacities. After a number of deadly encounters, the rebels and royalists signed the Pacification of Ghent in November 1576. The agreement did not last long. In 1579, representatives of the northern Dutch provinces concurred, via the Union of Utrecht, to assist one another militarily, to create a common army, and to tax their citizens collectively in order to keep the army. The southern provinces responded with their own treaty, the Union of Arras, and the decision to initiate negotiations with representatives from the Spanish monarchy.[50] The accords divided the country along religious lines.[51] Religion became "the binding force that held together the different interests of the different classes and provided them with an organizational and propaganda machine capable of creating the first genuinely national and international parties in modern European history."[52]

The potential for stability emerged in 1609, when the northern and southern provinces signed the Twelve Years' Truce.[53] It was a false signal; war ensued once again in 1621. The two parties continued to meet in the battlefield for the next twenty-five years, with neither side being able to impose its will on the other. Finally, in the early 1640s, the Spanish monarchy, which was also at war with Germany and France and finding it very difficult to finance all three conflicts, approached French and Dutch representatives with comprehensive peace proposals. After extensive negotiations, the Spaniards and the Dutch signed the Treaty of Münster in 1648. The accord recognized the Dutch Republic as an independent state and its right to retain control over the territories that it had conquered during the final stages of the conflict. The agreement was part of the greater Peace of Westphalia that brought to an end the Thirty Years' War.

The birth of the modern conception of sovereignty

The Thirty Years' War that started in 1618, along with the treaty that terminated it in 1648, transformed Europe's political landscape and the nature of politics in multiple ways.[54] First, the treaty divided Europe into three distinct regions. The east continued to be dominated by a landed aristocracy that would not experience a major challenge to its authority until the middle of the nineteenth century. The middle region broke into a large number of fragmented states, with each determined to protect its independence and to promote either Catholicism or Protestantism. Their uncompromising zeal transformed the Holy Roman Empire into a politically powerless actor. The region that gained the most from the prolonged war was the west. Dominated by England, France, and for a brief while the United Provinces, and aided by subsidies, tax exemptions, and new commercial laws, the area underwent rapid economic development. This region was also the principal beneficiary of other major changes.

By giving themselves spiritual authority over the residents of their respective kingdoms, the monarchs partially validated Jean Bodin's claim that territorial sovereignty was the key component in world politics. Sovereignty, according to Bodin, is a property controlled not by a ruler or rulers but by the state, and because it is vested in the commonwealth, it is both absolute and perpetual. The leaders of a commonwealth act only as "the lieutenants and agents of the sovereign ruler" and the sovereign "cannot in any way be subject to the commands of another" at any time.[55]

Bodin's sovereignty was nothing more than an ideal, unless its holders possessed the means to enforce and protect it.[56] The second effect experienced by the principal actors in Europe's western region was an alteration in the nature of their power and, thus, the capacity of states to protect their sovereignty. During the Thirty Years' War, monarchs relied mainly on hired troops to fight their battles. This practice proved to be costly and counterproductive. At the war's end, monarchs began to build their own armies and to assume the function of commander-in-chief. With the French monarch paving the way, other rulers in the region also began to set up the infrastructure necessary to train and serve their respective armies. Military camps and barracks, many with their own hospitals, and backed by administrative and judicial institutions, mushroomed throughout western Europe. To finance their development, monarchs took measures designed to stimulate economic growth and raised funds through taxation.[57]

The birth and application of a new ideology never materialize in tandem. The fragmentation of the Church, followed by lengthy and costly religious wars between Catholics and Protestants, freed monarchs to put into practice Machiavelli's contention that their interests always overrode morality, and Bodin's claim that territorial sovereignty was absolute and perpetual. Initially—and throughout much of western Europe—Machiavelli's argument that a leader had the right to define his state's interests according to his own political interests superseded Bodin's declaration that commonwealths, not their respective leaders, are sovereign. In spite of this discrepancy, 1648 marks the dawn of the state as Europe's chief actor, with its interests defined by its leader. From this time forth, interactions between states would be driven by their leaders' ideological conviction that their most important responsibility was to protect their states' sovereignty and that to succeed they had to, at minimum, ensure that their states' power did not decrease in relationship to the power of other states and, at maximum, augment their states' power whenever the benefits of doing so outweighed the costs.[58]

To contend that Westphalia freed monarchs to put into practice the idea that their interests always override morality is not to argue that religion became a less significant power tool. Political leaders of that period concurred with Machiavelli's dictum that no "institution is firm or lasting if its rests on man's strength alone ... Sovereignties, in particular possess strength, unity, stability only to the degree to which they are sanctified by religion."[59] For Machiavelli, which religion the prince promoted and supported was not important; what was essential was that he uphold the foundations of his country's religion. As such, religion was a tool of power. It functioned as an ideology to help increase the mutual trust and collective morale of the people of the prince's country. The shared norms propagated and supported by religion made it possible for the prince to not have to rely always on force to protect and boost his power.

An inauspicious beginning

Competition compelled Europe's leading actors to expand their territorial reach. England was no exception. Its initial drive was stimulated by Spain's imperial threat and the conviction that unimpeded access to, and control over, sections of America would help advance its trade interests, multiply its financial assets, and augment its regional power. Other contributing factors were the need of idle Englishmen to find jobs, the religious mayhem triggered by the split between Catholics and Protestants, and the belief by some members of the English elite community that it was their moral duty to propagate a more humane form of Christianity than the one promulgated by the

Spaniards. The role played by these factors did not remain constant, nor did England's policies towards its American colonies.

By the middle of the sixteenth century, many European leaders feared that Castile's imperialism would ultimately pose a direct threat to the continent. For most of the parties involved it was virtually impossible to separate power politics from religious rivalries.[60] Concern arose regarding the version of Christianity (Catholicism) Charles V, and subsequently his son Philip II, sought to enforce both in Europe and America. It was believed that rather than liberating people from internal and external threats and guaranteeing the survival of the Christian republic, the Castilian empire would use its superior power to annihilate the rights of all free men. As William Paterson, first governor of the Bank of England, noted at the start of the eighteenth century, "it has only been from accident and the unaccountable mismanagement of the Spaniards that any of the nations of Europe worth looking after have been left in a condition to preserve their liberty."[61]

Until the second half of the sixteenth century neither the English Crown nor Parliament estimated it was imperative for England to look westward in order to replicate Castile's maritime adventures. England's population and market had been growing steadily and sharing in the general economic prosperity of Europe. London, moreover, was rapidly becoming an attractive metropolis.[62] But then England's fortunes took a turn for the worse. Exports of cloth began to decline, generating an economic depression that resulted in the widespread displacement of workers. The continuing rise in population, in turn, helped spawn increases in food prices, unemployment, and landlessness.[63]

These ills were compounded by the religious turmoil that followed the passage of the 1533 *Submission of the Clergy* law. The law positioned the monarch at the head of the state and the church. This signified that the Church of England gave up its power and authority to formulate Church laws without the king's approval. It also meant that any form of religious dissent could be construed as both treason and heresy. As noted by a clergyman of that period, "[N]o subject may, without hazard of his own damnation in rebelling against God, question or disobey the will and pleasure of his sovereign." Of equal import was the king's decision to divorce his kingdom fully from papal authority. In *Restraint of Appeals Act,* Henry VIII's chief minister, Thomas Cromwell, wrote:

> [I]t is manifestly declared and expressed that this realm of England is an Empire, and so hath been accepted in the world, governed by one Supreme Head and King having the dignity and royal estate of the Imperial crown of the same, into whom a body politic compact of all sorts and degrees of people divided in terms and by names of Spirituality and Temporalty, be bounded and owed to bear next to God a natural and humble obedience.[64]

By declaring England an empire, Cromwell was declaring it a sovereign entity, no longer under the jurisdiction of the pope. Both acts had additional political intents. As the ruler of the newly created Anglican Church, the monarch sought to promote religious and political conformity. To underscore his dual authority, King Charles I declared in the 1620s that "People are governed by the pulpit more than the sword in time of peace."[65] The Anglican Church thus became one of the central supporters of regal authority.[66]

The increase in regal authority did not cultivate an outflow of civil harmony immediately. The most unyielding and determined Protestants in England were the "Calvinist/Perkins' Puritans," who, in their resolve to change the Anglican Church, wanted to transform society as well. This commitment to changing both the Church and society was inspired by Jean Calvin and modeled on the teachings of William Perkins.

Calvin published the first edition of his *Institutes of the Christian Religion* in 1536. That same year he moved to French-speaking Geneva, Switzerland, which a few months earlier had ordered its monasteries disbanded, mass abolished, and the authority of the pope renounced. After a fourteen-year effort, Calvin and his supporters had created a system in which the Church, though separate from the state, ruled on all moral and religious matters. The system's governing body—the Consistory—was composed of ministers and laymen elders elected by the city council. The Consistory imposed a strict religious and moral code on the citizens of Geneva and turned every conceivable sin into a crime. Excommunication and banishment from the community became common practices, and so did the execution of apostates, heretics, adulterers, pregnant single women, and rebellious children. Calvinism, thus, became an ideology designed to transform Geneva's society based on the claim that Rome's Church had become corrupt, and on the Renaissance assumption that "inspired" individuals, working as members of a "Reformed Church," could create a good society, one committed to serving God.

In England, the most influential Protestant doctrine was closely associated with the school of thought that supplied the main body of Puritan clergy in the early seventeenth century. The teachings of the school's founder, William Perkins, were respected by both the clergy and the laity, and studied at Cambridge. At the core of the doctrine lay the claim that Puritans cooperated with God's purposes and strove to bring about his kingdom, while Catholics were irresponsible men and women interested in serving the world instead of God. Puritan clergy taught that by studying the scriptures and searching their consciences in earnest, men would develop the courage to fight tenaciously in order to bring about God's wishes. Conscience, explained Perkins, serves as a control mechanism between God and Man. Each person's conscience responds to God and provides him a warning signal against wrong actions.[67]

Much of the Puritans' initial ire in England had been directed against Henry VIII's decision to keep the ecclesiastical structure of the Anglican Church mostly Catholic, but with the monarch instead of the pope as its leader.[68] By the start of the seventeenth century, King James I, weary of the ongoing challenges voiced by Puritans, warned that if they did not conform to his authority and that of the Anglican Church, he would force "them out of the land." Both sides tolerated one another until 1625, when Charles I succeeded his father. Determined to strengthen the hand of English Catholics, Charles I appointed as leaders of the Anglican Church bishops devoted to restoring Anglican orthodoxy and cutting back the role played by Puritan ministers. He weakened the capability of the Puritans to voice their opposition when he dissolved Parliament in 1629 and went on to rule arbitrarily for the next eleven years. During this period, the number of Puritans who moved to America increased substantially.[69] But by then, a number of the inhabitants occupying parts of North America had already been exposed to the Christian fervor of many Englishmen.

Two mindsets dominated the thinking of the first group of English explorers. For a short time, most assumed they would be able to accumulate great wealth rapidly and with little effort. As their search for gold mines and Spanish treasure ships failed to bring about the desired results, they turned their interests to the production of tobacco. Behind this change in focus, however, lay an important difference in perspective. For many Englishmen, America symbolized an opportunity to carry on the work of Jesus and to save souls. In the new land they saw an opportunity to reaffirm their interpretation of history as a progressive movement that would eventually result in the conversion of all mankind. They viewed America's natives as members of an uneducated society that deserved external assistance in order to realize their potential. "It is not the nature of men, which makes them barbarous and uncivil … change the education of men and you shall see their nature will be greatly rectified and corrected."[70]

Determined not to replicate Castile's cruel treatment of Native Americans, the colonizers assumed they could rely on kind actions instead. While the Spaniards conquered the West Indies "with rapiers point and musket shot, murdering so many millions of naked Indians," the English should use "fair and loving means, suiting to our English natures." Gentle actions, moreover, would help convince Native Americans to embrace Christianity, and conversion would lead to a successful colonial enterprise. "Godliness is great riches, and … if we first seek the kingdom of God, all other things will be given unto us." The Virginia Company of London, chartered in April 1606 by King James I to "make habitation plantation and to deduce a Colony … of our people into that part of America commonly called Virginia," also advocated, at least during the early years, the implementation of a non-violent and deferential approach. It claimed that by "way of peace and gentleness, then shall you always range them in love to your wards, and in peace with your English people, and by proceeding in that way, shall open the springs of earthly benefits to them both, and of safety to yourselves."[71]

Not every colonist in Virginia shared the belief that Native Americans would embrace Christianity if treated fairly. Just as many Spaniards had used their experience in the Canary Islands to guide their initial dealings with America's indigenous population, a significant number of Englishmen applied the knowledge they had acquired during their colonization of Ireland for the same purpose. Under its loose dominion since the twelfth century, the English kingdom decided four centuries later to widen and solidify its control over Ireland. The decision elicited violent responses from the Irish. Angered by the Irish's "barbaric" reaction and unwillingness to embrace England's "superior" civilization, the English waged on them a war of terror and intimidation. "[N]othing but fear and force can teach duty and obedience to such rebellious people." The reaction seemed to have its intended effect. As the publicist for an English leader boasted, the Irish were filled with terror "when they saw the heads of their fathers, brothers, children and kinsfolk, and friends, lie on the ground before their faces, as they came to speak to the colonel." With victory came control of great estates that would be colonized with Protestant settlers from England and Scotland.[72]

It did not take long for the second outlook to overtake the first one. When it became evident that Native Americans would not acquiesce peacefully, most of the colonizers, including those who had originally advocated humane treatment, began to accept the actions endorsed by the likes of Martin Frobisher and Ralph Lane. Informed by their own experiences in Ireland, Frobisher and Lane advocated the use of force, savagery, and harsh reprisals to achieve their ends. With neither the Native Americans nor the colonizers willing to acquiesce, violence arose. By 1624, the Virginia colonists, with London's full backing, had eradicated much of the native threat.[73]

Colonists in New England also underwent a change of heart. Many of those who contemplated a move to the region believed that England's latest troubling economic and social ills signaled that God disapproved of the place. The commitment on the part of the Puritans to migrate and to take on new risks was deepened by their conviction that in New England they would have a chance to "display the efficacy and power of the Gospel both in zealous preaching, professing, and wise talking under it, before the faces of these poor blind Infidels." This vow was publicly noted by the 1629 charter of the Massachusetts Bay Company, which stated that its principal objective was "to win and incite the natives of the country to the knowledge and obedience of the only true God and Savior of mankind, and the Christian faith."[74] But it was not to be. In 1636, the Pequot, whose hegemony in the Connecticut area had been severely undermined, went on the offensive. The settlers retaliated, and by the end of April 1637 they had nearly destroyed one of New England's most powerful tribes.[75]

During this period, King Charles II decided to use the American colonies to counterbalance the Netherlands's swift economic rise. England's power depended on its navy. To build a commanding fleet, the government needed to augment its overseas trade revenues. Between 1651 and 1663, the Parliament enacted several Navigation Acts. They tendered three commands. First, they stipulated that merchants trading with English colonies could use English ships only. Second, upon identifying the colonial commodities that yielded the greatest profits to merchants and the highest revenues to the state, they limited their shipment solely to England. And third, they required that all products originating in Europe and going to the colonies stop at an English port and pay custom duties.[76]

To tighten England's control over the colonies, its government established the Dominion of New England in the 1680s. The Dominion was designed to hold under its jurisdiction the five New England colonies, along with New York and East and West New Jersey. In the meantime, James II continued with his religious campaign in England. He promoted Catholics to high-status positions, and authorized the execution and torture of Protestant rebels. Protestant church leaders, along with members of Parliament, turned against their king. They proposed to William, the Prince of Orange and a Protestant alternative to the king's crown, that he invade the island. William accepted the offer. As the Prince of Orange moved toward London, James II fled. In his new role as monarch, and with the backing of Parliament, William promised to protect the Anglican establishment and tolerate religious diversity.

William's ascension to power prompted those in the colonies who had opposed James II's measures to try to nullify them. Eager to mobilize colonial resources for a war against France, William did not welcome the colonists' challenge. Nonetheless, sensitive to the fact that in a war against France he would need their united backing, he sought a compromise. With the exception of Connecticut and Rhode Island, all of the colonies eventually agreed to have royal or proprietary governors, and the councils and the military under English auspices, and to submit all legislation for approval first by their governors and then by the king and his council. The king, in return, authorized the formation of colonial assemblies chosen by property-holders, thus granting them the same liberties held by their counterparts in England. Discord between England and the colonies continued, but the compromise survived until the 1760s. The agreement helped transform England into a genuine transatlantic empire, with London retaining the authority to design political, military, economic, and cultural policies for the colonies.[77]

Islam and the slow disintegration of the Ottoman Empire

By the seventeenth century, the Ottoman Empire no longer posed a major threat to Europe's most powerful actors. Several factors contributed to this new state of affairs. First, the Ottoman Empire did not benefit from the wealth that poured into Europe as its leading actors ventured into, and colonized, new regions. Second, while the Ottomans began after the debacle of 1683 to fight wars designed to slow down the contraction of their empire, Britain and France were engaged principally in policies of imperial expansion.[78] Third, Europe's newly acquired wealth afforded its chief members the capability to develop military technologies much more sophisticated than those created by the Ottomans.[79]

The most detrimental impediment encountered by the Ottomans was the fourth one. After the Treaty of Westphalia in the 1640s, Europe's leading actors began to establish political, economic, and social institutions that would enable them to create the modern state. To strengthen their power and capacity to control their states' inhabitants and maintain order, leaders relied on religion. Their common practice was to expel those who shared a religion different from the one chosen by the state. The Ottoman Empire, composed of inhabitants practicing a variety of religions, speaking a multitude of languages, and adhering to a broad variety of customs, never managed to develop the type of governmental structure that would ultimately facilitate the propagation of a common identity—a self-equivalent to the identities fashioned by powers such as France, England, and Prussia.[80] Though Islam lay at the core of the Ottoman Empire's system of governance, it was not utilized to build the empire. Instead, Islam was applied as a "guise" by leaders whose principal interest was to survive as a group, increase their power, and prosper in the economic sphere.[81] Islam's marginal role as a political tool of the Ottoman Empire would become evident in the nineteenth century, as one national group after another broke away from the realm in order to create its own independent state.

Building the foundation for a new world system

A world system unlike the one that existed at the end of the fifteenth century had materialized by the dawn of the eighteenth century. Five conditions set the two systems apart. First, the number of actors that were part of the new system was substantially larger than the figure that had framed the old one. Second, the European actors' dominance of the eighteenth-century world system was vastly greater than their control of the earlier system. Third, the Treaty of Westphalia paved the road for the materialization of the modern state. As such, the modern state emerged as the dominant military and economic unit in the global arena.[82] These three conditions helped increase the potential for conflict between entities that previously had interacted little with one another. Fourth, while world leaders had always known that they could not afford to lose sight of power relations, this knowledge became Europe's leading ideological principle during the eighteenth century. Though this conviction continued to play a central role, it was modified temporarily during the nineteenth century, when Europe's leading actors believed that to protect themselves they had to maintain a power balance. And fifth, whereas during earlier times Christianity had served as an ideological tool of imperialism, by the eighteenth century its principal function, albeit in different forms, was to advance unity and stability within each state or empire.[83]

It would be unwise to claim that Christianity, and the tensions generated by its internal conflicts, spawned the major changes that resulted in the structure of meaning of the eighteenth-century world system. It would be equally injudicious, however, to claim that it had no effect. Likewise, it would be imprudent to ignore the indirect effect of Islam's weakness as a unifying political ideology. This weakness lessened the Ottoman Empire's ability to protect its integrity, and in time, it changed the overall structure and nature of the Mediterranean political system.

Christianity did not engender the early Iberian explorations. Commercial and financial aspirations, abetted by an adventurous spirit, were the initial catalysts. As recurring discoveries revealed unforeseen sources of great wealth, dreams of a universal empire under Castilian leadership mesmerized the Crown. Temporal and spiritual leaders drew on Christianity to rationalize Castile's territorial conquests, the imposition of Christian doctrine on the inhabitants of the occupied territories, and the design and enforcement of labor rules on the subjugated inhabitants. Though Hispanic colonists habitually abused the rights articulated by the Castilian crown and the papacy, they also relied on Christianity to validate their transgressions. Of no less significance is the fact that the interlopers brought with them a vision of the world that was completely at odds with a belief system that had guided the actions of their new subjects. Throughout the next three centuries, this new structure of meaning radically transformed the political, economic, and social nature of much of the Western Hemisphere. And this transformation eventually had an immense effect on the actions initiated by its members, the role they played in the world system, and their capability to affect it.

Material objectives, along with a hefty dosage of adventurism, spawned early English colonialism as well. Commitment to a distinct religious ideal, inspired by the doctrines of Reformists, motivated an appreciable number of English colonists. In Edmond Wright's words, "English North America was the distant legacy of Calvin and Luther, and of the turmoil in politics and in religion that followed their teaching. And, at least in intention, its crusading was by the Word, not the Sword."[84] Many of the colonists crossed the Atlantic convinced that it was their moral obligation to create a world social order that reflected the teachings of Jesus, and that Native Americans would hail their benevolence and welcome being exposed to a "superior" civilization. This idea, initially backed by the English Crown, faded on both sides of the Atlantic as Native Americans resorted to arms to protect their spiritual and material way of life. Nevertheless, just as in the case of Spain, in the long run the Protestant tenets the English intruders sought to promulgate throughout the Western Hemisphere's northern region affected both in the type of state their descendents created and the kind of world system they envisioned and tried to design.

As Spain and then England were trying their fortunes on the other side of the Atlantic, much of Europe was experiencing its own fundamental makeover. The transformation it experienced cannot be attributed solely to the schism that emerged between Christians. Nonetheless, its role was salient and multiple. The immediate, and obviously unintended, effect of the religious struggle was the restructuring of Europe's power distribution. The Holy Roman Empire, the actor with the greatest material potential to dominate

Europe if only its multiple entities were to unite, was kept disconnected in part because of each ruler's steadfast unwillingness to forfeit his sole right to dictate his state's religious practice. With Germany divided, other actors moved aggressively to exploit whatever opportunity might arise. Another related effect of the religious struggle was the decision on the part of Europe's leading monarchs to seek in secularism an alternative and rightful rationale for political action. Secularism, in turn, stressed that a monarch had to focus on his power relative to the might of his key foes. The promotion of secularist politics, however, did not signify the rejection of religion. Religion, in fact, became an outright tool of power. Monarchs used religion as a means to impose on their states' inhabitants normative values designed to cultivate stability, mutual trust, and efficiency. As monarchs agreed to respect each other's right to attend to his country's religious concerns without external involvement, they legitimized the concept of monarchical sovereignty, which helped set the foundation for the emergence of the modern state.[85]

The slow or rapid demise of an empire can have as much effect on a regional or world system as the actual growth of an empire. Sometimes both developments proceed in tandem, and when they do, the impact on the system is distinctly more momentous than if they ensue independently. Towards the end of the seventeenth century, the Ottoman Empire began to lose its power and luster. The empire was doomed by the absence of abundant material power and the lack of an ideological religion sufficiently compelling to overcome the diversity inherent in regions with unlike religions, languages, and customs.

Conclusion

Religion and politics intermingled in major parts of the world system from the sixteenth to the end of the eighteenth centuries. Religion was the political ideology of the era. It did not dominate every single facet of the political processes, but its presence was inescapable, and it helped transform the world system's structure of meaning. Actors used religion to justify the extension of their empires in territories far away from their home base, and to socialize their new subjects. They used religion to validate their decisions to fight within and against the Holy Roman Empire; to generate domestic stability; and to rationalize their reliance on power politics in order to curtail the strength of opposing religions. And in one instance, it was the failure to properly nurture religion as a political ideology that would eventually contribute to the demise of an empire that in earlier years had been exceptionally powerful.

3 The strengthening of an empire, the materialization of a new one, and the emergence of novel ideologies: 1750–1871

The births of a unique secular ideology and a would-be empire

Europe's political arena during the eighteenth century was characterized by power competition. By the close of the century Russia had advanced across the Urals all the way into Siberia, recovered West Russia from Poland, obtained much of the former state of Poland, acquired Kiev and the middle Dnieper lands, wrested Livonia and Estonia from Sweden, and gained control of the Black Sea's north shores. The Austrian Habsburgs, because of their need to cope with potential foes on a number of fronts, limited their imperial aspirations to the surrounding areas. They ruled Austria, Bohemia, Silesia, Moravia, Hungary, Naples, Milan, Sicily, and the southern Netherlands after 1714. Prussia and the Ottoman Empire faced distinct challenges. Though the Peace of Westphalia fragmented Germany into three hundred impoverished principalities, it also enabled Prussia to emerge as their dominant entity. Its aspirations did not transcend its region's borders and were more defensive than imperialist. With the support of a highly efficient and well-financed Junker-officered army, Prussia made the most of new opportunities. It seized Silesia, a significant industrial center in the east, in 1742; it secured its status as a power to be reckoned with after it defeated Austria in 1763; and it created a continuous Prussian territory stretching from Memel in the Baltic Sea's eastern coast and Magdeburg in the western side when it gained control over one of Poland's areas in the 1770s.

As Europe's empires endeavored to consolidate or enlarge their dominions, the Ottoman Empire underwent a period of almost uninterrupted decline. By the end of the eighteenth century the Ottoman Empire had lost Hungary, the Banat, Transylvania, and Bukovina to Austria, and the north coast of the Black Sea from Bessarabia to the Caucasus, including the Crimea, to Russia. As if to add insult to injury, the Austrians and Russians forced the Turks to grant both of them the right to intervene on behalf of the Ottoman Empire's Christians.[1] And then there were Spain, Britain, and France.

No two actors could reflect better the failing value of an old ideology and the rising worth of a new one than Spain and Britain. And no other pair could convey more aptly the effects their divergent destinies were about to have on the world system. Spain's and Britain's enterprises in the Americas had unfolded as discrete and distinct attempts to build their empires and to redesign the world system according to their dissimilar ideological images. Each had as a guide a deeply rooted, but different, Christian conviction, and each possessed the capacity and will, at least initially, to rely on Christianity to shape the affairs of its targets. But eventually, they would engage in very different journeys.

Spain appeared feeble by the end of the eighteenth century. It had not been able to replicate the political, economic, and social changes other European actors had been introducing, and it remained unwilling to accept that America was producing wealth not for the metropolis but for itself and for markets of its choice.[2] It took the Spaniards several more decades to recognize that the empire had become a burden, but by then it was too late. Most European states had already turned their backs on the Christian ideology of universalism and had replaced it with the belief that to attain global hegemony a state had to promote work and industry, accept religious diversity if not at home at least elsewhere, and gain command of the seas and major trade routes.[3]

Britain's power status changed swiftly during the seventeenth and eighteenth centuries. During much of the seventeenth century, its power was inferior to France's. By the time the War of Spanish Succession had ended in 1713, however, Britain had attained power parity with France and was on its way to becoming Europe's greatest maritime entity.[4] To develop its empire, Britain relied principally on its comparative advantages in financial and commercial services. The establishment of the Bank of Britain in 1694, the regularization of the national debt, the cultivation of the stock exchange, and the growth of "country banks" increased the moneys available to both government and business. Britain's comparative advantage solidified in 1763, when France agreed to relinquish control over Canada and all its claims east of the Mississippi, and over Dominica, Grenada, St. Vincent and Tobago in the Caribbean; over Senegal in West Africa; and over a major area in India. France was not Britain's only victim; during the same period London compelled Spain to cede Florida.[5]

With its latest triumph, Britain's leaders were pressed to figure out how they would protect their enlarged empire. In its drive to become Europe's principal entity, Britain had nearly doubled its debt, and was spending more than sixty percent of its budget on interest payments on the debt.[6] To address its burgeoning fiscal predicament, the British Parliament adopted a series of measures designed to strengthen its control over the colonies and to compel its inhabitants to help pay for the safeguarding of the enlarged empire.

France's forced exit transformed Britain into the landlord of a territory that extended from the Appalachians to the Mississippi and from Canada to Louisiana. Before London could decide what to do with its new asset, the Ottawas, infuriated by the colonists' practice of buying vast tracts of land at very low prices, removing Native Americans by force from lands they occupied, and disregarding existing treaties, launched a series of attacks on the settlers. Certain that the earlier colonists had made themselves susceptible to French challenges by abusing Native Americans, Britain issued a royal proclamation in 1763. Designed to prevent the further outbreak of conflict between the colonists and Native Americans, the proclamation granted the entire region between the Alleghenies and the Mississippi to Native Americans, and prohibited foreign settlers from buying land or settling in that area. Though the proclamation did not preclude the future expansion of the colonies, it stipulated that only representatives of the British government would be authorized to acquire new lands.[7]

Implementation of the declaration required a substantial increase in Britain's military presence in the colonies; and a sizeable growth in the number of troops entailed a considerable rise in cost. Britain's first step was to assign some seven thousand five hundred soldiers to patrol the posts in the Appalachians. To help pay for the deployment of additional forces, the British Parliament passed the Sugar and Stamp Acts. The first act entailed a three pence tax on each gallon of molasses and syrup imported by the colonists, while the second one imposed a duty on the colonists' newspapers, pamphlets, passports, cards and dice, liquor, licenses, wills, and legal documents.

The colonists were not angered by the costs imposed by the new taxes. The various new duties averaged only about seventy percent of their equivalent in Britain and were designed to cover only one-third of the annual army costs in the colonies.[8] What riled them was the British Parliament's assertion that it possessed the rightful authority to levy taxes on the colonists. The settlers found in John Locke's *The Second Treatise of Government* the rationale they needed to challenge the claim.

> Government cannot be supported without great Charge, and 'tis fit
>   every one who enjoys his share of the Protection, should pay out of
>   his Estate his proportion for the maintenance of it. But still it must
>   be with his own Consent, i.e., the consent of the Majority, giving it
>   either by themselves, or the Representatives chosen by them. For
>   if any one shall claim the Power to lay and levy Taxes on the People,
>   he thereby invades the Fundamental Law of Property, and subverts
>   the end of Government. For what property have I in that which
>   another may by right take, when he pleases to himself?[9]

Opposition to Britain's action began to mount shortly after the acts were approved. Bostonians voiced their discontent by asking: "If taxes are laid upon us [British subjects] in any shape without ever having legal representation where they are laid, are we not reduced from the character of free subjects to the miserable state of tributary slaves?"[10] Colonists in New York, Virginia, New Jersey, Rhode Island, and Connecticut also expressed their displeasure. Acts of violence followed.

Aware that individually the colonies could not match Britain's power, their representatives met in New York to design a response. With the adoption of a Declaration of Rights and Grievances, the thirteen colonies stipulated that no taxes could be imposed on the colonists but by their own consent, that the only ones who could levy taxes on the colonists were the representatives they chose and who served in the colonists' own legislature, that the colonists could not be represented by Britain's House of Commons, and that it was unreasonable and inconsistent for the people of Great Britain to give the monarch authority over the properties of the colonists. British merchants and manufacturers argued that if the Stamp Act were not repealed, the resultant rebellion by the colonists would harm their trade and generate high levels of unemployment. British legislators acquiesced, and in 1776 they withdrew both the Stamp Act and the Sugar Act.

The British Parliament's decision to rescind both acts symbolized a slight tilt in power in favor of the colonies. George Greenville, Britain's prime minister, noted in 1768 that if his country gave up under any condition its right to taxation it would be surrendering its sovereign right, which was "inseparable from it, in all ages and in all countries."[11] That same year, assemblies in Massachusetts, New York, Virginia, New Hampshire, Rhode Island, New Jersey, Pennsylvania, and Connecticut approved resolutions opposing Britain's attempt to reinstate "taxation without representation."[12] For the next five years, colonists debated whether they should sever their relationship with Parliament and the Crown and establish complete colonial self-rule, or should retain their connection with the Crown and strip the power of Parliament in the colonies.

Revolutions need a spark. The March 1770 "Boston Massacre," set off by a confrontation between English soldiers and colonists, reminded both sides that a contentious divide separated them. Many colonists cultivated the memory of the Massacre in order to stress that as free men they had an obligation to protect their personal sovereignty, but the event did not convince them that the time for taking drastic steps was ripe. An additional rationale for wanting to challenge Britain's authority was provided by the British Parliament when it passed an act designed to rescue the East India Company from bankruptcy in 1773.

The British imposed a heavy tax on tea sold in Massachusetts. Because of the high cost, five-sixths of the tea consumed by the colonists came from illegal imports. The 1773 act reduced the cost of British tea, with tax included, to a price lower than that charged for the smuggled tea. The policy incited criticism from the smugglers and from those who claimed that Parliament lacked the authority to impose duties on the colonists. In November, a group of colonists boarded three tea ships in the Boston harbor, spilled the contents of more than three hundred chests of tea into the water as some two thousand people watched, and then returned to the city to boast about their exploit. During the next year, as colonial newspapers expressed their anti-British sentiments, additional anti-tea demonstrations were initiated in almost every colony.

Convinced that some of the acts amounted to high treason, the Crown concluded it had no choice but to implement whatever measures it deemed necessary to preserve "the dependence of the said colonies upon his kingdom and for the protection of the subject in the exercise of his lawful commerce."[13] For the British Parliament the dispute transcended taxes; its gravest fear was losing the authority to rule the colonies. Certain that Boston was its chief adversary, Parliament approved a bill authorizing the closing of its port to all commercial traffic.

Unable to mount a united front, Boston temporarily relegated its leadership role to Virginia. To express its support of Massachusetts, the House of Burgesses issued a statement indicating that an "attack made on one of our sister colonies to compel submission to arbitrary taxes, is an attack made on all British America"[14] Soon after, all the colonies, except Georgia, agreed to hold a congress in Philadelphia in September 1774. As the delegates were debating, and while the British monarch was warning Prime Minister Frederick North that the government had to decide whether to master the colonists or leave them to themselves, Massachusetts' colonists were preparing for war. And so it began in Lexington and Concord in April 1775.

The war, along with the Treaty of Paris that brought it to an end on September 3, 1783, reaffirmed a couple of old, contradictory ideologies, planted the seeds of a few new ones, and sent a warning signal.[15] First, the war, which had started as a struggle between an empire and its rebellious colonies and became a world conflict when France, Spain, and the Netherlands joined forces with the USA in its struggle against Britain, reaffirmed the growing belief that world politics was power politics. To the European actors, the USA's claim that the war was a war of independence was immaterial; the only issue that drew them into the conflict was their distinct power interests. Second, the nearly united decision by the American colonies to confront Britain sent potent signals to both imperial actors and colonial subjects. It warned imperial actors that colonial subjects had the right to challenge their rulers, while it encouraged colonial subjects to stand for their rights. Third, the USA's declaration of independence strengthened the appeal of a new and evolving ideology—the doctrine of the sovereignty of the people. And fourth, it notified the globe's leading entities that a different type of world power was prepared to emerge in the not-too-distant future.[16] Though at the time of the signing of the Treaty of Paris no one believed that the new USA would transform itself into one of the world's dominant actors overnight, those attending the meeting recognized that its power potential was formidable.

The emergence of balance-of-power doctrine and nationalism

Some contemporary analysts of world politics, particularly in the USA, envisage the balance-of-power concept as an idea void of values. For them, a foreign policy built on a mature balance-of-power theory is the perfect anti-dote to a foreign policy erected on a set of ideological principles. Often, these same analysts try to validate their argument with the contention that balance of power is a concept that transcends space and history and, therefore, that it captures reality as it is. In the next few pages I contest the argument, and postulate that the idea of the balance of power is a modern one, and that a number of critical European actors sought to propagate it as an ideology starting in the early nineteenth century. Moreover, I propose that one of their objectives, but clearly not the sole one, was to use balance of power to counter the rising popularity of nationalism as a political ideology.

In the eighteenth century, many of Europe's leading thinkers, inspired by Isaac Newton's scientific theories, came to believe that in time someone would discover rules of rational behavior for human society. For a while, their hopes remained unfulfilled. Though after 1648 the European states had somewhat moderated their destructive tendencies, they continued to fight one another. Disillusioned by these developments, a number of them proposed that the most effective way to generate security and stability between actors in a particular region was by adherence by each actor to the balance-of-power principle. One of the central advocates of this idea was François Fénelon.

According to Fénelon, the rationale for creating a properly balanced power system was to prevent any one actor from becoming so powerful that it could misbehave with impunity and strive to achieve "universal dominion." He built the argument on the assumption that all states are inherently aggressive, even the small ones, and would indulge in conquests if the opportunity arose. To ensure that a balance was created and protected, the actors within a system had to be constantly vigilant in order to anticipate dangers and modify their alliances accordingly.[17] A country, emphasized Fénelon, must commit itself to the idea of balance of power in order "to preserve itself and its neighbours from servitude: 'tis to contend for the liberty, tranquility, and happiness of all in general: For the over-increase of power in any one influences the general system of all the surrounding nations."[18]

An idea rarely becomes a political ideology until a major event, often a costly one, persuades political leaders to reassess the ideas that guide their actions. The nationalism spawned by the French revolution, along with the Napoleonic wars, compelled the leaders of several of Europe's most important entities to heed Fénelon's advice.

The French Revolution

In 1786, a deficit that was nearly one-quarter as large as its revenue, and interest on the loans that would siphon off half of the revenue at payment time, convinced France's Comptroller-General to submit to the Paris Parliament—France's most important sovereign legal court because of its size—a land tax and stamp duty. The measure, if approved, would end the privileged standing of the clergy and nobility.[19] The Paris Parliament rejected the proposal and questioned the scope of monarchical power. Without an agreement as to how to address the deficit and with violent riots spreading rapidly throughout Paris, France's king, Louis XVI, called for a meeting of the Estates General.

The Estates General was composed of three entities. The clergy controlled the First Estate, the nobles made up the Second Estate, and "representatives" of the rest of the population ran the Third Estate. After a series of confrontations with the king and representatives of the other two Estates, speakers for the Third Estate named its institution "National Assembly" and asserted that as the sole representative of the "people" it personified the sovereignty of the nation. The National Assembly formalized this claim August 26, 1789, when it passed the *Declaration of the Rights of Man and the Citizen*.[20]

Europe watched carefully the struggle that ensued inside France. In Britain, some claimed that granting double representation to the Third Estate would lead to anarchy and violence because its members lacked the intellectual capacity to act rationally; while others advocated the supremacy of reason over submission to monarchical government. The people of Habsburg-controlled Belgium, energized by developments in France, proclaimed an independent United States of Belgium in early 1790. Their euphoria was short-lived; by the end of the year they were again under Habsburg rule. Other European monarchs began wondering how the events in France would affect their own legitimacy and power. To offset France's revolutionary path, Emperor Leopoldo II of Austria and Frederick William II of Prussia signed the Declaration of Pilnitz on August 27, 1791. France's rulers took notice and moved against counterrevolutionaries everywhere. Boasting that the French nation would grant fraternity and aid to all those who wanted to recover their liberty, France's army annexed Savoy, Nice, Belgium, and the Rhineland, overthrew their political regimes, and changed their social order in a little over a year. The early successes intensified France's resolve to rely on war as a tool of political and social change.[21]

As the war gained momentum, so did terror within France. After an extended period, a new group of French leaders, determined to institute stability and prevent the return of monarchical rule, destroyed the machinery of terror and designed a new constitution. Their success was fleeting. Burdened by the financial pressures incurred by the war, they were overthrown by Napoleon Bonaparte in late 1799. Europe experienced Napoleon's ascension to power almost immediately. Motivated by a deep sense of patriotism and guided by Napoleon's brilliant generalship, the French military inflicted crushing defeats on Austria in 1805 and 1809, Prussia in 1806, Russia in 1807, and Spain in 1808. Napoleon's glory began to wither after he and his troops invaded Russia in 1812. The routing of his army by an Austrian, Russian, Prussian, and Swedish alliance forced him to abdicate the throne in 1814. His attempt to return to power was spoiled when the same coalition, backed by Britain, trounced his army in 1815. Napoleon's ephemeral but impressive rise imposed on Europe two distinct, and often contradictory, political concepts: nationalism and balance of power.

Nationalism does not always refer to the people of a state, nor to members of a community, who belong to the same ethnic group, speak the same language, or practice the same religion.[22] As a symbol, it belongs to the realm of values.[23] The concept stands for a sentiment of solidarity held by one group in relation to other groups. In its most developed form, nationalism is a political ideology that uses the nation as its foundation and rationale for action.[24] It symbolizes the belief that a nation's interests are separate from the interests of other nations or the common interests of all nations.[25] In a state or an empire composed of different nations, political leaders have used nationalism as an instrument to invoke a nation's right to, at minimum, be autonomous or, at maximum, form its own distinct and sovereign state. When correspondence between the legal and the cultural entity, that is, between the state and the nation, is close, nationalism assumes the form of patriotism, either to protect the state from external threats or to augment its power.

One of the first non-French Europeans to appreciate the value of nationalism was Carl von Clauzewitz. As a soldier in the Prussian army who was defeated by the French at the Battle of Jena, von Clauzewitz proposed that Napoleon owed his victory, in part, to his ability to animate the French citizenry and soldiers with a nationalist passion. To cope with the threat of extinction, added von Clauzewitz, Prussia's ruling Hohenzollern had to cultivate a patriotic sentiment that would result in the unification of the various German provinces into a nation-state.[26] It was precisely this kind of belief that alarmed leaders of multinational empires.

Austria's principal negotiator, Count Klemens von Metternich, contended that the nationalists and the liberal tides sparked by the French Revolution and fostered by Napoleon would, if left unchecked, instigate anarchy throughout Europe and undermine the integrity and power of traditional states.[27] Though he sensed that in the long run it would be impossible to stop the forces of change, Viscount Robert Castlereagh, Britain's foreign minister, believed it was necessary to slow down its pace. As he noted in a letter to the British minister in Sicily in 1814, the attempts to promote the principles of freedom "are in full operation ...; but I am sure it is better to retard than to accelerate the operation of this most hazardous principle which is abroad."[28]

With the Napoleonic wars behind them, Britain, Austria, Russia, France, and Prussia sought to create in Europe a system based on the premise that their welfare depended on their willingness and ability to erect and maintain a power equilibrium. Advocated by France's main representative, Charles Maurice, Prince de Talleyrand, the tenet stipulated that because conquest did not make right, the only two things that could be relied on to legitimize a sovereign or a regime were dynastic right and general recognition.[29] Determined to protect the Austrian empire from the aspirations of nationalist groups within its realm, Metternich backed Talleyrand with the assertion that states only "existed in so far as they had shown themselves capable of maintaining their political independence for centuries." The builders of the 1815 balance of-power system then moved on to solidify its foundation either by conferring to certain states, preferably the oldest and most powerful ones, direct or indirect control over an array of different nations, or by curbing the capacity of any one nation partitioned into small provinces to integrate.

France was given back its monarchy, but its territory was shrunk to its 1789 size. Britain appropriated land from France, Holland, and Spain. The king of the Netherlands became Belgium's new ruler and the Grand Duke of Luxemburg. Sweden retained its power over Norway, while Switzerland acquired new cantons. Italy was still not Italy, and was kept that way by being divided into states, most of which remained linked to the Habsburg family. The German provinces were treated similarly. The thirty-nine states were incorporated into a German Confederation, with the emperor of Austria serving as its hereditary head. The intent was to create a framework that would both impede France and Russia's expansionary ambitions and hamper German liberal and nationalist aspirations. Poland was granted its own kingdom, but under Russian tutelage. The Austrian Empire continued to retain jurisdiction over a vast territory, encompassing a wide range of nationalities. As just noted, it presided over the loose German Confederation and controlled northern Italy. Moreover, its own princes ruled the key Italian duchies of Moderna and Parma. German, Magyar, Czech, Ruthven, Polish, Rumanian, and Serbo-Croatian nationals inhabited these various locations. And finally, bordering Austria and Russia, was the Ottoman Empire. Still ruled by Turks, in the nineteenth century its reach extended over present-day Turkey, Serbia, Bosnia, Romania, Bulgaria, Montenegro, Albania, and Greece. It continued over current Syria, Iraq, Lebanon, Israel, Jordan, northeastern Egypt, Saudi Arabia's western section, and Kuwait. Internal and external religious divisions crisscrossed these nationalist partitions. Some twelve million members of the Greek Orthodox Church lived in the midst of the Ottoman Empire's vast Muslim population, while on the other side of its northwestern frontiers, in lands occupied by European empires, Latin and Greek Christendom were the dominant religious practices.

The first set of nationalist salvos

Challenges to the agreements reached at the Congress of Vienna materialized quickly. In 1818, while discussing how to deal with France, which by then had fulfilled the conditions stipulated by the victors three years earlier, Tsar Alexander of Russia proposed to the leaders of Europe's major powers the creation of an alliance designed to safeguard each other's borders and possessions and help shield whatever form of government existed in each entity. Castlereagh rejected the proposal. He noted that to construe the original agreement as an instrument for the protection of established regimes and the suppression of revolutions was to broaden the intent of the original treaty, and that Britain was not willing to play such a role.[30] He reaffirmed his resolve two years later when, following the outbreak of a rebellion in Spain, the leaders of Russia, Prussia, and Austria proposed to act together to restore King Ferdinand VII's power. Castlereagh made it clear that because his country was governed by a representative regime, it would not use force to affect the internal affairs of another.[31]

In early 1822, a group of wealthy Greek expatriates declared independence from the Ottoman Empire. The war against the Turks, they noted, was not "that of a faction or the result of sedition." It was "a national war, a holy war, a war the object of which [was] to reconquer the rights of individual liberty, of property and honour."[32] Most of Europe's leaders did not welcome the revolutionary salvo. For them, Greece, which had been under Turkish rule since the fifteenth century, was just another province of the Ottoman Empire. They feared that Greece's independence would undermine the Ottoman Empire's power and spawn drives by the competing powers to exploit its weakness. By 1826, when it became evident that Russia would intervene on Greece's behalf in order to augment its own sphere of influence in the Balkans, Britain and France decided they could no longer remain inactive. The three parties agreed in June to use force against Turkey if it failed to sign an armistice with Greece. In 1833, Turkey granted Greece its freedom under the empire's suzerainty.

During this period, a second nationalist crisis erupted at the core of Europe's balance-of-power system. In 1830, the Belgian provinces that had been under Dutch rule since the 1815 Congress sought to gain their independence. While a wide range of issues drove the Belgian provinces to rebel, they were united by their unwillingness to accept Dutch as their official language and, as Catholics, King William's policy of equality for all religions. Their declaration at the opening Congressional session replicated the Greeks' earlier claim that the struggle was a national one. "In the name of the Belgian people," they stated, "the provisional government opens an assembly of the representatives of the nation. The nation has confided to these representatives the august mission of founding, on the broad and solid basis of liberty, the edifice of the new social order which will be the beginning and guarantee of durable happiness of Belgium."[33] King William appealed for outside support. Russia and Austria wanted to help him, but Britain and France warned that they would oppose any form of external intervention. France viewed an independent Belgium as a means to boost its own power in the region, while Britain objected to having troops from eastern entities in an area where London had traditionally played a central role.[34] The major powers recognized Belgium's independence at a meeting held in London in 1831.

Though the challenges initiated against the traditional principle of legitimacy by the forces of nationalism were still too weak to have a defining effect on the balance-of-power system, the leaders of Europe could no longer ignore their presence. The independence sought by the Greeks and the Belgians signaled that nationalism would not fade away. The effects of these events, however, would prove to be negligible when compared to the consequences generated by the uprisings that would afflict Europe's political arena during the rest of the nineteenth century.

The second set of nationalist salvos

Liberty had different meanings throughout Europe in the nineteenth century. British liberalism adhered to the belief that "the greatest good for the greatest number" would result if each individual were permitted to pursue his own economic self-interest with little meddling from the government. Governmental action against the natural properties of economic order were bound to be felt in the "shape of hardship and coercion somewhere."[35] In the continent, particularly where people had not yet attained political unity or were living under foreign rule, liberty meant freedom from foreign control or freedom for the nation. For the Greeks, it stood for freedom from Turkish dominance; for the Italians it meant bringing Austrian rule to an end and creating the Italian nation; and for many Germans it signified becoming members of the same state. In the continent, thus, liberalism and nationalism went hand in hand; and in some instances nationalist ambitions overpowered other liberal values.[36]

The 1848 revolts started in Poland with members of its aristocracy facing up to Russia's authority. The Congress of Vienna's decision to give Poland its own constitution while placing it under Russia's dominion angered Poles. In 1830, a group of officers in Warsaw took over public buildings and set up a Polish supreme national council. Russia retaliated with an invasion, and after putting down the opposition it revoked Poland's constitution and imposed stricter rule. Russia's intrusion did not extinguish the Polish revolutionary spirit. Even though the ideological range of those striving for independence extended from constitutional monarchists to socialists, they shared the belief that insurrection was the only way Poland would regain its independence. In 1846, Polish aristocrats and bourgeoisie in exile attempted to launch another national revolution. Once again, it failed. The uprising, however, enabled those arrested to present their political goals to a broader public during their mass trial.[37]

As the Poles' nationalist aspiration was being crushed, another nationalist rebellion was emerging in southern Europe. Italy was made up of eight different states inhabited by people who spoke a score of dialects and carried traditions that ranged from the French-oriented culture of Piedmont and the progressive leaning of Lombardy, to the clerical practices of the Papal States and the feudalism of Sicily.[38] Despite these and many other social, political, and economic differences, a common vision united them: to free themselves from the Austrian yoke. This hope gained momentum with the election of a supposedly liberal pope in 1846. Inspired by the belief that unity might be achieved under Pius IX, the cry "foreigners go home" became louder. Finally, in January 1848, an insurrection in Sicily forced the Bourbon monarch to accept the enactment of a new constitution.

The uprising created a domino effect, as other Italian princes followed suit with similar responses.[39]

As Italian nationalists struggled to free themselves, another wave of domestic unrest struck the French monarchy. These events did not surprise a keen observer of French and American politics. In late January 1848, Alexis de Tocqueville, then a member of the parliamentary opposition, warned his colleagues in the Chamber of Deputies that the passions of the masses were not political but social. The masses, he explained, were "gradually forming opinions and ideas [that] are destined to upset this or that law, ministry, or form of government, but society itself until it totters upon the foundation upon which it rests today."[40] His unease was warranted. In February, after enduring the 1845 potato blight, the 1846 poor grain harvest, the rapid increase in the price of foodstuffs, and the high unemployment in consumer good industries and construction, members of the "lower" bourgeoisie and the Parisian working class took to the streets once again.[41] The revolt soon led to the abdication of the king and the establishment of a republic sustained by universal male suffrage.

As the French struggled to restructure their political system, the Germans debated whether to engage in radical reforms. In early March, some fifty liberals from a number of German states met in Heidelberg and invited representatives from the German Confederation to join them in Frankfurt. By the end of the month some six hundred delegates from the German states had gathered to arrange elections for a Constituent Assembly. By the following March, the Frankfurt Assembly had designed a new constitution and introduced universal male suffrage.

The Germans were not the only ones influenced by events in France. In March, just a few days after Louis Philippe had abdicated the French throne, a Hungarian aristocrat called for the end of the "unnatural political system" that ruled Austria.[42] As the head of a group of Hungarian liberals, Lajos Kossuth demanded national sovereignty for Hungary under a Habsburg dynasty, the enlargement of the franchise, and freedom of the press.[43] As Kossuth was calling for a change in Hungary's standing vis-à-vis Austria, students in Vienna, with the support of workers, were drafting a petition asking the emperor to sanction freedom of speech and abolish censorship. These demands were soon followed by demonstrations and violent clashes with troops. The ensuing bloodshed convinced the emperor to give in. By April, the Austrian government had approved a set of thirty-one liberal laws that abolished censorship, ended the nobility's exemption from taxation, and proclaimed equality before the law. The Czechs in Bohemia, the Croats by the Adriatic, and the Rumanians in Transylvania launched similar nationalist initiatives.

Most of Europe's revolutionary movements had come to naught by 1850. Moderate French Republicans gained the upper hand during the April 1848 elections for the Constituent Assembly. With support from property owners, the new French government announced that young bachelors involved in public works in Paris would be dismissed or conscripted into the army, while the rest would have to find jobs in the private sector or in public enterprises in the provinces. Angered by the new policies, French workers took to the streets once again. By the end of June, their revolt had been crushed.[44] On December 10, 1848, Louis Napoleon, with strong support from a bourgeoisie, became president of France's Second Republic. A year later, he took over the Assembly and announced that he would retain the presidency for ten years. By the end of 1852, he had transformed the Second French Republic into the Second French Empire and had become its emperor.

Other European liberation movements experienced a similar fate. Italy's hopes for unification were temporarily razed with the defeat of Piedmont, the overthrow of the Roman Republic by French troops, and the takeover of Venice by Austrian troops, all between 1848 and 1849. In March 1849, the Frankfurt Assembly invited Frederick William IV of Prussia to become Germany's new emperor. He rejected the offer, and the Assembly crumbled shortly afterward. Subsequently, a military alliance between the rulers of Prussia, Saxony, and Baden crushed the German revolutionary drive and executed many of its leaders.[45] Prussia's January 1850 constitution placed responsibility for the ministers in the king's hands, and the army beyond the reaches of the law.

Liberation drives throughout the Austrian Empire encountered a comparable outcome. Influenced by the success of the Hungarians, Czechs in Bohemia called for the meeting of a Pan-Slav Congress in Prague in June 1848. Their voices did not elicit a positive response from Vienna. During the gathering of the Congress, the army suppressed the liberation movement and placed Prague under military control. This action marked the beginning of the end of the 1848 revolutionary movement in Austria. Austria declared war on Hungary in October; and though Hungary proclaimed its independence from the Habsburg dynasty in April 1849, it was back under Austrian control by August, after being forced to surrender to joint Austrian–Russian forces.

In spite of its initial failure to alter Europe's political structure, nationalism retained its importance, and by 1871 it had helped alter the 1815 balance-of-power system noticeably. The first dramatic success came in 1861, when Piedmont freed itself from the Habsburg dynasty and took over Lombardy, Sardinia, Parma, Modena, Romagna, Tuscany, the Papal States, Naples, and Sicily. In March of that same year, the first Italian parliament, composed of only the upper and middle classes, recognized Victor Emmanuel II as Italy's first king. Aware that the power of the Habsburg dynasty had been undermined by Italy's unification, Prussian forces invaded Austria in 1866. Austria acquiesced shortly afterward. As part of the peace treaty, Austria agreed to remove itself from the German Confederation and accepted the annexation by Prussia of Hanover, Hesse-Cassel, and part of Hesse-Darmstadt. These events encouraged the Magyars to demand the creation of a Magyar-ruled Hungarian state within the monarchy. The Habsburg emperor gave in and authorized the formation of two separate states in 1867. Austria and Hungary would be united under his rule as king-emperor by a treaty that regulated their commercial and financial relations; established joint administrative institutions responsible for defense, foreign affairs, and finance; and provided for a common army.

The nationalist impetus continued. In July 1870, France declared war on Prussia. By the end of the year, Prussian soldiers, with wide support from the other German states and united by the conviction that "[a]ny German, whoever he may be, who is not now on the side of his people, is a traitor," had defeated France and annexed Alsace and Lorraine. King William I of Prussia assumed leadership over the newly created German Empire in Versailles, France, in January 1871.

In sum, by 1871, after a little over half a century, nationalism had undermined the basic ideas on which Europe's 1815 balance-of-power system had been built, and as a result had altered the power distribution in the region measurably. With nationalism as the emerging norm, Europe in 1871 had at its core a very powerful Germany, and on its Mediterranean leg a united Italian kingdom yearning to make its mark. Bordering both was the newly structured Austrian–Hungarian Empire—a dominion whose monarchy, in order to survive, had forfeited some of its power and given it to its second-most-important nationalist group.

The other major actors would not remain impervious to these changes long. Britain, as the ever-present outsider, was still perceived by many of its peers as Europe's principal arbitrator. Its ability to continue exercising this role, however, would soon be challenged. In France, for nearly two decades Louis Napoleon strove to enlarge the power of its Second Empire through the establishment of new colonies. Following the defeat in the war against Prussia, France's leaders were immediately compelled to create a new republic and to deal with the strategic and economic challenges engendered by their new, powerful neighbor. Russia, led by one of the few European monarchies unaffected by the 1848 uprisings, viewed the new developments with a mixture of hope and fear. On the one hand its leaders wondered whether they could augment the power of their empire by exploiting the nationalist hardships of both the Ottoman Empire and the Austrian–Hungarian Empire. On the other hand they feared that Russia's freedom of action would be severely handicapped by the unification of the German states under Prussia's skillful leadership. And then there was the Ottoman Empire. As a creature of conquest, the Ottoman Empire, under Turkish leadership, was being forced to cope with the yearnings of Balkan nationalists to shape their own destinies, and with Russia's readiness to capitalize on Constantinople's hardships. But as the events of the next four decades would show, these desires were not unique.[46]

The creation of a quasi-global economic system

By 1815, Britain, because of its naval might, the strength of its financial institutions, its commercial expertise, and its control of the Indian, Chinese, and Southeast Asian inter-port trade, was in an excellent position to promote liberalism and develop free trade without augmenting its territorial possessions.[47] For Britain, explained the poet and historian Thomas Macaulay in 1833, it would be far better if "the people of India … were ruled by their own kings, but wearing our broadcloth, and working with our cutlery, than that they were performing their salaams to English collectors and English magistrates … To trade with civilized men is infinitely more profitable than to govern savages."[48] Lord Palmerston, Britain's foreign secretary, restated the argument several years later in response to France's suggestion that the two countries partition North Africa. "We want to trade with Egypt and to travel through Egypt but we do not want the burden of governing Egypt … Let us try to improve all these countries by the general influence of commerce, but let us abstain from a crusade of conquest."[49]

Britain's rationale for promoting free trade had a couple of distinct pragmatic foundations. At the start of the nineteenth century, Britain had an abundance of skilled and unskilled labor, and capital. Its main problem was that because it did not have enough land to produce primary products at relatively low prices, it faced the risk of having its own economic development derailed. Developing regions, on the other hand, had plenty of land and natural resources, but not the labor and capital they would need to develop them. For Britain, the importing of primary products under free trade conditions would signify expanding its own land area, while for the developing regions, the importing of manufactured commodities would represent access to capital and labor.[50]

Before it could promote the open exchange of goods worldwide, Britain had to repeal legislative restrictions on freedom of trade, especially tariffs designed to protect its grain market. In 1846, it abandoned the Corn Laws, which had protected domestic grain against foreign competitors. In Macaulay's words, scrapping the act would enable Britain to "supply the whole world with manufactures and have almost a monopoly of trade of the world," while other nations raised "abundant provisions for us." Shortly after breaching the protectionist dam, Britain disposed of the Navigation Acts and Sugar Acts.[51] These actions required, in turn, the breaking of the landowners' control over parliament and the extension to the commercial classes of political power more proportional to their economic significance.[52] By diminishing the economic significance of Britain's agriculture, free trade decreased the wealth and political influence of its landed aristocracy.[53]

The above changes were not the only significant ones. During that period, the call for a small and economical government became louder.[54] Commercial and financial leaders saw government as a corrupt institution that diverted income and savings from their "natural" channels, and spent the taxpayer's money unwisely and on behalf of those with political influence.[55] This challenge did not go unanswered. Between 1814 and 1870, government expenditures fell from an equivalent of twenty-nine percent of gross national product to nine percent.[56] In sum, though free trade and limited government had different roots, after 1840 low taxation and free trade became one voice. Their advocates argued that implementation of both policies was necessary in order to eradicate corrupt vested interests, cut off politics from the foul influence of commerce, and award the public a common benefit—cheap food.

Britain's decision to create an empire of trade meant, at one level, initiating a massive shift of capital and labor from Britain and other parts of Europe. It is estimated that while Britain's balance of credit abroad increased from 24.6 million pounds in 1816 to 3989.6 pounds in 1913, approximately 21.5 million people left the British Isles during that same period.[57] At another level, it signified setting up a network of transport and utilities in various regions in order to facilitate economic and financial transactions.[58] What is more, to contain the risks it would encounter, Britain created a set of norms and rules of behavior designed to dictate the conditions under which international commercial and financial interactions would be conducted.[59]

Britain's relationships with some of South America's new republics help capture the type of global economic system the former endeavored to create and the ideology that guided its construction. As proven by Britain's failed attempt to occupy Buenos Aires in 1806, military intervention presented overwhelming political and logistical problems. Britain's new undertaking would be to help establish in the peripheries "like-minded" cooperative elites who would demonstrate that economic progress was compatible with individual liberty, differential property rights, and political stability.[60] South American republics would implement reforms designed to set up monarchies, foster domestic order, and curb the "evils of democracy." In the words of Britain's colonial secretary, Viscount F. J. Goderich, the task of the British was to "transfer to distant regions the greatest possible amount both of the civil liberty and the forms of social order to which Great Britain is chiefly indebted for the rank she holds among the civilized nations."[61] Much of this would be accomplished via the expansion of commerce and the repercussions it would generate. Commerce, explained Earl C. J. Canning, Britain's undersecretary for foreign affairs in the 1840s, would promote prosperity; prosperity would spawn the establishment of friendly states; and a number of sympathetic entities would help maintain stability in an international arena inhabited by the exhausted monarchies of continental Europe and the new revolutionary states led by the USA.[62]

In its drive to create a liberal world system, Britain established self-policing and self-regulating mechanisms, and demanded discipline from those governments requesting loans if they hoped to remain credit-worthy. Aware that the penalties would be severe if they did not play by the rules imposed on them by London, the loan recipients began to develop a remarkable degree of "like-mindedness" with their creditors.[63] In most cases, London's main requirement was that the loan recipients honor their debts, even under difficult circumstances. In 1873, for instance, though Argentina faced a major financial crisis, its president announced that his country would implement an austerity program and was prepared "to suffer privations and hunger" in order to protect its international reputation and the national government's credit rating.[64]

Britain's free-trade ideology had a moral and religious tone. Certain that no other actor had climbed as high as Britain had on the ladder of progress, its leaders proudly claimed that it was their country's duty to improve the material and moral conditions of others. Their duty, declared the head of Britain's Foreign Affairs Office, Lord Palmerston, "is not to enslave, but to set free; and I may say without any vainglorious boast, or without great offense to anyone, that we stand at the head of moral, social and political civilization. Our task is to lead the way and direct the march of other nations."[65] With one of the world's most religious societies and a Protestant doctrine that believed in salvation by good works, the British missionaries formulated comprehensive plans designed to evangelize "heathens" globally. "Go to the conquest of all lands. All must be at His length," became their motto.[66] Britain's missionaries and political leaders did not always agree on values and methods, but they concurred that the moment "natives" were converted to Christianity, they began to show a desire for the "advantages of the civilized life."[67] Everyone's interest, thus, was attended.

Britain's global system eventually gave way to greater economic and financial competition. From the 1840s until the early 1870s, Britain benefited greatly from Western Europe's and the USA's drive to industrialize their economies, and from the overall growth of markets in underdeveloped countries, including those within its empire. Britain served as their principal provider of semi-finished manufactures and as their financier. The framework of the interactions began to change in the early 1870s. Less developed countries remained dependent on Britain, largely because to acquire enough sterling to pay their debts and preserve their credit-worthiness, they needed Britain to continue importing their goods. But despite their dependency, the more powerful countries began to break their British ties. As their economies grew, many Western European states and the USA started to erect sizeable trade barriers in order to protect their own nascent industries. Faced with a world less willing to play according to the norms and rules of behavior it had envisioned and proposed in the 1840s, Britain reneged on its earlier claims that it would rather trade with distant territories than rule them. Its decision helped launch a new race for territorial partition.

The materialization of a power imbalance in the Americas

Introduction

The effects of Napoleon's military adventures at the start of the nineteenth century reached beyond Europe's boundaries. In North America, they enabled the recently born USA to force both France and Spain to sell, respectively, Louisiana and Florida. This action augmented the USA's territorial power considerably. South of the Rio Grande, Napoleon's power drive in Europe enticed the Spanish king's American colonies to strive for independence. Though by the middle of the 1820s most of them had fulfilled this goal, their success did not give way to the formation of stable and powerful Latin American states. For the next fifty years, as the USA continued to enlarge its territorial power and create a solid sovereign state, Spanish–American states, burdened by ethnic, class, and state–church divisions, their inability to generate a unifying nationalist ideology, and the economic and political aspirations of external entities, gradually destroyed their chances of becoming new leaders of the world system. The emergence of this exceptional American power imbalance would begin to affect the nature and structure of the world system as the nineteenth century moved through its final stages.

The rise of a new world giant

From its early days as a republic, the USA understood that if it ever hoped to become a powerful actor, it first had to cope with the threats emanating from the world system, and that to counter those threats it had to take advantage of its geographical remoteness and develop unique relationships with Europe's leading entities.[68]

The first opportunity materialized at the start of the nineteenth century. In 1801, after Spain had sold the Louisiana territory to France, Thomas Jefferson concluded that if the USA ever hoped to incorporate the region west of the Mississippi all the way to the Pacific Ocean, it first had to control the area just purchased by France. Two years later, convinced that France and Britain were about to be entangled in another war, and that Napoleon could ill afford to be caught at the same time in a major dispute with the USA, Jefferson pressured him to sell the Louisiana territory. For a paltry $15 million, the USA doubled the size of its territory.

Napoleon's second contribution to the aggrandizement of the USA's area came about indirectly and was not realized until several years after he had been toppled. His forces occupied Spain and dethroned its king and son in 1808. With the fall of the Spanish crown, the Spanish–American colonies were forced to decide whether they wanted to retain their allegiance to the deposed king or seek independence.[69] Those who advocated complete independence carried the day, and by 1818, Spain, though no longer under French control, was embroiled in a number of wars against its American colonies. Aware of Spain's predicament, President James Monroe demanded that it relinquish control of Florida. With much of its power depleted, Spain acquiesced.[70]

Time did not moderate the USA's determination to exploit the weaknesses of its neighbors. Few former Spanish–American colonies were able to take positive steps towards the creation of strong and legitimate states after they had gained their independence from Spain. Mexico was not an exception. In 1845, Texas, which fewer than ten years earlier had freed itself from Mexico, asked to be annexed as part of the USA. The US Congress accepted the request. After a short war, a weakened Mexico agreed to sell to the USA all the territory presently encompassed by California, Nevada, Utah, most of New Mexico and Arizona, and parts of Colorado and Wyoming for $15 million.

For a state to become an important world player, it must first create a united front. Though the USA had tripled the size of its territory during the first fifty years of the nineteenth century, significant internal divisions slowed down its efforts to act as a united actor and become a solid competitor in non-American regions. The North, dominated by a mixture of an urban culture and a family-oriented agricultural one, came into conflict with a system of beliefs, values, and ideas structured by a slave-based economy that grew quickly as new land became available and industrialization generated an increase in demand for cotton. In time, without a strong, unifying, nationalist ideology, the presence of two competing forms of nationalist sentiments helped push the USA towards a major civil war.[71] Success by the North did not result in the immediate purging of Southern nationalism. Nevertheless, it helped Washington signal other states that if necessary the USA possessed the material capacity to build a very powerful military force and prevent any one of its members from seceding.

Latin America's breakdown

By the middle of the 1820s, most Spanish–American colonies had gained their independence.[72] Free, they now faced the formidable task of creating stable, sovereign states. Upon achieving independence, leaders of distinct regions often try to protect their power with the support of regional militias. Failure on the part of the central government to counteract and destroy regional militias will typically impede the state-building process. During the state-building process, moreover, local power holders must forge political agreements and build institutions capable of extracting resources for common defense, maintaining internal order and adjudicating disputes, protecting established rights and privileges, and creating elementary economic and political infrastructures. Cooperation ensues when rivals adjust their behavior to the actual or anticipated preference of each other.[73] The distance between the preferences of two or more adversaries affects their chances of cooperation— the greater the gap, the smaller the likelihood of cooperation.[74]

Economic inequality per se does not obstruct the creation of a legitimate state. The leaders of a state with severe economic inequity, however, will find it very difficult to legitimize and consolidate their rule if the division is reinforced by ethnic, racial, and/or regional cleavages. Their efforts will be further undercut if their drive to create an all-encompassing nationalist ideology is defied by the rise of multiple nationalist subcultures. The effects of the actions by powerful world entities on newly created states are sometimes difficult to gauge. All other things being equal, when leaders of a recently formed state with great economic potential have been unable to design a framework of domestic political and economic cooperation, they would prefer not to have a powerful actor as one of their neighbors. Nevertheless, a newly created state's economic potential and the extent to which its leaders worked with one another played much more important roles in dictating whether a powerful entity would intervene. Paradoxically, while a powerful actor's first decision to act against a deeply divided newly born state could slow down the targeted state's consolidation and legitimization processes, in due course it could help generate a unifying nationalist ideology if intervention became a nearly common practice.

The conditions just identified aided or hindered the efforts by the leaders of Chile, Peru, and Mexico to create solid and legitimate states.[75] Of the three, the leaders of Chile were the first to consolidate and legitimize the power of the state. The struggles that followed Chile's independence were comparatively minor, largely because members of its political and economic elite were not as divided as those of other former colonies.[76] By 1833, after concluding that Chile was too young and inexperienced to adopt a document that focused principally on individual liberties, its political and economic elites ratified a constitution that made the observance of laws its central tenet, and that extended extraordinary powers to the central government. These two conditions were interconnected. The observance of laws, argued the creators of the new constitution, "is the very foundation of the social order."[77] Social order in a new state would be maintained only if there was a "strong, centralizing Government, whose members [were] genuine examples of virtue and patriotism."[78] Moreover, with a strong central government, capable of maintaining social order, Chile would be able to create a business climate attractive to its own economic elite and to foreign capital.[79]

The creators of the new Chilean constitution sought to consolidate and protect the power of the executive branch, control political competition, and curb regional divisiveness by: i) limiting the service of the Congress to three months; ii) granting the president control over the military, the authority to appoint provincial governors, and the right to declare a state of siege in any part of the country while the Congress was in recess; and iii) ruling that voters had to be at least twenty-five years old, be able to read and write, and possess a certain amount of property or enjoy a certain income.[80] They applied similar rules to citizens interested in running for office. To instill continuity and further restrict opposition, they extended to members of both houses the right to seek reelection as often as they wanted, and permitted the president to seek reelection for one additional five-year term.[81]

Chile's elite determination to create a unified state was aided by the presence of an ethnically homogeneous society. By the time Chile had gained independence, out of a population of approximately nine hundred thousand people, some seventy-four percent of the inhabitants were categorized as Spanish and another ten percent as mestizo. Most of Chile's indigenous population, unlike those in the other former colonies, lived in their own separate territory and maintained a high level of autonomy.[82] This division created a sense of cohesion among those residing within Chile's boundaries (excluding the Arauco region in the south) that made it easier for those seeking to consolidate and legitimize the power of the state to contend that they were pursuing a vital and common objective.[83]

These conditions helped Chile's initial political and economic development. From 1831 to 1861, it had three presidents, each serving two five-year terms. The relationships between the economic elites remained stable. They generally agreed that their interests were closely linked to the preservation and protection of an economic system that facilitated commerce with foreign countries.[84] Government revenues went up from two million pesos in 1835 to sixteen million four hundred thousand in 1875,[85] which helped improve Chile's transportation and communication systems. This development, in turn, helped the state to promote its authority among the inhabitants of outlying regions, and to stimulate further Chile's export-oriented economy.[86]

The post-independence period proved to be difficult to every Spanish-American colony, but few of them encountered greater problems than Peru.[87] Much of the wealth acquired by the Spanish colonists in Peru came from the mining of silver and the production of mercury.[88] The effective extraction and refining of silver demanded economies of scale and vertical integration.[89] With the development of the mines came also the expansion of other sectors of Peru's economy. Stock ranching and agriculture were established near the border with Chile to provide sustenance for the mining areas of Potosi. In the upper part of Peru's coastal zone, the dominant products were sugar, tobacco, and cacao, while wine was the main commodity in the area south of Lima. Because the Spaniards depended heavily on the indigenous population to work the mines, and on men and women of African origin to farm the land either as servants or slaves, it was not long before rigid ethnic and racial inequalities took hold.[90]

Independence did not eradicate either division. Peru remained divided for several years into two economic clusters: a protectionist camp and a liberal clique.[91] Each group favored the creation of a state designed to promote and protect its own set of economic interests. The economic elites of the north created a common front against direct trade with the North Atlantic area and endorsed the establishment of a protected trade area in the Pacific corridor.[92] On the other hand, the south, which encompassed the coastal provinces and the sierra hinterlands, advocated the establishment of close ties with the Atlantic regimes and the British, and revival of the Bolivian markets.[93]

The division came to an end in the late 1840s, when the north imposed its military superiority on the south.[94] Moreover, by then the oligarchs of the north had concluded that they wanted unencumbered and inexpensive access to the sea.[95] The impetus for the reduction in the commercial conflict between both regions came from changes in Peru's economy and the international economic system. In 1826, goods from Britain took one hundred and two days to reach the Peruvian port of Callao. After 1840, when steamships began to navigate the eastern waters of the Pacific, the same trip was reduced to forty-five days.[96] At the same time, guano, which existed in great abundance in Peru's coastal islands and had been used as a fertilizer by Peru's indigenous Indians prior to the colonial period, became a commodity in high demand. The age of advanced farming in Britain and the beginnings of agricultural chemistry in Germany helped turn guano into Peru's most important export. Its production increased from seven thousand tons in 1830 to about four hundred thousand in 1860. Guano export was responsible for an average annual growth rate of exports of 4.5 percent between 1840 and 1852, and of 5.2 percent between 1852 and 1878.

The advent of guano production incited a demand for repayment by those who had granted Peru loans to fight the war of independence. Peru agreed. To ensure payment its government committed itself to placing in the Bank of Britain half of its guano earnings. Since this pledge curtailed the resources available to the Peruvian government to expand and centralize its administration, its leaders began to solicit loans, placing as guarantee the earnings derived from future guano exports.[97] The decision had disastrous consequences. Peru had drawn one major loan in 1822 and another in 1824 to the value of nearly two million pounds. Because of the economic repercussions of the war, it was forced to cease paying the service on its debts two years later. By 1848 the interest accumulated reached more than two and a half million pounds. The surge of guano in the international market motivated foreigners to demand that Peru renew the service of its debts. In 1856, the Peruvian government agreed to begin repayment of the consolidated debt.[98] The agreement, in turn, spurred native Peruvian creditors, who had never been paid by the government for previous loans, requisitions, and services, to demand that their claims be observed. In 1850, the Peruvian government concluded that if it hoped to protect Peru's credit standing, it would also have to recognize and service its domestic debt.[99]

The new decision restricted the availability of revenue to centralize, augment, and legitimize the power of the state. Hoping to compensate for this shortcoming, Peru began to offer foreign creditors earnings to be derived from future exports as collateral for loans.[100] The availability of large amounts of revenue did not lead to an increase in reinvestments in the decayed mines and haciendas and to a rise in employment. Instead, it led to the further concentration of wealth and to the additional appropriation of land held by indigenous communities. To make things worse, just as the production of guano began to decline, the government was forced to channel additional revenues derived from its sale to increase the size of the military in order to contain social unrest. Between 1854 and 1862, more than fifty percent of the revenues elicited from the sale of guano were lost as a result of internal conflicts.[101] In the midst of these tribulations, delegates to Peru's Congress formulated a constitution designed to curtail drastically the power of the Executive. The passage of the new constitution spawned a new set of revolts. Finally, in 1860, the Peruvian Congress acquiesced one more time, and returned to the Executive much of its lost authority.[102] By then, however,

Peru's troubles were too deeply rooted in its social and economic structure to be assuaged by any constitution, regardless of the amount of power it placed in the hands of the Executive.

During this period, two other factors undercut the ability of Peru's elite to consolidate and legitimize the power of the state. Peru's main elite controlled the coast, but to rule they depended on the backing of regional oligarchies in the highlands. The relationship between the elites was precarious, and throughout much of the nineteenth century they were unable to concur on a nationalist ideology. Moreover, during this same period, the ideology they sought to generate was one that purposely excluded substantial portions of Peru's indigenous population. It was nationalism that strove to perpetuate the ethnic and racial hierarchies designed and implemented during the colonial period.[103]

Mexico's state-creating experience differed little from Peru's, except in one important way. The social system of Mexico (originally named New Spain by the Spaniards) changed significantly during the colonial period. The hierarchical structure originally imposed by the Spanish monarchy placed Spaniards at the top, indigenous people in the middle, and blacks at the bottom. Miscegenation changed the caste system. By the eighteenth century, four ethnic mixtures had been added to the original hierarchy: mestizos (Euro-Indians), mulattos (Euro-Africans), zambos (Afro-Indians), and chinos (Asians of various mixtures). For quite some time, New Spain's leaders relied on two criteria to dictate social rank. The first criterion was whether the person was black; blacks invariably were placed at the bottom of the social hierarchy.[104] The second one focused on the "purity" of an individual's blood. Purity determined whether an individual would have access to higher education, the Church, the professions, the craft guilds, bureaucratic employment, and other major elite positions.[105] Economic growth, however, foiled this second criterion to the point that it became possible for a black person, or one of "mixed" blood, to purchase a "patent of whiteness." With the royal order of *gracias al sacar* (grateful for deliverance) institutionalized in 1795 but practiced since at least 1773, the Crown established standard fees for seventy-one categories regulating the amount persons with different levels of "purity" had to pay in order to become "white."[106]

Mexico's drive towards independence following Napoleon's dethroning of the king of Spain in 1808 was lengthy, chaotic, and destructive. A compromise ensued in 1820, when Colonel Augustin de Iturbide, a criollo and the commander of the royalist forces in southern Mexico, and General Vincente Guerrero, an anti-royalist indigenous guerrilla leader, signed the Plan of Iguala. The program's major planks were delineated in its first three articles. The first article stipulated that Roman Catholicism would be the only religion practiced in New Spain, the second one called for the independence of New Spain, and the third one recommended the creation of a monarchy moderated by a constitution.[107] Prepared by Iturbide, the plan was a political compromise that brought together the various factions in New Spain.[108] Rebels accepted the plan because it called for independence and equality of all citizens. Criollos who wanted separation from Spain but feared the radicalism of the indigenous and castes, viewed the plan as a moderate alternative. Conservatives who did not favor autonomy believed it was a wise compromise because it advocated the protection of their rights and property. And the clergy supported the plan because it was convinced that without self-government its interests in New Spain would be undermined by the latest anti-clergy measures adopted by the junta in Spain.[109]

Hopes for a peaceful state-creation process faded rapidly. In September 1821, New Spain's leaders signed the Act of Independence and chose Iturbide as their first chief executive. Less than a year later, the army named him emperor of Mexico. He retained the post for less than twelve months. Burdened by a faltering economy, a nobility who yearned for a European prince who would free them from their fiscal responsibilities, a territory subdivided into regions led by leaders with conflicting interests and unwilling to relinquish their power to a central government, and a population structured hierarchically along racial and ethnic lines, Iturbide became Mexico's first of many leaders to be forced out of power prematurely.[110]

Concerned that Mexico would not be able to protect its independence unless it resolved its economic ills, a group of leaders in Mexico City granted Britain access to Mexico's mineral resources. Well over twenty million pesos were injected into Mexico's ailing economy shortly afterward. With the monarchy no longer an acceptable political form, Mexico designed its first federalist constitution. The 1824 Mexican constitution divided governmental powers between the executive, the legislative, and the judicial bodies, and the country into nineteen states, with each state being granted control over the election of its own governor and legislature.[111] It also stipulated that citizens could not be classified by racial origins in governmental documents,[112] declared Roman Catholicism Mexico's official religion, and prohibited the practice of any other religion.

The period of tranquility came to an end in 1828. From then until the late 1840s, a major divide separated two groups. One group argued that the only path to modernity was via the formation of a powerful centralized government. Their opponents claimed that in order to break the autocratic dependency that it inherited from Spain, Mexico had to grant its provinces and citizens extensive freedoms. Caught in between were the various indigenous groups that had little use for the government and the institutions Mexico's leaders were attempting to shape.[113]

A country deeply split along economic and ethnic lines must sometimes face a series of crises before its people accept that unless they unite and act with a common purpose, powerful foreign actors will exploit the divisions to advance their own interests. Texas, which had been under Mexican dominion, declared its independence in 1836 after a brief war. But it was not until the end of the 1846–1848 Mexican–American war, when Mexico was forced to accept the USA's incorporation of Texas and to surrender control over all the territory of the present states of California, Nevada, Utah, most of New Mexico and Arizona, and parts of Colorado and Wyoming, that its leaders began to grasp the impact engendered by their inability to consolidate and legitimize the power of the state.

To acknowledge that it would be in Mexico's interest to develop a national spirit was one thing; to agree on how to attain it was a different matter. The war, in fact, intensified the ideological divide. Mexican liberals argued that it was imperative to remove all vestiges of colonialism. They called for the creation of a federal democratic republic, governed by representative institutions that addressed the needs of small proprietors, yeoman farmers, and master craftsmen, but not those of the Church.[114] Conservatives advocated the revival of the colonial heritage, with the Church acting as the unifying bond, and called for the eradication of excessive regionalism.[115]

The struggle between the two factions continued through the 1850s, buttressing the power vacuum that had afflicted Mexico almost since its conception. Its plight did not go unnoticed abroad. Foreign actors began to press the new government to pay the debts accrued by previous Mexican regimes. With Mexico's reserves nearly exhausted, its government refused to pay. In October 1861, Spain, Britain, and France agreed to intervene militarily. Spain hoped to regain some modicum of control over what used to be one of its richest colonies; Britain was interested solely in collecting its claims; and France wanted to augment its power by expanding its colonial reach.[116]

Shortly after Spanish and French troops landed in Mexico, with British naval protection, France demanded full payment of its claim. Knowing that Mexico did not possess the means to fulfill the demand, Britain and Spain refused to support France and withdrew their forces.[117] Although a number of conservatives viewed the French invasion as a way to rid Mexico of liberals, most put their rancor aside and joined liberals in the struggle against the invaders. The issue was no longer conservatives against liberals, but whether Mexico would be independent or ruled by a foreign power. The Mexican Congress agreed that the liberal government should govern "with no other restriction than the salvation of the independence and integrity of the Nation, the constitutional form of government, and the Reform Laws."[118] By the end of 1865, the French forces had the Mexican army on the run and seeking protection from the USA. But just as it seemed that the French would succeed, Napoleon III, troubled by Prussia's expansionist warnings, recalled his troops from Mexico. This action forced the invaders to rely on an army composed mostly of Mexicans. Nineteen months later, the leaders of Mexico's liberal government marched triumphantly into Mexico City and restored the liberal republic.[119]

The war forced Mexican leaders to recognize that without a strong, unified state, they would always be at the mercy of foreign powers. During the conflict, the president, with nearly omnipotent powers, was able to expunge the internal opposition and unite Mexicans in a common cause. By the war's end, accustomed to ruling with little opposition, he began to search for ways to increase his power vis-à-vis conservatives, regional leaders, and the Mexican Congress. The design became so encompassing that by 1871 his government had created a state in which the president had the power to pursue order at the expense of liberty.[120] He did not succeed fully. Mexico would have to wait another half century before it would benefit from the emergence of a strong unifying nationalist ideology—one that would make it possible for a set of core leaders to build a state strong enough to thwart the power ambitions of rival domestic actors and foreign entities.

Anglo America versus Latin America

A successful war of independence does not guarantee the swift creation of a stable sovereign state. The nature and intensity of the domestic and international obstacles it encounters in its next political journey will determine, in part, whether it succeeds at crafting a safe and sound state.

Despite their many political and economic differences, the leaders of the thirteen American colonies ruled by Great Britain agreed that their prospect of success would be greater if they created a united state than if each went its own separate way. For a period after independence, the conflicting interest groups within the USA managed to prevail over their differences. They were even able to spawn a non-imperialist ideology of imperialism. As expressed by John O'Sullivan, the editor of the *Democratic Review*, the USA, "the nation of many nations is destined to manifest to mankind the excellence of divine principles; to establish on earth the noblest temples ever dedicated to the worship of the Most High—the Sacred and the True."[121] The voicing of a manifest destiny was not sufficient to persuade the competing domestic interest parties to put aside their differences and rally around a common nationalist sentiment. The Civil War disclosed this fact. Victory by the North, moreover, did not result in the immediate birth of a strong nationalist sentiment. Time and new crises would have to ensue before the USA would experience the unifying conditions harvested by nationalism. Comparatively, however, the tribulations faced by the USA were less severe than those encountered by the newly created Latin American states.

Simón Bolívar's vision for Spanish-America did not differ noticeably from that articulated by the early leaders of the USA. Convinced that the USA and the great powers of Europe would attempt to fill the vacuum left by Spain's departure and that the newly born Spanish-American states would be too weak to weather their assault, he crisscrossed sections of South America, helping the colonies achieve independence and fostering the formation of a large post-independence confederation. In late 1819, he proposed the creation of a greater Colombia composed of Ecuador, New Granada, and Venezuela. By the end of 1821, he had liberated Cartagena and had established a constitutional government in Cúcuta. Subsequently, he marched south to help liberate Bolivia and Peru, and persuade their leaders to form a Spanish-American confederation.

Bolívar did not fulfill his grand vision. He helped free Peru and Bolivia, but he failed to persuade their leaders that their ability to design their countries' destinies was dependent on the formation of a united front. By 1829, the regionalism and centrifugal elements that had been kept partially dormant during the colonial period, but had surfaced during the wars of independence, forced him to abandon his dream. Some of the conditions that obstructed the creation of a Spanish-American confederacy also impeded several of its entities from crafting stable sovereign states. Inside several of the newly established Spanish-American states, regional elites with competing political and economic interests either battled one another or struggled to ensure that the central government would not undermine their own power. In many of them, this problem was compounded by the presence of a society structured unequally along ethno-racial lines, and by the absence of a strong nationalist political ideology. Chile proved to be the exception. Chilean nationalism emerged early and quite easily partly because its society was relatively homogeneous, confined to a small area, and threatened for a substantial portion of the nineteenth century by indigenous rebels occupying part of the country's southern region. The setting up of a strong executive body with supremacy over a deferential armed force also helped. In Peru, ethno-racial cleavages and regionally divided economic interests undermined attempts by elites to foster coalescing nationalist sentiments. In Mexico, which was also burdened by political and economic regionalism, nationalism did not begin to emerge as a revered political force until its people had experienced multiple humiliations in the hands of foreign actors.

One question remains unanswered. Did the political and economic structures imposed by the Spanish colonists and the culture they introduced help undermine their elites' attempts to create stable and legitimates states? It depends on whether structural conditions challenged the existing culture or reinforced it. The Spaniards introduced the same culture in both Peru and Chile. And yet, by the time the two colonies had gained independence, their respective political and economic structures and cultures had changed considerably. Economic necessity helped generate a spirit of economic cooperation in Chile prior to independence—a spirit that did not die with independence. Peru's experience was different. Its colonists never developed a sense of economic interdependence, largely because they could exist as separate and independent economic entities. Independence did not persuade them to change their outlook. Their attitude towards cooperation began to change only as changes in the domestic and international economies forced them to recognize that their well-being was dependent on their ability to work with one another.

Argentina is another case in point. During most of the colonial period, Spain paid little attention to the territory presently encompassed by Argentina. Spain's lack of interest extended the colonists and criollos a freedom rarely experienced by their counterparts in other colonies. Likewise, the territory's vast, agriculturally rich pampas enabled its inhabitants to survive without having to develop deep roots in any one area, and allowed the regions to subsist without needing to design a common set of economic goals. The gaucho, the symbol of the pampas, was an uncooperative creature; his definition of sovereignty meant himself above all others.[122] Though the various provinces joined Buenos Aires in the struggle against the Spaniards, they refused to surrender some of their economic autonomy to the capital the moment they attained independence. It was not until the 1860s, when they finally recognized that without Buenos Aires's active leadership their economies would continue to falter, that the provinces agreed to yield to the capital's dictates.

Simon Bolívar best depicted the initial effect of culture on state creation when he decried the failure on the part of the Spanish colonists to teach criollos the basics of self-government and to instill in them a culture of political, economic, and social responsibility. A citizenry that lacked this culture, he complained, could ill afford to create a federal government that sought to adhere to the "exaggerated precepts of the rights of man; this form, by authorizing self-governments, disrupts social contracts and reduces nations to anarchy."[123] Bolívar acknowledged that the level of internal discord within the various Latin American colonies differed substantially. More importantly, as political, economic, and social conditions changed throughout the newly established Latin America states, so did the beliefs and values of their inhabitants, and especially of their leaders.

Conclusion

The balance-of-power doctrine designed at the 1815 Congress of Vienna assumed the form of a political ideology. As an ideology it had its own distinct set of cognitive, affective, evaluative, programmatic, and social-base dimensions. It was constructed on two broad assumptions. Its central idea was that regardless of how moderate a state's behavior had been, it would dispose of its old inhibitions if it were allowed to rise to a position of predominance.[124] Its second premise was that the only legitimate states were those that had demonstrated for centuries they had the capability to maintain their political independence. The affective and social base dimensions of the balance-of-power ideology were clear and narrow. As an ideology, balance of power was designed to appeal to the sentiments and emotions of Europe's most important leaders. It sought to generate amongst them both fear and support by denouncing Napoleon's immoderate ambitions, and nationalism's destructive potential.[125] Its programmatic dimension was two-sided. To prevent the emergence of a predominant power, Europe's leading actors had to be farsighted and flexible in order to form and change alliances. To offset the rise of nationalism, those same entities had to avoid supporting nationalist causes. Their refusal to support national causes would generate two positive effects—it would help protect both the security of traditional empires and the power equilibrium that existed between them.

The repeated clashes between the balance-of-power doctrine and national-ism affected greatly the structure of Europe's system. After more than half a century of espousing the virtues of the balance-of-power doctrine and attempting to contain the effects of nationalism, some of Europe's original leading entities found themselves facing two highly unpleasant realities. On the one hand, nationalism had assisted in the formation of two new actors, one of which was primed to redesign Europe's power distribution. On the other hand, nationalism had enfeebled and would continue to weaken the legitimacy and power of two traditional multinational empires: the Austrian–Hungarian Empire and the Ottoman Empire. With no single actor able to moderate the tensions generated by these two forces, it was only a matter of time before one or more entities in the region would resort to war to try to change the structure of the European system.

The Western Hemisphere was not immune to developments in Europe. By the middle of the nineteenth century it was not uncommon to assume that the USA would eventually emerge as one of the leading actors. Still, like many other newly created states, the USA had yet to develop a unifying nationalist ideology. The Civil War did not resolve the problem, and nationalism would not materialize as an effective coalescing ideology until the USA was forced to meet head-on powerful international adversaries. Nevertheless, the Civil War catapulted the USA to a higher level in the world system's material structure. It warned other international actors that Washington, if provoked, possessed the will and economic capacity to build a very powerful military force.

During this period, newly created states south of the USA's border were not able to replicate its overall success. Most Latin American leaders encountered serious obstacles as they endeavored to legitimize and solidify the power of their respective states, and create stable political regimes. Acute regional, ethnic, and class divides, moreover, hindered their attempts to generate a coalescing nationalist ideology. Their recurring failures did not go unnoticed. Britain supplanted Spain as Latin America's strongest external force during much of the nineteenth century; and the USA would, in turn, displace Britain as the new century approached. The new imbalance would remain unaltered through the entire twentieth century.

4 A world system destabilized by five ideologies: 1871–1914

Prancing towards world war

The collision between a frail, ideologically built balance-of-power doctrine and a rising nationalist ideology assumed a new dimension not long after Germany became one of Europe's most formidable states. No entity experienced the impact of this clash as strongly as did the Ottoman Empire—the "sick man on the Bosporus."

By the time Prussia, with the aid of nationalism, had formed a united Germany, the Ottoman Empire had already endured several setbacks. Serbia, Bessarabia, and Greece had, for all practical purposes, freed themselves from the Ottoman Empire by the start of the 1830s. During this period, Muhammad Ali established himself as Egypt's new ruler and built an army powerful enough to threaten the Ottomans' hold on the sultanate.[1] The Ottoman Empire's major territorial losses, however, did not come about until after its 1887–1888 war with Russia.

In August 1875, Christian Slav rebels in Bosnia and Herzegovina, an area northwest of Serbia, launched a nationalist insurrection against Turkish rule. Serbians, hoping to expand their own territory, supported the rebels. Their action did not generate the expected results, and Serbia was forced to appeal for international protection. Russia was the first to respond. Upon learning that the Turks had defeated the Serbs, Russia, driven by its desire to become the dominant force from the east coast of the Black Sea to the Adriatic Sea, moved against the victors. Russia's victory in 1878 compelled Britain, Austria–Hungary, and Germany to intervene to ensure that the balance of power would not be altered radically. At the Congress of Berlin held in the summer, the major parties agreed that Serbia, Rumania, and Montenegro would gain full independence from Turkey; Austria–Hungary would rule Bosnia and Herzegovina; Britain would take over Cyprus; and Russia would gain control over the Bessarabian provinces that had been under Rumania's dominion since 1865. The Treaty of Berlin reaffirmed the belief on the part of some of Europe's principal leaders that in order to protect the "balance of power," and thus stability, they had to preserve the integrity of the Ottoman Empire as much as possible.[2] This signified the need to contain the power aspirations of some of Europe's actors, and to offset whenever possible the nationalist aspirations of groups clamoring for independence and the creation of their own distinct state.

In 1890, Germany no longer had Bismarck to help it resolve its countless foreign policy challenges. Its neighboring states, moreover, were apprehensive about its future plans. Russia, thus, signed a pact with France in 1894. Britain, concerned about Germany's rapidly growing economy and by its leader's claim that "Germany had great tasks to accomplish outside the narrow boundaries of Europe," agreed to form an entente with France in 1903, and reached a similar agreement with Russia three years later. Germany, in the meantime, retained the defensive pact it had reached with Austria–Hungary in the 1880s.

For a brief moment near the end of the nineteenth century it seemed as if temperance would win the day. It did not. In 1901, Serbian officers shot their king, Alexander, a client and protégé of Austria–Hungary, and his wife and several high-ranking officials. Peter Karageodjevic, a Pan-Serb pro-Russian who wanted to end Serbia's dependency on Austria–Hungary and unite all Serbs and Croatians under a common state, replaced Alexander. Clubs and secret societies committed to the liberation of Slavs in southern Austria–Hungary and in the adjacent provinces of Turkey sprang into action immediately.

Austria–Hungary did not take these activities lightly. Convinced that its problems in the Balkans would not lessen until it subordinated Serbia, Vienna decided to take advantage of Serbia's diplomatic and commercial dependency on Austria–Hungary. In 1906, after Serbia had signed a customs treaty with Bulgaria, Vienna stopped the import of Serbia's largest export, livestock. The action did not alarm Serbia. Within a year's time, Belgrade had developed more profitable trade agreements with Egypt, Germany, Greece, and Turkey. Angered by the turn of events, Vienna announced that it would link Austria–Hungary with Salonika by railroad on the shore of the Aegean Sea. If laid down as proposed, the new railroad would bypass Serbia and cut it off from the Adriatic Sea.

Russia and Britain opposed the plan, but just as Berlin was about to join Vienna to reject the objection, junior officers stationed in Salonika launched a revolt against the Ottoman Empire's sultan, Abdul-Hamid. The intent of the junior officers was to stop the sultan's despotism, the further crumbling of the empire, and the continued intervention by foreign powers. They did not succeed, and a small domino effect ensued. Bulgaria declared its independence of the Ottoman suzerainty; Crete joined Greece; and Austria–Hungary annexed Bosnia–Herzegovina, a region it had administered since 1878. Russia objected to Austria–Hungary's action but chose to acquiesce after Berlin informed St. Petersburg that it supported Vienna's decision.

Europe's political milieu did not improve as the twentieth century moved on. Its level of stability was affected by Serbia's nationalist aspiration and its impact on Austria–Hungary's power, and by Germany's need to protect Austria–Hungary's status as a major power. The success of Serbia's nationalist drive depended in no small measure on the Ottoman Empire's ability to arrest its continuing downfall.

It has been stated that during the eighteenth century and early part of the nineteenth century, the Ottoman Empire "did not realize that it was falling ever more behind Europe."[3] By the time Abdülmecid I came to power in 1839, however, some of the leaders of the empire had already concluded that unless they adopted drastic measures they would never be able to breach the gap. Unlike the previous ruler, the new one was prepared to adopt the Western philosophy that a state, in addition to keeping civil order and protecting its citizens from foreign powers, had to provide a broad range of additional services.[4] Though many changes were brought about, the reformers were unable to increase the empire's revenues enough to finance the economic and social reforms they advocated.[5]

In 1909, the same young Turkish officers who earlier had tried to bring about a change in the empire's regime marched into Constantinople, deposed the sultan, and created a government committed to "Turkifying" the empire. Their initiative spawned counteractions. Italy invaded Libya. In the Balkans, Montenegro, Serbia, Bulgaria, and Greece declared war on the Ottoman Empire. Their victory did not produce the intended results. Although each was able to enlarge its own territory, none gained as much as it had expected. Serbia was the most displeased. During the war against the Turks, Serbia had secured control of Scutari, an area on the Adriatic Sea, and was hoping to make it part of its state. During peace negotiations held in London in 1913, Vienna vetoed Serbia's request and proposed instead the creation of an independent Albania. Upon learning that St. Petersburg would not come to its aid, Serbia acquiesced.

The London conference exposed the deep divide between some of Europe's leading actors. St. Petersburg, though it had not assisted Serbia, believed that Russia's power aspirations were tightly linked to Belgrade's own territorial ambitions. As a Russian leader noted in a letter to his Serbian counterpart: "Serbia's promised land lies in the territory on present day Hungary."[6] Vienna, in turn, concluded that it could no longer tolerate any attempt on the part of Serbia to expand at Austria–Hungary's expense.

The assassination of the heir to the Habsburg throne, Archduke Franz Ferdinand, and his wife, in Sarajevo in June 1914, was the pretext Vienna needed to issue an ultimatum to Serbia. Serbia countered with a reasonable compromise. Vienna discarded Belgrade's rapprochement and declared war on Serbia near the end of July. St. Petersburg, averse to renouncing its power ambitions in the Balkans, ordered the full mobilization of its troops against Austria–Hungary and along the Russian–German border. Berlin, wary that a war against Russia would expose Germany's western flank, demanded that Paris affirm its neutrality if a war between Germany and Russia were to ensue, and that it transfer to Germany custody over two border fortresses as evidence of good faith. Paris made it clear that it was prepared to abide by the terms of its defense alliance with St. Petersburg. By early August, war had been declared between France and Russia on one side, and Germany and Austria–Hungary on the other. Britain entered the struggle against Germany and Austria–Hungary the next day. In time, the Ottoman Empire and Bulgaria joined Germany and Austria–Hungary, while Japan, Italy, and the USA linked up with the other camp.

In sum, from its inception the 1815 balance-of-power doctrine was destabilized by nationalism. Nationalism, however, served different purposes. In certain instances, as in the case of Britain, leaders used nationalism to invigorate patriotism in order to augment its own power relative to that of other empires or states. In the case of Germany, which did not exist as a state prior to 1871, Prussia relied on nationalism to bring together the various German entities under its leadership. In the case of the Ottoman Empire and the Austrian–Hungarian Empire, however, nationalism helped engender their own destruction.[7] The challenge faced by both empires was exploited not only by relatively small national groups striving to free themselves and create their own states on the basis of ethnic and/or linguistic ties, but also by other major actors hoping to boost their own relative power.[8]

In the latter part of the nineteenth century, the leaders of the Ottoman Empire relied extensively on Islam to both increase unity among its population and prevent its fragmentation into national territorial states. Ironically, though they opposed the notion of nationhood "defined by an attachment to a territorial fatherland and/or to ethnicity or language," their Islamism, when linked to Ottomanism, was anchored on the same foundation they contested. This contradiction did not go unnoticed. It intensified the commitment on the part of Christian Ottomans, who had been ruled by the Muslim leaders of the empire for some five centuries, to view everything in religious terms and thus to seek independence. Likewise, Ottomanism–Islamism was not compelling enough to offset the aspirations of non-Turkish Muslims to create their own nation-states.[9]

Opposite sides of the same coin—imperialism and nationalism

The emergence of a unified Germany in 1871 ended the process of creating powerful states in the European continent. This development, in turn, inspired its principal actors to expand and accelerate their rivalry beyond their continent's boundaries. In time, the USA and Japan, determined not to be left behind, began to copy some of the policies of the European powers.

The drive to reach the most remote corners of the world was motivated by more than strategic and economic aspirations.[10] It was also stimulated by the belief that those with superior intellectual and moral capacity had the right and obligation to transform less-developed societies. Paradoxically, in their push to globalize imperialism, the imperialists exported nationalism, that is, the doctrine that holds that humanity "is naturally divided into nations, that nations are known by certain characteristics that can be ascertained, and that the only type of government is self-government."[11] Imperialism, thus, "created both the conditions [that] formed anti-imperialist leaders and the conditions [that] ... began to give their voices resonance."[12]

The imperialist explosion of the 1870s would not have ensued had it not been preceded by a series of "European revolutions." As explained earlier, the state became the globe's principal actor in the seventeenth century, and nationalism became the legitimating principle of politics and state-making around the middle of the nineteenth century. Three revolutions facilitated the emergence of the modern nation-state in the Western world. The first one was marked by the shift from feudalism to capitalism near the end of the fifteenth century. During the transition, entities with strong central authority began to control economic exchanges within their territories. This expansion benefited states in the form of receipts from taxes, monopolies, and customs; control over important natural resources; and regulations of commodity exchange and trade. One of the end results of this process was the creation of a "single territory-wide occupational system ... , and the erosion of persistent regional divisions."[13] As this transformation took place, a second revolution began to materialize.

Between the late fifteenth century and the eighteenth century, bureaucracies in England, France, Spain, Sweden, Prussia, and Russia increased in size, and in order to maximize their resources they augmented their reliance on technical expertise. These changes were carried out simultaneously in military and civilian organizations. The revolution in artillery and planned warfare, accompanied by the emergence of a specialized professional military force, made it easier and less costly for European dynasties to enlarge their territorial and political dominion. To ensure that their martial forces were properly equipped and supplied, monarchs sponsored the establishment of bureaucratic personnel with technical expertise. Both of these developments, in turn, spawned the founding of institutes of higher education, technical academies, scientific societies, and military academies and staff colleges.[14]

The third revolution took place in the educational and cultural arenas. Determined to gain greater control over the church and clergy, free the state from ecclesiastical and traditional constraints, and achieve religious conformity, monarchs called for the development of an educated elite schooled in the classics and adept in secular learning. Those who pursued this path and showed loyalty to the state and the dynasty were rewarded with bureaucratic appointments. To broaden their reach and strengthen their control, Western states encouraged cultural uniformity and a standard mode of communication. They enhanced their role as educators of the middle classes with the implementation of national education projects and the founding of new universities, academies, and museums. States did not reach their peak as the leading educators until the latter half of the nineteenth century, when they adopted mass compulsory primary education. One of the objectives of the latest revolution was to produce citizens committed to, and mindful of their obligations toward, their respective states.[15]

A state's ability to project its power beyond its borders has always depended in part on the strength of its economy. By the start of the last quarter of the nineteenth century, Europe was already beginning to experience another major industrial makeover. Persons with little scientific training, interested mainly in increasing productivity and improving the quality of products, set off the first major industrial change; individuals with deeper scientific understanding, attracted to the idea of introducing new commodities, bred the second one. It was a revolution led by steel, oil, electricity, and chemicals, and was "far quicker in its impact, far more prodigious in its results, far more revolutionary in its effects on people and outlook."[16] Though private individuals and firms were the principal forces behind the two industrial transformations, the notion of a completely independent economy, unaffected by the actions of the state, held little attraction.[17] Entrepreneurs and financial leaders understood that the strength and performance of a state's economy had a measurable effect on whether the state was a strong or weak international actor, and that their own fortunes depended substantially on the state's willingness to be an engaged and reliable associate.

With the most important consequences of the different revolutions in place, Europe's dominant states were ready to launch a new form of imperialism. Britain, Spain, Portugal, the Netherlands, Russia, and France had established colonies throughout Africa, Asia, the Middle East, the Americas, Australia, and New Zealand long before the 1870s. Few colonial holders, however, revered their possessions. Some feared that the holding of colonies would incite jealousy from other powers; others were concerned that as colonial powers they would endure a fate similar to that experienced by Spain in Latin America, while a third group voiced moral objections. From the 1870s on, most of these concerns were put aside, and European colonial imperialism, induced by fervent nationalist sentiments, "became more open, chauvinistic and competitive."[18] Similar sentiments surfaced in the USA and Japan.

From west to east—imperialism attended by nationalism

By the late nineteenth century there was no other state in the world system that had become as dependent on imperialism as Britain. Though between 1815 and 1865 Britain's leaders repeatedly claimed they favored free trade over direct territorial control, during that same period they expanded British territory at an annual rate of about one hundred thousand square miles.[19] By the 1880s, Britain had become the greatest exporter of industrial products and capital, as well as financial, commercial, and transport services.[20] But as Britain's imperialist dominion increased, so did the challenges. First, industrialization throughout the European continent and the USA undermined Britain's ability to retain its quasi-monopolistic control of the world market. Second, the economic depression of the 1870s and 1880s led the USA and many of the industrialized European states to erect sizeable trade barriers.[21]

Third, militant working-class organizations and cycles of large strikes reemerged throughout Britain.[22] And fourth, returns from British domestic and foreign investments shrank significantly.

With fewer markets and more commercial and financial competition in the industrialized world, there was a demand for greater governmental intervention in non-European societies and the imposition of stricter laws to provide protection from the challenges emanating from other European states and the USA. Initially, not every British leader was prepared to jettison free trade and embrace the launching of a new wave of overseas possessions. In the 1880s, for instance, Prime Minister William Gladstone argued that what was important for Britain was not the possession of a formal empire but the physical and mental powers of the British people. Still, he and other leaders were not ready to propose that Britain should renounce its colonial policy. More to the point, the converse argument gained momentum. As Britain's leaders realized that its hegemonic status was being challenged by the power aspirations of other European actors and the USA, their willingness to resort to force to retain or to gain control of overseas territories increased.[23] As explained by art critic John Ruskin during his 1870 inaugural lecture at Oxford, England must establish "colonies as fast and as far as she is able," seize "every piece of fruitful waste ground she can set her feet on," and teach the "colonists that their chief virtue is to be fidelity to their country, and their first aim is to advance the power of England by land and sea."[24] Cecil Rhodes, who by the time of his death in 1902 had helped increase Britain's domain by almost one million square miles of African territory, inserted a strong dose of pragmatism to Ruskin's message by contending that in order to "save the forty million inhabitants of the United Kingdom from a murderous civil war the colonial politicians must open up new areas to absorb the excess population and create new markets for the products of the mines and factories." To avoid a civil war, he added, the British Empire "must become an imperialist."[25] The British government concurred. It promoted the idea that Britain's destiny as a major political and economic power depended heavily on its ability to continue enlarging its empire in Asian and African territories.[26]

Foremost among the modern determinants of a state's power, alongside the strength of its military and economy, was a government's ability to harvest support for its foreign policy from the public at large and from influential political, economic, financial, and cultural figures. With nationalism at its peak by the 1870s, the leaders of the world's dominant powers were ready to use it to help promote their own version of imperialism. Benjamin Disraeli, who led Britain as prime minister briefly in the late 1860s and then from 1874 until 1880, linked nationalism to patriotism and used the association to popularize and legitimize imperialism. In the early 1870s, he remarked that the "people of England and especially the working class of England, are proud of belonging to a great country ... are proud of belonging to an Imperial country."[27] A few decades later, Prime Minister Lord Archibald

Rosebery glorified the linkage when he referred to "that greater pride in Empire which is called Imperialism and is a larger patriotism."[28]

The British media also played a role. Determined to enlarge their readership beyond the upper and middle classes, several of Britain's newspapers simplified and sensationalized the news. During the last years of the nineteenth century, the *Daily Mail* claimed that it was the "Voice of Empire in London journalism," while the *Daily Express* advertised that its policy was "patriotic" and its faith was "the British Empire."[29] Both newspapers called Britain's 1899–1902 war against the Boers patriotic, chastised those who opposed it, and helped convince lower middle-class and white-collar youths to enlist.[30]

Public schools performed a similar function, but with a smaller audience. They became the means for persuading members of the ruling class that it was their duty to devote themselves to the protection and advancement of the empire. As noted by a Harrow headmaster: "The boys of today are the statesmen and administrators of tomorrow. In their hands is the future of the British Empire. May they prove themselves not unworthy of the solemn act."[31] Ironically, late-Victorian public schoolboys began to shun trade and industry, the two fields that had helped transform Britain into an empire, in favor of becoming military officers, senior civil servants, clergymen, barristers, or colonial administrators.[32] By the start of the next century, nationalism and imperialism had become so intertwined that the British government agreed to establish an "Empire Day."

British leaders did not rely solely on nationalism to foster imperialism. Constantly they declared that superior civilizations or races were morally obligated to elevate the life value of "inferior" members of the human race. Convinced that Britain's economic might was indicative of a God-extended authority, many of its most illustrious citizens asserted that their nation had the duty and responsibility to export Christianity and the rule of law to those who lacked them.[33] The British politician Sir Charles Dilke summed it up when he claimed that because Britain was in the vanguard of real progress and its people were racially and culturally superior to the people of other countries, it was their duty to assist the less fortunate.[34] In 1893, Joseph Chamberlain, at that time one of Britain's most able politicians, applauded its decision to become Uganda's protectorate. Those who were about to assume such responsibility, he noted, were influenced by the traditions of the past and by the spirit of "adventure and enterprise"—a characteristic that made the Anglo-Saxon race "peculiarly fit to carry out the working of colonization."[35] Rudyard Kipling took the argument a step further when he suggested that the British Empire was the trustee of a divine purpose.

> God of our fathers, known of old,
> Lord of our far-flung battle-line,
> Beneath whose awful Hand we hold
> Dominion over palm and pine.[36]

Many of Britain's concerns and sentiments resonated on the other side of the Atlantic. Between 1893 and 1898, the USA experienced a severe double-cycle depression. Washington came under intense pressure from members of the business and financial community to help find new markets. In 1897, the president of the National Association of Manufacturers in the USA stated that manufacturers "have outgrown or are outgrowing their home markets and the expansion of our foreign trade is their promise of relief." That same year, the US Department of State made it clear that it had not ignored the clues. To its embassies abroad it wrote:

> It seems to be conceded that every year we shall be confronted with an increasing surplus of manufactured goods for sale in foreign markets if American operatives and artisans are to be kept employed the year around. The enlargement of foreign consumption of the products of our mills and workshops has, therefore, become a serious problem of statesmanship as well as of commerce.[37]

The message was echoed by Secretary of State James G. Blaine, who remarked:

> [T]he United States has reached a point where one of its highest duties is to enlarge the area of its foreign trade. Under the beneficent policy of protection we have developed a volume of manufactures which, in many departments it overruns the demands of the home market. In the field of agriculture, with the immense population given in it by agricultural implements, we do far more than produce breadstuffs and provisions for our own people ... Our great demand is expansion. I mean expansion of trade with countries where we can find profitable exchanges. We are not seeking annexation of territory.[38]

Blaine was not candid. During that same period, Cuba and the Philippines, after enduring nearly four centuries of Spanish colonial domination and battling for years their shared oppressor, were close to gaining their freedom. But it was not to be. Washington, after helping defeat Spain, pressed Cubans to insert in their constitution provisions that would grant the USA the authority to intervene in their domestic affairs.[39] Though resentful, Cubans acquiesced. For the next two decades, Washington forced several other Caribbean Basin nations to endure a similar fate. On the other side of the globe, the USA imposed a more visible form of domination. Convinced that the Filipinos could not govern themselves and that if left to their own devices other powers would try to control them, Washington established a commonwealth-type rule in the Philippines.[40] Washington also believed that domination of the Philippines would improve the USA's ability to reach other markets in the region. As explained by a leader of the Republican Party, Senator Henry Cabot Lodge, "We believe in trade expansion ... [and the] greatest of all markets is

China. Our trade there is growing by leaps and bounds. Manila, the prize of war, gives us inestimable advantages in developing that trade."[41] Even President William McKinley, who initially had opposed involving the USA in a war with Spain over territory, in due course conceded that returning the Philippines to Spain would be "cowardly and dishonorable," and giving it to France or Germany, "our commercial rivals in the Orient," would be "bad business and discreditable."[42]

A strong nationalist sentiment also helped infuse Washington's determination to broaden the USA's political and economic horizons. Americans, like the British, believed that they were the "success race." As noted by John Fiske, a popular lecturer:

> The work which the English race began when it colonized North America is destined to go on until every land on the earth's surface that is not already the seat of an old civilization shall become English in its language, in its religion, in its political habits and traditions, and to a predominant extent in the blood of its people.[43]

Albert Jeremiah Beverdige, a future senator from Indiana, unabashedly said to his audience in Boston as the USA prepared to go to war against Spain: "We are a conquering race. … American law, American order, American civilization and the American flag will plant themselves on shores hitherto bloody and benighted, but by those agencies of God henceforth to be made beautiful and bright."[44] Theodore Roosevelt, who in a few years would assume the presidency, presented a stark Darwinian argument shortly after being appointed assistant secretary of the navy: "All the great masterful races have been fighting races, and the minute that a race loses the hard fighting virtues, then, no matter what else it may retain, no matter how skilled in commerce and finance, in science or art, it has lost its proud right to stand as the equal of the best."[45] McKinley added his opinion when he asked, rhetorically: "Shall we now, when the civilized world applauds and waits in expectation, turn timidly away from the duties imposed on the country by its great deeds?"[46] Some years later, another president, Woodrow Wilson, left very little doubt that he shared the sentiment of his predecessors. He stated:

> [N]ations and people who have stood still the centuries through are to be quickened, and to be made part of the universal world of commerce and of ideas which has so steadily been a-making by the advance of European power from age to age. It is our peculiar duty … to moderate the process in the interests of liberty; to impart to the peoples thus driven out upon the road of change … our own principles of self-help; teach them order and self-control in the midst of change.[47]

In Germany, the connection between nationalism, patriotism, and imperialism assumed a complex form. In the early 1880s, as the worldwide depression of prices, interest, and profits became acute, Bismarck, who originally considered himself a free-trader and an anti-colonialist, modified his outlook. With Germany's economy hampered by a rapidly growing population, Bismarck used colonialism as a way to create an ideological consensus among big business, the trading interest, and the lower middle-class anti-industrial groups.[48] During this period, however, Germany had constrained its drive to increase its colonial possessions. After the 1890s, without Bismarck at the helm, Germany altered its rhetoric and behavior. William II, who viewed himself as "an instrument of God" and believed that Germany had to push hard to gain its due "place in the sun," argued that to become a world empire Germany needed colonies, and to establish and protect its colonies Germany had to become a sea power. His claim concurred with the opinion of upper- and middle-class Germans, who pressed on for the creation of a powerful navy, the development of the world's largest and fastest ships, the economic penetration of distant areas, and, most importantly, the radical expansion of its colonial reach.[49]

German leaders understood that the government could not expect the population to support the enlargement of the empire unless their basic needs were met. Berlin, thus, continued to carry out and broaden the social reforms initiated during Bismarck's tenure. Its leaders, however, also argued that failure on the part of Germany to enlarge its empire would undercut its ability to foster social advancement. This meant that in return for their extended rights and privileges, Germans were expected to respect the law, renounce revolution, and support unconditionally the imperial actions of the state.[50] Friedrich Naumann explained it best when he wrote:

> We stand on nationalism in our belief that the unfolding of economic and political power by the German nation abroad is the prerequisite for all far-reaching social reforms at home. At the same time we are convinced that external power devoid of national consciousness cannot in the long run satisfy the political interested masses. We therefore seek a power policy abroad and reform at home.[51]

France's drive to enlarge its empire during the latter part of the nineteenth century also had its own unique rationale. Most French citizens were not interested in overseas expansion and viewed the colonies as costly luxuries.[52] With a population of some thirty-nine million people, France's overseas empire contained only eight hundred and fifty-five thousand French citizens, with some seventy percent of them concentrated in Algeria.[53] Moreover, though protectionist legislation encouraged French colonies to trade exclusively with the national market, most French financial institutions and private investors invested principally in developed economies. France's investors outlaid only nine percent of their overall overseas investments to the colonies, while Britain's allotted close to forty-five percent.[54]

This aversion was not shared by some of France's most important figures. Eager to restore some of his nation's lost international luster, Napoleon III launched an aggressive expansionist policy shortly after assuming power in late 1848. His effort came to naught in 1870, when Prussia routed France's armed forces. The humiliation brought about by the defeat divided France's population into two general groups—those who believed that reconstruction, revenge, and restoration of national prestige should take place on the domestic front, and those who claimed that only the creation of a world empire would give France back its vanished glory and security.[55] Despite the division, the French empire grew considerably during the next forty years.

The principal backers of France's imperialist policy were the military, centrist republicans, and a dynamic, but loosely organized, colonial party. Like the inhabitants of other European states and the USA, the French believed that they were vastly more civilized than the native inhabitants of their colonies and had an ethical obligation to assist them. In the words of Jules Ferry, a French premier from 1879 to 1885, the "superior races have a right vis-à-vis the inferior races ... because they have a responsibility, the responsibility to civilize the inferior races." French patriotism, claimed the French, differed meaningfully from that of other European countries. As explained in a French 1904 textbook for primary teachers, the patriotism of France's neighbors was aggressive, narrow, and mediocre because it was "founded on national pride, on ideas of territorial aggrandizement, on a notion of material grandeur." France's patriotism, on the other hand, was superior because it was based on "the moral ideal of respect for others" and its foreign policy was designed to elevate others to a higher plane of civilization. It was France's destiny to stand above other nations; it was its responsibility to "spread, wherever it is able, its language, culture, its arms, and its genius."[56]

A first overview

Different rationales spawned late-nineteenth-century imperialism. The leaders of Great Britain and the USA used imperialism to address some of the economic and financial problems afflicting their respective countries. Bismarck, aware that as a new, united state Germany still faced substantial internal divisions, relied on imperialism to diminish the political, economic, and social pressures brought about by a rapidly growing population, and to bring together competing factions while it addressed their separate needs. During the post-1890 period, imperialism became a means of transforming Germany into a world power and enhancing its prestige. In the case of France, despite the fact that most of its people had little interest in its overseas possessions, some of its most influential members argued that imperialism would enable it to reemerge as a global power and regain some of its lost glory.[57] In all four cases, political, economic, financial, and cultural leaders used different forms of nationalism to engender domestic support. In addition, the leaders of each state were convinced that their country, because it possessed a superior culture, had the moral obligation and right to educate and enlighten less sophisticated societies.

The effects of their ideologies and behavior were widespread. From the early 1870s until the beginning of the First World War, Europe's dominant states and the USA distributed or redistributed around one-quarter of the world's surface. Britain increased its land possessions by some four million square miles, France by approximately three and a half million, Germany by a little over one million, Belgium and Italy by just under one million each, and Portugal by a little over three hundred thousand. Russia continued its long-standing tradition of taking over adjoining territories, while outside Europe, the USA expanded by close to one hundred thousand square miles.[58]

Japan's imperialist nationalist response to imperialism

When studying late-nineteenth-century imperialism, Western analysts focus principally on the goals sought and policies implemented by Europe's leading powers and the USA, and tend to overlook Japan's international political, military, and economic aims and practices. This has been a grave omission for two reasons. First, Japan was the one major non-European target of Western imperialism to both stand against it and respond with its own form of imperialism. As noted by one analyst: "Japan began its career as a modern imperial power under the imperialist gun, escaping its aggressor by becoming an aggressor itself."[59] Second, Japan, like the USA, expanded its territorial dominion by close to one hundred thousand square miles.[60]

From the fourth decade of the seventeenth century until the middle of the nineteenth century, Japan adopted a policy of seclusion.[61] At first, Japan banned Christianity, expelled most foreigners, including overseas missionaries, and outlawed all travels abroad by Japanese. For the next two centuries, Confucian ethics helped establish a hierarchically ordered society consisting of, in descending order of importance, the nobility, with nominal power; the daimyo and their warriors (samurai); the farmers; and at the bottom, the artisans and merchants.[62]

Despite the fact that during the isolationist period contact with the external world was limited, Japan's leaders remained interested in contrasting their country with China and the West. For a time the Japanese viewed themselves as barbarians and deemed China's Ming dynasty to be superior. Following the Manchu conquest of China in the seventeenth century they began to modify their perception, and by the nineteenth century they had become convinced that Japan, not China, was the culturally superior civilization. Their attitude was not confined to China. "Our Divine Land," wrote a nineteenth-century influential member of a nationalist school of thought, "is situated at the top of the world ... The various countries of the West correspond to the feet and legs of the body ... As for the land amidst the seas which the Western barbarians call America, it occupies the hindmost region of the earth; thus its people are stupid and simple, and are incapable of doing things."[63]

In February of 1853, a squadron of ten warships, including three steam-propelled frigates, led by Commodore Matthew Perry, entered Tokyo Bay and demanded that Japan open its market to American commerce. Mindful that it lacked the means to offset the USA's naval might, Japan opened two ports. Four years later, Japan granted the USA access to additional trading harbors and agreed to freedom of trade and a schedule of tariffs.[64]

The USA's behavior forced Japan's leaders to reassess their perceptions of the external world. Still guided by the belief that countries could be classified as civilized, half-civilized, and uncivilized, and determined to escape domination by the West, Japan's leaders placed it in the middle category and relied on the designation to persuade their compatriots that the country needed to modernize in order to advance to the highest rank. To succeed, Japan had to restructure its political, economic, and social systems. In 1868, reformers overthrew the Tokugawa regime. In the ensuing years, they wrote a new constitution based on the Prussian–German model; reformed the legal system; expanded the educational scheme; instituted a new banking structure; created a modern Japanese fleet; encouraged the creation of a railway network, telegraphs, and shipping lines; and helped Japanese entrepreneurs modernize textile productions and develop heavy industry, iron, steel, and shipbuilding.[65]

Restructuring the government and encouraging major changes in the financial, commercial, and educational arenas were not enough. In order to survive and prosper in a world surrounded by potential enemies, a small country also had to generate a new spirit of "collective patriotism." The arrival of the Western powers did not transform the Japanese into patriots overnight. After two decades of revering and using Western technology and methods, however, many Japanese leaders had developed strong misgivings about the type of nation-state Japan was becoming, and advocated the development of a distinctively Japanese "national ideology."[66] Japan, explained a journalist of that period, should continue to westernize so long as the process did not "damage the national character." Nationalism, he added, was the "basic element" necessary to preserve and develop "a unique culture."[67] In 1890, Inoue Tetsujiro, a scholar who had studied in Germany, delineated the relationship between nationalism and international threats. "[I]n the Orient today," he stated:

> Japan and China alone have an independence stable enough to vie for rights with the powers. But China clings to the classics and lacks the spirit of progress. Only in Japan does the idea of progress flourish, and Japan has it within its means to anticipate a glorious civilization in the future. Japan, however, is a small country. Since there are those that swallow countries with impunity, we must consider the whole world our enemy. [W]e can rely only upon our forty million countrymen. Thus any true Japanese must have a sense of public duty, by which he values his life lightly as dust, advances spiritedly, and is ready to sacrifice himself for the

sake of the nation. [We] must strengthen the basis of the nation by cultivating … and … prepare for an emergency by nurturing the spirit of *collective patriotism.*[68]

By the 1890s, Japan's leaders had concluded that the time had come to alter the nature of their relationship with the outside world. In 1894, Japan's foreign minister informed the British minister that the Japanese would not accept "a system of relations with foreign Powers which they no longer considered to be compatible with the progress and changed institutions of the country."[69] Though for years Britain had refused to renegotiate its treaty with Japan, it agreed to relinquish its extraterritorial rights in exchange for a commercial treaty. The USA, Germany, Russia, Italy, and France also altered the terms of their agreements shortly afterward.[70] But by then, two new major international events had helped intensify Japanese nationalism.

For some time Japanese leaders had viewed the Korean peninsula as a place to set up military bases and as a bridge to link Japan to Manchuria's rich resources.[71] The press, with ample support from the government, sought to popularize the idea that war against China was a meaningful endeavor. Tokutomi Soho, the founder of *Friends of the Nation*, a group that advocated the bold application of Western models to lift Japan to the ranks of civilized societies, argued that it was imperative to go to war against China in order to "transform Japan, hitherto a contracting nation, into an expansive nation."[72] War between the two ensued in 1894. The following year China called for a truce and agreed to comply with many of Japan's demands.

The victory altered the way both nations were perceived. In Japan, China became a source of passionate contempt and hatred during and after the war.[73] Local orators, the press, popular magazines, and schoolteachers depicted the Chinese as the "cowardly Chinamen" from "pigtail land" who "ran from battle disguised in women's clothes."[74] Japan's perception of self also changed. Tokutomi Soho wrote: "Before, we did not know ourselves, and the world did not know us. But now that we have tested our strength, we know ourselves and we are known by the world. Moreover, we know we are known by the world."[75] Takayama Chogyu, a leading proponent of *Japanism*, proposed that the war helped transform an empty theory about loyalty and patriotism into a concrete "national consciousness."[76] Abroad, the USA's secretary of the navy, impressed by Japan's victory, acknowledged that the country had leaped "to a place among the great nations of the earth."[77]

The war with China, however, did not generate the rewards Japan had expected. According to the peace settlement reached by the two governments, China recognized Korea's independence, and Japan got from China the southern portion of the Fengtien province in the Liaotung peninsula, a substantial war indemnity, and access to four cities and ports. Russia, Germany, and France opposed the accord immediately. Lacking the means to stand against the three powers, Japan agreed not to serve as Korea's protectorate and accepted Russia's decision to occupy Manchuria and northern China.[78]

The reversal did not undermine Japan's resolve. "At present," said one of its leaders, "Japan must keep calm and sit tight … [it] must watch and wait for the opportunity in the Orient that will surely come one day. When this day arrives, Japan will decide [its] own fate."[79]

A new opening materialized at the dawn of the new century. After China's defeat, the foreign powers, certain that its ruling regime was about to collapse, sought to carve out spheres of influence and lease territories as bases. These interventionist measures generated a wide wave of xenophobia throughout China's northeastern region that was followed by a series of attacks by Chinese nationals on missionaries and on members of the foreign legations in Beijing and Teintsin. Though all the foreign powers occupying China sent troops to suppress the uprisings, Russia went a step further and took over three eastern provinces in Manchuria. Britain, fearful that Russia's action would unbalance the power distribution in the region, but unable to take a forceful stand because of its struggle against the Boers in South Africa, asked Japan to increase its military presence in northern China. This request paved the road for the signing of an alliance between Britain and Japan in early 1902. The treaty served Japan's interests well. In addition to stipulating that Britain would remain neutral if Japan were to become involved in war, the accord acknowledged Japan's peculiar interests in both China and Korea.[80]

Russia's refusal to withdraw its forces from Manchuria played into the hands of those in Japan who advocated a bellicose policy toward Russia. Most of the Japanese media urged their readers to "overcome the mental malady of fearing Russia" and called for a war against the occupiers of Manchuria. In February 1904, Japan launched a surprise attack on Russia's fleet based in Port Arthur. Though after months of heavy fighting Japan's triumphs seemed to indicate that victory was at hand, its military and civilian leaders, aware that their country lacked the means to wage a prolonged war, authorized the government to ask the president of the USA to help negotiate a peace settlement. On September 5, 1905, Russia recognized Japan's rights to "guide, protect and control" Korea, and ceded southern Sakhalin, the territories around Port Arthur and Tailen, and the railways between Port Arthur and Chanchung. Russia, however, refused to pay indemnities to Japan.

The agreement was not well received throughout Japan. Domestic newspapers criticized it and helped incite riots in several Japanese cities. Both actions signaled that most people throughout Japan were at ease with the notion of robbing Korea of its sovereignty and viewed imperialism as a fitting nationalist device.[81] The war, moreover, gave Japan what it had coveted since its humiliation half a century earlier—a victory over a major Western power, control over valuable territories, and worldwide prestige. Other actors throughout East and Southeast Asia, along with the Western powers, acknowledged that henceforth they could not afford to ignore Japan.[82]

In short, an amalgamation of concerns and interests triggered Japan's imperialist policies. Averse to surrendering its sovereignty to the Western powers, Japan's authorities employed imperialism to accelerate its economic development, become a major strategic power, and gain recognition as one of the Far East's leading players. To achieve these goals, they relied on more than a strong economy and "fortifications and warships." Steered by the belief that if they were united, "even a million formidable foes [would] be unable to harm [them]," they used a wide range of means to create a strong sense of "collective patriotism" among the forty million Japanese.

The rise of nationalism in four corners of the world

Japan was not the only state that tried to free itself from foreign domination. Anti-imperialist reactions elsewhere, however, were not followed by a new wave of imperialism piloted by the victims. Inspired by strong nationalist and, in some cases, religious ideologies, a number of the affected actors mounted revolts. Though their levels of success varied, most did not gain independence until after the Second World War. The ideas that inspired their responses against their foreign rulers did not die with the initial disappointments. Because China had a long-standing status as a world power, and because its actions would ultimately help transform Asia's power distribution, this study will focus first on its struggle to formulate a united nationalist response to Western and Japanese imperialism.

China's downfall as a world power and the rise of nationalism

China's decision in the fifteenth century to discontinue its extensive naval expeditions did not mark the start of an isolationist period. For the next four hundred years China became part of a world system defined mainly by Europe's leading entities. Being a member of a system defined by others did not signify that China had become one of their dominions. Following the expansionist policy launched by some of Europe's chief actors during the late fifteenth century, China continued to develop and maintain its political, economic, and cultural autonomy. Two factors contributed to its success. First, during much of this period no European state possessed the means to challenge an empire that embraced five million square miles and three hundred million people. Second, many in Europe were impressed by China's "civilization." It was not unusual for European leaders to state that they planned to inject their own societies with the spirit of China.[83]

Of critical significance in a highly competitive world environment is how rapidly and effectively a member of the system develops in comparison to others, and how well it adapts to changing conditions and challenges. Britain, though it did not disparage the old, was unafraid of the new. China remained affixed to a culture that valued old over new. The difference in their world outlooks is reflected in their distinct approaches to science. Since Isaac Newton, British and European scientists had adhered to the idea that what distinguishes a scientific hypothesis from a non-scientific one is whether it is falsifiable. Repeated attempts to falsify a hypothesis accomplish two things.

First, failure to invalidate a hypothesis with a broad range of additional "negative" information enhances its relevance, the willingness by others to accept it, and its utility. Second, a successful drive to refute a hypothesis often facilitates the discovery of alternative hypotheses and solutions. Successful refutations, in other words, spawn change and, as a result, new discoveries. In addition, heavy reliance on abstraction and mathematics help enrich hypotheses. Chinese scientists placed little value on testability, abstraction, and mathematics. They focused, instead, on gathering information that reinforced existing knowledge. Moreover, though science in China was empirical, it was not experimental. The absence of experimentation undercut the ability of Chinese scientists to test hypotheses and the opportunity to move along uncharted waters.[84]

By the 1830s, Britain had attained substantial superiority over China in three vital areas. With a population of three hundred million people, China, during the Ch'ing period, raised revenue of one hundred million taels, while Britain, with seventy million people under its dominion (including the inhabitants of North America and India) collected the equivalent of seventy-five million taels in revenue. This meant that China's revenue-collecting capacity was only one-third that of Britain's. Without a central bank, national debt, or bill market, China's ability to borrow in order to back up major projects was also inferior. Second, though China had a military establishment visibly larger than Britain's, its horsepower, firepower, artillery, and navy were not on a par with Britain's. Third, Britain's per capita energy consumption, a reasonable measure of levels of industrialization during that period, was five times greater than China's.[85]

These discrepancies had a direct effect on their relationship in the 1830s. With the USA no longer a part of its empire, Britain, after decades of relying on diplomatic measures to persuade China to open its mostly self-sufficient economy, opted for an aggressive approach. By then, British merchants had discovered that opium, easily imported from India, was in high demand and commanded a high price. Unhappy with the domestic effects brought about by the trafficking of opium, China sought to control its trade. The destruction of twenty thousand chests of opium by the Chinese extended Britain the rationale it needed to take an uncompromising stand. A war that started in November 1839 came to an end three years later when China, unable to match Britain's military superiority, signed the Treaty of Nanking. With the signing of three additional accords, Western powers created the common basis they would rely on to deal with China. When the Treaty of Nanking expired more than a decade later, the Western powers demanded that China provide a more open market, access to its interior, freedom of navigation on inland rivers, and permanent residency in Beijing for their diplomatic representatives. Because of China's unwillingness to acquiesce to the new demands, British and French forces marched into Beijing, burned its Summer Palace, and imposed the Convention of Beijing. The 1860 Convention delineated China's new diplomatic, territorial, and commercial obligations toward the West.[86]

Raised in a long-standing tradition of implicit cultural preeminence, China's leaders initially were unable to mount an effective counter-imperialist policy. Their failure spawned the creation of secret societies throughout south and central China and revolts. Though the goals sought by the societies varied, they shared a strong anti-Christian and anti-Western-imperialism outlook. Animosity against Christian missionaries and Chinese converts meant more than tension between two competing cultures. It stood for conflict between Chinese culture and a foreign ideology that advocated political, economic, and cultural penetration.[87] The "Proclamation of Warning," issued in 1898 by a coal miner and leader of a secret society, is a good example of the anti-Christian and anti-Western-imperialism sentiments. It stated:

> Nowadays, foreign merchants come for trade, and Christian missionaries come to preach Christianity. They have stripped us of our means of livelihood on the land, destroyed the sacred relationships between the emperor and his subjects and between father and son. They used opium to poison China and fancy technology to delude the people ... Our national debt is heavier than a mountain. They burned down our summer palace and seized our tributary states. They forced the court to open treaty ports and wished to dismember our country as if it were a melon. From antiquity to the present, there have been no barbarians like these.[88]

Japan's defeat of China in 1895 strengthened the resolve of Chinese leaders and intellectuals to offset the pressures from the foreign powers. Influenced by the belief that societies evolve in a linear fashion, but still committed to the concept of universal harmony for "all-under Heaven," members of China's scholar-official class proposed a "one world" vision. By claiming that democracy, equality, and human liberation were humanity's most worthy objectives, Chinese scholars argued that the movement towards those goals was evolutionary. The former barbarians—Europe and the USA—occupied the highest place, *Great Peace*, and autocratic China resided in the early phase of a lower stage, *Approaching Peace*. Because interaction between members that had evolved differently ensued in a state of *Chaos*, it was China's mission and responsibility to guide others toward a global *Great Peace*.[89]

When several foreign entities decided to exploit the growing power vacuum and joined forces to demand additional rights and concessions, Chinese rebels responded with a series of attacks.[90] The foreign powers met the rebellion with their own aggressive measures, and it was not long before the interlopers started to extort additional concessions and large compensations. The reaction by the foreign powers to the rebellion convinced many Chinese that they could no longer afford to continue dreaming about the past. Impressed by Japan's success at building a powerful nation in a short time, China launched its own set of reforms. It began to modernize its state structure, institute elected assemblies, build a modern army, design a modern law code, and revamp the educational system.[91] While the reforms were being implemented, a number of Chinese intellectuals suggested that China form a racial bond with the inhabitants of other Asian states, especially Japan, in preparation for a "struggle between the white and yellow races." The idea died rapidly. Russia's defeat in 1905 persuaded many in China that Japan's pan-Asianism was nothing more than an attempt to disguise its own imperialist aspirations. Confronted by the competitive nature of world politics and by the realization that the powers that were infringing on China's sovereignty possessed their own distinct identities, China's scholars advocated the development of a unifying "national consciousness."[92]

Two competing "nationalist" perspectives evolved. The centralists contended that it would be impossible to create a solid nationalist foundation if rival provincial interests, with their own distinct traditions and interpretations of autonomy, attempted to create a nationalist sense of awareness. The federalists, in turn, proposed that a national constitution could be designed only on the foundations of previously established provincial constitutions. As explained by a leader of Guangdong province:

> The people of Guangdong are truly the masters of Guangdong. It is appropriate that with respect to Guangdong, its political, financial, military, educational affairs ... should all be controlled and managed by the people of Guangdong. When the people of Guangdong manage their own affairs and complete their own independence, then it is the beginning of the independence of all of China.[93]

Disillusionment with imperial authority continued to grow. In 1911, a small army mutiny broke out in one of China's provinces and forced its governor to leave. Shortly afterward, nearly every province declared its independence. On January 1, 1912, Sun Yat-sen became the Republic of China's provisional president. During the second week of February, the emperor abdicated, Sun stepped down, and a new provisional president was sworn in. The end of the Qing dynasty, however, did not mark the beginning of a stable political alternative.[94] The change not only failed to end the internal discord but also enticed the foreign powers to enlarge their diplomatic, strategic, and economic authority throughout China. With the Treaty of Versailles to back them up, the foreign powers set up a total of sixty-nine ports throughout China. The ports became the permanent residences of Westerners, centers for trade and commerce, and sites of consulates and military barracks, all protected as semi-independent units with their own tax and legal-judicial systems.[95] The foreign powers also appropriated China's entire customs revenue, and Tibet and Mongolia were given autonomy under the watchful eyes of Britain and Russia, respectively.[96]

Though the first revolution failed, the establishment of the provisional government and the abdication of the emperor marked the break with the most enduring political tradition the world had ever known. The revolution "was motivated not by traditional values, but by adapted foreign ideologies and political theories such as national sovereignty, citizenship, nation-state, nationalism, Republicanism, and Social Darwinism."[97] In his inaugural speech, Sun noted that the revolution would be guided by the principles of nationalism, democracy, and people's livelihood.[98] Sun framed nationalism to correspond with two revolutionary objectives. Its first one was to free China from foreign political and economic domination. "Government," stated Sun, "is progressing in every other country today; in China, it is growing backwards. Why? Because we are under the political and economic domination of foreign nations."[99] Sensitive to the fact that during the Qing dynasty its emperor ruled over five different groups of people, Sun hoped to ensure that they would remain part of the newly created Republic of China. "The people," he noted, "are the foundation of the state. Unifying the Hun territories, Manchuria, Mongolia, the Muslimlands, and Tibet means uniting the Hun, Manchu, Mongol, Hui [Muslim], and Tibetan ethnicities as one people. This is called the unity of the nation."[100]

By the 1920s, a fresh generation of Chinese Western-oriented intellectuals and students had emerged. One of their first steps, under Sun's leadership, had been to reorganize the Nationalist (Kuomingtang) Party. With China's small Communist Party as its ally, the Nationalist Party launched a major anti-foreign campaign in 1925. As the movement gained momentum, the Nationalist Party, by then under Chiang Ka-shek's leadership, sought to weaken the Communist Party.[101] The move paid off, at least initially. Outnumbered, the Communist Party sought refuge in China's northwestern region. The struggle between the two factions eased Japan's move into Manchuria. In 1936, however, Chiang was forced to concede that to offset Japan's imperial aspiration he would need to form a common front with the communists. Resolution of their domestic differences would have to wait.

In short, China's repeated failures to free itself from the foreign powers were precipitated largely by the unwillingness on the part of its imperial authorities to forgo the long-standing belief that its civilization was superior to all others, and by its provincial leaders' refusal to forfeit some of their freedoms in order to create a united national consciousness. China's initial inability to construct a unified nationalist ideology mirrored the experiences that many other victims of imperial policies underwent, or would undergo, during their early attempts to expel interlopers. In the case of Mexico, the struggle to create a united front against foreigners would prove to be less taxing.

Mexico's nationalist revolution

On September 16, 1910, a century after Father Miguel Hidalgo y Costilla had asked Mexicans to revolt against the Spaniards, General Porfirio Díaz, Mexico's president since 1876, stepped onto the balcony of the National Palace in

Mexico City and called on his compatriots to commemorate their hard-won freedom.[102] Díaz's exhortation seemed justified. After decades of internal strife and intervention by foreign powers, Mexico had attained a modicum of political and economic stability.[103] With a population increasing at the rate of 1.4 percent per year, Mexico's economic production had grown at an annual rate of 2.7 percent, and exports at an annual pace of 6.1 percent. In the 1890s, moreover, the Díaz regime had balanced the budget, reformed the treasury, abolished internal tariffs, overhauled the banking institutions, placed Mexico on the gold standard (thus eliminating fluctuations in the value of the peso), and accumulated substantial reserves.[104] And yet, some eight months later he was forced to resign. His resignation launched the initiation of steps that in time would alter radically the nature and structure of Mexico's political and economic systems.

Like all of his predecessors, Díaz endeavored to solidify his power from the moment he became president. He relied on fraud, graft, and nepotism to constrain factionalism and curtail the power of potential adversaries. He muzzled Mexico's press and prevented the election of his opponents to Congress. He reduced the overall size of the military, and relied on paramilitary forces that answered directly to him to engage in repressive activities. Aware that any attempt on his part to further undermine the authority of the Church would generate hostility from the Conservatives, he allowed it to recover some of its lost political, economic, and social relevance. Determined to prevent his own allies from appropriating his power, he rejected the formation of a political party. At the provincial level, moreover, he turned rival political leaders against one another. He selected around seventy percent of the governors and made sure that they remained loyal to him by choosing individuals who, though lacking political, economic, or social roots in the provinces they were assigned to govern, would be able to amass substantial wealth in their assigned posts.[105]

Díaz could not have transformed Mexico into a nearly closed hegemonic regime without foreign assistance. Convinced that the members of Mexico's political and economic elite would not challenge the system they lived under so long as they were plentifully compensated, Díaz found his saving device outside his country's borders. By the time Díaz was forced to abdicate the presidency, foreign investors controlled one-seventh of Mexico's land surface and two-thirds of Mexico's accumulated investment (outside of handicraft and agriculture). By 1910, assets owned by US investors were larger than all other foreign holdings combined, while ninety-eight percent of Mexico's arable land consisted of haciendas, and ninety percent of Mexico's peasants, most of whom were illiterate, were landless.[106]

Eventually, Díaz's autocratic ways and Mexico's heavy dependency on foreign investors spawned revolts. In early 1909, Francisco I. Madero proposed the creation of an independent Anti-Reelectionist Party. Committed to the idea that Mexicans had to revive their public spirit and shed their chaotic political inheritance, he traveled the country promoting himself as the

w/ alternative ideologies

alternative presidential candidate. As expected, Díaz retained the presidency. In early November 1910, however, Madero denounced Díaz, named himself Mexico's provisional president, and set November 20 as the date when the revolt against the government would be launched.[107] The unanticipated became reality. On May 25, 1911, Porfirio Díaz was forced to resign and leave the country.

Initially, the presidents who succeeded Díaz were reluctant to fully break Mexico's link to the external world. Each assumed that such a step would inflict heavy costs on Mexico. Still, each one steadily sought to weaken the economic hold foreigners had on Mexico. Despite the fact that often there were significant political differences between Mexico's political leaders, strong nationalist sentiments made attacks on foreign investors a powerful and reliable source of popular support. The imposition of new taxes on large agricultural and mineral operations became a common practice. The foreign-dominated oil industry became one of the most attractive targets. In 1913, the Mexican government raised the special oil tax from twenty cents to seventy cents per ton. Two years later, a different Mexican government ordered state approval on all transfers of ownership in the oil zone, imposed new taxes, and stopped additional exploration and development until new legislation had been enacted. One of the articles of the 1917 constitution vested subsoil rights in the state. The same constitution, moreover, sought to reduce the job insecurity experienced by most Mexican workers by stipulating their rights and the employers' responsibilities.[108] A year later, a new petroleum law imposed higher taxes. For the next ten years, Mexico and the USA addressed their differences via negotiations until they reached a major accord in 1928. A steep drop in the production of oil in Mexico, and in the petroleum sector's contribution to Mexico's gross national product, helped ease their differences.[109] With the agreement, Mexico acknowledged the ownership of concessions held by foreign companies before 1917, while the foreign companies recognized Mexico's ownership of subsoil rights.[110]

The agreement did not mark the end of Mexico's anti-foreign sentiment. During his presidency, Elías Calles persuaded Mexico's power-holders to put their differences aside and support the creation of a party that would centralize authority for the regime. His successor, Lázaro Cárdenas, strengthened the party by creating and incorporating mass organizations within it.[111] One of Cárdenas's major triumphs was to bring thirteen thousand oil workers (out of nineteen thousand) into a single union and place it under his party's tutelage. His next major success was the nationalization of most railroads, which had been mostly under foreign control. But his coup de grâce came in 1938, when he nationalized the oil industry.[112]

Cárdenas's success was facilitated by the attitudes and behavior of foreign proprietors. The head of Royal-Dutch Shell, Sir Henri Deterding, for instance, "was incapable of conceiving of Mexico as anything but a Colonial Government to which you simply dictated orders." As the foreign companies continued to pursue a policy of "passive unhelpfulness," oil increasingly assumed an emotional dimension involving both "race and nationality."[113] The Mexican president, mindful of the strong nationalist sentiment generated by the behavior of the foreign oil companies, noted in a speech in 1938 that for the 1911 revolution to continue, Mexicans had to "be prepared at all times to resist, even at a cost of serious sacrifice, attacks by those who do not understand the justice of the Mexican cause and those who seek to bring about its failure by creating a situation of uncertainty and alarm."[114] As a Mexican radio announcer would explain shortly afterward, Cárdenas's decision to expropriate the oil companies was "tantamount to a declaration of economic independence in the same way as the one issued in 1821 marked the political independence of Mexico." "[T]he political revolution," he added, "had produced – dialectically – the economic revolution."[115] But the second one could not have transpired without the unifying force of nationalism.

The evolution of nationalism in Britain's "jewel"

In the early 1500s, Portuguese sailors and traders set up several trading posts on India's western coast. They retained dominance over the trade in spices and Far Eastern textiles until a century later, when Dutch and English merchants and ship owners began to make inroads. England's leading interloper was the East India Company, a company established in 1600 by a small number of merchants in London who wanted to bypass middlemen in the eastern Mediterranean and deal directly with spice suppliers in the East Indies. By the middle of the 1670s, the Company's yearly export of English manufactured goods amounted to a value of nearly one hundred and fifty-five thousand English pounds. During that same time period it was importing Indian goods, largely textiles, worth eight hundred and sixty thousand English pounds.[116]

Britain's relationship with the East India Company changed after the American Revolution. Determined to avert another debacle, England's prime minister, William Pitt, submitted in 1784 an act that made the British government a partner of the East India Company. Thirty years later, the Company had the most powerful army in India and ruled, directly or indirectly, Bengal, much of the upper Ganges basin, and large portions of eastern and southeastern India. The remaining territories in the subcontinent were governed by native princes who feared the Company's power and in many instances sought, if not its friendship, at least its protection.[117]

Until the early nineteenth century, British rule had depended extensively on the willing participation of Indians, either as allies or as employees working as revenue collectors, merchants, and sepoys. The rulers owed their initial success in no small measure to their readiness to integrate themselves with the Indian modes of government. After 1813, however, educational reformers, known as Anglicists, argued that because India was fundamentally a backward place, its ways had to be changed. Indians, they claimed, would attain salvation only if they learned English and adopted English customs through an English education. Despite the fact that the British sought to change India's ways and customs by making English the subcontinent's official language, creating an educational system along English lines, and designing a penal code based on English law, the administration of India remained dependent on Indians and their institutions.[118]

For symbolic reasons, entities that have been under the control of empires want to identify the moment their war of liberation began. For many, the 1857 mutiny by the Indian Army stands as India's First War of Independence; for others it does not, because they contend that it lacked a coherent ideology.[119] A more balanced view would propose that the mutiny was less than a national revolution but more than just another military uprising.[120] The defiance and the response it generated pushed India into the forefront of British political life and helped develop a concept hitherto largely unheard of throughout the subcontinent—Indian nationalism.

The rebellion broke out in an area just northeast of Delhi in May 1857, after members of sepoy regiments freed from jail comrades who had been found guilty by a court for refusing to use a new greased cartridge.[121] Following their release, the rebels burned down bungalows and offices, killed many Europeans, and marched towards Delhi. Twenty-four hours later, some five thousand men occupied the city and declared its titular king the emperor of Hindustan. The action did not challenge British supremacy. While a quarter of the sepoys in the Army of Bengal joined the revolt, the armies of Bombay and Madras did not. In July, however, an event changed the nature of the conflict dramatically. A rebel leader, after imprisoning two hundred women and children in a house in Cawnpore, ordered their execution. For the next year, the British carried their retribution to an extreme. After they regained control of Delhi, they slaughtered its occupiers indiscriminately, claiming that God authorized them to show "no mercy to murderers."[122] In the words of India's viceroy, Lord Charles Canning, "the sympathy which Englishmen ... felt for the natives ... changed to a general feeling of repugnance."[123]

With the change in attitude came the belief that Britain alone should be India's master. The 1858 Government of India Act took away the East India Company's power and placed it entirely in the hands of the Crown. Subsequently, Britain created the post of Secretary of State for India and restored the legislative functions of the largely white councils of Bombay and Madras. It restructured the Indian military by placing all the troops under the Crown, increasing the proportion of British soldiers, and recruiting more reliable men. By the 1870s, much of India had been pacified and become more British.[124]

The value placed on India continued to increase during the rest of the nineteenth century. By the 1880s, it was the Indian Army, with its massive reserve forces, that enabled Britain to project itself, at no additional cost to its citizens, as a great military power capable of competing with the ground forces of continental Europe's dominant actors.[125] India's military significance became most evident during the First World War, when 1.3 million of its men participated on behalf of the empire.[126] Moreover, as Europe's principal economies moved aggressively to catch up with Britain's, the latter's economic dependence on India rose. British exports to India (and Burma) increased from 9.4 percent in the 1846–1850 period to 12.9 percent during the 1881–1885 phase. By the start of the First World War, India was absorbing one-tenth of Britain's overseas investments.[127]

In the absence of a well-organized political unit, nationalism will not rise. India, with a population of more than two hundred million people, was a political map composed of more than five hundred princely states and a number of provinces governed directly by British officials. In Karl Marx's words:

> Hindustan is an Italy of Asiatic dimensions ... the same rich variety in the products of the soil, and the same dismemberment in the political configuration. Just as Italy has, from time to time, been compressed by the conqueror's sword into different, national masses, so do we find Hindustan, when not under pressure of the Mohammedan, or the Mogul, or the Briton, dissolved into as many independent and conflicting states as it numbered towns or even villages.[128]

What is more, by then racial and religious tolerance throughout the subcontinent had ebbed measurably. Indians saw themselves as Hindus or Muslims first, and Indians second. Religion, as Jawaharlal Nehru would note years later, was to become India's greatest burden—it spawned dogmatism and narrow-mindedness.[129]

The early growth of nationalism in India was tightly linked to the development of a unified national economy and an elite that was taught to believe that an education based on knowledge of Western philosophy and science would give rise to a class of enlightened men able to run their own country. During the second half of the nineteenth century, India witnessed the steady growth of educated Indians who had been taught in English in government schools, colleges, and universities, and had been exposed to British political ideas that emphasized the rights of the individual and the limitations of the legal power of the state.[130] Following widespread protests in 1883 against a government proposal to extend the jurisdiction of Indian local magistrates to Europeans, a number of affronted educated Indians formed an association for the purpose of addressing issues related to their country. In its early days, the Indian National Congress met only once a year and took stands that were not particularly revolutionary. The attitude of its members changed substantially during the 1898–1905 viceroyalty of George Nathaniel Curzon.

Lord Curzon arrived in India certain that its population and those of other Asian countries were members of an inferior race that did not act according to the canons of morality and truth, and that had relied on deception to advance their interests. He did little to conceal his prejudice. English opinions regarding lying, he stated in 1905, "are strong, distinct and uncompromising in the abstract; Hindu and Mohammedan opinions on this subject are fluctuating, vague and to a great extent dependent upon times, places and persons ... I know no country where mare's nests are more prolific than here."[131]

For Lord Curzon, questioning the integrity of Indians did not seem enough. The British Parliament had passed in 1833 a statute stating that the criterion for eligibility for holding employment under British ruling would be capability and not religion, place of birth, or color. Though the declaration was reaffirmed in 1858, it was not until 1870 that the British government allowed an Indian to enter the British civil service. Five years later, India's viceroy, Lord Litton, acknowledged in a private letter that the initial claims could not be fulfilled and that when faced with "the choice between prohibiting them (the Indians) and cheating them," Britain had "chosen the least straight-forward course."[132] During his tenure as viceroy, Lord Curzon went a step further by stating in public that Indians would never be recognized as equals so long as Britain ruled them:

> You base your claims for equality on the Queen's Proclamation. But what does it promise you?
> It says that you will have equality when you are qualified for it. Now here we have certain qualifications which can only be obtained by heredity or race. Therefore, as you cannot acquire race, you cannot have equality in India as long as Britain's rule lasts.[133]

Tired of tempering their discontent, an increasing number of Indians began to challenge Britain's authority. In 1906, just after Muslims had announced the creation of the Muslim League, many members of the Indian National Congress sided with one of its delegates when he stated that they had to denounce "in every part of our country this new principle of imperialism that the White man has a sort of 'divine right' to rule over the Coloured man."[134] Two years later, members of the National Congress found themselves divided between "moderates" and "extremists." Determined to curtail the discontent that was rapidly brewing throughout India, Britain introduced reforms that increased the number of elected Indians on the provincial and central legislative councils of the Raj.[135]

The next major nationalist impetus for change started just before the First World War. In 1915, India extended a hero's welcome to one of its own: Mohandas Gandhi. The previous year, Gandhi and General Jan Christian Smuts, South Africa's Minister for Defense and Native Affairs, had reached an agreement that led to the passage of the Indian Relief Bill. The bill met all of Gandhi's demands—the abolishment of a three-pound annual tax on Indians, the legal recognition by South Africa of marriages considered legal in India, and the acceptance of a domicile certificate as the only document Indians would be required to present to enter the Union. Despite the considerable significance of the agreement to Indians in South Africa, the manner in which Ghandi sought to bring it about was of greater import to those outside the country.[136]

In 1906, Gandhi, who had been working with the Natal Indian Congress since 1894 to help protect the rights of Indians in South Africa, decided to adopt a new strategy. Until then, he and others had pursued their goals by relying on a mixture of conventional legal and political devices. With only modest success to show for their efforts, Gandhi launched a new campaign. He called it *Satyagraha* (the force of truth), and built it on the belief that evil could be defeated only if one abandoned aggressive acts and relied on restraint. Non-cooperation and civil disobedience thus became *satyagraha's* two principal campaign instruments.

In 1918, Gandhi put into practice *satyagraha* in Ahmedabad, an impoverished mill town that had been hit by a plague epidemic. In an attempt to keep the weavers from leaving the town while the plague raged, mill owners had offered them bonuses—up to seventy-five percent of their wages. When the plague began to subside, the mill owners ended the bonuses; weavers, in turn, demanded a fifty to sixty percent wage increase. Gandhi joined the cause of the weavers, and in March he began the first of the seventeen fasts "to death" that he would undertake throughout the rest of his life. Four days later the disputing parties reached a compromise. The nature of the compromise was less important than the fact that Indians began to view Gandhi as a representative of their aspirations—a future that did not involve Britain.

Gandhi's *satyagraha* came at an inopportune time for the British. In 1917, India's viceroy, Lord Frederic Chelmsford, and the Secretary of State for India, Edwin Montagu, cognizant that the war had become very costly to the Allies, concluded that in order to persuade India's educated classes to continue supporting the war effort they would have to be offered some reforms. They put forward the Montagu-Chelmsford Declaration, which proposed extending the franchise to one-third of India's population, establishing eight fully autonomous provincial governments, and setting up a Legislative Assembly of one hundred and forty members—one hundred and five of which would be elected—and a Council of State, or Senate, composed of sixty members. The Government of India Act was approved two years later. Its intent was to create the machinery required to implement the principles delineated in the 1917 Declaration.[137]

The goals of the Montagu-Chelmsford Declaration were immediately undermined by a new set of acts—the Rowlatt Acts. During the First World War years, the Raj had imposed severe restrictions on political activities throughout the subcontinent. The Rowlatt Acts were approved in order to continue the clamp-down on "political subversion." In April 1919, Gandhi called for a nationwide *satyagraha* to protest the acts. Gandhi hoped his call would set off a peaceful protest, but it soon turned into riots that led to the destruction of property and attacks on, and killing of, Europeans. Shortly afterward, Brigadier General Reginald Dyer and his forces moved into

Amritsar, a place where the government had lost control and Europeans had been murdered, with orders to restore civil order and impose martial law. After the local Congress defied Dryer's ban on public meetings, his troops moved against a crowd and fired on it. By the time the soldiers had finished carrying out the attack, three hundred and seventy-nine Indians lay dead and hundreds wounded. Gandhi called off the *satyagraha*.[138]

For the remainder of the 1920s both sides pursued competing goals. The aim of the National Congress and Gandhi was self-government and total independence. All along, however, Gandhi rejected armed revolution and relied on peaceful resistance. The British, though willing to concede on a number of important issues, were opposed to broaching the subject of full independence. Britain's refusal to relinquish control was incited by the fear that without India there would be little left to the Empire.

The opposing parties continued to disagree. Despite the ongoing demands by Britain's conservatives that the Raj reestablish its moral authority in the face of Indian nationalism, and in spite of the divisions that existed among nationalists in India, the die was cast. By 1937, following the first provincial elections held under the 1935 Government of India Act, Congress's spectacular victories granted its leaders the right to claim that it was the principal representative of the Indian people. By the time the world heard the first sounds of the new world war, there were few in both Britain and India who doubted that independence would come to India soon.[139] But as India prepared to attain its freedom, most Indian leaders became convinced that it would be very difficult to do so as a single actor. They realized that even though Muslims and Hindus had ignored many of their differences during their struggle against the British, the closer they got to independence the harder it would be for both sides to disregard them.

Hindus and Muslims did not always live in harmony prior to the arrival of the British. During much of the fifteenth and sixteenth centuries, they coexisted under Mughal rule.[140] Towards the end of the seventeenth century, however, their relationship changed when a Muslim leader seized control over the Mughal Empire, imposed on Hindus taxes that had been previously eliminated, forced them to convert to Islam, and ordered the destruction of Hindu temples.[141] Friction between Muslims and Hindus did not disappear while they were under British dominion, but their differences did not prevent their leaders, particularly those who had been educated in the West, to unite in the pursuit of a common goal—the eviction of the British.

Though Muslims and Hindus were both negatively affected by the revolt of 1857, following the event Muslims rapidly lost much of their influence. Hindus, especially the high-caste Bengalis, emerged as a sub-elite working first for the East India Company and then for the British Raj, while Muslims, with the exception of a small commercial class, were generally the least educated and poorest amongst Indian communities. In spite of the inequity, Muslim leaders decided that they would be better off joining the Hindu effort than siding with the British. As violence between Muslims and Hindus increased, concerns about their ability to remain united mounted, particularly after Muslims had decided to create their own distinct political organiza-tion—the Muslim League. Still, both sides continued to cooperate. In 1916, the Muslim League and the Indian National Congress reached an accord to act jointly against the Raj, and did so during the 1919 disturbances.

After 1924, Muslims progressively worried about how well they would fare as a minority in an Indian state. This fear intensified following a deadly riot that ensued in early 1930, when Muslim shopkeepers in Calcutta refused to participate in a massive disobedience campaign prompted by Gandhi.[142] By the middle of the 1930s, few Muslims trusted the Indian National Congress, and most had made the Muslim League their new political home. It also was during this period that Muslim intellectuals began to think about creating a separate Muslim state. Finally, in 1940, members of the Muslim League announced that they were determined to create an independent Pakistani state. The intense nationalist sentiment that enabled Hindus and Muslims to join forces in order to evict the British, would ultimately be replaced by equally powerful, but enormously divisive, religious sentiments.

"The cemeteries are the only colonies that continually prosper in Algeria"[143]

By the time the negotiators at the Congress of Vienna had finalized their agreements in 1815, there was little left for the leaders of the French empire to boast about. Its non-European dominion consisted mainly of a scattering of Caribbean islands and a few trading stations in Africa, the Indian Ocean, and along Indochina's coast. France's mediocre post-Congress of Vienna monarchs did little to regain some of the empire's lost aura. Sometimes, however, potential challenges, either domestic or international, can engender unexpected opportunities. In 1827, a representative of Charles X's govern-ment became involved in a minor altercation with an Algerian local ruler over a debt France had amassed during Napoleon's Egyptian mission decades earlier. Aware that it had been losing the support of France's middle class, the government of Charles X reasoned that a dazzling victory in Algeria, fol-lowed by the opening of new markets and the creation of outlets for trade, would help regenerate domestic support. France invaded Algeria in 1830 with some thirty-four thousand troops and occupied its most important city, Algiers.[144]

The arrival of the French brought to an end Algeria's three hundred-year loose association with the Ottoman Empire. Algiers, though a province of the Ottoman Empire, was for all practical purposes an independent entity con-trolled by Turks. Algiers's leader, the pasha, ruled a territory of approximately sixty thousand square miles and made political decisions without consulting the sultan in Constantinople. As rulers, the Turks had no interest in the wel-fare of their subjects and refused to mix and socialize with them. Their two principal goals were collecting the largest possible amount of taxes and maintaining order.

Arabs and Berbers, who with the exception of a small urban population had traditionally grouped themselves in tribes, were Algeria's principal inhabitants.[145] The tribes were either nomadic or sedentary, depending on their location; either Berber or Arabic; either rich or poor; either powerful or weak; and either independent or dependent. Though most indigenous Algerians regarded themselves as Sunni Muslims, their religious attitudes and conduct varied.[146] The Berbers were the least observant, the Moors the strictest, while sedentary rural Arabs were more committed than Arab nomads to following the injunctions of the Shari'a. In contrast with Muslims in other Arab regions, popular saints typically overshadowed the religious, social, economic, and political roles played by the *ulamas* (official Islamic scholars). Marabouts (popular saints) were believed to be holders of Baraka—defined as a "beneficent force, of divine origin, which causes superabundance in the physical sphere and prosperity and happiness in the psychic order." They and their disciples were the sole providers of education in the countryside, offered charity and shelter for the needy, consecrated marriages, and pronounced divorces. They often served as mediators between conflicting parties and imposed peace settlements. The prestige of marabouts was conditional. To be acknowledged as one, an individual had to prove his religious and moral worth, and could lose his position if he wandered off the permitted path.

At the start of the nineteenth century, a number of Sufi orders and independent marabouts began to voice their discontent with the level of taxation imposed on native Algerians by the Turks.[147] During the next twenty-five years, the displeasure translated into open acts of rebellion.[148] One of those affected by the actions of the Turks was Mulhi al-Din, the leading marabout of the province of Oran. Fearful that Mulhi al-Din would join the rebellion, the Turks imprisoned him and his son, Abd al-Qadir, for two years. Following their release, both traveled to Mecca twice and decided to spend their time in solitude. Their seclusion was short-lived.

After the arrival of the French, Mulhi al-Din mounted a jihad against the new intruders. A year later, in May 1832, Arabs, under Abd al-Qadir's leadership, launched a series of attacks against the French. Though the attacks were not successful, they helped establish Abd al-Qadir as his father's rightful successor. In November 1832, an assembly made up of sharifs, marabouts, shayks, and other notables proclaimed Abd al-Qadir *Amir al-Mu'minin* (Commander of the Believers). The struggle between Abd al-Qadir and the French continued, on and off, until December 1847, when the amir surrendered to the French troops commanded by General Thomas-Robert Bugeaud.[149] Despite the defeat, Abd al-Qadir's revolt proved to be significant in three ways. First, for a number of years he ruled a substantial part of the territory that today is considered to be part of Algeria. Second, his revolt was the most successful campaign of resistance launched against the French in the nineteenth century. And third, he organized both the war and the nascent state under the banner of Islam.[150]

By the time Abd al-Qadir surrendered, commitment on the part of the French to colonize Algeria had developed firm roots. A commission dispatched in 1833 to study France's future role in Northern Africa contended that colonizing Algeria was a "question of national self-respect," that the abandonment of such a task would be interpreted by others as "an act of weakness," that possession of Algeria would fortify French influence, that "a new population will consume the products of our manufacturers," and that "the development of a new people [would be] beneficial to the civilized world."[151] One of this view's most ardent advocates was Alexis de Tocqueville, who in 1841 wrote: "I do not think France can think seriously of leaving Algeria. In the eyes of the world, such an abandonment would be the clear indication of our decline ... Any people that easily gives up what it has taken and chooses to retire peacefully to its original borders proclaims that its greatness is over. It visibly enters the period of decline."[152] De Tocqueville also declared that France should not "separate domination and colonization and vice-versa." As he explained:

> There are two ways to conquer a country: the first is to subordinate the inhabitants and govern them directly or indirectly. That is the English system in India. The second is to replace the former inhabitants with the conquering race. This is what Europeans have almost always done ... Colonization without domination will always be an incomplete and precarious work ... If we abandon the Arabs to themselves and allow them to build up a proper power at our backs, our establishment in Africa has no future. Either it will dissolve bit by bit through the permanent hostility of the natives or will fall suddenly at the hands of those natives aided by a Christian power.[153]

By 1849, France had taken over Algeria's most productive lands around the coastal area and encouraged and supported the settlement of Europeans from France, Corsica, Spain, Italy, and Malta, and declared Algeria an integral part of France.[154] As noted by Napoleon III: "Algeria is not a colony properly speaking, but an Arab kingdom; the natives like the settlers have equal rights to our protection, and I am equally the emperor of the Arabs as of the French."[155] But clearly he did not mean to suggest that Arabs would have equal right. During the next fourteen years the French acquired some three hundred and seventy-seven million hectares of Algeria's most productive farmland and forest.[156]

It took France until 1879 to gain full control of Algeria. Before that time, a number of uprisings came to pass. Two of them are worth noting. The most notable one, in the late 1840s, was led by Bu Ziyan, who asserted that the Prophet Muhammad had told him that he was a Mahdi (a prophet or messiah who is expected to appear in the world sometime before it ends). His drive came to naught when he was defeated in 1849. The last major Algerian revolt of the nineteenth century occurred in 1871. Set off by economic adversity and famine, and inspired by the downfall of the French Second Empire, Muhammad al-Hajj al-Muqrani, with the backing of the powerful Rahmaniyya Sufi Brotherhood, launched a jihad. The drive experienced the same fate as those that preceded it.[157] All of this came at a very high cost for both the Algerians and the French. In the words of a French investigating commission: "We have surpassed in barbarism the barbarians we came to civilize."[158] Or, as the French often remarked during that period: "The cemeteries are the only colonies that continually prosper in Algeria."[159]

After crushing the 1871 revolt, the French moved aggressively to change Algeria's society. In addition to imposing on Arabs taxes higher than those levied on Europeans and using the revenues to further colonize Algeria, the French denied Arabs access to French schools, weakened Algeria's existing Muslim educational system, and replaced the Muslim system of justice with one based on French legal precepts and principles. France's most important change, however, did not come until 1881, when it approved the *Code de l'Indigénat*. The code was a statutory mechanism designed to control Muslims. Some of its provisions stipulated that Algerian Muslims were prohibited from speaking against France and its government, becoming schoolteachers without proper governmental authorization, traveling within Algeria without a permit, giving shelter to strangers without permission, and holding meetings attended by more than twenty people.[160]

Afraid that the aforesaid measures might not be sufficient to consolidate its control over Algeria, France launched an attack against what it considered to be the gravest threat: Islam. For many of the first colonizers, their task in Algeria was "to reopen ... the door of Christianity in Africa." Providence, they noted, had bestowed on France the responsibility of converting Algerian Muslims to Christianity.[161] Though this commitment did not necessarily diminish with time, by the 1880s it was being accompanied by the belief that it was imperative to debilitate the Arab-Muslim identity. Conscious that it could not eradicate Islam, France curtailed its practice, monitored and controlled religious festivals and pilgrimages, and replaced many of the existing religious schools with its own Islamic colleges. Moreover, towards the end of the nineteenth century it started providing French education to small numbers of Algerian Muslims. Its intent was to fashion a Muslim Algerian elite—*évolués*—that in time would identify closely with France and its civilization.[162]

The strategy did not work. The First World War forced France to recruit men from its various colonies, including Algeria. During the war, some two hundred thousand Algerian Muslims fought under the leadership of French commanders, and some twenty-five thousand lost their lives. After the war, ideas promoted by the Russian Revolution and Woodrow Wilson reached Algerians. For some, the Russian Revolution symbolized the overturning of a regime by the working class and the possibility of establishing a classless society in the future. For others, Wilson's support for self-determination stood for a call for arms against the colonists.[163]

Three groups assumed responsibility for voicing Algeria's discontent: the
Ulama (legal scholars), the Young Algerian movement, and the Etoile Nord-
Africaine. Toward the end of the nineteenth century, a group known as *salafiya* had emerged in Egypt. The movement stressed that the best way to
respond to Western domination and the sense of moral inferiority that Muslims had been developing was by returning to the original practices of the
Muslim forefathers (*salafiya*). In the early 1900s, a young Algerian by the
name of Abdelhamid Ben Badis established the Association of Algerian
Ulama (often referred by its French acronym—AUMA). The organization's
motto was: "Arabic is my language, Algeria is my country, Islam is my religion." Algeria's emerging liberal bourgeoisie found a voice in the Movement
of Young Algerians. According to one of its leaders, Ferhat Abbas, there were
two Frances and two policies: one was a nation with an enlightened civilization and great moral fortitude; the other was an oppressive colonial power.
Convinced that there had never been an Algerian nation and, thus, that there
was no need to be a nationalist and strive for independence, Abbas demanded
that the first France thrust aside the second one, give Algerians the same
rights it extended to the French, and accept that a person could be both
Muslim and French. Members of Algeria, Morocco, and Tunisia's immigrant
communities in Paris established the third group—the Etoile Nord-Africaine
(ENA)—in 1926. As the most radical nationalist movement, the group advocated complete independence for the three North African countries, confisca-
tion of all property acquired by the colonists, withdrawal of all French troops,
and creation of an army. The French government disbanded it in 1929. After
an attempt by the communists to gain control of the movement, the ENA
reconstituted itself in 1933.[164]

The ascension to power in metropolitan France in 1936 of the Popular
Front, a left-wing regime under the leadership of the socialist Léon Blum,
raised the hopes and expectations of Algerian reformists. In June of that same
year, AUMA convened a Muslim Congress in Algiers with the increasingly
influential Movement of Young Algerians and the Algerian Communist Party.
In spite of their differences, they agreed on demands that included the granting of political and economic equality to Algerians. Specifically, this meant
replacing the existing arrangements with a unified system that gave native
Muslims, the colonizers (*colons*), and metropolitan Frenchmen the same rights.
Shortly afterward, a delegation of the Muslim Congress traveled to Paris to
present the charter. Towards the end of 1936, Blum and Maurice Viollette,
who had been given responsibility for Algerian affairs, submitted a plan that
would extend French citizenship to some twenty-one thousand Algerian
Muslims, including university graduates, elected officials, army officers, and
professionals. The plan did not discuss independence. The *colons* immediately
opposed any attempt on the part of the Popular Front government to give in
to the demands presented by the Muslim Congress, and convinced the government to dissolve the Etoile Nord-Africaine. Forced to further curtail the
activities of the reformists, the French authorities refused to allow those few

Algerians who had been granted citizenship to retain Muslim personal status, ordered the arrest of AUMA members, placed individual associations under official control, and banned the opening of any unauthorized schools.

The measures did not have the desired consequences. In 1938, Ben Badis, after calling the law against schools "the darkest day in the history of Islam in Algeria," put an end to his cooperation with the French authorities. Other reformist groups followed suit. By the start of the Second World War, the policy of assimilation advocated by moderate reformists was no longer a viable option. A new era of nationalist opposition would begin after the landing of the Allied forces in Algeria in late 1942.[165] But before Algerian nationalism could declare victory, both sides would have to endure dreadful human costs.

Anti-imperialist nationalism

Nationalism in China, Mexico, India, and Algeria emerged as responses to the imperialist activities of Western actors (along with an East Asian entity in the case of China). The evolution of their actions and the results they generated, however, varied. A few conclusions can be derived from their distinct experiences.

All four cases shared at least one element. In each instance, one of the greatest obstacles to expelling the foreign master was the extended inability of the affected actor to generate a unified nationalist front. The obstacles that obstructed such a development differed. China, with a long-standing tradition of independence and self-rule, labored under the untenable assumption that its superior culture freed its leaders from the burden of consistently having to reexamine their world outlook. The feudal leaders' unwillingness to renounce part of their freedom made their task of generating a united anti-foreign spirit considerably more difficult. In the case of Mexico, for nearly a century, provincial leaders' determination to protect their narrowly defined interests hindered their capacity to safeguard their hard-won independence from Spain from new foreign political, financial, and capital challenges. It was only after they had lost large portions of their northern territories to the USA, had been invaded and ruled by the French, and had allowed foreign nationals to control vast portions of their natural resources and commercial and financial interests, that Mexicans developed a united nationalist front.

India and Algeria encountered their own distinct problems. India, like Mexico, was not an entity per se until the arrival of the Europeans. But unlike the Spaniards in the case of Mexico, the English did not exactly govern the Indian subcontinent as a unit. Even after Britain took over the East India Company, India remained a mixed organism made up of princely states and of provinces directly governed by the British. Religious differences, moreover, were deeply infused in the subcontinent's political environment. In some ways, Algeria's experience may have been the most troublesome of the four cases. For an extended period, Algeria was under the dominion of Turks who, though part of the Ottoman Empire, ruled with few constraints from the core, barely interacted with the indigenous population, and did little but maintain order and ensure that Algerians were taxed. The arrival of new conquerors did not mark the beginning of a better era for Algeria. Determined to regain some of their lost glory and certain that their subjects were members of an inferior civilization, the French moved aggressively to control their new dominion's political, economic, and social environments. Though for a brief while a few Algerian leaders were able to use Islam to mount armed operations against the colonizing forces, effective military responses by the French enfeebled its symbolic value. As time went by, attempts to create a unifying front were thwarted repeatedly by tribal rivalries and ideological differences.

Ironically, events generated outside the realm of the colonies were what finally impelled anti-imperialist groups to forge united fronts. The First World War, Western education, Woodrow Wilson's fourteen points, and the Russian revolution were the principal stimulators. Compulsory participation in a war that was not of their making, along with Western education, heartened the resolve of many Indians and Algerians to demand that they no longer be treated as lesser citizens and that their ability to perform private or public tasks be determined by merit, not religion, color, or ethnicity. Woodrow Wilson's call for post-war self-determination, as part of his fourteen-point program, did not persuade either Britain or France to repudiate its colonial history. However, it helped nationalists in China, India, and Algeria to project their struggle among potential Western sympathizers in a manner that was no longer alien to them. Regrets among Westerners for many of the exploits by the colonial powers afforded nationalists new opportunities. In turn, the Russian revolution, by being cast as an uprising designed to assist the masses, made it easier for nationalist leaders in China, Mexico, and Algeria to generate badly needed popular support in their respective domestic milieus.[166]

Because an actor's prospects for gaining its freedom is also affected by external factors, it should be noted that the greater the value, whether real or symbolic, that an imperialist power places on a subject, the harder it is for the affected party to gain its freedom. Though a number of foreign actors, with the USA at the lead, coveted Mexico's natural and economic resources, its value to them, though substantial, was never exceptional. Mexico's foreign investors, moreover, never staked their international reputation on their ongoing ability to dominate it. That was not the case for Britain and France. India for Britain and Algeria for France were more than materially valuable colonies. Each colonial power believed that without its colony its repute as an empire would be severely harmed. A similar case can be made for Japan and its relationship with China. While most of the Western intruders viewed the mainland empire as an important strategic and economic entity, Japan also regarded it as a crucial symbol of its prestige. With China under its command, Japan would be able to rightfully claim recognition as Asia's principal entity and could demand the same deference and privileges conferred on other great empires.

An imperialist and nationalist world system

By the time the sounds of war began to reverberate throughout the world arena in 1914, the 1815 world system designed by Europe's main actors had already experienced major changes. By 1919, it would undergo another substantial restructuring.

Determined to ensure that the power aspirations of Europe's principal entities would not reach menacing levels and that nationalism would not threaten the vitality of traditional multinational empires, Europe's core actors sought refuge in the balance-of-power doctrine. By 1871, a doctrine that had been an ideology since its inception could no longer withstand the multi-directional forces of nationalism. On the one hand, nationalism brought together multiple independent provinces to create two distinct, potentially powerful actors, Germany and Italy; on the other hand, it helped destroy the Ottoman and Austrian Empires.

Some forty years later, the mounting tension generated by the conflict between both ideologies helped give birth to a world war. By then, Europe's interests, passions, and ills had transcended its immediate borders. With Britain as the leading promoter, members of disparate political communities slowly became addicted to the belief, or were forced to believe, that a world interconnected by trade was a commendable goal. Conscious that their superior military, economic, and organizational powers nearly always made it possible for them to dictate the terms of trade agreements, other European actors, along with the USA and Japan, were quick to copy Britain's method. Very few corners of the world escaped their reach. In a short time, they transformed the world system into a highly competitive arena, with each major actor dominating large portions of territory not adjacent to its own borders. In the process, they delineated the types of principles, norms, rules, and procedures that members of the system would have to adhere to during their interactions.[167] They also set up criteria that entities had to meet in order to be accepted as a "civilized" member of the international society. This meant, among other things, that new states had to prove they possessed the means to guarantee "the life, liberty, and property of foreign nationals"; create "suitable governmental" organizations; and "adhere to the accepted diplomatic practices."[168]

During this period, nationalism played two additional roles. Imperialists used nationalism to generate both the justification and the public support they needed to implement imperialism. Targets of imperialism, in turn, relied on nationalism to engender both the rationale and popular backing they needed to confront the imperialists. Until the First World War, the first group was the more effective one; afterward, the second one began to gain the upper hand. The actions by the second group would help restructure the world system fundamentally.

nationalism going a ways

5   A world still burdened by multiple conflicting ideologies: 1919–1990

Incompatible ideologies during the post-First World War period

The stability of a regional or world system depends on the intensity of the tensions generated by contradictory forces, and on the capacity of its most influential members to understand the nature and causes of the strains, and control or defuse them. A more peaceful and stable international environment did not follow the end of the First World War. Instead, it gave way to the rise of distinct and cacophonous ideologies, advocated by some of the world's leading powers.

American liberalism

By the time the USA entered the First World War, few leaders questioned its economic and military might. By the time the war had come to an end, few were unaware of the type of world system the president of the USA hoped to craft. The ideologically entrenched balance-of-power doctrine created and promoted by Europe's dominant actors, argued Woodrow Wilson, had not constrained the power aspirations of states and reduced intra- and inter-state conflict. The new world system, he added, had to have at its core an international organization with the power and authority to regulate the use of military force, and it had to be populated with democratic states. The new international organization would be formed for "the purpose of affording mutual guarantees of political independence and territorial integrity to great and small states alike."[1] Democratic regimes would aid the international organization by providing people the opportunity to express their will. In democracies, explained Wilson, representatives have no choice but "to follow the opinion of mankind and to express the will of the people rather than of leaders."[2] Autocratic governments, on the other hand, are untrustworthy, because they commonly disregard peace covenants. Mindful that democracies are fragile during their early developmental stages, Wilson advocated the creation of an open world market system. Protectionism, he argued, encourages complicity and enables big business to further strengthen its power. Big-business dominance of the domestic market, in turn, undermines democracy. An open world market system, on the other hand, abets global economic advancement, which is a condition for the spread of democracy worldwide.[3]

Wilson's global vision was founded on two concepts—freedom and equality. The concept of freedom he and other Americans advocated had its roots in the Reformation and began to gain momentum after the seventeenth century. Typically referred to as "freedom from" [the state], it assumed that man was more than a citizen of the state; he was a private self with the freedom to be different and to dissent.[4] For the individual to be able to exercise his freedom, the state, which existed as a supra-ordinate entity, had to protect him against any attempt on its part to abuse its power or use it arbitrarily. This type of protection enabled the individual to choose, and was guaranteed by laws.

Inequality, rather than equality, is natural. Equality does not ensue if things are permitted to follow their course; it can result only if an external agent intervenes. The Greeks and the Romans entertained the idea of equality without ever assuming that men were the same, alike, or equal. They derived it, instead, from the belief that "he who wants to establish justice tries to make equal things that are unequal."[5] The drive to make unequal things equal has assumed various forms. In its most extreme incarnation it called for economic sameness ("the same wealth to each and all"). In earlier days, however, the emphasis was on the juridical–political aspect of equality—on granting citizens the same legal and political rights.

"Freedom from" and the juridical–political aspect of equality formed the conceptual foundations of liberal democracy in the USA. Without the presence of both conditions, political competition and political participation could not have happened. In the absence of political competition and political participation, moreover, there would have been no democracy. Democracy, thus, functioned as a mechanism designed to facilitate open competition in the electoral market by ascribing voting power to the people and forcing leaders to be responsive to their needs and interests.

Democracies are not equally competitive. Afraid that personal liberties would energize too much political rivalry and set up factions, the USA's founding fathers crafted a system that would restrain divisions. They designed a plurality electoral system (winner-takes-all) that automatically curbed the number of parties that would emerge, thus forcing each party to gather under its umbrella a relatively wide range of groups, interests, and demands.

A plurality system is not appropriate for all societies, at least during their early developmental stage. The chances of surviving and thriving are greater the smaller the spread of opinion within a society. The success of the USA's plurality system can be attributed in no small part to the narrow dispersion of the interests of its citizens. Throughout much of the nineteenth century, the people of the USA focused on bettering their own standard of living and electing politicians that favored limited government. In Alexis de Tocqueville's words, "The inhabitants of the United States alternately display so strong and so similar passion for their own welfare and for their freedom that it may be supposed that these passions are united and mingled in some part of their character." Americans believe "their chief business is to secure for themselves a government which will allow them to acquire the things they covet and which will not debar them from the peaceful enjoyment of those possessions which they have already acquired."[6]

Markets differ with regard to the freedom individuals have to enter them and the extent to which buyers and sellers can determine the terms of exchange. A self-regulating, or perfect, market is one in which all interested buyers and sellers are free to participate and no one buyer or seller can determine the terms of exchange. No society has ever had a perfect market. A market's distance from perfection is determined by the nature of the political system to which it belongs. For a market to be nearly self-regulating, its political system must prevent the government from becoming the market's sole player, and it must provide the government the power to thwart attempts by a single private supplier from becoming the market's sole definer of the terms of exchange.

Contemporary democracies always have free-market economies.[7] The association is not coincidental, for the two are the materialization of constitutional liberalism. During its early days, constitutional liberalism was a movement designed to enlarge and protect the liberties, first of nobles and then of a merchant middle class, by imposing constitutional restrictions on a government's prerogatives. The personal liberties these groups sought to expand and safeguard reached beyond the right to be different and to dissent. They wanted the freedom to engage in trade, set up their own enterprises in order to pursue the benefits that trade generates, and keep as much of the earnings as possible. In short, though liberal democracy was conceived to win and protect a variety of liberties, some of the most important ones were the rights to private property, free enterprise, free contract, and occupational choice. The outcome of the drive to secure these freedoms has been competition—competition between individuals free to decide what they want to do with their own energies and skills in both the political and economic arenas.[8]

It is one thing to create an open and competitive political and economic system at home; it is a very different matter to replicate the deed worldwide. Success in the second endeavor depends on the disseminator's abilities to persuade its domestic community that it can and must alter the world environment, and to persuade the other world actors that they will be better off if they carry out the proposed changes. Emboldened by the USA's power and earlier feats, Wilson traveled to Europe convinced that his actions were shepherded by God's will and that his intellectual and moral faculties were superior to anyone's in the US, Congress. He was certain that the American public would accept his rationale for creating the League of Nations and heightening the USA's profile in the world arena. In the process, he failed to bear in mind that as the ruler of a democracy he had to keep a watchful eye

on the US Congress, and that most of its members rarely welcome fundamental changes, especially when they are excluded from the decision. As a
result, the belief that US membership in the League would have meant "an
increase with the poison-infected areas of the world" won out over the conviction that the League was the only antidote able to protect the American
people from the "poison of disorder, the poison of revolt" roaming through
the world arena.[9]

By the time a new leader had assumed the US presidency in 1921, few in
the USA's domestic political arena favored Wilson's world vision. Warren G.
Harding made it clear that he disagreed with the former president's contention that the "Great War" had been fought to eliminate future wars, or that
the League of Nations would help abolish the long-standing dependency on
war as an instrument of politics. According to the new president, wars would
persist; the Great War differed little from previous wars; and the League of
Nations was nothing more than a different sort of alliance that might serve
the interests of other states, but not those of the USA. Harding, however,
shared his predecessor's conviction that the USA should strive to craft a more
liberal international economic system. This belief was rooted in the idea that
the prosperity of the US economy was tightly linked to its ability to import
large quantities of raw materials and semi-manufactured goods at relatively
low prices, and that the international community would benefit from a system
that enabled the USA to thrive. Americans accepted this vision for a while;
but just as Wilson had failed to persuade them that they should strive to
create a more democratic international political system, his successor was
unsuccessful at convincing them that they should endeavor to liberate the
international economic system.

Responses from the international community were mixed. Horrified by the
immense costs they had absorbed during the war, men and women throughout Britain demanded the right to determine their own destinies. Armed with
new voting powers, they commanded their leaders not to embroil Britain in
the affairs of other states. Their anti-war posture remained unaltered almost
until the end of the 1930s. The French, having undergone a distinctly more
severe experience during the war, focused on electing governments committed
to preventing Germany from ever posing a major threat.[10] They experienced
a setback in 1923, when their support of their government's occupation of the
Ruhr elicited worldwide criticism. In view of the strong anti-war sentiment
that had spread throughout parts of Europe and the USA, France had little
choice but to reach an agreement with Germany in 1925 whereby the two
parties established a system of guarantees along the Belgian–German and
Franco–German borders.

As the leaders of the USA, Britain, and France labored to cope with the
growing powers of their respective constituents, other world actors had been
designing and voicing ideologies whose core tenets were different from those
of free-market democracies. In the early 1920s, no ideology posed a greater
challenge to free-market democracy than Soviet Marxism–Leninism.

Soviet Marxism–Leninism

The forefather of Marxist–Leninist ideology did not posit a theory of world politics. Marx focused, instead, on the nature of social change within societies. Social change, he contended, was the result of struggles between classes. Every society has its haves and have-nots. The ruling class uses the government, laws, and society in general to protect its property rights.[11] Capitalism reflected the culmination of different forms of class struggles that had been ensuing throughout history. Like previous forms of economic arrangements, capitalism would in turn be destroyed by its own set of internal contradictions. "The centralization of the means of production and the socialization of labor," wrote Marx, "reach a point where they prove incompatible with their capital husk. This husk bursts asunder. The knell of capital private property sounds. The expropriators are expropriated."[12]

Russia's 1917 revolutionary spirit was born a number of decades earlier. During the 1860s and 1870s, Russia's Left repeatedly attempted to restructure society according to the tenets of utilitarianism, positivism, materialism, and realism. Its members hoped to create a society based on knowledge and reason rather than on metaphysical, religious, aesthetic, and historical approaches to reality. By the 1870s, the Left stopped emphasizing individualism and personal emancipation and began to advocate populism. It assumed that by turning to the peasants it would uncover the purity and probity it had not found within its own environment.[13]

Though the masses did not respond to the populist crusade, the flames of insurgency remained alive. As Russia continued its rapid development into a capitalist society, the need to defend the afflicted peasant community gained moral stature. This drive provided Marxists their rationale. They presented themselves as a "tough" alternative to the "soft" vision of the populists, claimed to offer an objective perspective on history, and promised that the practice of their dictates would bring about victory.[14]

Russian Marxists failed to maintain a united front. In 1903, the Russian Social Democrats split into the Bolsheviks and the Mensheviks. The breakup was set off by differences in party strategy. The Bolsheviks advocated the establishment of a party with well-defined lines of command, guided by professional revolutionaries committed to imposing military discipline, while the Mensheviks favored a larger and less structured organization.[15] This is not the place to discuss the domestic and international conditions that enabled the Bolsheviks, led by Vladimir Lenin, to stage a successful revolution in Russia in 1917. It suffices to say that upon assuming power they sought to gain complete control over Russia's political, economic, and social affairs. A brief discussion of three of Lenin's written works should help clarify their rationale for action.

In *What is to Be Done,* published in 1902, Lenin argued that the proletariat needed a revolutionary party to lead them. Without leadership, the proletariat, instead of pursuing its historic revolutionary mission, would give in to limited gains. Politically, however, Lenin needed an alternative justification to rationalize the extraordinary power he claimed the revolutionary party should assume. In *Imperialism, the Highest Stage of Capitalism*, published at the height of the First World War, he forwarded a series of interrelated arguments. He started with the claim that in its advanced stages capitalism becomes monopolistic, enabling banks and financial institutions to gather massive surpluses of capital. To maximize profits, these organizations export their capital to countries where it is in short supply and where labor, raw materials, and land are cheap. In time, the main capitalist countries divide the world into colonies. This division did not mark the end of the road. The need of their economies to continue growing forces imperialist states to confront one another in the battlefield for control of each other's possessions.[16] The First World War, along with imperialism, served Lenin's last argument well. Imperialism, he proposed in *State and Revolution*, aggravated the structural disparities in the world system. These disparities spawned the impetus and conditions necessary for popular liberation through social revolution. However, because most members of the proletariat had yet to gain a high level of consciousness, they would most likely fail to seize the opportunity. The revolutionary party of the proletariat, thus, had to solidify its power in order to, first, create solidarity within the working class and, second, overthrow the imperialist, capitalist order.[17]

The October 1917 revolution generated a number of domestic and international challenges. Shortly after taking over Petrograd and declaring Russia a soviet republic, the Bolsheviks were defeated in the elections for the Constituent Assembly. This setback did not force them out of power. In January 1918 they dissolved the assembly, and two months later they signed the Peace of Brest-Litovsk with Germany. For Lenin, the success of the revolution depended partly on whether Russia was able to end its war with Germany. The treaty, he explained, would give the Bolsheviks the respite they needed to "heal the very severe wounds inflicted by the war upon the entire social organism of Russia and bring about an economic revival."[18]

The end of the war against Germany was followed by a period marked by uncertainty. At home, the Bolsheviks battled a loose alliance made up of army officers and Cossacks, political groups covering much of the ideological spectrum, and members of the Russian bourgeoisie. In the midst of this internal struggle they were thrust into an international crisis spawned by invading forces from Japan, Great Britain, France, Greece, the USA, and several other nations.

The invaders did not share a common rationale. Japan wanted to exploit Russia's frailty in order to take over part of the island of Sakhalin and much of east Siberia. Some of the European nations hoped to prevent Germany from seizing war material from ports such as Archangel and Murmansk. The USA had its own motivation. Shortly after the Bolsheviks had gained power, Wilson suggested that other states yield to Russia's legitimate need to develop freely its own political system and national policy. It was their obligation to extend Russia "a sincere welcome into the society of free nations under institutions of [its] own choosing ... and assistance also of every kind that [it] may need and [itself] desire."[19] Even so, Wilson feared that his chances of helping create a new, stable, international system at the end of the First World War would be lessened by Russia's transformation from an autocratic, anti-revolutionary realm to a dogmatic, revolutionary regime determined to promote communism as the antidote to free markets and democracies. His concern deepened following Lenin's decision to sign a peace agreement with Germany and the claim that Russia would finally "be able to render effective assistance to the socialist revolution in the West which had been delayed for a number of reasons."[20] Thus, in July 1918, Wilson agreed to send US troops to Vladivostok and Murmansk.

Though the intervention did not undermine the power of the Bolsheviks, it reinforced their hostility towards outsiders, especially the USA. For them, the civil war was more than a struggle between competing Russian groups. They viewed their main adversary, the Whites, as pawns acting on behalf of Russia's capitalist enemies.[21] As Nikita Khrushchev, a future Soviet leader, would state many years later, the civil war was "thrust on us by the bourgeoisie, our own [and that of] the world at large, which was instigating counterrevolution and intervention against us."[22]

With few opponents able to challenge their authority and power, the Bolsheviks hastened to create a cadre of true believers. Their commitment to educate the proletariat was rooted in the belief that they had to inculcate a common perspective about the world. *The ABC of Communism*, written by N. Bukharin and E. Preobrazhensky as a popular version of the 1918 Party program, became the most widely read political piece in Soviet Russia.[23] Peaceful coexistence was outright rejected. "We might as well hope for petting a tiger to persuade the animal to live upon the grass and to leave cattle alone ... [C]apitalism cannot exist without a policy of conquest, spoliation, violence and war."[24]

Lenin's death in 1924 exposed the Party's deep ideological divisions. Ultimately, it was Stalin's "Socialism in One Country" doctrine that emerged victorious.[25] After consolidating his power, Stalin proceeded carefully. Determined to buy time to enable the Soviet Union to restore its lost power, Stalin sought to lessen whatever fears the birth of the Soviet regime might have generated in the capitalist world. In 1925, during his report to the Fourteenth Congress, he noted that "a certain temporary equilibrium of forces has been established between our country ... and the countries of the capitalist world: an equilibrium that determined the present period of 'peaceful coexistence.'" At the Sixteenth Congress, after discussing the deep economic crisis faced by capitalist states, and warning that some of them would attempt to address their own internal contradictions at the expense of the USSR, he emphasized that the Soviet regime was committed to a "policy of peace" with capitalist nations.[26]

Caution did not mean a change of mind. As Stalin stated to a group of visiting American labor leaders in the late 1920s:

> In the course of further development of international revolution there will emerge two centers of world significance: a socialist center, drawing to itself the countries which tend toward socialism, and a capitalist center, drawing to itself the countries that incline toward capitalism. Battle between these two centers for command of the world economy will decide the fate of capitalism and of communism in the entire world.[27]

Still, the Soviet leader continued to believe that in the immediate future wars would be spawned by the rivalry between capitalist states. "The principal arena of the struggle is South America and China, the colonies and dominions of the old imperialist states." He added, "The bourgeois states are furiously arming and rearming. What for?" "[T]he imperialists need war, for it is the only means by which to redivide the world, redivide the markets, sources of raw materials and spheres for the investment of capital."[28]

In the 1930s, the USA and the Soviet Union agreed that it would be in their mutual interests to reach a modus operandi. Franklin Roosevelt extended to the Soviet Union full diplomatic recognition shortly after becoming president. Moscow, in turn, pledged to "respect scrupulously the indisputable right of the United States to order its own life within its own jurisdiction and to refrain from interfering in any manner in the internal affairs of the United States, its territories, and its possessions."[29] Throughout the rest of the decade, Stalin continued to adjust carefully his country's foreign policy to new developments in the world arena. He sought to form "a united front against fascism and war" as Germany's, Italy's, and Japan's power and imperialist aspirations increased.

Fascism and Nazism—ideological antidotes to liberalism and communism

Using nationalism as its pedestal, Italy designed fascism, and set up the foundation for the formulation of Nazism by one of Europe's most powerful and volatile actors—Germany. Though unlike in one important respect, both ideologies formed a common front against Soviet Marxist–Leninism and US free-market democracy. Across the globe, Japan continued its imperial expansion, backed by its own type of fascist dogma.

Fascism in Italy

By the second half of 1922, Italy was enduring the same pains experienced by other European states—a soaring rate of inflation that had wiped out the salaries, pensions, and savings of the middle class, as well as mounting insurrectionist violence. In October, the king of Italy invited Benito Mussolini, a former Marxist and the leader of the Fascist Party, to become Italy's new prime minister and form a government. By 1925, Mussolini had imposed his will over the Italian Parliament, stifled the opposition, gained control of the media, curbed freedom of speech, struck a compromise with the Catholic Church, eliminated labor strikes, and brought to an end the widespread disorder that had been afflicting Italy since the end of the war. Dreams of building a powerhouse as magnificent as the Roman Empire motivated him to try to expand Italy's industrial and military capacity and to announce his penchant for war.[30] "War," as one of the slogans written on the walls of buildings throughout Italy proclaimed, "is to the male what childbearing is to the female."[31]

Fascism was born as a reaction to liberalism and socialism, both of which are offshoots of the Enlightenment. Though distinct, liberalism and socialism agree on a set of premises. They assume that: i) each human being is an end in himself/herself, not to be used by others as a tool to accomplish their own selfish ends; ii) despite differences, human beings share the same essential nature—the ability to use reason to resolve problems; iii) religion is a private matter that can be used by individuals as a source of comfort but not as absolute truths to guide public affairs; and iv) human history is the history of progress.[32] Many of these ideas came under attack. Sexual, racial, linguistic, cultural, religious, and national differences, argued some of the challengers, do matter. Others added that superstition and prejudice are strikingly more common than reason. Reason, they claimed, is used not to examine problems critically but to excuse desires and justify prejudices. Without religion, moreover, it would be impossible to create and protect a civilized and orderly society. Based on these challenges, the anti-Enlightenment thinkers depicted a critically different picture. Humans are basically non-rational. Conflict between them is typically sparked by racial, sexual, religious, national, and linguistic differences.[33]

The human reality portrayed by anti-Enlightenment theorists provided the foundation on which Mussolini erected his fascist ideology. Individuals, he proposed, are by nature social animals. Alone they accomplish little, but as members of a collectivity they have the potential to accomplish much. It is the nation, with its history, culture, and cohesiveness that enables individuals to achieve fulfillment. In the modern world, however, it is the state that functions as the "political, juridical, and economic organization of the nation"[34] Or, as Mussolini noted, the "Fascist conception of the state is all-embracing, outside of it no human or spiritual values can exist, much less have value. Thus understood, the fascist State is totalitarian."[35] Though the Italian state, as an organic unit, assumed responsibility for the nation's political, economic, and social activities and well-being, it relied on the leaders of a group—the Fascist Party—to ensure that the necessary functions were carried out effectively. The task of the Fascist Party was to erase the divisions that had weakened Italy. Individual freedoms were considered destructive; only by believing and obeying the leaders of the Fascist Party, and fighting for the state, could individuals attain freedom.

Convinced that Italians would not obey unless they received tangible rewards, Mussolini sought to create a new relationship among workers, owners, and the state. He divided the economy into twenty-two corporations, established the Ministry of Corporations, and granted it the authority to supervise them. He then assigned administrative responsibilities for each corporation to representatives of the Ministry of Corporations, the workers, and the owners. Though the three groups were expected to share decision-making responsibilities, representatives of the Ministry, acting on behalf of the general public, were the ones who typically had the last word. Their actions, however, generally reflected the interests of the owners.[36]

During his early days in power, Mussolini did not view fascism as "an article for export." Several years later, after consolidating his power and that of the Fascist Party, he renounced his initial claim.[37] "If every age has its own characteristic doctrine," he noted, "there are a thousand signs that point to Fascism as the characteristic doctrine of our time."[38] Mussolini's international aspirations differed little from those of earlier Italian leaders. In 1915, Britain, France, and Russia sought to enlist neutral Italy in the war against Germany and Austria–Hungary. An agreement was reached only after the three Allied powers had accepted that, once the war had been won, Italy would secure control over Dalmatia, Gorizia, Istria, Southern Tyrol, and Trent. At the Paris Peace Conference, however, though Italy gained control over territories in the Alps and along the northern shore of the Adriatic, its claims to Dalmatia and Fiume, Albania, and some of the colonial territories in Africa and Asia, were rejected.

Nationalists soon argued that Italy had been cheated of its rightful rewards. After solidifying his own power, Mussolini began to use nationalism to strengthen Italy's position in the world arena. Initially, he focused on protecting Italy from Hitler's expansionist aspirations. When Hitler declared that Germany would no longer adhere to the Treaty of Versailles and would start re-arming, Mussolini met with Britain and France's leaders to form a united counter-front. Though the meeting was unproductive, Mussolini understood how badly Britain and France wanted Italy's continuing support, and he exploited their need. With the contention that it was "better to live for one day as a lion than a hundred years like a sheep," he ordered Italy's armed forces to move aggressively against Ethiopia.[39] His calculations proved correct. Italians applauded the act; Britain and France, along with the rest of the international community, criticized it but did not take the steps necessary to alter Italy's behavior. In May 1936, Italy annexed Ethiopia.

By then, Italy's relationship with Germany had changed. Indebted to Hitler for his willingness to remain neutral during the Ethiopian crisis and for supplying Italy with iron, coal, steel, and other scarce material, Mussolini informed him that if Austria were to become a German satellite, he would not object. In July, Germany and Austria, with Mussolini's blessing, reached a secret understanding, freeing Hitler to act in Austria and other parts of southeastern Europe as he saw fit. A few months later, Italy and Germany announced a cooperative agreement. Mussolini flaunted it as the "Rome–Berlin Axis," and declared that the "Wilsonian ideology" was in ruins. Mussolini's final acquiescence to Hitler's imperialist drive came when he quietly accepted Germany's invasion of Austria in March 1938, and its annexation less than a month later.[40]

Mussolini's change of mind had both a strategic and an ideological foundation. Though still influenced by Europe's long-standing imperialist traditions, as well as by fascist theories of autarky,[41] he recognized that in order for Italy to expand its power into the Mediterranean basin it would have to accept Germany's move eastward. At the same time, he had grown to respect and admire Hitler. Impressed by the social Darwinian belief that states could be categorized as either rising or declining, the Italian leader became increasingly convinced that Germany, like Italy, belonged to the first category. Italy and Germany, he noted, shared "a common fate" and were "congruent cases."[42]

Nazism in Germany

Though Mussolini was the first to popularize fascism, Italy's inferior material power status prevented him from significantly affecting Europe's regional system. Nazism proved to be not only a much stronger ideological force but also one that called for the creation of a world somewhat different from that advocated by Mussolini's fascism.

In late August 1939, Germany and the Soviet Union signed a neutrality agreement. In the summer of 1941, Adolf Hitler invaded the Soviet Union. It was not a careless act. "Everything I do is directed against Russia. If the West is too stupid and blind to understand that, I shall be forced to come to an understanding with Russia in order to defeat the West and then, after its defeat, to turn against the Soviet Union with all my forces."[43] His strategy was rooted in his theories of race and geopolitics. Combined, they capture the essence of Hitler's ideologically embedded foreign policy— *Lebensraum*.

Hitler's *Lebensraum* had several components. First, for Germany to fulfill its great destiny, the German *Volk*—"folk" or "people"—had to protect their racial purity and move aggressively against those who had betrayed them and sought to divide them. Second, because Germany lacked enough arable land to feed a rapidly expanding population, its only real alternative was to move abroad a substantial number of Germans. Third, based on the belief that emigration to distant lands was certain to be obstructed by France and Britain, would devalue the consciousness of the German people, and would enfeeble the Aryan race, he advocated the takeover of adjacent lands. Those lands—Eastern Europe and the western part of the Soviet Union—were rich in agriculture and minerals and inhabited by inferior races. And fourth, the takeover of such territories would enable Germany to transform itself into Euro-Asia's leading power.

Hitler's racial conviction had a number of progenitors, but none was more influential than the ideas of Count Joseph Arthur de Gobineau. In his *Essay on the Inequality of Human Races*, published in 1854, Gobineau wrote that the only variable that could significantly explain human progress and decline was race. Upon dividing and ranking the human species into three basic racial groups, with white at the top, yellow next, and black at the bottom, Gobineau proposed that only whites were endowed with nobility, freedom, honor, and spirituality. The white race, however, was not entirely pure; it was subdivided, in descending order, into Aryans, Slavs, and Semites. Based on this typology, Gobineau postulated that "the basic organization and character of all civilizations are equal to the traits and spirit of the dominant race."[44]

Gobineau's ideas influenced Hitler profoundly. "Any crossing of two beings not at exactly the same level," Hitler wrote in his autobiography, "produces a medium between the level of the two parents." "Such mating," he added, "is contrary to the will of Nature for a higher breeding of all life." He went on to argue that history offered countless proofs of the ill effects generated by the mixing of Aryans with members of an inferior race. History.

> shows with terrifying clarity that in every mingling of Aryan blood with that of lower peoples the result was the end of the cultured people. North America, whose population consists in by far the largest part of Germanic elements who mixed but little with the lower colored peoples, shows a different humanity and culture from Central and South America, where the predominantly Latin immigrants often mixed with the aborigines on a large scale. By this one example, we can clearly and distinctly recognize the effects of racial mixture. The Germanic inhabitant of the American continent, who has remained racially pure and unmixed, rose to be the master of the continent; he will remain the master as long as he does not fall a victim to defilement of the blood.[45]

At the core of Hitler's argument about race rested his deep anti-Semitism.[46] The Jew throughout history, he wrote:

> has lived in the states of other peoples, and there formed his own state, which, to be sure, habitually sailed under the disguise of "religious community" as long as outward circumstances made a complete revelation of his nature seem inadvisable. But as soon as he felt strong enough to do without the protective cloak, he always dropped the veil and suddenly became what so many others previously did not want to believe and see: the Jew." Jews, stressed Hitler, were "members of a *people* and not of a *religion*."[47]

Could Germans on their own recognize the significance of protecting and promoting the Aryan race? According to Hitler, Germany's main problem in the 1920s was that its leaders and people incorrectly assumed that economic necessities or the urge for power were the state's principal culture-creating forces. To fulfill their potential, Germans first had to accept the leadership provided by the Nationalist Socialist German Workers' Party (or Nazi Party in its abbreviated form). The Nazi Party would help them recognize and understand that their unique racial qualities would enable them to create the "folkish (völkish) state" and thus to realize their glorious destiny.

From the basic ideas of a general folkish world conception the Nationalist Socialist German Workers' Party takes over the essential fundamental traits, and from them, with due consideration of practical reality, the times, and the available human material as well as its weaknesses, forms a political creed which, in turn, by the strict organizational integration of large human masses thus made possible, creates the precondition for the victorious struggle of this world view.[48]

With the preconditions in place, Hitler went on to explain the kind of foreign policy Germany would have to design and implement in order to achieve greatness. Germany's 1914 frontiers "were in reality neither complete with respect to the inclusion of people of German nationality, nor intelligent with respect to geo-military appropriateness."[49] He was referring, in part, to his belief that Germany had been experiencing for some time the "Malthusian curse"—the inability to feed its rapidly expanding population based on the amount of arable land under its control.[50] Faced with such a challenge, Germany had but four choices: i) intensify the cultivation of the available arable land; ii) reduce its birthrate; iii) promote a colonial and trade policy; or iv) take over new soil in Europe proper.[51] After explaining why it would be inappropriate to implement either one of the first two alternatives, Hitler discussed why the fourth alternative was preferable to the third one.

Colonialism would have entailed sending German settlers to overseas lands. Hitler dismissed the option because "a colonial policy could only have been carried out by means of a hard struggle" and did not guarantee that German settlers would retain their racial and national identity.[52] The last option was much more sensible for several reasons. First, control over the productive agricultural land and valuable mineral resources located adjacent to Germany would enable Germans to stay alive and flourish. "The right to possess soil," Hitler explained, "can become a duty if without extension of its soil a great nation seems doomed to destruction ... If we speak of soil in Europe today, we can primarily have in mind only Russia and her vassal border states."[53] Linked to this argument was his belief that Germany's adjacent eastern lands were being occupied by Slavs, an inherently inferior group that lacked organizational ability[54] and was dominated by Jews, who had to be suppressed and, possibly, wiped out.[55] During the latter part of the nineteenth century, he added, Germany's chancellor, Otto von Bismarck, had been able to establish an alliance with Russia because it was led by a non-Slavic, Germanic, upper stratum. Russia's 1917 revolution, along with the war, had destroyed its government, which was now dominated by "world Jewry."[56] "In Russian bolshevism, we must see Jewry's twentieth century effort to take world dominion unto itself." "The struggle against Jewish bolshevism of the world requires a clear attitude towards Soviet Russia. You cannot drive out the Devil with Beelzebub."[57]

The last option concurred with Hitler's belief that those who ruled the "heartland" (Russia and Eastern Europe) would control Euro-Asia.[58] In 1937, while discussing with his top military leaders possible ways of taking over new territory, he stated that by annexing Austria, which had a large German population; destroying the Czechoslovakian state, which had failed to protect its minorities; and expelling millions of "racially unsuitable persons" from the two states, Germany would be able to both feed part of its own rapidly growing population and be partially surrounded by friendly governments. Subservient regimes in some of its eastern borders would, in turn, free Germany to move its armed forces against Soviet Russia.[59]

World leaders normally think in terms of what they believe are "achievable" political objectives; Hitler deplored this approach. "The task of a program-maker," he wrote, "is not to state the various degrees of a matter's realizability, but to demonstrate the matter as such; that means, he has to care less for the way but more for the goal." He acknowledged that the program maker's chances of succeeding in the short term were minuscule; still it was his obligation not to buy into what he referred to as the "art of the possible." The "greater a man's works for the future are, the less is the present able to understand them, and the more difficult also is the fight and the more rare the success."[60]

Hitler's political decisions were not entirely divorced from immediate political realities.[61] The Treaty of Versailles had restricted Germany's armed forces to a size no larger than one hundred thousand officers and men; dissolved its General Staff, the War Academy, and the cadet schools; denied its army the right to manufacture military aircraft, tanks, and other offensive weapons; and ordered that the navy be limited to a nominal force with no submarines and no vessels exceeding ten thousand tons. By 1932, Germany's former enemies, especially Britain, were willing to eliminate some of the military restrictions. Britain's prime minister, Ramsey MacDonald, drafted a plan that granted Germany equal status with regard to armaments. In October 1933, Hitler rejected the proposal and withdrew Germany from the disarmament talks and the League of Nations. In early 1934, Germany and Poland signed a non-aggression pact, which was followed by a trade concordat. In June, Germany signed a naval pact with Britain. The agreement both legitimized Hitler's earlier repudiation of the Treaty of Versailles's military clauses and freed Germany to build a fleet thirty percent as large as Britain's and as many submarines as it wanted.[62]

Hitler continued to execute his aggressive, but measured, steps during the second half of the 1930s. In 1938, he implemented the next stage of his *Lebensraum* doctrine. On March 12, he returned to his birthplace, Branau, one day after German troops had marched into Austria. "If Providence once called me from this city to assume the leadership of the Reich," he stated in a speech, "it must have charged me with a mission, and that mission can only have been to restore my dear homeland to the German Reich." With Austria part of Germany, he turned toward Czechoslovakia. His first attempt was thwarted when Prague, convinced that a German attack was imminent, ordered the partial mobilization of its troops. When Britain, France, and the Soviet Union announced that they would help the beleaguered state, Hitler held back. Nonetheless, he warned that he would even the score. By the end of September, he had German forces prepared to march into the Sudetenland. Britain and France's leaders, eager to avoid another war, met with Mussolini and Hitler in Munich. All four agreed that Czechoslovakia would evacuate its troops from the Sudetenland and redraw its borders. By March of the following year, Hitler had transformed the western part of Czechoslovakia into a German protectorate, converted its eastern side into a satellite state of Slovakia, and brought Hungary, Bulgaria, Rumania, and Yugoslavia under Germany's political umbrella. The German drive continued. In late August, a week after Germany had signed the Non-Aggression Pact with the Soviet Union, German troops attacked Poland. In his address to the German High Command prior to the invasion, Hitler stated: "Eighty million people must obtain what they have a right to. Their existence must be guaranteed. The stronger is in the right. Supreme hardness." This time, however, Hitler's action elicited a different response. On September 3, Britain and France declared war on Germany. Less than two years later, Hitler attacked the Soviet Union. "During the war I had no more difficult decision to make than the attack upon Russia. I had always said that we must avoid a two-front war at all costs." But by the middle of June 1941, we:

> had lost hope of being able to end the war by a successful invasion on English soil ... Consequently the war would have to go on forever, with moreover increasingly active participation of the Americans ... In order to persuade the English to surrender, in order to compel them to make peace, we consequently had to dispel their hope of confronting us on the Continent with an enemy of our class, that is, the Red Army ... Our sole chance to defeat Russia consisted in anticipating her ... If we seized the initiative we could defeat her in her own country.[63]

Last of all, he declared war on the USA four days after Japanese carrier planes had attacked it by surprise at Pearl Harbor. In little more than two years, Hitler had "gambled away a dominant political position and united the most powerful countries in the world, despite all their previous enmities, in an 'unnatural alliance'."[64]

Military-style fascism in Japan[65]

Japan's transformation into a fascist system differed fundamentally from Italy's and Germany's. In the latter two cases, the changes proceeded rapidly, following the failure by their respective democratically elected governments to address the economic and social ills afflicting their societies. In both instances, moreover, magnetic political leaders induced the changes. In the case of Japan, the adjustment came about gradually, without a persuasive leader at the helm, and with the army, backed by business and political leaders and intellectuals, playing the central role. Though the manner and pace in which the changes ensued differed, the leaders of Japan and Germany did share a number of beliefs and attitudes. Both were dissatisfied with their countries' standing in their respective regional systems and attributed their troubles to actions by external actors. Both were concerned with their countries' rapidly expanding populations and the shortage of arable land, and believed that in order for their economies to continue growing they needed to enlarge their territorial power. Both were certain that communism and liberal democracy threatened the foundations of their own societies. And both were convinced that their racial superiority bequeathed them the right to establish permanent domination over other races and peoples.

By the beginning of the twentieth century, Japan had already adopted, with some modifications, several Western political practices. Its 1889 constitution established a bicameral national assembly. The House of Peers, modeled after the British House of Lords, was composed almost entirely of former court nobles, feudal lords, and associates of the new leadership groups. Members of this house either were appointed or inherited their posts. Members of the Diet were elected by one percent of the population—male taxpayers who paid more than fifteen yen in taxes. From its inception, the Japanese Diet used its control over the budget to wrest a substantial share of the political power from the governmental cabinets. The cabinets gained dominance over the political system in the first half of the 1910s, when the same party that ruled the Diet controlled the cabinet.

Japan's zeal to "Westernize" its political system was matched by its determination to become Asia's leading actor. The Chinese revolution of 1911–1912 destroyed the Qing dynasty. Its successor, rather than turning to Japan for financial assistance as its predecessor had done, approached Europe. Japan did not welcome China's change of heart, but there was little it could do, at least initially. With Europe caught in a military impasse in late 1914, Japan seized all of Germany's possessions in the Far East and presented to the Chinese government what became known as the "Twenty-One Demands" document. It called for the establishment of a de facto protectorate in the form of Japanese advisers attached to the Chinese government, as well as Japanese control over China's most valuable natural resources. Britain and the USA rejected the idea of a Japanese protectorate but accepted many of Tokyo's economic demands. Two years later, Britain, Russia, and France formally recognized Japan's wartime gains in East Asia. Washington, afraid that such a decision would undermine its trade and investment interests in China and its drive to attain naval supremacy in the Pacific, balked. After extensive negotiations, Washington and Tokyo agreed to accept China's territorial integrity and Washington's "Open Door" principle, and to recognize Japan's special interests in China accorded by its geographical proximity.[66]

The agreement did not resolve the implicit struggle for hegemony in the Far East between Japan and the United States. Determined to derive some benefit from every new opportunity, Japan became one of the principal negotiators during the Peace Conference held in Paris. During the talks, Japan's representatives persuaded the other main actors to have the League of Nations grant Japan control over the German Pacific islands north of the equator in the form of a mandate, and the same economic privileges previously enjoyed by Germany on the Shantung peninsula of China. The success experienced in the international environment was not replicated in the domestic arena. Burdened by extensive domestic economic problems and social unrest, the Diet counteracted in 1925 by approving the Public Order Preservation Act. The Act was designed to curtail the spread of "dangerous" views—ideas that threatened private property and promoted the overthrow of the emperor system and the capitalist social order.[67]

By late 1932, it had become evident that the Japanese armed forces would not acquiesce quietly to the will of the civilian government. The rift between the two deepened during and immediately after the 1930 Naval Conference in London. With the crashing of the world economy, Japan's civilian leaders searched for budgetary cutbacks and strove to develop friendlier relations with the other major naval powers.[68] Japan's naval representatives, however, refused to yield unless they secured an accord that would allow Japan to increase the size of its navy substantially. The accord reached in London granted Japan the right to increase its naval power considerably; nevertheless, it failed to satisfy many of the navy's principals.[69] Army leaders were equally unyielding. By the time the Japanese army had consolidated its power over Manchuria, its senior officers were prepared to disregard the foreign policy dictates that did not concur with their expectations.[70] As explained by Admiral Keisuke Okada: "After the occupation of Manchuria, the Kwantung Army was the real government there ... The government of Japan had no way of learning what the plans and activities of the Kwantung Army were in those years. The Army was completely beyond the control of the Japanese government and remained so until the Great War in 1941."[71] The Army's rationale for wanting to control Manchuria was simple. "To secure Manchuria as a market for our commodities," wrote General Muto Nobuyoshi, the commander-in-chief of the Kwantung army, "seems to be a way of breaking the [economic] impasse ... and of removing various causes of unrest at home."[72]

The fissure between the Japanese government and the military began to lose its edge as both sides started to discuss ways to approach the impending naval conference in London. In 1934, the Japanese Naval General Staff convinced the cabinet that at the next meeting with representatives of the major world powers Japan should demand the removal of restrictions imposed on the size of its fleet. In September, the Japanese government informed Washington and London that it planned to renounce the Washington Naval Treaty before the end of 1934. The second London Naval Conference opened near the end of 1935, and Japan's representatives immediately showed no desire to compromise on the parity issue. When the other members refused to address it, the Japanese mission walked out.

The Japanese delegation returned to a tumultuous domestic political arena. Following the February 1936 general election, a military faction led by junior officers took over the Diet and the administrative district of central Tokyo, murdered three members of the cabinet, and nearly killed its prime minister. Its basic goal was to get rid of the "effete leadership" advising the emperor. The Emperor called on loyal troops to crush the mutineers. The rebels surrendered on the last day of February. Out of the one thousand four hundred and eighty-three personnel involved in the attempted coup d'état, seventeen were condemned to death. By the summer of 1937, all seventeen had met their fate, including Kita Ikki, one of Japan's most influential advocates of Japanese fascism and someone who was greatly admired by the young officers who mounted the attempted overthrow.[73]

Kita presented his ideas in two major works—*National Polity and Pure Socialism*, published in 1906, and *General Outline of Measures for the Reconstruction of Japan*, published in 1923. Like other socialists, Kita viewed history as an evolutionary process. "There is no socialism," he wrote, "without previous evolution in individualism, no world federation without evolution in imperialism, no communist society without evolution in private property." In his first book he connected socialism with national policy. Social democracy, led by the state, was part of the evolutionary process. To bring about social democracy, however, the state had to be transformed. It had to be changed from an emperor system that served the interests of selfish business and governmental leaders to one that addressed the needs of its citizens. In the new system, the emperor and the people would each play separate and distinct roles in order to ensure that privileges were granted "to each of its components."[74]

In his second book, Kita advanced two proposals. On the domestic front, he called for the elimination of the ruling political party, and of the bureaucratic, military, and financial elite, in order to pave the road for the establishment of the real union between the emperor and the people. To break the existing system, Kita advocated a coup d'état led by young military officers and backed by a committed civilian elite. The new leaders would immediately declare martial law and suspend the parliament. With no one to undercut their power, they would then reconstitute the imperial government, institute state control over the economy, destroy the financial and landed interests of the wealthy, guarantee private property for all the people but only up to a certain amount, carry out major land reforms, extend legal protection to tenant farmers, introduce profit sharing and the eight-hour day into industry, and grant suffrage to all men. Through its production ministries the state would operate all the large firms and enterprises appropriated for surpassing the allowed limit of private wealth, and through its Ministry of Labor it would protect the rights of workers and settle labor disputes.[75]

With regard to the international arena, Kita presented two views. He argued that Japan, like any other nation, had the right to protect itself, and to start war in self-defense. He added that Japan had an obligation to resort to war to evict the colonial powers that had infringed on the rights of Asians. In Asia, the villains were Britain, "a multimillionaire standing over the whole world," and Russia, "the great landlord of the northern hemisphere." Because the seven hundred million people inhabiting "China and India [had] no path to independence," it was Japan's duty to guide and protect them.[76] "Japan as an international proletariat," he emphasized, "should be unconditionally allowed to start a war in order to rectify the injustice of the present international boundaries."[77] It should "lift the virtuous banner of an Asian league and take the leadership in a world federation." There was a practical rationale behind Kita's argument. Japan's population, like Germany's, had increased rapidly in the previous decades. Tokyo had no choice but to take over areas that would be able to "support a population of at least two hundred and forty millions" in the not too distant future.[78]

Though it is difficult to measure the overall effect of Kita's work on Japan's people, government, and military, it is fair to note that after the February 1936 failed coup d'état, many of the changes he recommended were realized. Prior to February 1936, the military had been divided into two blocs—the Imperial Way faction and the Control faction. Each one believed that Japan had to become "purer" and more powerful. The first group placed greater weight on the struggle against a communist Soviet Union; on cooperation with China, but on Japan's terms; and on an emperor-centered polity. The second group advocated major changes to prepare Japan for global warfare. Influenced by the thinking of Ishiwara Kanji, the army's leading theorist on strategy at the staff college, the Control faction argued that Japan, with the military as its foremost organization, was fated to create a new world order. To succeed, Japan had to go to war against those actors advocating some of the world's most shameful ideologies—first the Soviet Union, then Great Britain, and finally the USA.

In August 1936, the Japanese inner cabinet adopted a foreign policy program titled *Fundamentals of National Policy*, which advocated some of the same goals sponsored by the Control faction. In order to strengthen its national defense and attend to its population problem, Japan should divide its imperialist designs into an inner ring comprised of Manchuria, north China, and Korea, and an outer ring consisting of the Dutch East Indies, Malaysia, the Philippines, and French Indochina. The designers of the plan emphasized that the expansion would have to be conducted gradually and peacefully. Caution was necessary because Japan imported great amounts of iron ore from Malaya and Indonesia, tin and rubber from Malaysia, coal from French Indochina, and oil from the Dutch East Indies. Also, Britain, the Netherlands, France, and the USA would resist any attempt on the part of Japan to boost its presence in the region.

The commitment on the part of Japan's military to alter the structure of the regional system came to full light in July 1937 when, following a clash between Chinese and Japanese troops outside Beijing, it launched its solution to the China problem. By late September, Japan's North China Army had deployed some two hundred thousand soldiers in China. It was not long before the Japanese army had gained control over China's ports, waterways, main cities, and railways. Confident that its action would not lure the USA to retaliate militarily, but concerned that it could generate a reprisal from the Soviets, Japan signed with Germany and Italy the Anti-Comintern Pact near the end of 1936.

The Japanese military was mindful that in order to succeed with its international endeavors, the government had to undertake major organizational reforms, bring about the systematic allocation of raw materials so that strategic industries would be able to perform their manufacturing tasks efficiently, and foster popular harmony. Therefore, the Japanese military and its civilian backers launched a number of initiatives on the domestic front.[79] One of the Army's first major steps was to assign to itself confirmatory powers regarding the selection of prime ministers. This change predisposed prime ministers to pursue a policy of acquiescence to the military's leading members.[80] The military also moved aggressively to alter its portion of the government's expenditures. In 1936 it was already absorbing forty percent of the government's spending; following the attempted coup, its share jumped to seventy percent.[81] The next year, the military strengthened the war-coordinating capabilities of the army and navy chiefs of staff by activating the Imperial Headquarters. And in March 1938 it pushed for the approval by the Diet of the National Mobilization Law. The law granted the Japanese cabinet the power to control "human and material resources in such a way as to enable the State to give full scope to the efficient use of its strength for ... national defense in time of war."[82]

Part of the process of reshaping Japan's domestic arena involved engendering a collective vision of the country's international task and destiny. The creation of such an image took two forms. As in the past, Japan's military leaders understood that modern war entailed more than struggle on the battlefield; it also involved "a war of ideology." In order to carry out this war, Japan had to boost its "national spirit, and under this spirit the people [had to] be unified."[83] Japan's Home Ministry assumed formal governmental responsibilities for this charge. With the language of race as its principal tool, the Home Ministry sought to reach the masses via publications, films, radio programs, lectures, and rallies.[84]

Japan's racial rationale was delineated in a six-volume study written by researchers from Japan's Population and Race Section of the Research Bureau of the Ministry of Health and Welfare, and was collectively entitled *An Investigation of Global Policy with the Yamato Race as Nucleus*. To rely on racial views to act against others, they claimed, was not uncommon. Historically, peoples throughout the world had differentiated themselves according to racial characteristics. To acknowledge a biological hierarchy based on intrinsic qualities and capabilities was both moral and just.[85] "To view those who are in essence unequal as if they were equal is in itself inequitable. To treat those who are unequal unequally is to realize equality."[86] It followed that the Japanese, as Asia's foremost race, had an obligation to reach beyond their immediate borders in order both to evict the imperialist Western powers from the region and liberate their Asian brothers. They would break the pattern of nationalist and capitalist expansions introduced by the Western powers and replace it with a self-sufficient Asian community where tasks and responsibilities would be allocated racially, according to criteria designed by the Japanese.[87] Or, as Japanese officials often stated, "Japan is the stem family and Manchuria is the branch family." One day, Manchuria would become a "splendid nation just like Japan."[88]

Japanese leaders, like their German counterparts, feared that they would not be able to generate a strong, loyal, nationalist sentiment amongst their people by simply accentuating the qualities of their race and their obligation to serve the nation. They were convinced that, along with political indoctrination, they needed to restrain the manifestation of views that questioned state actions or weakened the will to fight. To centralize and strengthen its censorship capabilities, the government established the Cabinet Information Division in September 1937. One task of the newly created division was to prevent the media from expressing anti-war or pessimistic sentiments that could, according to the government, confuse the public and incite public disturbances. Another duty was to ensure that the media continued to "inspire an enduring, untiring spirit into the mind of the people."[89] In February 1941, some nine months before Pearl Harbor, the Justice Ministry submitted to the Diet a Peace Preservation Law. The new law was designed to curtail activities by communists and religious groups involved in politics. It would also enlarge the government's authority to detain and interrogate suspects, and it would keep in custody until it "reformed" them those individuals who had been found guilty of engaging in anti-state activities.[90]

By 1939, Japan's domestic political, economic, and social arena had undergone major changes. Its leaders, however, had yet to fulfill one of their central foreign policy goals—control of Southeast Asia. Germany's invasion of Poland and the rapid expansion of the war throughout Europe provided Japan the opportunity it had coveted. The war hampered severely Britain's, the Netherlands', and France's capacity to prevent Japan from encroaching on their Southeast Asian colonial interests. Moreover, because the three European colonial powers had been forced to redirect many of their Southeast Asian resources to offset some of the losses engendered by the war, Tokyo recognized that Japan's access to a number of critical goods would soon be curbed. This understanding came almost on the heels of Washington's decision to cancel the 1911 USA–Japan commercial treaty by the end of the year.[91]

In October 1939, a study by Japan's Cabinet Planning Board rephrased one of the arguments posited in the 1936 *Fundamentals of National Policy* document. It proposed that in order to cope with the restrictions placed on exports to Japan by the European colonies and the USA, Japan had to integrate into its economic sphere "areas on the East Asian mainland and in the southern region." In the summer of 1940, with the war in Europe demanding the full attention of its leading contenders, Japan's foreign minister announced his country's determination to unite in "a single sphere" the peoples of East and Southeast Asia. As the region's stabilizing force, he noted, it was Japan's "mission and responsibility" to bring together peoples who were related to each other "geographically, historically, racially, and economically."[92] By then Japan had already extracted major economic, trade, and strategic concessions from the Netherlands and France.[93]

Washington objected to Tokyo's confrontational policy. To convey its anger, it prohibited the sale of aviation fuel and the highest grades of iron and scrap steel to Japan by US corporations. Undaunted, in August 1940, Tokyo announced its *Outline of a Basic Policy*. In addition to stressing the creation of a strong national defense state, the document emphasized that the immediate objective of Japan's foreign policy was to form a "Greater East Asia Co-Prosperity Sphere."[94]

During the first half of 1941, Tokyo and Washington seemed determined to resolve their differences peacefully. By July, however, it had become evident that they would not succeed. Shortly after learning that Germany had invaded the Soviet Union, Japan widened its control of Indochina by occupying its southern part. Washington counteracted by freezing Japan's assets in the USA and placing an embargo on oil exports to Japan. The Netherlands and Great Britain took similar steps.[95] In early September, members of the Japanese cabinet and the military agreed to continue negotiations with Washington but go to war if the two parties failed to reach an accord by the end of October. Japan's Navy Chief of Staff, Osami Nogano, explained their rationale.

> A number of vital military supplies, including oil, are dwindling day by day. This will cause a gradual weakening of our national status quo, the capacity of our Empire to act will be reduced in the days to come ... By the latter half of next year, America's military preparedness will have made great progress, and it will be difficult to cope with her. Therefore, it must be said that it would be very dangerous for our Empire to remain idle and let the days by.[96]

On October 18, Tojo Hideki, who just a few days earlier had opposed Washington's demand that Japan withdraw its troops from China, became his country's new prime minister.[97] With Tojo as Japan's leading decision-maker, and with a navy reluctant to oppose the war, it was only a matter of time before the conflict that had started in Europe in 1939 would officially become the Second World War.[98]

A liberalist US foreign policy

The day after the Japanese attack on Pearl Harbor, Roosevelt vowed that the USA and its allies would win the war. Winning the war, however, was not Roosevelt's sole objective. In August 1941, after a meeting with Britain's prime minister, Winston Churchill, the two leaders released the Atlantic Charter communiqué, in which they delineated the world system they envisioned after the war. The first two principles stipulated that neither country would seek to enlarge its territory, and recommended that other actors conform to the same code of behavior. The third called for the affirmation of the right of all people to select their own form of government, and insisted on the restoration of sovereign rights and self-government to those who had been forcibly deprived of them. The fourth and fifth principles underscored the USA's and Britain's commitment to help other states acquire access to trade and raw materials, and promised greater economic collaboration in order for them to procure economic development, better labor standards, and social security. The last principle expressed the two countries' determination to disarm those states "that threaten, or may threaten, aggression outside their frontiers [Japan, Italy, and Germany]" and encouraged other states to lighten "the crushing burden of armaments."[99]

Roosevelt's imagined world system differed significantly from the one envisioned by Wilson. Where Wilson advocated democracy, public opinion, and diplomacy, Roosevelt called for the creation of a security organization led by "four policemen"—the USA, the Soviet Union, Great Britain, and China. Roosevelt recognized that in order to create such an organization he had to get the backing of two different actors. He had to persuade the American public that the USA had no choice but to assume the leadership role it had refused to embrace in the interwar period, and he had to convince Stalin that it would be in the interest of the Soviet Union to work closely with the USA in order to prevent the destabilization of the world system.

Ideological enmity in a bipolar nuclear world

Roosevelt's death near the end of the war transferred the burden of fulfilling his goals to his vice president, Harry Truman. By the summer of 1945, however, the new US administration had become convinced that Roosevelt's goal of establishing a long-term association with the Soviet Union was unattainable. Secretary of State James Byrnes summarized the change in attitude as follows: "There is too much difference in the ideologies of the U.S. and Russia to work out a long term program of cooperation."[100]

In January 1946, at the behest of Secretary of the Navy James Forrestal, Edward F. Willett submitted a study of the effect communism had, and would most likely continue to have, on Soviet foreign policy. In the foreword, Willett painted a disquieting picture. He warned that "[s]trict application of Communist doctrine to the settlement of [the problems facing the contemporary world] leads by force of logic to the possibly unexpected and certainly unwelcome conclusion that violent conflict between Soviet Communism and Capitalist Democracy seems inevitable."[101] After discussing dialectical materialism and its relationship to communism, and communism's philosophy of history, morality, revolution, and society, Willett reached several conclusions. Upon asking: "What will be the future development of relations between Soviet Russia and Capitalist Democracy?" Willett acknowledged that in spite of Moscow's dependence on communist ideology, it was unlikely that it would ever go to war against the USA over an abstract principle. Russia, he noted, was weary of war, and its leaders were "realists." Moscow, he explained, knew that the USA was a powerful adversary and that a war against it would exact incalculable costs on the Soviet Union. Moscow's goals were to transform the Soviet Union into a powerful economic entity, establish communist governments in the ring of states surrounding it, and encourage the worldwide creation of communist governments. Willett predicted that "two major spheres of interest will gradually develop: one a Capitalistic Democratic sphere in the western hemisphere grouped around the United States and the second, a Communist sphere embracing a substantial part of the rest of the world around Russia." The USA, he warned, could not afford to ignore the lessons of history by "thinking that generous treatment converts potential enemies into friends." Any reliance on such thinking "invites only disaster so long as a nation with the apparent principles of Russian Communism and the tremendous power of Russia continues to exist."[102]

It was around this time that George Kennan, the US embassy charge d'affaires in Moscow, sent a long telegram to Washington delineating the effects of communist ideology on Soviet behavior and the steps the USA would have to take to contain Soviet imperialism. Kennan was contemptuous of the target of his analysis. After contending that communism did not represent the Russian people's natural outlook and that its predictions had been proven wrong by history, he noted that the Soviet leadership used Marxist dogma to justify its fear of the outside world and relied on dictatorial rule.[103] For the Soviets there could be no modus vivendi with the USA. The Communist Party was driven by the conviction that in order to secure its internal power, it had to disrupt the internal harmony of the USA's society and destroy its traditional way of life. He recommended that Washington design its foreign policy cognizant of these unpleasant facts, and approach the task with the "same thoroughness and care as solution of major strategic problems in war, and if necessary, with no smaller outlay in purpose."[104] The US government had to: i) study the Soviet problem objectively; ii) educate the American public to the realities of the Russian situation; iii) address US internal problems in order to deny Moscow the chance of using them to its own advantage; iv) assist other nations, but especially the European nations, to gain greater security; and v) not sacrifice its methods and conception of human society as it struggled to cope with Soviet communism.[105]

Moscow was equally concerned about Washington's global aspirations. As Stalin realized that the Soviet Union would emerge from the Second World War as one of the world's two most powerful entities, he commenced to shed the covers with which he had concealed his ideological creed from the outside world for much of the 1930s and first half of the 1940s. His willingness to pursue this course of action was assisted partly by Washington's new drive to redesign the international economic system.

One of the Atlantic Charter's principles underscored the USA's and Britain's commitment to help all states have access to trade and raw materials. Another principle emphasized their commitment to foster greater economic collaboration in order to procure economic development, better labor standards, and social security. In July 1944, Roosevelt and Churchill invited officials of more than forty countries to attend a meeting in Bretton Woods, New Hampshire. At the meeting, the representatives agreed to create an international system that would not hold domestic economic activities captive to the stability of the exchange rate, as had been the case with the gold standard system. Further, the system would not sacrifice the stability of the international economic system to the domestic autonomy characteristic of the interwar period. They also agreed to set up the International Monetary Fund and the International Bank for Reconstruction and Development (World Bank).[106]

Persuading Moscow that it would be in the Soviet Union's interest to become part of this new economic arrangement proved impossible. The Soviet leaders viewed the Bretton Woods agreement as but another device used by Washington to protect and enhance the USA's dominance over the world's capitalist economy. This sentiment gained intensity in 1947, when the Truman administration acknowledged that the measures adopted at Bretton Woods would not help Europe resolve its economic problems. Washington reasoned that the costs absorbed by the major industrial states during the war had been so great that the financial goals it had helped design three years earlier could not be realized without substantial economic assistance from the USA. Washington's apprehension had an additional rationale. The Truman administration feared that the European communist parties, which had gained substantial popularity after the war, might rely on the economic and social dislocation engendered by Europe's economic woes to gain power. Washington's foreign policy-makers were particularly concerned with the fate of France's and Italy's governments, where the communist parties had gained considerable popular backing.

To shield its western European allies, Washington proposed that they join the USA in the design of a plan for the recovery of Europe. In June 1947,

Secretary of State George C. Marshall announced that the USA was prepared to offer up to $20 billion in relief if the European states got together and drew up a rational plan on how to use the aid. "It is logical that the United States should do whatever it is able to do to assist in the return of normal economic health in the world, without which there can be no political stability and no assured peace." He emphasized that the policy was not "directed against any country or doctrine but against hunger, poverty, desperation, and chaos." Though Stalin sent representatives to Paris to discuss Marshall's proposal, their stay in the city lasted only a few days. Viacheslav Molotov, head of the Soviet delegation, concluded during early negotiations that the Marshall Plan would subordinate his country and Eastern Europe to Western capitalism.[107] Stalin shared Molotov's fear. The Soviet leader believed that acceptance of the plan would relegate the Soviet Union to the role of a supplicant state and would solidify the hegemonic status of the USA in the world economy.[108] "We shall be dependent on the West," he noted bluntly during a discussion with one of his associates.[109]

By the end of 1947, thus, the leaders of both the USA and the Soviet Union had developed views about each other that were "ideological mirror images." Much of the American leadership had accepted Winston Churchill's pronouncement that "[f]rom Stettin in the Baltic to Trieste in the Adriatic, an iron curtain has descended across the continent" and that all the countries behind that line "lie on the Soviet sphere and all are subject in one form or another not only to Soviet influence but to a very high and increasing measure of control from Moscow." Stalin, in turn, agreed with his ambassador in Washington that the USA's "monopolistic capital" was "striving for world supremacy."[110] Until his death in 1953, however, the Soviet leader remained convinced that though Japan and the most advanced capitalist countries in Europe had acquiesced to the USA's economic leadership, ultimately they would try to break away. As he noted in his *Economic Problems of Socialism in the USSR*, "Germany (Western), Britain, France, Italy and Japan have fallen into the clutches of the U.S.A. and are merely obeying its commands." But he then asked, rhetorically, whether those countries would be compelled "to break from the embrace of the U.S.A. and enter into conflict with it in order to secure an independent position and, of course, high profits?" Unsurprisingly, his answer was: yes.[111]

At the start of the 1950s, as the US public and Congress labored to accept that the USA no longer held a monopoly over nuclear weapons and that China had moved into the communist camp, President Truman ordered the reexamination of his country's security objectives and strategic plans. In April, Paul H. Nitze, who had replaced Kennan as director of Policy Planning at the Department of State, and his associates produced a document that would be referred to as NSC-68. As others have already analyzed it extensively, this section will focus mainly on its ideological character.

The document revealed its writers' determination to place the Soviet Union's political system under a harsh light. "The Kremlin," noted the writers, regards the United States as the only major threat to the achievement of its fundamental design. There is a basic conflict between the idea of freedom under a government of laws, and the idea of slavery under the grim oligarchy of the Kremlin ... The idea of freedom moreover, is peculiarly and intolerably subversive of the idea of slavery. But the converse is not true. The implacable purpose of the slave state to eliminate the challenge of freedom has placed the two great powers at opposite poles. It is this fact which gives the present polarization of power the quality of crisis.[112]

The writers of the document went on to argue that the insecurities experienced by the USA manifested themselves both physically and psychologically. Though Washington had to remain vigilant about Soviet attempts to alter existing military and economic distributions of power, it also had to be alert about Moscow's worldwide efforts to humiliate and intimidate the USA, and to undermine its credibility. Ultimately, the survival of the USA depended on the recognition by its government, "the American people, and all free peoples, that the cold war is in fact a real war in which the survival of the free world is at stake."[113] With this perspective as its foundation, NSC-68 called for a vast increase in the number and variety of interests the USA should be prepared to protect and the amount of resources it would need to invest in order to succeed. Truman approved it not long after North Korean troops had crossed the border that had been dividing their country from South Korea since 1945.

In short, by the early 1950s the sentiment that the conflict between the USA and the Soviet Union was a struggle between two competing world views—one committed to freedom, the other to slavery and oligarchy—was embedded in the minds of most Americans and their leaders. In the words of Henry Kissinger, Soviet behavior was "conditioned by the element of Marxist-Leninist ideology which emphasizes the inevitability of world revolution and the economic collapse of capitalism."[114]

Ideology does not always blind foreign policy-makers to the harsh realities that surround them. By 1956, the Soviet leadership had recognized that the USA had been successful at uniting Europe's strongest states under NATO, that it dominated the United Nations, and that it had "saved" South Korea. At the Twentieth Party Congress held in 1956, Nikita Khrushchev, the Soviet Union's new leader, acknowledged these facts when he stated that war with the USA was avoidable. Still, he added, the Soviet Union could not deny the possibility that the "imperialists" may choose to start one. For this reason, he concluded, the Soviet Union had to continue augmenting its military might and, like the USA, adopt the strategy of mutual assured destruction.

That same year Khrushchev faced a major international challenge, and his reaction did not differ significantly from the one the authors of NSC-68 would have advocated for the USA had it encountered a similar crisis. In October, Hungarian university students launched demonstrations demanding greater freedom for their country, which had been under communist rule and

Soviet supervision since the end of the Second World War. Hoping to avert a political confrontation, the Hungarian government abolished the one-party system and freed a very popular and active anti-communist Catholic cardinal. The responses did not quiet the protesters. Fearful that Washington might exploit the situation, Khrushchev and the other Kremlin leaders ordered Soviet troops to crush the revolt. They achieved their objective immediately. In Khrushchev's mind, the Soviet Union did not have a choice. "If we let things take their course," he commented, "the West would say we are either stupid or weak, and that's one and the same thing. We cannot possibly permit it, either as Communists and internationalists or as the Soviet state. We would have capitalists on the frontiers of the Soviet Union."[115]

La Havana and Berlin tested the resolve of both adversaries in the late 1950s and early 1960s. In 1959, Fidel Castro marched triumphantly into Cuba's capital. His entrance brought to an end the struggle he had launched in the early 1950s against the dictatorial rule of Fulgencio Batista, an avowed supporter of the USA. In February 1960, President Dwight Eisenhower decided that the new Cuban regime had moved too close to the Soviet camp and that its continued existence challenged the authority of the USA in the Caribbean Basin. New presidential elections delayed military action against Cuba until 1961. During the campaign, John F. Kennedy promised that he would return Cuba to the "Cubans" and that under his leadership the USA would intervene in the domestic affairs of developing states to ensure that they developed "along lines broadly consistent with our concepts of individual liberty and government based on consent." In April, President Kennedy authorized the launching of an ill-conceived plan to overthrow Castro. Despite the fact that the invasion did not topple the Castro regime, it warned other Latin American leaders that the USA took its struggle against communism seriously. The 1962 Cuban missile crisis enabled Kennedy to notify the Soviet Union and Latin American states that Washington was prepared to resort to war, even nuclear war, to retain its hegemonic status in the Western Hemisphere. Subsequent subtle and not-so-subtle interventions by the USA in Brazil in 1964, the Dominican Republic in 1965, Chile in 1973, and Nicaragua and Grenada in the 1980s, helped reinforce the message.[116]

In Germany, Moscow faced its own challenges. Berlin, which is located in Germany's eastern side, was split into East and West Berlin and divided into political zones. Responsibility for the protection of opposing areas was assumed principally by the Soviet Union and the United States. This political environment created a highly visible cause for dispute. After the partition, West Germany declared Berlin to be a land under its jurisdiction, while East Germany proclaimed it its capital city. By the late 1950s, Moscow was fretting about two matters regarding West Germany and Berlin. First, it feared that the USA would deploy nuclear weapons in West Germany. This fear was justified. In late 1957, the NATO council announced that it had accepted the USA's offer to position medium-range ballistic missiles throughout Europe, including West Germany. Second, Moscow worried that West Germany's astonishing economic recovery would hinder East Germany's own economic progress. As East Germans learned about the accomplishments of their western counterparts, they crossed the divide in search of better opportunities. Many of them proved to be those East Germany needed the most—the talented and educated. Moscow used a number of tactics to stop the departures. When none managed to prevent the flight, Khrushchev ordered the building of a wall along the boundary with West Berlin. The wall achieved its immediate intended objective—to stop the East–West flow. Symbolically, however, it failed. Its presence served as a daily reminder that to compete with market democracy, communist East Germany had to deny its own people the right to choose.

Khrushchev's days as leader of the Soviet Union came to an end in October 1964. He was replaced by Leonid Brezhnev as first secretary and Aleksei Kosygin as prime minister. The new leadership in Moscow did not bring about a noticeable transformation in the Soviet Union's foreign policy. Peaceful coexistence, sponsored first by Khrushchev, became part of Brezhnev's foreign policy vocabulary. Both Soviet leaders concurred that nuclear weapons had radically altered their country's relationship with the USA. This inference did not prevent the Soviet Union from competing for the hearts and minds of the foreign masses. Asia, Africa, the Middle East, and occasionally Latin America, became targets of opportunity. As time went by, however, Moscow began to realize that bringing socialism to developing countries exacted high costs. Soviet Foreign Minister Andrei Gromyko conceded this much when he stated that "the Soviet Union's potential for rendering economic assistance is not infinite." The Soviet Union, he added, would continue to allocate funds to developing countries, but only "on the basis of its own capabilities."[117]

Moscow's decision to curb economic assistance did not mean it was prepared to surrender control over those entities that were already part of its sphere of influence. In the spring of 1968 it used force to suppress the Prague uprising in Czechoslovakia. As Brezhnev explained in his *Brezhnev Doctrine*, the freedom of foreign socialists "to determine their country's path of development remained secondary to the cause of universal Marxism-Leninism." Actions by foreign socialists "must damage neither socialism in one country nor the fundamental interest of other socialist countries nor the world-wide workers movement." Every "Communist party is responsible not only to its own people but also to all socialist countries and to the entire Communist movement."[118]

Washington also worried about overextending the USA's capabilities. The war in Vietnam, which upon reaching its crescendo forced President Lyndon Johnson to announce that he would not seek reelection, alerted Washington that its foreign policy framework might require a change. This sentiment was compounded by the belief that the nuclear arms race with the Soviet Union was imposing exorbitant economic and social costs on the USA, and that their countries' respective nuclear capacities had become so cataclysmic that these weapons had lost some of their usefulness as instruments of deterrence.

Responsibility for altering the USA's foreign policy framework was assumed by Richard Nixon and his national security adviser, Henry Kissinger. The two shared the belief that the Kennedy and Johnson administrations had overextended the USA. "In the life of nations, as of human beings," wrote Kissinger, "a point is often reached when the seemingly limitless possibilities of youth suddenly narrow and one must come to grips with the fact that not every option is open any longer." The USA, he continued, had to "set its priorities, both intellectual and material."[119] Based on this thinking, they committed themselves to undoing the bipolar system that had emerged at the end of the Second World War. A bipolar system, argued Kissinger, tempts its two leaders "to maintain its preeminence among its allies, to increase its influence among the uncommitted, and to enhance its security vis-á-vis its opponent."[120] A multipolar system, on the other hand, though harder to manage, distributes responsibilities for preserving order in a more equitable manner than a bipolar one. To alter the structure of the system, the Nixon–Kissinger team had to fulfill two goals. First, it had to persuade Moscow that it would be in their mutual interests to shift the emphasis from nuclear superiority to nuclear efficiency, and restrain their attempts to pursue unilateral advantages and exploit crises. The end result of this policy was détente. Second, a multipolar world would emerge only if some of the European powers agreed to assume greater responsibility for their own security. With much of their economic health regained—in no small measure thanks to the extensive assistance provided by the USA—it was time for the leading European states to rely more on themselves for defense.

The tension that had dominated the relationship between the USA and the Soviet Union since the Second World War reached its lowest decibels during the period when both sought to curb their ideological passions. Psychologically and physically fatigued, the two states agreed that it would be in their mutual interests to lower the tone of their rhetoric, at least temporarily. Détente was the temporary end result of this acknowledgment.

Ideology regained its second wind in the USA during and following the 1976 presidential elections. Though it rose from the same foundation, it assumed two distinct faces. From the moment he assumed the presidency, Jimmy Carter tried to implement a foreign policy that met his moral standards. According to Carter, the USA had to implement a foreign policy that emphasized the same values it stressed at home—morality and commitment to freedom and democracy. He also suggested that the USA could not continue to assume that communists instigated every challenge initiated against governments friendly to the USA. During his first year in office he criticized the Soviets and the Czechs for the way they treated their dissidents, insisted that South Africa abandon its policy of apartheid, sought to persuade the white government of Rhodesia to accept majority rule, and urged the governments of several Latin American countries, including those of Argentina,

Chile, Brazil, and Nicaragua, to renounce dictatorial rule and pave the way for democracy. Certain that the arms race with the Soviet Union was both irrational and immoral, he tried to persuade Moscow that together they should freeze the further production and modernization of nuclear weapons and, if possible, reduce drastically their numbers.[121]

One of the major consequences of the Carter presidency was exposure of the dangers of relying on ideological righteousness to erect a foreign policy, without first thinking seriously about the contradictions it may generate. By the end of his presidency in 1981, Carter handed over to his successor a series of foreign policy failures. Iran and Nicaragua were under the leadership of new political regimes, both intensely anti-American; Soviet troops were on Cuban and Afghan soil; the SALT II agreement abetted further the division in the USA between supporters and opponents of arms control; and oil prices worldwide had reached new heights.

Carter was elected president, in part, because he campaigned as a Washington outsider, one who would bring to politics a new sense of moral integrity. However, as already noted, in the USA morality wore different masks. Those who had rebuked Nixon's policy of détente were as persuaded about the righteousness of their moral claim as those who believed that the USA should adopt an anti-military stand and stop bolstering dictatorial regimes that violated human rights. Those in the second group did not condone communism, but they argued that it was less baneful living with it than promoting an arms race that held the world hostage to terror. They also believed that an excessive fear of communism had led the USA to disregard those values on which its identity was based, to tolerate ruthless dictatorial regimes, and to ignore the woes of those who, because they were left with no other choices, viewed communism as the only way out of their misery. Members of the first group, in turn, viewed communism, and any state that adhered to its ideology, as the gravest imaginable political evil. They did not excuse non-communist dictatorial regimes, but they considered them less threatening and less immoral than communist ones.

The 1980 presidential election brought the leading representative of the USA's conservative ideology to the White House. Ronald Reagan assumed the presidency committed to resurrecting the anti-communist fervor of the early Cold War days. He and members of his administration summoned Americans to confront communism with a new sense of purpose. One of Reagan's first steps was to call for the restoration of America's global power and prestige. The USA, noted Reagan, was an "Island of Freedom" empowered by "Divine Providence" to protect peace and liberty throughout the globe.[122] The Soviet Union, on the other hand, was "the most evil enemy mankind had faced in his long climb from the swamp to the stars"[123] This "evil empire" was committed to creating a single political world with the Kremlin as its hegemon. "I know of no leader of the Soviet Union since the revolution, and including the present leadership, that has not more than once repeated in the various Communist congresses they hold their determination that their goal must be the promotion of world revolution and a one-world socialist or Communist state, whichever word they want to use."[124] And, as he would state often, the "Soviet Union underlies all the unrest that is going on. If they weren't engaged in this game of dominoes, there wouldn't be any hot spots in the world."[125]

In spite of believing that the Soviet Union posed a horrific threat, Reagan was convinced that the USA's nemesis was facing a major crisis. On June 8, 1982, during an address to members of the British Parliament, he stated:

> We are witnessing today a great revolutionary crisis, a crisis where the demands of the economic order are conflicting directly with those of the political order ... [T]he crisis is happening ... in the home of Marxist-Leninism, the Soviet Union ... [The Soviet Union] is in deep economic difficulty. The rate of growth has been declining since the fifties and is less than half of what it was then ... The constant shrinkage of economic growth combined with the growth of military production is putting a heavy strain on the Soviet people. What we see here is a political structure that no longer corresponds to its economic base, a society where productive forces are hampered by political ones.[126]

Reagan and his advisors made the most of the perceived opportunity. They reasoned that Washington would be able to create fissures in the Soviet system and force Moscow to curtail its foreign activities by increasing the USA's overall military budget and by backing with "money and political muscle" the various movements throughout the world battling communism.[127] With these measures, the USA would be able to reverse "Soviet expansionism by competing effectively on a sustained basis with the Soviet Union in all international arenas, particularly in the overall military balance and in geographical regions of priority concern to the United States."[128]

Reagan wasted little time in implementing his radical foreign policy. He persuaded Congress to support a major increase in the Defense Department budget and proposed a plan for modernizing and strengthening the USA's strategic nuclear arsenal. He also approved the execution of two far-reaching directives. The first order, NSDD 32, would provide funds to anti-communist movements committed to battling the "Soviet empire" on the periphery. By periphery, the document meant mainly Eastern Europe. The second one, NSDD 75, called for rolling back the Soviet Union's sphere of influence. Most importantly, on March 23, 1983, Reagan announced a new Strategic Defensive Initiative. The plan called for switching the emphasis placed originally on the development of offensive nuclear weapons to the development of defensive weapons. It entailed the development of a space-based ballistic missile defense that would rely on new technology such as laser and particle beams to destroy Soviet missiles in flight before they reached their targets.[129]

Reagan's gamble paid off. In 1991, following the demise of communist rule in Poland, Hungary, East Germany, Bulgaria, Czechoslovakia, and Romania,

Moscow formally agreed to replace the multinational Soviet state with a loose federation of republics known as the Commonwealth of Independent States. Finally, in early October 1993, President Boris Yeltsin disbanded Russia's Communist Party. The collapse of the Soviet "evil force" had not come about overnight. The Soviet Union had been facing an internal crisis engendered by the cumbersome imbalance between its political structure and its economic base since the 1960s. This imbalance eventually eradicated the Kremlin's capability to continue competing effectively in the global arena.[130]

Balance of power versus balance of terror versus "star war"

In Chapter 3, I proposed that the balance-of-power doctrine designed in 1815 assumed the form of a political ideology, with its own distinct set of cognitive, affective, evaluative, programmatic, and social-base dimensions. The ideology was built on two ideas. It began with the assumption that any state, regardless of how moderate its behavior might have been, would dispose of its old inhibitions if it were allowed to rise to a position of predominance. Its second contention was that the only legitimate states were those that had demonstrated for an extended period that they possessed the capability to maintain their political independence. The doctrine's affective and social-base dimensions were closely linked. The ideology was designed to appeal to the sentiments and emotions of Europe's most important political leaders. It sought to generate amongst them both fear and support by criticizing Napoleon's immoderate ambitions, and nationalism's destructive potential. Its programmatic dimension was two sided. To prevent the emergence of a predominant power, Europe's leading actors had to be farsighted and flexible in order to form and challenge alliances. To offset the rise of nationalism, those same entities had to avoid supporting nationalist causes. Their refusal to support nationalist causes would generate two positive effects—it would help protect both the security of traditional empires and the power equilibrium that had existed between them.

The First World War affected the world system and attitudes toward the balance-of-power doctrine in distinct ways. Though by the war's end the world system remained multipolar, some of the players from the earlier system had vanished, while the powers of other actors had changed substantially. The war moved the USA and Japan to, or closer to, center stage, while it destroyed the Ottoman Empire and the Austro–Hungarian Empire. Moreover, it diminished Britain's and France's respective material powers measurably, but not as much as Germany's; and compelled a different Russia to pull back temporarily while its leaders restructured its political, economic, and social systems. In this newly restructured world system, nationalism gained substantial prominence.

The human and material costs engendered by the war fostered intense antiwar sentiments in Europe and the USA. Though arguments took different forms, a great many questioned the rationale behind the balance-of-power doctrine. They echoed Woodrow Wilson's claim that, rather than containing the power aspirations of states, the implementation of the balance-of-power doctrine encouraged them to augment their military might and craft secret alliances. Distrust, fear, and uncertainty soon permeated their relationships.

Disparagement of the balance-of-power doctrine by a number of important international actors helped free others to inflame nationalist sentiments, and to use them to justify their expansionist policies. The drive to enfeeble the doctrine and manipulate nationalist passions resulted in another world war. As the new one began, scholars and makers of foreign policy revived their interest in power, its distribution, and how it ought to be controlled. But in the world system that rose from the Second World War, the ideology that had defined the previous balance-of-power doctrine was no longer pertinent.

The emergence of the USA and the Soviet Union as the leading powers at the end of the Second World War, the development of the nuclear bomb, and Washington's decision to use it twice against Japan, destroyed the central premises of the balance-of-power doctrine designed in 1815. During the early days of the Cold War, Washington did not devise a policy that would enable the USA to use its nuclear advantage vis-à-vis the Soviet Union. As explained by Henry Kissinger, the USA failed because its leaders treated nuclear power and diplomacy as discrete phenomena.[131] Stated differently, the USA was unable to develop a nuclear doctrine with its own distinct set of cognitive, affective, evaluative, programmatic, and social-base dimensions.

By the 1950s, with the Soviet Union in possession of its own set of nuclear weapons, Washington tendered an unremarkable idea. It proposed that the "way to deter aggression is for the free community to be willing and able to respond vigorously at places and with means of its own choosing."[132] Though John Foster Dulles made it clear that Washington had no intention of turning every local war into a world war, he emphasized that it would retaliate massively if it concluded that the actions of other actors were threatening the interests of the USA. He added that by not disclosing in what regions and under what circumstances Washington would use the nuclear weapons to retaliate, it hoped to force potential aggressors to think carefully before they initiated offensive acts.

The nuclear power disparity between the USA and the Soviet Union in the early 1960s was substantial. Towards the end of 1962, the USA possessed a total of two hundred and ninety-four intercontinental ballistic missiles (ICBMs), one hundred and forty-four submarine-launched ballistic missiles (SLBMs), and six hundred long-range bombers. The Soviet Union, on the other hand, only had seventy-five ICBMs, only a few SLBMs, and one hundred and ninety long-range bombers. The imbalance, however, did not undercut the Soviet Union's ability to deter the USA from initiating a nuclear attack. With each superpower in possession of a second strike capability, the USA's secretary of defense, Robert McNamara, announced a new nuclear strategy. Known as mutual assured destruction (MAD), the strategy's cognitive dimension took it as a given that leaders on both sides were rational and unwilling to trigger the destruction of millions of people to boost their country's political or strategic stand. It sought to instill amongst American and Soviet political leaders, and their respective publics, the deep fear that Armageddon would result if either side acted irrationally. Its programmatic dimension was built on two ideas. To promote stability and avert a nuclear war, leaders on each side repeatedly sought to persuade their counterparts that they would respond automatically with a nuclear counterattack if their country were to experience a first nuclear strike. To ensure that their commitment would not be overlooked or questioned, both tried to make certain that their country would not be outpaced in the development of new nuclear devices and delivery systems. They also worked hard at persuading weaker actors that building their own nuclear arsenals would not serve their own interests and those of the world system.

Over much of the rest of the course of the Cold War, most American strategic thinkers, and almost by default the American public and the rest of the world, continued to accept MAD as the only viable doctrine of deterrence. Still, from the start of the nuclear age, a small group of critics, composed primarily of scientists and intellectuals, insisted that the only way to avert a nuclear disaster was by banning all nuclear weapons. In the 1980s, the number of people supporting the ban increased measurably, particularly following the publication of Thomas Shell's best-selling book: *The Fate of the Earth* (1982). Though heavily criticized by specialists on nuclear strategy and arms control, the book struck a chord worldwide. The influence of the ban-the-bomb movement did not wane until the late 1980s and early 1990s, when Washington and Moscow agreed to sharp reductions in their strategic nuclear arsenals.

Of greater significance was President Ronald Reagan's stand vis-à-vis MAD. In 1983, he criticized MAD's moral foundation. The USA's dependency on mutual assured destruction, he argued, was "a sad commentary on the human condition." "Wouldn't it be better," he added, "to save lives than to avenge them? Are we not capable of demonstrating our peaceful intentions by applying all our abilities and our ingenuity to achieving a truly lasting stability?" As an alternative, he proposed the Strategic Defense Initiative (SDI). Three ideas guided his thinking. At the outset, he refused to accept the notion that vulnerability to attack represented a superior moral and strategic position for the USA. Second, he believed that to fulfill its national security and foreign policy goals the USA had to operate from a position of strength. By consistently operating from a position of strength, Washington would be able to steadily undercut the rationale by potential adversaries to attack. Third, with the advent of new and highly sophisticated technology, more international actors were gaining access to space. The proliferation of space-launch vehicles and ballistic missiles increased the capacity of adversaries to attack the USA and its vital interests. To offset their threat, Reagan accepted the advice of scientists who proposed that one of the most effective ways to protect the security of the USA would be to control space militarily via the development and use of space-based interceptors.[133]

SDI remains an unfinished strategy. Scientists have yet to master the technology needed to create a system capable of both tracking incoming missiles and destroying them before they hit their assigned targets. The demise of the Soviet Union, moreover, has lessened the need, at least temporarily, to resolve the various technological puzzles that have encumbered its development. And yet, despite its multiple shortcomings, SDI stands apart from MAD. The two are built on different moral standards and rely on different instruments to achieve the same goal—protecting the USA from a nuclear attack.

In sum, the balance-of-power doctrine experienced substantial changes during the 1815–1980s period. In each alteration, what the doctrine postulated was not the result of an objective reflection of world realities but of an interpretation dictated by the interests the interpreters sought to protect and promote. Such interests, moreover, were defined by the interpreters' beliefs, values, and ideas. From this contention one ought not to assume that changes in the material world did not affect the nature and structure of balance-of-power doctrines. Clearly, scientific and technological discoveries, along with changes in the material distribution of power throughout the world system, repeatedly forced political leaders, scientists, and international relations analysts to alter the way they interpreted reality. But their interpretations were never independent of their values, beliefs, and ideas. Had they been, it would be impossible to explain the positing of competing doctrines under the same set of material conditions.

Conclusion

The actor with the capacity to absorb the costs of intense competition longer and respond to emerging challenges faster won the ideological struggles that arose from the ashes of the First World War. Although both conditions are interlinked, the first one is principally a function of an actor's material capability, whereas the second one is chiefly determined by its ideological flexibility.

A comparative analysis of the war capacities of the major powers explains why the Allied forces defeated the Axis military. By 1943, the combined war capabilities of the USA, the Soviet Union, and Great Britain were more than three times greater than the aggregate capabilities of Germany, Japan, and Italy. It was this simple fact that led Winston Churchill to state, upon learning that the USA was entering the war: "Hitler's fate was sealed. Mussolini's fate was sealed. As for the Japanese, they would be ground to powder. All the rest was the proper application of overwhelming force."[134]

The above discrepancies raise questions as to why Germany and Japan would resort to war when the odds of winning or reaching a favorable compromise were so much against them. With respect to Germany, John J. Mearsheimer, one of today's most esteemed Realists, writes that had Hitler restrained himself after the fall of France and not invaded the Soviet Union, "conquest probably would have paid handsomely for the Nazis." He then adds that the "trick for a sophisticated power maximizer is to figure out when to raise and to fold."[135] Mearsheimer is right to contend that power maximizers must know when to stop. The problem with the argument is that it fails to concede that often power maximizers are ideologues. For Hitler, expanding east was dictated not just by his conviction that Germans needed the additional land to prosper, but also by his deeply ingrained racist dogma that viewed Slavs as a biologically inferior people who had to be coerced to service a superior race. When Hitler wrote, "Germany will be a world power or there will be no Germany,"[136] he was essentially saying that a race cannot prosper unless it is prepared to risk defeat.

For some Realists, Japan's decision to go to war against the USA was not part of an irrational process. Mearsheimer claims that Japan "opted to attack the United States, knowing full well that it would probably lose, but believing that it might be able to hold the United States at bay in a long war and eventually force it to quit."[137] To strengthen his argument, Mearsheimer quotes Scott D. Sagan, who writes: "[T]he Japanese decision for war appears to have been rational. If one examines the decisions made in Tokyo in 1941 more closely, one finds not a thoughtless rush to national suicide, but rather a prolonged agonizing debate between two repugnant alternatives."[138]

Both Mearsheimer and Sagan are right when they observe that before deciding on war Japan's leaders wrestled over the decision, and that when they finally made it they knew perfectly well that the odds of winning were against them. It was Tojo Hideki, the war minister, who summarized Japan's dilemma when he said to Prime Minister Konoe Fumimaro, "Sometimes a man has to jump, with his eyes closed, from the veranda of Kiyomizu Temple."[139] What neither Mearsheimer nor Sagan seems able to recognize is that Japan's leaders created the dilemma—they could have chosen not to expand into China and Southeast Asia—and that their own ideological rigidity deprived them of the choice. As the superior race, Japan's leaders repeatedly noted, they were obligated to destroy the unjust order imposed on much of Asia by the Western powers and create one that adhered to the tenets of the Imperial Way. Or, as explained by Chihiro Hosoya, during the 1930s the Japanese leaders were filled with a sense of mission and considered war a worthwhile risk.[140]

The impact of the ideological inflexibility of the leaders of the Soviet Union took longer to unfold, but in the end its consequences were also devastating. The Soviet Union lost the competition with the USA not on the battlefield but in the economic area. Article 16 of the 1977 Soviet Constitution defined the Soviet economy "as a single public economic complex embracing all sectors of social production, distribution and exchange on the country's territory." This meant that the Soviet Constitution, with very few exceptions, prohibited individuals or groups from owning the means of production or from engaging independently in entrepreneurial activities.[141] The Soviet Union accumulated and invested capital for economic return and development.

Unlike market-oriented economies, however, the Soviet Union owned capital and allocated it among the various sectors of the economy based on priorities determined by governmental officials.[142] Though initially, centralized planning enabled the Soviet Union to develop many of its industries at a very rapid pace, in time the rate of growth diminished. Soviet economists recognized the economic downturn relatively early and proposed measures that would grant factory managers the freedom to decide what style, assortment, quality, and quantity of goods to produce. They also suggested that factories be evaluated in terms of profits. After an extensive debate, the Soviet leadership agreed to give factory managers some measure of freedom over production. All in all, however, the economic system remained highly centralized, and its impact was measurable.[143] Between 1966 and 1970, the Soviet economy grew at an annual rate of five percent; between 1981 and 1984 it grew by only two percent. During those periods, Moscow, in addition to investing in defense an estimated fifteen to seventeen percent of its gross national product, compared to approximately seven percent for the USA, was highly active in the developing world.[144]

Konstantin Chernenko's death in March 1985 finally propelled to the leadership those who for quite some time had been calling for major changes. With Mikhail Gorbachev at the helm, they moved swiftly to reinvigorate the economy and alter the makeup of the ruling party. They relied on a policy of openness (*glasnost*) to apply pressure on ministers, factory managers, and economic officials. As the idea gained momentum, Gorbachev and his associates began to use the term "crisis" to describe the Soviet Union's social and economic predicaments. They spoke forcefully in favor of decentralizing the planning of the economy by extending greater decision-making authority to factory managers, and they demanded that greater attention be paid to housing, health care, education, and consumer needs.[145] They also moved aggressively to consolidate their power in the Politburo. By September 1989, they had succeeded in removing from the supreme ruling body the last member of the "old guard."

Adjustments in the domestic arena were carried out with an eye on the world environment. The new leaders deduced that unless they altered the foreign policy of the Soviet Union, their new domestic economic and political measures would not be enough to bring about the results they desired. In their view, the militarization of Soviet foreign policy implemented by the former leaders had thwarted the development of the Soviet economy.[146] Gorbachev explained the relationship between the two during an interview with the editors of *Time* magazine in 1985. "You ask what changes in the world economy could be of benefit to the Soviet Union. First of all, although this belongs more to politics than economics, an end to the arms race. We would prefer to have every ruble that today goes for defense to meet civilian, peaceful needs."[147] He made a similar argument at the Twenty-Seventh Party Congress in 1986, when he stated that changes in the international arena were so profound and significant that the Soviet Union had to rethink, and conduct a

comprehensive analysis of, all its factors—"The situation of nuclear confrontation calls for new approaches, methods, and forms of relations between
different social systems, states and regions ..." [war, he added] "had ceased to
be the continuation of state policy by other means"; that the Soviet Union
could not continue to advocate the export of violent revolutions; that states,
even socialist ones, had to determine their own fate without Soviet direction;
and that the rapid decline of the Soviet economy compelled it to bring to an
end its isolation from the rest of the global economy.[148]

Gorbachev's readiness to expose and disparage earlier policy mistakes
continued. During a visit to Yugoslavia in 1988, he repudiated the *Brezhnev
Doctrine*. With the Yugoslav leader at his side, he stated that socialist countries should "have no pretensions of imposing their concepts of social development on anyone ... [and] prohibit any threat or use of force and
interference in the internal affairs of other states under any pretext whatever."[149] Shortly afterward, he criticized the Soviet invasion of Afghanistan.
The incursion, he explained, had been very costly—it had undermined the
reputation of the Soviet Union and moved its main Asian rival, China, closer
to the USA. To underscore his commitment to improve his country's international image, Gorbachev ordered the withdrawal of Soviet forces from
Afghanistan and informed Washington that he was suspending all military
and economic aid to Nicaragua.

And yet, almost as a final valiant attempt to save Marxism–Leninism from
the dustbins of history, Gorbachev continued to support the ideology that had
guided his country's domestic and international behavior for more than half a
century. He steadfastly held to the belief that "Marxism-Leninism [was] the
greatest revolutionary world view" and that "[b]ourgeois ideology [was] an
ideology of service to capital and the profits of monopolies, of adventurism
and social revenge, the ideology of a society with no future."[150]

What he thought no longer mattered; by then most Eastern European
states had rescinded their allegiance to the Soviet Union and started to mold
their own political courses. On December 21, 1991, eleven republics issued a
joint statement noting that "[w]ith the formation of the Commonwealth of
Independent States, the USSR ceases to exist." Four days later, Gorbachev
resigned as president of a state that had already stopped existing.[151] Unable
and unwilling to question its own unyielding ideological dictates for some
seventy years, and burdened for more than forty years by a competition that
it could ill-afford, Soviet Marxism–Leninism finally surrendered to the forces
of a much older, and more powerful, ideology—nationalism.

With no one to challenge its authority, the USA moved swiftly to dis-
seminate its ideological principles. Little did Washington realize at that time
that the vanishing of the Soviet Union would free an array of repressed
groups to rely on violence to fulfill their nationalist, ethnic, or religious goals,
and that the USA's own drive for ideological hegemony would help instigate
aggressive and brutal reactions.

6 The resurgence of forgotten ideologies

[M]any old gods ... are rising from their graves. They strive to gain power over our lives and again they resume their eternal struggle with one another.[1]

The impetus to globalize market democracy

Shortly after the end of the Cold War, Washington left little doubt that it intended to create a world system that reflected the USA's ideology. In 1993, Anthony Lake, President Bill Clinton's national security advisor, announced that the USA was determined to carry out Woodrow Wilson's mission. "[E]nlargement of the world's free community of market democracies," noted Lake, lay at the heart of Wilson's foreign policy. Finally, after a long and arduous struggle, first against fascism and subsequently against communism, the USA was on a position to realize the former president's dream. "The expansion of market-based economies abroad," explained Lake, "helps expand our exports and create American jobs, while it also improves living conditions and fuels demands for political liberalization abroad. The addition of new democracies makes us more secure because democracies tend not to wage war on each other or sponsor terrorism ... "[2]

From early on, the Clinton administration moved rapidly to regain the ground the USA had surrendered in the global economy during the Cold War. Paradoxically, it was Japan, one of Washington's savviest competitors, that first granted the USA the opportunity to reclaim its standing as the world's most efficient economy.

By the late 1980s, much of the world had concluded that the East Asian economies, led by Japan, had crafted a new political economic model—one that guaranteed political stability and rapid economic growth with relative equity. Their success was built on a rather simple formula. To become an effective participant in the global market, the state had to shield its home market from foreign competition and help its domestic firms become powerful and effective international competitors. The state intervened not by taking over the economy, but by erecting trade barriers, facilitating credit and investment, ensuring high saving rates, keeping inflation low, promoting

exports, and fostering education attentive to the skills required by industrialization. Moreover, the state promoted political stability by relying on
varying degrees of regulated politics, from dictatorship to a one-party system,
and by rewarding their citizens' commitment to the common cause with
relatively equitable economic reforms from the proceeds of economic growth.[3]

The strategy enabled the East Asian economies to catch up with their more
advanced counterparts. In 1989, however, as Japan's "bubble" economy burst,
the dominoes began to waver. It was not long before the International
Monetary Fund (IMF), with US backing, insisted that Japan revive its economy by: i) reducing the power of the "iron triangle" (business leaders, politicians and bureaucrats); ii) lowering market barriers; iii) permitting foreign
ownership of domestic companies, including the banking sector; iv) relying on
economic criteria rather than favoritism when granting loans and putting
together financials deals; v) deregulating capital and product markets; vi)
persuading firms to focus on maximizing profits rather than on market shares;
and vii) pressing companies to replace their seniority and lifetime employment with a Western-style merit system. The USA toughened its demands in
1998. Afflicted by fragile banking systems loaded with bad loans, the stock
market indices of Indonesia, Malaysia, the Philippines, Singapore, South
Korea, Taiwan, and Thailand underwent substantial drops in 1997. Shortly
afterward, each economy was forced to devalue its currency and dig deep into
its reserves in an attempt to stop the economic plunge. It was not long before
the same Asian states that just a few years earlier had scorned the USA as a
"has-been" economic power, came knocking on Washington's doors asking
for assistance. The IMF, with strong backing from the Clinton administration, forced the distressed parties to undertake liberalizing reforms in finance,
corporate governance, and labor markets; and it insisted that they restrict
domestic demand through higher interest rates, lower government spending,
and stiffer taxes.[4]

The Clinton administration also took aggressive steps on the trade front.
As the 1990s unfolded, it pressured other core actors to open their markets
more. In addition to demanding that they lower tariffs and quotas, it
denounced loose anti-trust enforcement, government regulations that constrained competition, deficient implementation of intellectual property rights,
and the limited access to product distribution systems. Furthermore, it intensified its efforts to assist US-based economies to attain contracts abroad. To
show foreign competitors that they should take its stipulations seriously, the
Clinton administration often enforced Section 301 of the US trade law—a law
that permits the USA to retaliate against actors that refuse to open their
markets.[5]

Though the economic and financial policies implemented by the Clinton
administration often spawned criticism and counteractions from overseas,
none of the challenges was severe enough to endanger the USA's relationship
with its core allies in Europe and Asia. For the most part, they agreed that
ultimately no one could afford to rebuff the world's most powerful economy.

The significance of the USA's economy became particularly evident by the end of the first quarter of 1999, when even the most doubtful parties acknowledged that the 1998 financial crisis could have spun into a world depression had it not been for the USA's superior economic capacity. At that time few were prepared to question the assertion by former secretary of state Henry Kissinger that the USA was "enjoying a pre-eminence unrivaled by even the greatest empires," or the claim that there "has never been a system of sovereign states that contained one state with [the United States's] degree of prominence."[6]

Despite the USA's unmatched military and economic power, many of its leading "movers and shakers" belittled the manner in which the Clinton administration handled foreign policy. They contended that, rather than relying on multilateralism, which according to critics places too much emphasis on support from the international community and on humanitarian interests, US foreign policy-makers should bear in mind that global interests are not always in accord with national interests. As Condoleezza Rice noted shortly before becoming George W. Bush's national security adviser, "there is nothing wrong doing something that benefits all humanity, but that is, in a sense, a second order effect." The USA, she continued, had to reinvigorate its military in order to give it "the capacity to carry out its missions," focus on the numerous challenges posed by China, reshape the defense identity of the North Atlantic Treaty Organization, "mobilize whatever resources it can" in order to remove Saddam Hussein from power, and develop with South Korea and Japan a resolute and decisive policy of deterrence toward North Korea.[7]

It was not long before the Bush administration was given the opportunity to try to promote its own world vision. With the shocking attacks of September 11 behind him, Bush ordered two invasions, and designed an uncompromising national security doctrine. Despite the intense worldwide rebuke that he received following the invasion of Iraq, the president continued his initial course and announced in May 2003 that his administration had accomplished part of its initial mission—the toppling of the Saddam Hussein regime—and was moving swiftly to transform the country into a model democracy. Five years later, the initial optimism had vanished. As many observers had forecasted, creating a stable democratic system in Iraq proved to be a much more complex and costly task than initially believed. Though by 2008 Iraq's internal conditions had improved substantially, the Bush administration was still trying to dispel the perception that, despite its incredible material power, the USA lacked the competence to lead the world system.

Nationalism, ethno-nationalism, and fundamentalism

Every world system houses a variety of contradictory forces, but the tensions they breed rarely evoke the same level of interest from the world's leading actors. The end of the First World War did not give way to a more stable system. The unwillingness or inability on the part of the USA to try to generate a consensus among the leading competing actors produced a power vacuum that was exploited by Germany, Japan, and Italy. The main promoters of democracy and communism eventually counteracted with a united front, but the end of the Second World War was followed by a struggle between the two ideologies that had defeated Nazism and fascism. This new rivalry defined world politics for more than four decades, and led its principal instigators to the brink of a nuclear encounter on more than one occasion.

The tensions generated by the above dissensions, however, were not the only ones that afflicted the world system during the periods that followed the First and Second World Wars. The forces of nationalism continued to multiply in peripheral regions under the shadows of the more compelling ideological battles. It was only after the end of the Cold War that they started to regain their previous political value and draw the attention of the world's leading actors. Ethnicity and religion, alongside nationalism, had swelled as sources of political change. To trace their evolution, a brief analysis of the 1919 Paris Peace Conference is in order.

From the moment the rulers of the most powerful states gathered in Paris, they agreed that they would apply the principle of self-determination solely to the successor states of the German, Russian, Austro–Hungarian, and Ottoman empires. Under the watchful eyes of London, Paris, Tokyo, and Washington, numerous states were born or reborn. Poland reemerged as a sovereign entity by regaining control over territories it had ruled near the end of the eighteenth century. Czechoslovakia became a multinational state by uniting portions of territories previously controlled by Austria and Hungary. Finland, Estonia, Latvia, and Lithuania broke away from Russia and formed their own separate nations. Similarly, Yugoslavia absorbed Serbia, Montenegro, Croatia, the former Turkish provinces of Bosnia and Herzegovina, and the Habsburg provinces in Slovenia and Dalmatia. However, when the time came to decide the fate of the colonies controlled by Britain and France, both left little doubt that they intended to keep them. Likewise, US congressional leaders notified President Woodrow Wilson that they would vote against membership in the League of Nations unless he was assured that the Monroe Doctrine would be excluded from the legal jurisdiction of the League of Nations. Britain and France retained their colonies, and the USA was not asked to renounce its political canon towards Latin American states.[8]

In addition, the major powers agreed to create a system of "mandates" for the territories outside Europe previously controlled by those defeated in the First World War, mainly Germany and the Ottoman Empire. Based on the "level of development" each population was assumed to have achieved and on the claim that because of their superior civilization the victors had a moral responsibility to guide the less developed, Article 22 of the Covenant of the League of Nations stipulated that the mandates would be divided into three groups. Class A mandates referred to peoples in areas formerly controlled by the Ottoman Empire who had "reached a stage of development where their existence as independent nations can be provisionally recognized subject to the rendering of administrative advice and assistance by a Mandatory." Britain became the mandatory of Iraq, Palestine, and Transjordan, while France assumed the role of temporary caretaker of Lebanon and Syria. Class B mandates were imposed on populations in Central Africa. Populations in that region were deemed to be distinctly less developed than those in Class A mandates and, thus, in need of substantially greater direct supervision by the colonial powers. Britain assumed full authority for Tanganyika, and divided jurisdiction with France over Togoland and the Cameroons. Belgium became the sole mandatory power in the Rwanda–Burundi area.

Based on the assertion that the populations in South West Africa and some of the South Pacific islands were extremely underdeveloped, Article 22 classified them as Class C mandates and stipulated that they would be "administered under the laws of the mandatory as integral portions of its territory." Henceforth, South Africa administered South West Africa; New Zealand took over the former German colony of Samoa; and Australia gained control over Nauru and New Guinea. Tokyo took over Germany's Pacific islands north of the equator, and retained control of Shantung, an area in China inhabited by some thirty million people.[9]

From nationalism to ethno-nationalism in Africa

By the start of the 1960s the consensus throughout the world system was that the lack of political, economic, social, or educational preparedness on the part of certain colonies to exist as independent, sovereign entities would no longer be accepted as a rationale for delaying independence.[10] This change in attitude had a radical effect on the structure of the world system. In the Middle East, a mixture of war exhaustion, financial troubles, and nationalist pressure persuaded Britain and France to leave the area. By the mid-1970s there were no European colonies left in South and Southeastern Asia (with the exception of Hong Kong), and the entire African continent had freed itself from direct European domination. In the Republic of South Africa, Namibia, and Zimbabwe, however, the descendants of the European colonizers retained nearly absolute power for a number of additional years.[11] And yet, though of the vast array of sovereign states that emerged from the defunct European empires almost none experienced political stability and financial prosperity immediately, few were forced to live through the destruction endured by the inhabitants of the newly born African states.

It has been proposed that sooner or later colonization compels its victims to ask: how can we free ourselves from colonizers and ensure that no one else will attempt to overpower us again? In the case of Africa, its leaders transformed the general question into a set of explicit queries. Can we, Africans, stand on our own? How can we generate self-reliance? How can we forge a racial identity in an environment that is racist and discriminates against us? How should we, as elites, distribute power? As Africa's indigenous elites sought answers, they also conjectured as to whether there could be a balance

between continuity with the past, change, and adaptations to new circumstances; and they wondered where the balance would lie if it did exist.[12]

Though nationalist movements had started to emerge throughout Africa
prior to 1914, the one that received the greatest international attention materialized outside the continent. In 1900, H. Sylvester-Williams, a West Indies
lawyer practicing in London, called for a "Pan-African" Conference to protest the "stealing of land in all colonies, racial discrimination and [to] deal
with other issues of interest to blacks."[13] The attendees, most of whom were
from England, the West Indies, and the USA, sent a letter to Europe's leaders
requesting that blacks in all areas under colonial rule be granted "the right to
responsible governments."[14] The appeal received little attention. In 1918, W.
E.B. Du Bois, an African-American activist and scholar, helped revive Sylvester-
Williams's idea by pressing Wilson to address Africa's problems during his
trip to Paris in 1919. As explained by *The Chicago Tribune* in its January 19,
1919, edition, Du Bois, along with Robert R. Moton, the head of the Tuske-
gee Institute, hoped that leaders attending the Paris Peace Conference would
agree to "modernize the dark continent."[15]

Though *The Chicago Tribune* noted that the request would in all likelihood
be disregarded, Du Bois persisted. While in Paris, he set up the First Pan-
African Congress and brought together fifty-seven delegates from fifteen
countries, including several from Africa. The participants did not demand
outright emancipation. Instead, they requested the establishment of a "code
of law for the international protection of the natives of Africa." They stipulated that the land in Africa and its natural resources be held in trust for the
natives, that the investment of capital in Africa be regulated to prevent the
exploitation of its natives and the exhaustion of its natural wealth, that slavery and capital punishment be abolished, that every native African child be
given the right to receive an education at public expense, and that Africa's
natives be permitted to participate in local and tribal governments.[16] Three
additional congresses were held during the 1920s, each with the intent of
creating a solid organization, expanding its African membership, promoting
the principle of absolute equality of races, and reemphasizing or refining the
principles stipulated at the first congress. By 1929, the Pan-African movement
had lost much of its original impetus, due to internal divisions, a substantial
drop in the number of African participants, and the quiet, but firm, opposition by the colonial powers.

Africa's intellectual elites, however, did not remain idle. Emboldened by
their Western education, they averred that the continent's liberation had to be
guided by a philosophy. Of the numerous and varied ideas they had assimi-
lated from Europe, they placed nationalism above all others.[17] To contest
effectively Europe's rule, they argued, they had to engender a nationalist sentiment that would authenticate the voices of the "natives."[18] Notions about
the kind of nationalism that they should adopt evolved. Members of the ear-
liest modern intelligentsia, grateful for their conversion to Christianity and for
the fact that the acquirement of a Western education had helped them

improve their own social standing, proposed that they reject African culture and emulate the civilization of their masters. Convinced that their past practices had failed to prevent the trespassers from enlarging their power, the early intelligentsia came to believe that Europeans were "technically powerful and intellectually superior," and that the best way to offset their control was by adopting their ways. In time, new members of the intellectual elite rejected this perspective and contended that the Europeans would never stop discriminating against Africans, even those who were educated and whose social standing had improved. A movement emerged in the second half of the nineteenth century partly as a response to the claim in some of Europe's leading intellectual centers that different races possessed dissimilar levels of intellect and that Africans, as a whole, had the lowest. The movement, named "Ethiopeanism," called for the development of race consciousness, together with African solidarity and autonomy. Advocates of Ethiopeanism did not reject the West wholeheartedly. Rather, they argued that to achieve emancipation Africans had to strive for self-discovery, which entailed both eliciting the constructive elements of their cultures and traditions, and taking advantage of the knowledge imparted by Western education. The convergence of the two mores gave rise to new religious and cultural movements throughout Africa.[19] Neither of these two perspectives, however, suited Africa's traditional elites. Traditionalists, composed principally of Africans chiefs and kings who had ruled prior to the arrival of the colonists and who continued to lead during the colonial period, insisted that Western civilization should be avoided, because Africa's old ways were better.[20]

Italy's 1935 invasion of Ethiopia, an actor that for Africans stood as the embodiment of freedom, helped strengthen the nationalist fervor throughout Africa. For those who had long focused on the "evils" of imperialism, the assault reaffirmed their claim that European imperialism was motivated by the demand for markets and raw materials.[21] Ethiopia's inability to repel the attackers, moreover, warned them that if they hoped to expel the colonizers, they had to acknowledge that Europe was exploiting them not as members of any one particular ethnic group but as blacks.

It took another world war for African nationalism to become a commanding anti-colonial force. The war had two distinct complementary effects. First, the demand to partake in a conflict not of Africa's doing, the repeated racial abuses experienced by many of the African soldiers who participated in the conflict, and the knowledge that the colonizers were relying on Africa's own natural resources to carry on the struggle, helped fuel further an anger that was already intense. Second, the rationalization put forward by the Americans, the British, and the French that the war was being fought for self-determination and the right of all people to choose their own form of government, helped legitimize the calls for independence voiced by African nationalist groups.

By 1945, with the winds of war favoring the Allied forces, advocates of Pan-Africanism intensified their campaign. At the Pan-African Congress held in Manchester, England, they composed the *Declaration to the Colonial People*, which stated: "We affirm the right of all colonial peoples to control their own destiny. All colonies must be free from foreign imperialistic control, whether political or economic."[22] Independence did not follow immediately. Britain, the European actor most attuned to Africa's nationalist movements, intended to engage in a measured devolution of its colonies to friendly successor states. France and Portugal, on the other hand, sought to foster the notion that their colonies were integrated into the homeland. Belgium, however, showed little interest in addressing the issue. By the second half of the 1950s, some of these actors had been forced to accept that independence would come about much faster than they had originally estimated.[23]

A number of factors helped accelerate the process. Relinquishing control of India in the case of Britain, and of Indochina in the case of France, impelled both European empires to concede that their heydays as two of the world's leading powers existed only in their memories. Furthermore, by the latter part of the 1950s, with their economies mending rapidly, Britain and France recognized that they had done so with little contribution from their colonies. The Cold War also had a critical effect. Aware that in its effort to enlarge its prestige worldwide the Soviet Union had been siding with Africa's nationalist forces, neither Britain nor France wanted to make Moscow's venture easier. As explained by Kwame Nkrumah, Ghana's leading political figure, had "it not been for Russia, the African liberation movement would have suffered the most brutal persecution."[24]

The initial movement towards independence came in Northern Africa. Libya, a former colony of Italy, provided the breakthrough by gaining its independence in 1951. After Libya, there was a five-year interlude before Tunisia, Sudan, and Morocco replicated its achievement. Ghana's independence in 1957 encouraged surrounding colonies to press for their own. The gates broke almost wide open in 1960, when Nigeria and most of the former French colonies became states in their own right. As the 1960s moved on, so did the movement towards independence throughout the rest of Africa. In the meantime, the state of euphoria that overtook Africans in 1960 ran its course quickly.

In December 1958, at the *All African People Conference*, Du Bois declared: "If Africa unites, it will be because each part, each nation, each tribe gives up a part of the heritage for the good of the whole." Nkrumah claimed to share Du Bois's dream. In his work *Consciencism: Philosophy and Ideology for Decolonization*, Ghana's new president called for the creation of a new harmonious society from the multiple heritages of indigenous people, Muslims, and Euro-Christians, after they had all freed themselves from colonial rule. The move towards a United States of Africa took its first formal step when Ghana and Guinea formed a political union in 1961. At that time, the expectation was that Mali and Liberia would soon join them; eventually, only Mali did.

By 1963, a total of thirty-one colonies had gained their freedom; but in their new condition, they refused to surrender part of their sovereignty to an African union. The Pan-African dream came to an end in 1966, when a coup d'état ousted Nkrumah. An explosion of civil wars and political takeovers throughout other parts of Africa both preceded and followed his political demise. By the end of the twentieth century, Africa had become "the most conflict ridden region of the World and the only region in which the number of armed conflicts" was on the increase.[25] The nationalist ideology that had helped unite competing interests during the struggle against the colonial powers gave way to civil strife between antagonistic groups within each state.[26] More to the point, the various nationalist ideologies that helped give rise to a kaleidoscope of African states proved to be nothing more than a colonial superstructure that in many instances was eventually overwhelmed by ethnic and religious schisms. It was not long before African states that had shown economic potential at their inception found themselves nearly bankrupt and, once again, dependent on the developed world. Short analyses of four cases should help explain why so many African states were soon overtaken by internal anarchy.

Rwanda

Rwanda, like many other African colonies, had the misfortune of being ruled during different periods by two rival European powers. In 1890, at a conference in Brussels, Europe's main leaders agreed to grant Germany control over Rwanda and Burundi. From the moment they assumed possession of their new colony, the Germans differentiated their subjects according to certain physical characteristics. For them, the Tutsis, who during that time amounted to no more than sixteen percent of the population, "were as unlike as they could be to the common order of the natives of the surrounding districts. They had fine oval faces, large eyes, and high noses, denoting the best blood of Abyssinia." Many of those who possessed those features had been serving the leaders of the African kingdoms in the Great Lakes region, and therefore they were presumed to be more powerful and more capable than the Hutus.[27] Germans portrayed the Hutus as having "flat noses, thick lips, low foreheads, and brachycephalic heads," as being "both timid and lazy," as being afflicted by a "childlike character," and as belonging to "the class of serfs."[28] By the time it was forced to surrender its colony at the end of the First World War, Germany had laid the foundation of a pyramid-style feudal system, with the colonists and "Tutsi lords" at the top.[29]

With the First World War over, Belgium became Rwanda's new overlord. Determined to ensure that its outpost would provide a profit, Belgium reinforced the belief that the Tutsis were superior to the Hutus, and increased its reliance on the former. As reward for their services, Belgium extended the Tutsis considerable privileges, particularly in education. It was not long before a class partition between the two indigenous groups had emerged, followed by intense ethnic resentment.[30]

The Second World War and the USA's increasing global role forced Belgium to reconfigure Rwanda's social infrastructure and encourage the establishment of democratic political institutions. As the 1950s moved along, the Hutus became emboldened by their expanding freedom, and the Tutsis became troubled by their gradual loss of power. In late 1959, an increasingly restive Hutu population sparked a revolt that resulted in the overthrow of the last Tutsi monarch. Enraged by the action, a group of Tutsis retaliated with an assassination attempt on the leader of the largest Hutu political party. The Hutus responded with direct attacks on the Tutsis. During the struggle, between twenty thousand and one hundred thousand Tutsis died and more than one hundred and fifty thousand fled to neighboring countries. Conscious that other European powers were abandoning their colonies and that any further attempt to retain control over Rwanda would be exceedingly costly, Belgium granted the colony its independence in 1962. By then, Tutsis had become convinced that the Hutus intended to dominate the political arena fully. One of the Hutus' first measures was to install a system of quotas that limited the access Tutsis could have to education and the civil service.

A coup that installed a military dictatorship in 1973 was followed by elections in 1978, 1983, and 1988 that brought to power, and retained in power, the same leader. By 1990, with the economy in disarray and displaced Tutsis demanding the right to return to their native land and be recognized as Rwandans, the country found itself once again facing an uncertain future. In October, with the backing of their newly formed Rwandan Patriotic Front, rebel Tutsi forces invaded Rwanda. Rwanda's president responded with a pogrom against Tutsis and any Hutu who assisted them. The war continued until the middle of 1992, when both sides agreed to a cease-fire and the commencement of negotiations sponsored by the Organization of African Unity. But in 1994, after a plane carrying the presidents of Rwanda and Burundi was shot down, violence erupted once again. This time, its magnitude reached horrendous proportions. Between early April and the start of July, some nine hundred and thirty-seven thousand Tutsis and moderate Hutus died at the hands of Hutu militia groups. The rebel Tutsi forces renewed their attacks on the Rwandan government, and brought its downfall swiftly.

Blame for the conflict that developed between the Tutsis and the Hutus cannot be placed solely on their respective shoulders. Prior to the appearance of the colonialists, the Tutsis dominated the governing system and perceived themselves as being smarter and braver than the Hutus, but they still viewed both groups as Rwandans. For them, the terms "Tutsi" and "Hutu" reflected not racial differences but distinct social castes or classes. A Tutsi, according to one of their proverbs, was "a Hutu with 10 cattle." Both "[spoke] the same language, [had] the same culture, [lived] on the same hills, ... [were] the same people."[31] However, upon their arrival the Europeans referred to their own racial prejudices to reinforce the dissimilarity. They relied chiefly on the Tutsis to rule, and favored them when conferring privileges.

In October 1959, Gregoire Kayibanda created the Party of the Movement of Emancipation of the Bahutu (PARMEHUTU). The party's political objective was to defend the "humble people" (the Hutus) from the abuses by the "feudals" (the Tutsis). PARMEHUTU made it clear that its intent was to "restore the country to its owners" and suggested that if the Tutsis were unhappy they could "return to Abysinnia." Rwanda, it remarked, "is the country of the Bahutu (Bantu) and all of those, white and black, Tutsi, Europoean, and other provenance, who abandon feudo-colonialist ambitions." As time went by, and Rwanda's Hutu leaders encountered many of the economic, political, and social problems typically faced by ethnically divided, newly created states, they passed on the blame to the Tutsis. "Tutsi domination," stated PARMEHUTU in a pamphlet published in the 1970s, "is the origin of all evil the Hutu have suffered since the beginning of time. It is comparable to a termite mound teeming with every cruelty known to man."[32] And thus, the Tutsis became the "cockroaches" who had "infested Rwanda" and had to "be eliminated." Only after the total elimination of the Tutsis, emphasized those Hutus who had adopted a radical stand, would it be possible to create a just system in Rwanda.

In sum, Rwanda's post-colonial period was steadily overtaken by a radical form of ethno-cultural nationalism, one that progressively rejected the accommodation of different ethnic groups under the state's umbrella and advocated, instead, the creation of a community that shared the illusory ethnic attributes of the Hutus.[33]

Congo

West of Rwanda and Burundi, another source of ethnic conflict emerged. In 1955, the common perception among Belgium's leaders was that they would rule Congo for the next thirty to fifty years. They reasoned that it would take them that long to create an educated Congolese elite capable of taking over the reigns of government. Members of the Congolese elite disagreed as to whether the decolonization timetable was realistic. In a document titled *Manifesto of Conscience Africaine*, a group created by Catholic missionaries supported the view that Belgian Congo would need additional time before it became fully independent. Another organization, named *Alliance des Bakongo* (ABAKO), which was committed to the promotion of the interests of the Bakongo (or Kongo) people, called for an immediate transfer of power. Eventually, some of the competing parties agreed that Congo should achieve this end between 1962 and 1964. During that same period, the Belgian and the Congolese were not of one mind regarding whether the newly independent state should assume a federalist or a unitary structure. As tension in Congo mounted, with ABAKO inciting violence in order to accelerate the independence process, Belgium's leaders decided to cut their losses. They announced that Congo would become an independent state on June 30, 1960, and would adopt a federalist constitution and a parliamentary form of government.[34]

These decisions plunged Congo into chaos. In Congo, just as in Rwanda, a number of political leaders and groups advocated ethno-cultural nationalism. Patrice Lumumba, the creator of the *Mouvement National Congolais*, was not one of them. From his early days as a politician, Lumumba, who assumed the role of prime minister in Congo's first independent government, tried to build a national party that minimized regional and ethnic differences. Under the new system, however, political leaders and groups determined to promote their own regional and ethnic interests immediately sought to undermine Lumumba's effort.

On July 5, the Congolese army revolted in Leopoldville, and the conflict spread rapidly to other barracks throughout the country. Several factors engendered the rebellion. That the army was still led by white Belgian officers played a critical role. So did the fact that during the colonial period the Congolese soldiers had been indoctrinated in the view that their civilian kin were barbarians and savages who needed to be controlled, frequently by violent means. Further, the army was made up of ethnic groups, such as the Bakongo, the Bangala, the Batetla, and the Baluba, who were often hostile to one another. Five days after the start of the mutiny, Belgium claimed that its citizens were being threatened, and intervened militarily. The day after the invasion, Moise Tshombe, a long-time adversary of Lumumba and a close ally of Belgian industrial companies that mined copper, gold, and uranium, announced the independence of mineral-rich Katanga, a region located in the southeastern portion of Congo.[35] As violence continued to mount, and fearful that Belgium would attempt to regain control of its former colony, the Congo's government requested that the United Nations (UN) intervene militarily in order to evict the foreign forces. With Washington acting as the leading advocate of UN intervention, the first set of troops arrived on July 15. A series of actions and counteractions, which in time drew the involvement of the Soviet Union, led the USA's Central Intelligence Agency (CIA) to orchestrate the assassination of Lumumba. By 1963, the UN forces, with support from the USA, retook Katanga and reinstalled Tshombe, who was in exile in Angola, as president. Tshombe's term in power came to an end in 1965, when Joseph Mobutu, backed by Western military forces, seized power. Mobutu, with the approval of Washington and its Western European allies, established a one-party system and promoted himself as the one leader who could maintain stability and contain the spread of communism in Congo. In 1971, he changed Congo's name to Zaire and ruled the newly named state until May 1997, when Laurent-Desire Kabila deposed him. During his rule, Mobutu amassed a personal fortune, while his country, rich in minerals, plunged into poverty.

Congolese nationalism did not bring independence to Congo; it was brought, instead, by Belgium's fear that an attempt to retain control of its colony would prove to be exceedingly costly. In the absence of a common nationalist ideology that might have helped them unite, and unable to refer to a common language, history, and culture of their own, Congo's various political groups searched for their identities in the pre-colonial period. Ethnic divisions engendered antagonism, which was buttressed by great disparity in wealth between regions. Any ethnic group that controlled a resource-rich region sought to limit the extent to which it would have to share its wealth. Under such conditions, it was not uncommon for a political leader to try to assume dictatorial powers and to suppress any form of political opposition.

Nigeria

A third African entity afflicted by ethnic and regional divisions during the immediate years after independence was Nigeria. Nigeria's path to independence was the by-product of internal and external forces. Internally, educated Nigerian elites began to criticize the colonial administration and demand constitutional progress toward self-rule as early as 1934. Nigeria's participation in the Second World War, and the human and material costs inflicted on its people, strengthened its leaders' resolve to force Britain to institute major constitutional reforms, advance education, Africanize the civil service, promote economic development, and liberalize the native authorities.[36] Nigeria's nationalist drive had its intended effect. The very high human and material costs incurred by the Second World War on Britain diluted its capability and eagerness to remain a colonial power. As explained by Sir Arthur Richards, Britain's governor to Nigeria for the 1943–1948 period, to "have deferred constitutional reform [in the case of Nigeria] would have required a degree of direct moral and financial support which the British Government" was not prepared to provide.[37]

In view of Nigeria's ethnic, regional, and religious composition, British and Nigerian leaders agreed to design a federalist constitution. Three large ethnic groups—Hausa in the northern area, Yoruba in the southwestern region, and Igbo in the southeastern section—dominated Nigeria's political environment. These regional ethnic cleavages were further exacerbated by two other problems. First, Nigeria depended for its revenues and its balance of payments on its oilfields, most of which were located in Biafra. And second, most of the Igbo were Christians, while the majority of the Yoruba and Hausa were Muslims.[38]

The establishment of a "federal system of government is a result of compromise. It is a compromise between centrifugal and centripetal forces. It rests on a particular attitude on the part of the peoples of federating units who desire union but not unity."[39] By the time Nigeria attained its independence, its leaders had achieved the needed compromise. Three separate regions granted the central government the authority and power to create an army and a police force, and to assume responsibility for external relations. Each region, in turn, was dominated by a party that drew support from one home ethnic base and peripheral backing from minorities elsewhere, designed its own constitution, and had its own premier, governor, public service, judiciary, and marketing boards.[40]

Chaos did not follow independence right away; it took some six years to simmer. During that period, the northern region controlled the federal parliament, while each of the three regions sought to protect and enhance its own autonomy. In the first month of 1966, however, several Igbo army officers, certain that the interests of their region and ethnic group were not being properly served, assassinated the prime minister of the federal government and the prime ministers of the northern and southwestern regions, and installed an Igbo general as the new head of state. The opposition retaliated, and after six months of intensive fighting it killed the Igbo leader and replaced him with a northern Christian officer. The leader of the southeastern region responded by seceding from the federation and creating the new independent state of Biafra. Determined not to lose oil-rich Biafra, the federal government moved aggressively against the rebel forces and was able to reintegrate the region back into the state.[41] A military regime ruled Nigeria until 1979, when it returned power to civilian leaders. By 1983, however, politics at the state level had once again become localized, clientelistic, and corrupt, compelling the military to seize power "to save [Nigeria] from imminent collapse."[42]

Immanuel Wallerstein once wrote that the "subordination of private and sectional claims to the needs of the whole, is inevitably diminished" after independence is attained.[43] Nigeria exemplifies his argument. Following independence, Nigerians replaced the nationalism that helped them free themselves from British rule with ethno-cultural nationalism. For many in Nigeria, ethno-cultural nationalism became "another mechanism for protecting local and regional interests."[44]

Ghana

Students of Africa's post-independence experience often wonder whether Ghana during its early decades as a free state could have avoided the trauma encountered by many of the other actors in the continent. Many attribute Ghana's initial inability to elude the same ordeal to the political performance of its leader, Kwame Nkrumah. Such a conclusion may seem reasonable at first light, for, in the words of a keen student of Ghana's politics, the "story of Ghana during its first decade of independence is primarily the story of ... Kwame Nkrumah."[45] Though the argument has some merit, it fails to give sufficient weight to Ghana's domestic composition. Its internal makeup enhanced noticeably the likelihood that the state, despite its leader's best intentions, would have to endure substantial internal volatility during its early life as an independent actor.

Ghana's nationalist movement gained momentum immediately after the end of the Second World War. In 1947, Nkrumah was asked to become secretary general of the United Gold Coast Convention (UGCC), an organization originally designed "to address the problem of reconciling the leadership of the intelligentsia with the broad mass of the people."[46] Nkrumah, who had spent ten years studying and teaching in the USA and then had moved to London, arrived in the Gold Coast (as Ghana was known prior to independence) determined to speed up the move towards sovereignty. Divisions within the intelligentsia, and between members of the intelligentsia and the colonial leaders, ensued immediately. As the strain provoked by the fracture rose, so did the zeal on the part of Nkrumah and some of his closest associates to support the use of violence in order to accelerate the liberalization process. Confident that they would be able to work more effectively with the Gold Coast's traditional leaders, the British authorities called for the creation of a committee composed of British representatives and UGCC leaders, minus Nkrumah, in order to propose constitutional reforms. The committee generated recommendations that included the establishment of an all-African legislature, elected directly by the people in the more developed areas, and the formation of a cabinet led by eight individuals selected from the Ghanaian legislature and three appointed by the British governor. Nkrumah, who by then had formed the Convention People's Party (CPP), referred to the proposed constitution as "an imperialist fraud," and called for a series of strikes and boycotts. He and a few of his associates were soon jailed, but they were released when his party won the general elections held in early 1951. Aware that they had no choice but to work with Nkrumah, the British asked him to form the new government. He did, and ruled until 1957, when the Gold Coast became the independent state of Ghana.[47]

Ghanaians did not proceed towards independence with a common vision. During the three years preceding 1957, Nkrumah had to contend with a compelling challenge led by the National Liberation Movement (NLM), which was backed by the Northern People's Party, the Muslim Association Party, and the Togoland Congress. The core stipulation of the challengers was that the power of the central government be restricted with a federal constitution. In view of Ghana's population distribution, along with its ethnic and religious composition, the demand carried considerable political credence. Ghana's population, which is concentrated in the area along the coast, in the northern areas near the Cote d'Ivoire, and in the cities of Accra and Kumasi, is divided into small ethnic groups. The members of the various groups speak more than fifty languages and dialects. The most important linguistic groups are the Akans, the Guans, the Ga, the Ewe, the Moshi, and the Dagomba, and each dominates a particular region. About forty-two percent of Ghanaians are Christians, twelve percent are Muslims, and some thirty-eight percent practice some form of indigenous religion.

Nkrumah's opposition to the creation of a federalist state was built on the belief that in order to succeed, Ghanaians had to combat external and internal enemies simultaneously. The external enemies, he claimed, were the capitalist states and their multinational corporations; the internal adversary was the African bourgeoisie, who had joined forces with the Western bourgeoisie to prevent Africa from developing. In this struggle, explained Nkrumah, Ghanaians had to be led by an individual and a party intensely committed to a "nationalist socialist" ideology and determined to use force whenever necessary to destroy internal enemies. As Nkrumah noted when he sought to explain his willingness to resort to armed force to achieve his internal goals, "constitutions are powerless before guns."[48] Thus, shortly after independence, Nkrumah pressured the legislature to pass a number of highly repressive measures. The legislature, under the leadership of Nkrumah's party, approved the Deportation Act, the Avoidance of Discrimination Act, and the Preventive Detention Act. The first one was used to deport anti-CPP aliens in Kumasi; the second one, to ban all the existing political parties; and the third one, to imprison political foes for up to five years. In addition, Nkrumah suspended the pro-NLM Kumasi City Council, and declared a state of emergency in Kumasi.[49]

Deeply influenced by Marxist and socialist ideologies, Nkrumah advanced policies designed to provide social services, such as education, community development, health, and nursing. He also promoted public services that included electricity, water, and communication. Eventually his policies proved to be too costly. Ghana, which in 1957 had a robust balance of payments and a substantial foreign currency reserve, was bankrupt by 1966. It was afflicted by the absence of food and consumer goods and effective governmental services, and it was burdened by governmental corruption and oppression.[50] On February 24, 1966, the Ghanaian army and police overthrew Nkrumah and his cabinet, suspended the constitution, and dissolved the legislature and the CPP.

The first Ghanaian military regime ruled until October 1969, when it transferred power to a newly elected civilian government. Failure by the civilian government to control inflation led the military to intervene once again in early 1972. Futile attempts to engender internal stability and to create a reliable government resulted in a violent military coup in June 1979. The Third Republic, with a new, Western-styled constitution, and under the leadership of a newly elected president and parliament, was inaugurated later that same year. The restructuring did not have the intended effects, so in 1981 Flight Lieutenant Jerry John Rawlings, the same leader who orchestrated the 1979 coup, deposed the civilian government, assumed power, and banned all political parties. Rawlings ruled unchallenged until 1992, when Ghana adopted a new constitution and restored multiparty politics. Rawlings was elected president that same year and was reelected in 1996. John Kuffor succeeded Rawlings, who could not run for a third term, in a free and fair election in 2000.

Ghana's problems were distinctly less destructive than those encountered by some of the other newly freed African states. It started with a healthier economy and was led by a leader who recognized from the beginning the difficulties he would encounter in governing citizens who had deeply insular interests and who viewed the state as a distant and impersonal entity. And yet, to retain Ghana's unity, Nkrumah, in addition to promoting a national-ist–socialist ideology, imposed measures that immediately contradicted the traditional inclinations of its people and, at the same time, made it possible for those in power to abuse it.

A bird's-eye view

Throughout much of Africa, those who gained power in the early post-independence days rapidly unveiled their opposition to creating a competitive political system. Based on the contention that their intent was to build nation-states, they favored the formation of autocratic regimes. In such systems, few had access to power; patronage dictated appointments and promotions to state jobs, the judiciary, and state corporations; violence was used repeatedly to oppose organized opposition; and a single political philosophy was applied to procure the backing of the masses.[51] As these measures were applied, those excluded from the process—typically, the members of a different regional, ethnic, or religious group—mounted counter-steps designed to restructure the parceling out of goods.

From the analysis of the post-colonial experiences of four African states, one cannot encapsulate the fortunes of the continent's other states under a single generalization. A number of patterns, however, can be discerned. First, most African colonies had little difficulty attaining independence after the end of the Second World War. Two factors contributed to this development. Most of the European actors were deeply concerned about the political, material, and human costs of retaining control of their colonies. The import of this condition was boosted by the creation in virtually each African colony of a nationalist ideology in the form of an anti-European consciousness.

Second, as the leaders of many of the newly formed African states assumed their responsibilities, they were convinced that the post-independence period would be marked by considerable accomplishments. This sentiment was generally shared by the masses. Third, in several cases, the nationalist sentiment that helped many of the African colonies gain independence was displaced by a narrower form of identity—ethnicity. Fourth, the arousal of ethnic identity stimulated rancor between different groups. Fifth, when control of a region's material resources was at stake, hostility between contending ethnic groups instigated civil wars. Sixth, a number of African leaders used the continued threat or presence of violence as a pretext to reinstate the same kind of authoritarian-type system imposed by the colonial powers on their colonies. In time, one-party regimes became the rule rather than the exception. And seventh, failure on the part of individual African states to create a unifying nationalist ideology able to override ethnic and regional differences, placed them at the mercy of patently more powerful non-African states, multinational corporations, and international financial institutions.

The rise of anti-neoliberalism in Latin America

Latin American states have pursued their own distinct, and sometimes conflicting, interests since the end of the nineteenth century. Despite their differences, they have generally shared one grievance: Washington's propensity to
meddle in their domestic affairs. From the end of the Spanish–American war
until the early 1930s, the USA demanded the establishment of stable and pro-
business regimes in Cuba, Nicaragua, Mexico, the Dominican Republic,
Haiti, Honduras, Costa Rica, and Guatemala. Washington's methods varied.
In some cases it relied almost entirely on rhetorical statements or feeble diplomatic actions; in other instances it took forceful steps, such as engaging in
direct military intervention, reorganizing local military forces, favoring specific political groups, supervising elections, or pushing for specific civic and
social reforms.[52] In 1928, Latin American leaders, tired of Washington's
ongoing disregard for their countries' sovereignty, demanded at an Inter-
American Conference held in Cuba that the USA renounce its policy of
intervention.

Aware of the strong anti-American sentiment its involvement in Latin
American affairs had generated, and realizing that no extra hemispheric
challenge lingered over the horizon, Washington opted for a less brazen
approach. In 1934, President Franklin D. Roosevelt expressed formally the
USA's decision not to intervene in the domestic affairs of Latin American
states. The pledge, however, did not signify that the USA was ready to permit
its southern brethren to act without any form of external supervision. Thereafter, and until the end of the Second World War, Washington made allow-
ances for Latin American states led by pro-US dictatorial regimes; or it relied
on diplomatic channels to voice its discontent of, and challenge, leaders
whom it considered untrustworthy or feared were German sympathizers. In
short, throughout much of this period, Washington continued to intercede if it
estimated that the strategic and economic interests of the USA were being
threatened.

The overall format of the foreign policy of the USA toward Latin America
changed little during the post-Second World War period. Fearful that communism would encroach on Latin America, Washington warned its weaker
partners that it would resort to force, if necessary, to contain its spread in the
region. It conveyed the message in no uncertain terms in 1954, when President Dwight Eisenhower authorized the CIA to topple Guatemala's government. Though Washington's covert operation against Cuba in 1961 failed to
depose the new Castro regime, it reminded potential Latin American foes that
the USA was prepared to infringe on their sovereignty if its interests were
threatened. Anyone who doubted Washington's resolve was forced to recon-
sider her or his initial estimation following the 1962 Cuban missile crisis.
Subsequent interventions, either political or military, took place in Brazil in
1964, the Dominican Republic in 1965, Chile in 1973, Grenada in 1983,
Nicaragua throughout much of the 1980s, and Panama during the 1989–1990

period. These interventions simply reaffirmed Washington's long-standing conviction that, as the Western Hemisphere's hegemon, it was entitled to shape the domestic political structure of the regimes south of the USA's borders.

During the early years of the 1970s, Washington adjusted its ideology. Keynesianism, which promotes international trade and "productive" capital flows while overtly limiting short-term "unproductive" capital flows, was modified by neoliberal ideas. Advocated by the likes of Milton Friedman and Friedrich Hayek, the neoliberal model opposes government intervention in markets as prescribed by Keynesianism. It contends that the most effective way to slow inflation, stimulate economic growth, and improve the financial position of the state is by improving the mobility of capital. The neoliberal model gained substantial backing in the 1980s, following France's failed attempt to reenergize its economy.[53] By the middle of the 1990s, very few analysts throughout the USA and Latin America questioned Washington's new approach. Democracy seemed to flourish, and economic and financial structural changes appeared to generate the kind of advances so many had predicted. But then came the financial crises in Asia, Russia, Brazil, and Argentina. Soon, few throughout Latin America could fail to realize that major social dislocations had accompanied the rapid political, economic, and financial changes advocated by Washington. Sizeable increases in poverty, unemployment, and underemployment suddenly gave way to political discontent and to the accusation that the "Washington consensus" was not the right or just way. Left-wing populist political leaders won the presidencies in Brazil, Venezuela, Argentina, Uruguay, Bolivia, and Ecuador, by contending that neoliberalism was the cause of their countries' ills.

Not all of the new leaders rejected outright their countries' neoliberalist policy reforms. Still, a few made it clear that henceforth they, not Washington, would design the rules that would regulate their behavior, and they insisted that the new system would prioritize the needs of their own industries and the citizens they represented. Backed by rising nationalism, a number of Latin American leaders questioned the claim by the USA Treasury Department, the World Bank, and the IMF that the best way to stimulate growth was to lower trade barriers and deregulate markets quickly.[54] Though they agreed that changes had to take place, they stressed that to facilitate growth, Latin American states had to protect their own markets during the initial stages. The pace at which they opened and deregulated their markets, moreover, had to correspond with the development of a solid infrastructure—such as the creation of banks, roads, and schools. Latin American leaders noted that China did not lower its trade barriers until after it had achieved substantial economic growth. They also emphasized that states in the developed world, including the USA, were hypocritical, because they continued to protect their own textile producers, fund their own farmers, and safeguard their own maritime and construction industries. Failure on the part of leaders of the developed and developing nations to address their differences at the international meetings held in Cancun, Mexico, and Mar del Plata, Argentina, in 2003 and 2005, respectively, indicated that many throughout Latin America would continue to defy Washington's dictates. The rise to power of populist figures in Venezuela, Bolivia, Ecuador, and Nicaragua—leaders who were unafraid to use fiery rhetoric to rebuke George W. Bush and extol Fidel Castro—was another indication that certain Latin American states were determined to be the designers of their own destiny.

Political Islam versus nationalism

The power vacuum that emerged in several African states, and the rise of anti-neoliberal sentiments throughout several Latin American and other less-developed states, generated strain. However, it was not as severe as the international tension spawned by the upsurge of radical Islam. To uncover the modern roots of Islamic radicalism, it is necessary to begin with agreements formulated by two of Europe's leading powers during the First World War.

In 1915, as it became evident that the First World War would splinter the Ottoman Empire, Britain and France began to negotiate ways to partition its territory. Shortly afterward, the British and French cabinets secretly formulated the Sykes–Picot Agreement. The accord stipulated that after the war France would rule Lebanon and exert exclusive influence over Syria, while Britain would gain control over the Mesopotamian provinces of Basra and Baghdad, and the Palestinian ports of Acre and Haifa. By 1917, Lloyd George had changed his mind. In April, the prime minister informed Britain's ambassador to Paris that he considered the Sykes–Picot Agreement unimportant and intended to advocate the development of a Jewish homeland in Palestine under British control. On the last day of October, the British cabinet approved the Balfour Declaration, which stated that Britain would establish under its dominion "a national home for the Jewish people" in Palestine.[55]

Lloyd George and his associates based their decisions on three rationales. First, they were convinced that a Jewish Palestine would give Britain a land road from Egypt to India, and would link its empires in Africa and Asia. Second, they believed that Britain had a moral responsibility to help Jews return to their ancient homeland. And third, they were certain that were Britain to assure Arabs living in the region that their civil and religious rights would be protected, they would accept the decision.[56] Soon after announcing the Declaration, British forces captured Jerusalem.[57] Less than a year later, they marched into Damascus. And on October 29, 1918, Turkish delegates from the Ottoman Empire signed an armistice with Britain. Germany's decision to call for a truce in November compelled the Turks to relinquish control of the Arab territories they had governed for centuries to France and Britain.[58]

The agreements reached by Britain and France in the Middle East left little doubt that Wilson's call for an end to power politics had fallen on deaf ears. In fact, in the case of Britain, it was common for some of its leading figures to claim that its citizens "never had a better cause to look the world in the face; never did our voice count for more in the council of nations, or in determining the future destinies of mankind."[59] For a brief while, the hubris seemed warranted. Germany was temporarily out of the power game; the USA remained unsure about how it should comport itself in the world arena; the Bolsheviks were struggling to consolidate their power in Russia; and the Ottoman Empire was in tatters. Based on these developments, it was not unreasonable for France and Britain to assume that they would be able to strengthen their hands in the Middle East, Africa, and Asia. But it was not long before some of these same leaders recognized that their assumption was unjustified. With Egypt's anti-British revolt as his reference point, Arthur Balfour wrote in a letter to Britain's high commissioner in Egypt that the unrest "is doubtless part of a world movement which takes different forms in different places, but is plainly discernible on every continent and in every country. We are only at the beginning of our troubles and it is doubtful whether, and how far, the forces of an orderly civilization are going to deal effectively with those of social and international disintegration."[60]

Balfour had good reason to be concerned. At the First Palestine Congress meeting in Jerusalem, attendees rejected the Balfour Declaration, considered Jerusalem to be part of Syria, and demanded Arab independence. In Turkey, Mustafa Kemal Atatürk launched a nationalist movement with the intent of expelling the Allied occupiers. In the region bordering southern Turkey and northern Iraq, Kurds revolted against the British and proclaimed Kurdistan's independence. In another part of Iraq, Shiite Muslims launched an uprising and called for independence under Hashimite rule. In Palestine, non-Jews rioted and attacked Jews. In Syria, rival nationalist groups formed a coalition against the French. And in Morocco, groups mounted attacks against the Spaniards who, unable to withstand the onslaughts alone, soon became dependent on the support of French troops.

Eventually, the nationalist challenges generated results. In 1921, Britain conferred a constitutional monarchy on Iraq, but assigned every Iraqi minister a British adviser with the authority to approve or reject the minister's decision. The following year, while under intense pressure from the Wafd, an Egyptian nationalist party, Britain accorded Egypt formal independence and authorized the establishment of a constitutional monarchy. Britain, however, reserved the right to reject the composition of Egypt's government, and it used the prerogative in 1924 to force the dismissal of a Wafdist ministry. Nonetheless, Egypt gained its full independence twelve years later with the signing of the Anglo–Egyptian Treaty Alliance. In 1923, Britain recognized Transjordan as an independent constitutional state, but retained control of the military. In 1926, Lebanon pronounced the state a republic and approved a French-style constitution. Britain agreed to grant Iraq full independence in 1930, but the final step was not taken until two years later. That same year, Iraq was formally admitted to the League of Nations. During this general period, Mustafa Kemal Atatürk created the Republic of Turkey, and Abd al-Aziz ibn Saud established the Kingdom of Saudi Arabia. Inadvertently, thus, the Europeans had provided their colonial subjects "the form, the language, the very goals of resistance and rejection – 'independence'."[61] Nationalism in the aforesaid places, as elsewhere, was two sided. It was directed inwardly to help construct a community and legitimize the authority of the state to be, and outwardly to garner support from potential allies and undermine the power and legitimacy of the colonial authorities.[62]

The structure assumed by the new states varied according to the principles favored by their elites. At one end of the spectrum stood those who refused to conform to the Western model. Saudi Arabia became an Islamic state by adopting the Quran as its constitution and the shariah as its law.[63] At the other end was Turkey, an entity that formally ended the caliphate, suppressed or marginalized religious institutions, and created a secular state. In between were the vast majority of states. Egypt, Syria, Iraq, and Iran were actors that, despite the fact that they remained committed to Islam, equated political, legal, economic, and educational development with the secularization and westernization of the state and society.[64] Their leaders shared with their former colonial rulers the belief that in order to generate socioeconomic change, they first had to reform their culture via the introduction of Western values. The promotion of a secular vision of development in many of the new states generated a major disjunction, principally because their societies remained deeply rooted in their Islamic tradition.[65]

As Muslims gained their independence from the colonial powers, the new leaders accepted, often with little choice, the territorial boundaries drawn by, and imposed on them by, their previous masters. But as they advocated Western-style development, many Islamic fundamentalists began to reject the "primacy of the nation-state as the universal political form" and to criticize the action as a Western imposition.[66] Nationalist sentiments, they argued, were splitting "the land of Islam" into secular communities determined to push aside the religious establishment.[67]

Challenges to the secularization of the state took different forms. For present purposes, it suffices to discuss a few of the most important ones. One of the key thinkers who hastened the revival of radical Islam in modern times was Jamal al-Din al-Afghani. Born in Iran in the late 1830s, al-Afghani sought from early on to abridge the divergences between Muslims, and to mobilize them against European hegemony and corrupt leaders at home. Three ideas guided his actions. First, he contended that by going back to their origins, Muslims would end their backwardness, and would regenerate and purify Islam. Second, he argued that it was imperative to bring the different Muslim states under a single caliphate. Under a single caliph, Islam would regain its earlier wealth and dynamism. Third, he emphasized that Muslims had to battle all "Muslim sovereigns" who opposed internal "reforms and did not sufficiently resist European encroachments." To succeed in the struggle against their own corrupt leaders and the European countries that sought to seize Islamic lands, Muslims had to be attuned to the dangers of materialism in all its manifestations. As he noted in *The Refutation of Materialism*, "religion is the mainstay of nations, and their prosperity comes through it; in it is their happiness, and it is their pivot." "The beginning of the weakness of the Muslims goes back to the day that the lying opinions and beliefs of materialists appeared as a kind of religion." al-Afghani's most important example was the Ottoman caliphate, which "saw its position weakened in recent times only as a result of suggestions the materialists wheedled into the souls of its mighty and its military leaders."[68]

One of al-Afghani's most reputable disciples, Muhammad Abduh, born in 1849, became a chief figure in the teaching and interpretation of Islam in Egypt. Eventually, however, Abduh came to believe that, despite the need to bring together Muslims against their Western enemies, they would not be able to form a single, united, Muslim state. More importantly, upon his return to Egypt, Abduh proposed that Islam, when properly understood, was compatible with the liberal, democratic, and scientific values of the modern world.[69] Abduh's ideas were rejected by Egypt's militant political elites. By the late 1920s, a new radical voice emerged in Egypt's political arena. Hassan al-Banna, born in 1906, created the Muslim Brethren, capitalizing on the domestic discontent generated by Britain's presence and the suffering brought about by the rapid exodus from the countryside to the city. Mindful that Egyptians were yearning for security and answers to the questions of whom they should oppose and what they needed to do in order to improve their lives, al-Banna rapidly filled the void by establishing thousands of Muslim Brethren branches throughout the country.[70] From early on, he sought to neutralize local brands of nationalism built on Western secular models. His chief contentions were that nationalism and Islam were complementary if the former worked within the parameters of the latter, and that all places inhabited by Muslims were part of one Islamic fatherland.[71] In October 1938, he stated: "Islam does not recognize geographical boundaries, nor does it acknowledge racial and blood differences, considering all Muslims one *umma* ... The Muslim Brethren consider this unity as holy and believe in this union ... They support Pan-Arabism ... [T]he Muslim Brethren see the Caliphate and its re-establishment as a top priority."[72]

Hassan al-Banna was assassinated in 1949. By then he had transformed the Muslim Brethren into a mass movement that reached the urban lower middle classes, whose lives were guided by deep religious convictions.[73] The organization, however, experienced a major blow shortly after Gamal Abdel Nasser and his associates took over Egypt's government in 1952. Though for a while it seemed as if the narrow nationalist agenda of the new leaders would not be threatened by the Brethren's fundamentalism, their uneasy coexistence came to an end in October 1954, when one of its members tried to assassinate Nasser. The Egyptian leader and his colleagues moved rapidly to disband the Muslim Brethren and incarcerate some of its chief members. By then, Sayyid Qutb, also born 1906, had emerged as one of the Brethren's most articulate and important ideologues. His argument has been summarized as follows:

God's sovereignty (hakimiyya) is exclusive. Men are to obey God alone. Men are to obey only rulers who obey God. A ruler who obeys God faithfully follows God's mandate. The mandate is clear and comprehensive. It is available for mankind's guidance in the Shariah. To set aside that clear and comprehensible divine mandate is to lapse into jahiliyya. Rulers who so act are to be resisted. Resistance under these circumstances is a legitimate act of jihad. The ruler's claim to being a Muslim ruling a Muslim state is null and void.[74]

Qutb was one of those imprisoned in 1954, following the attempt on Nasser's life. He was released ten years later, jailed once again shortly afterward, sentenced to death in April 1966 during a trial designed to depict as un-Islamic his radical ideology, and hanged four months later. His trial and death did not quiet the radical voices; instead they provided a new martyr, an Islamic *shahid*.[75]

Another major political figure was Abu A'la al-Maududi (1903–1979), who played a central role in fostering the cause of Islam and Pan-Islam, first in India and then in Pakistan. Pakistani nationalists who had sought independence from the British and separation from India had advocated the creation of a "Muslim state" instead of an "Islamic state." Such a state would bring together Muslims from the entire Indian subcontinent, regardless of the intensity of their religious beliefs, and would institute political structures similar to those found in Great Britain. In his book *The Patriotic Appeal and the Islamic Union,* al-Maududi questioned this stand.[76] Based on the contention that politics was "an integral, inseparable part of the Islamic faith," he called for the "Islamization from above," and the creation of a state that would rule in the name of Allah. To promote the ideology of political struggle, al-Maududi founded the Jamaat-e-Islami, a political party that, ironically, used as its model avant-garde European political parties of the 1930s.[77]

The effects of these ideas took time to germinate, and when they did, they did not engender a singular and cohesive outlook. Israel's routing of the combined Egyptian, Syrian, and Jordanian forces in 1967; the loss of Sinai, Gaza, the West Bank, and Jerusalem to Israel; the failure on the part of Pakistan to prevent its partition into two states in 1971; and Lebanon's civil war in the mid-1970s helped spawn calls for the rebirth of an ideology that gave prominence to Islamic identity, history, culture, and values. But it would take the 1978–1979 revolution in Iran for Islam to regain some of its earlier allure as a political force.[78]

The revolution's leading figure, Ayatullah Ruhallah Khomeini, was to the "Islamic Revolution what Lenin was to the Bolshevik, Mao to the Chinese, and Castro to the Cuban revolutions."[79] Born into a family with solid religious credentials, Khomeini ventured into the political arena in the early 1940s when he published an unsigned article titled *Kashf al-Asrar* (*Secrets Unveiled*). Concerned that Iran's leaders might attempt to replicate the republic created by Mustafa Kemal Atatürk in Turkey, Khomeini argued that the "government of God" was the only true government. Islam, he emphasized, dealt with all types of difficulties, from the "most general problems of all countries to the specifics of a man's family."[80] In a carefully worded rebuttal to the claim that Muslims must always obey their rulers, Khomeini referred to Iran's leader, Riza Shah Pahlavi, when he wrote:

> God sent the Prophet of Islam with thousands of heavenly laws and established His government on the belief in the uniqueness of God and justice ... Would this same God order men to obey Atatürk who has disestablished state religion ... and in general, opposed the religion of God? Moreover, would he order us to obey Pahlavi who, as we all know, did all he could to uproot Islam?[81]

Khomeini continued to voice his opposition as Riza Shah's son, Muhammad Riza, began to implement an autocratic modernization program. The reforms, though substantial, did not bring about even development, nor did they generate solid and widespread political support from their principal beneficiaries. Thus, with the strong backing of an organization composed of regimented disciples recruited from among Iran's mullahs; with the advantage of Iranian secular nationalists' inability to create a united front, despite the presence of xenophobic nationalism; and with the use of a combination of religious, nationalist, and populist messages, Khomeini managed to place himself as the only viable alternative to the Pahlavi regime.[82]

The Pahlavi regime, however, was not the sole target of the Iranian Revolution. Many Iranians had not forgotten that the USA had helped mount the coup that overthrew the popular nationalist leader, Muhammad Musaddiq, or that its support of an increasingly despotic shah never wavered. The storming of the US Embassy in Tehran by radical Islamists on November 4, 1979, initiated a four hundred and forty-four-day crisis between Iran's new regime and the Jimmy Carter administration. The act on the part of Iran exacted a measure of revenge, but more importantly it symbolized the anger Washington's behavior had fueled throughout Iran. The Ronald Reagan administration's subsequent decision to aid Iraq during the Iraq–Iran war in the 1980s did little to alleviate this emotion. Unsurprisingly, the image of the USA as the "great Satan" soon became part of the common parlance, not just among Iranians but also throughout the Muslim world.[83]

By the end of the Iran–Iraq conflict in the late 1980s, the Iranian Revolution had lost some of its earlier aura. The exorbitant human and material costs exacted on Iranians, along with the chronic domestic clashes between competing ideological factions, led many, both inside and outside Iran, to question the role of the clerics. Still, despite internal divisions, the likelihood that the clerical regime would be toppled in the near future and replaced by a secularly oriented entity remained very small. As the transition from the old to the new millennium proceeded, new leaders, often known as "transnationalist jihadists," called for the waging of an armed struggle against Islam's leading enemy—the USA.

A couple of international crises helped provide the rationale for this directive. Both crises, however, must be viewed within the context of a clash that has been ensuing for quite some time. The creation of the Jewish state and the steadfast backing it received from the USA in the form of direct and indirect political, military, and economic assistance since Israel's 1967 defeat of Arab states, have helped Muslim extremists to "rally popular support and to attract recruits."[84] With regards to the kind of impact the creation of the Israeli state would have on Arabs, few explained it better than one of its most important early leaders. David Ben-Gurion once said to the president of the World Jewish Congress:

> If I were an Arab leader I would never make terms with Israel. That is natural: we have taken their country ... We come from Israel, but two thousand years ago, and what is that to them? There has been anti-Semitism, the Nazis, Hitler, Auschwitz, but was that their fault? They only see one thing: we have come here and stolen their country. Why should they accept that?[85]

To understand how the association between Washington and Israel is viewed among many in the Muslim world, one need not go further than the words of an al-Qaeda member, who said:

> The close link between America and the Zionist entity is in itself a curse for America. In addition to the high cost incurred by the U.S. Treasury as a result of this alliance, the strategic cost is also exorbitant because this close link has turned the attack against America into an attack against the Zionist entity and [vice versa]. This contributes to bringing the Islamic nation together and pushing it strongly to rally around the jihad enterprise.[86]

Though it is impossible to explain how much other events encouraged some Islamic groups to call for Muslims to direct their energies against the USA, it is commonly acknowledged that the war in Afghanistan against the invading Soviet forces acted as the opening salvo. For the first time in the modern era, Muslims from a vast array of countries converged in an Islamic state to fight an actor that was both an "infidel" and a "superpower," and they succeeded. Their victory helped transform the "Afghan war into a religious struggle between the *ummah* (the community worldwide) and godless Communism."[87] Or, in the words of Ayman al-Zawahiri, one of the first senior jihadis to fight in Afghanistan, "the jihad battles in Afghanistan destroyed the myth of a (superpower) in the minds of young Muslim mujahedeen. The Soviet Union, a superpower with the largest land army in the world, was destroyed, and the remnants of its troops fled Afghanistan before the eyes of the Muslim youths and with their participation."[88] This event, thus, in addition to producing a hardened and skilled transnational force of Muslim fighters, helped nourish the belief that inadequately armed but devoted men could confront a more powerful foe. As explained by al-Qaeda's leading figure, Osama bin Laden, using very meager resources and military means, "the Afghan mujahedeen demolished one of the most important human myths in history and the biggest military apparatus. We no longer fear the so-called Great Powers. We believe that America is much weaker than Russia." One of the interesting points in bin Laden's comment is his rationale for thinking that the USA was more vulnerable than the Soviet Union. How leaders use history to rationalize decisions helps explain bin Laden's conclusion. "[O]ur brothers who fought in Somalia," noted bin Laden, "told us that they were astonished to observe how weak, impotent, and cowardly the American soldier is ... America's nightmares in Vietnam and Lebanon will pale by comparison with the forthcoming victory in al-Hijaz."[89]

A second very important event was the Gulf War and the stationing of US forces in Saudi Arabia. Few Muslims throughout the world decried the decision by the USA and its allies to expel Saddam Hussein's forces from Kuwait in 1991. In fact, those who for years had advocated the creation of authentic Islamic states and societies also accused Saddam Hussein of creating an apostate regime in Iraq. Some of them even relied on more abrasive measures. bin Laden, for instance, for a time sponsored Islamist extremists operating in Iraqi Kurdistan against Saddam Hussein's autocratic regime.[90] It was also bin Laden who volunteered to senior members of the Saudi Arabia regime to put together a large force of mujahedeen in order "to get the Iraqi forces out of Kuwait."[91] After rejecting bin Laden's proposal, the Saudi monarchy authorized the USA to deploy its own forces in Saudi territory and sanctioned their permanent stationing after the Iraqis had been forced to leave Kuwait.[92] bin Laden repudiated the last decision. In his 1996 *Declaration of War Against the Americans* he wrote:

> It is out of date and no longer acceptable to claim that the presence of the crusaders is a necessity and only a temporary measure to protect the land of the two Holy Places ... Today it is seven years since their arrival and the regime is not able to move them out of the country. The regime made no confession about its inability and carried on lying to the people claiming that the Americans will leave. But never-never again; a believer will not be bitten twice from the same hole or snake! Happy is the one who takes note of the sad experience of the others.[93]

Though highly critical of the Saudi regime, bin Laden did not call for its overthrow, or for the ousting of other "lackey" regimes. Instead, his target became the USA. In fact, since then, bin Laden has worked hard to redirect Muslim ire away from their states to the USA. He considered the Saudi monarchy, and other Muslim regimes, nothing more than tools and agents of the USA. As he explained in 2002:

> The priority in this fight and at this stage should be given to the pagans' leaders, the Americans and Jews who will not end their aggression and stop their domination over us except with jihad … Take care not to be pushed into fragmenting your efforts and squandering your resources in marginal battles with the lackeys and parties but concentrate the blows on the head of the unfaith[ful] until it collapses. Once it collapses, all the other parts will collapse, vanish and be defeated.[94]

Conclusion

In 1990, John Mearsheimer proposed that some day in the not-very-distant future we might wake up "lamenting the loss of order that the Cold War gave to the anarchy of international relations."[95] In a sense his prediction proved to be right, but for the wrong reason and in the wrong place.

A proclaimed Realist, Mearsheimer posited that with the end of the Cold War the likelihood that Europe would face major crises, even wars, would increase dramatically in the next forty-five years. He based his pessimistic conclusion on a set of logically connected arguments. His two general theoretical lines of reasoning are that the "distribution and character of military power among states are the root causes of war and peace," and that multipolar systems are more likely to generate "dangerous geometries of power" than bipolar systems. After the Cold War, continues Mearsheimer, Europe began to revert "to a state system that created powerful incentives for aggression in the past," and moved towards becoming a multipolar system, with Germany, France, Britain, and perhaps Italy, emerging as its most powerful actors. These actors, along with a less powerful Soviet Union, will experience the "problems endemic to multipolar systems"—instability.[96]

Since the end of the Cold War and the demise of the Soviet Union, Europe has not moved in the direction predicted by Mearsheimer. Differences between its chief actors remain, but they are not of the nature that dominated their relations in the nineteenth century, nor are they addressed in the same way they were dealt with during that period. More to the point, none of the symptoms typical of a multipolar system have materialized in Europe, and neither power nor power imbalances dictate their interactions. Because of the European Union, the interactions between its members are shaped by an agreed structure of meaning, one that adheres to and advocates the idea that they will settle their disputes not by force but in some other ways.[97]

Of equal significance is the failure on the part of Realists, and thus of Mearsheimer, to predict that the principal sources of turmoil and instability in the world system would be engendered by actors that received inadequate consideration during the Cold War. Parts of the world system of the twenty-first century remain plagued by ethnic conflict. States that were formed when the European powers renounced control of their colonies, and those that came into being when the Cold War ended, too often find themselves encumbered by intense domestic ethnic and religious cleavages. Overwhelmed by internal divisions, a great number of African actors have squandered the opportunity to play even a nominal role in the design of the new world system. Their failures freed the more developed and stable entities to dictate the type of structure of meaning the world system would assume.

Outside Africa, a somewhat more balanced dispute has gained momentum. On the one hand are Western actors who advocate the worldwide creation of democratic regimes and neoliberal markets; opposing them are leaders of several developing states who contend that attempts to rapidly transform their domestic political and economic systems have spawned high human and material costs. Despite their repeated failures during the first decade of the twenty-first century to design reasonable settlements, both sides, including the USA, recognize that ultimately it is in their mutual interests to reach an accord. The ideological distance between the quarreling parties, moreover, is not profound enough to prevent them from formulating a relatively even-handed agreement.

The future of the world system looks decisively more ominous when the focus is directed to the struggle between actors who aspire to spread democracy and neoliberal economic policies, and jihadis who aim to evict Westerners and apostates from Muslim lands in order to create Islamic states. The material means possessed by the USA and its allies are substantially greater than those controlled by their Muslim rivals. However, there are too many intangibles for anyone to postulate a sound prediction of who will succeed and what ideology will take the lead in tomorrow's world. History has repeatedly demonstrated that in long drawn-out struggles the actors with the greatest material capabilities do not always emerge victorious. Victory has often come to the side of the actor with the deepest commitment to a cause and the greatest capacity to withstand exceedingly high costs for lengthy periods.

The USA's saving grace so far has been its ability to reflect on its mistakes, derive lessons from them, and design and implement suitable corrective measures. Whether it will retain this quality following the chaos the Bush administration spawned in Iraq, only history will tell. In any event, it is reasonable to assume that the type of radical Islam ideology that al-Qaeda-like groups are promoting will not vanish swiftly from the international political scene. As a counter-ideology, it has two core purposes: i) a call to action against those who, in the minds of its leading advocates, are striving to destroy Islam and the holy land where it was born; and ii) to create an *umma*, a large community of the faithful unhindered by geographical, tribal, ethnic, or language divides. Whether these aspirations are rational or realizable is beside the point. For its advocates, it is not so much a matter of whether they succeed at defeating their enemies—although such an objective is never belittled—but whether they adhere firmly to what they consider to be their religion's central tenets. Such an ideology, even in defeat, does not disappear entirely.

7 The dialectical nature of political ideologies in the world system

History teaches to doubt in order to know and to continue doubting.[1]

Introduction

For much of the second half of the twentieth century, the analysis of world politics has been dominated by the argument that material forces, in the form of power and interests, generate the best explanatory theories. The common contention has been that interests, not values, guide actions in world politics. Advocates of the Realist and Neorealist schools of thought have proposed that when the political stakes are high, pragmatism always overrides morality, and that any value, or set of values, is related to egoism.[2] They have also argued that when ideologies play a role in world politics, they do so only as a mediating factor between international structures and domestic institutions. In other instances, ideologies are "mere rationalizations for changes that would have occurred anyway."[3]

This study's intent has been not to cast doubt on the significance of material power and interests, but to give substance to the assertion that the content and meaning of power and interests are constituted by beliefs, values, and ideas.[4] Power and interests define international politics, but it is ideology that gives interests, and thus the use of power, meaning and purpose.[5] As Nigel Gould-Davies has noted, power "and ideology are not inherently antagonistic goals; they may even be mutually reinforcing. It is all a matter of how much power is pursued, what kinds are exercised, and how it is used."[6]

The analysis presented throughout these pages has tried to authenticate the critical role played by ideology by demonstrating that leaders, at least since Constantine ruled the Roman Empire, have consistently relied on some type of system of beliefs, values, and ideas to help:

i) create a political community;
ii) transform a political community into a state or empire;
iii) protect or augment the power of a state or an empire;
iv) free a political community from a state or an empire in order to establish a separate state;

v) create and protect a regional or world system;
vi) destroy an existing regional or world system and replace it with a new one;
vii) validate the use of violence to realize any of the aforesaid goals.

In this closing chapter, I put forward several interrelated lines of reasoning. In the first part, I present in summary form the various paths different ideologies have traveled and the tensions they have generated as they encountered one another. From that précis I derive four arguments. I first propose that though attempts to create a world system structure can be traced to the middle of the sixteenth century, it did not materialize until some three centuries later. Second, I contend that the structure of today's world system owes its existence, albeit partially and indirectly, to an ideology—more specifically, to Confucianism. Third, I claim that the major thrust to impose on the world arena a system of beliefs, values, and ideas was initiated by Spain's monarchy in the early sixteenth century, and that though the ideologies relied on in subsequent centuries by Britain and the USA differed markedly from Spain's, their intent did not. Each actor's goal was to propagate throughout the world arena a structure of meaning that reflected its own system of beliefs, values, and ideas. Each actor's action was driven by two interrelated impressions. Each one believed that such an act would help protect and promote its material interests. And each one was convinced that it had a moral obligation to spread its system of beliefs, values, and ideas because it was vastly superior to that of others.

The idea that Pax Britannica created the ideological foundation on which Pax Americana was built is not novel. Some defenders of the policies initiated by both states, however, have been inclined to assert that their success can be attributed to the superior quality of the values both actors sought to propagate worldwide. In the fourth section I present a less sanguine argument. I propose that liberalism's core characteristic is the advocacy of political and economic competition, and that success in competition demands flexibility and adaptation. In a Darwinian world, only those ideologies that foster flexibility and rapid adaptation to new circumstances prosper. Catholicism, Confucianism, Fascism, Nazism, Communism, Islamism were built on systems of beliefs, values, and ideas that stood firm against adaptation. Their inflexible characteristics foiled whatever hopes their advocates might have had to create a world system that echoed their values.

Ideology: a bridge between foreign policy and the structure of the world system

Time is a social construct. When historians fix their eyes on events, they force on them artificial beginnings and ends. They construct their analyses on the assumptions that causal relationships between events exist and can be uncovered. By choosing the demise of the Roman Empire in the fourth century as this work's starting point, this study has imposed on it a synthetic beginning. Certainly, its downfall had started earlier; but it was not until the fourth century that the leaders of the Roman Empire searched for an alternative formula—Christianity as a political ideology—to avert or, if possible, reverse the course. Though as a political ideology it did not prevent the breakup of the Roman Empire, Christianity facilitated the emergence of beliefs, values, and ideas that in due course would play very important roles, not just in Europe, but throughout the world.

In the early years of the seventh century, Muhammad drew on earlier religions to proclaim a series of tenets that covered the spectrum of political, economic, and social conduct. They pertained concurrently to relations between Allah and the believer, and between the believer and the rest of mankind. The interactions between both relationships set the foundation not only for the emergence of a different theological system, but also for the rise of a new political community and, eventually, of an empire whose extraordinary material capabilities would help alter the distribution of power in the regional system. The Islamic Empire came into being not just because a group of Arabs controlled the material capabilities necessary to create it, but also because they wanted to design an empire that would reflect their particular system of beliefs, values, and ideas. In time, the emergence and propagation of Islam as a religious and political instrument in a geographical area contiguous to an empire that had adopted Christianity as its own political device helped generate a power/ideological battle and define the structure of regional system encompassed by the Mediterranean area.

Christianity seemed to have a doubtful future as a political ideology in the latter part of the ninth and tenth centuries. It was advocated by leaders of a divided domain that, in addition to being challenged by an empire with an incompatible religious/political ideology, was being forced to battle barbaric tribes. Feudalism extended Christianity the opportunity to enlarge its power and strengthen its legitimacy in one of Europe's principal areas. With the demise of the western part of the Roman Empire and the emergence of competing centers of power, the Christian church moved to fill the political vacuum. It claimed that its political authority was greater than that of lay kings and emperors. With this argument as its foundation, it ordered Christians to stop fighting one another and use their human and material resources to free the land of Jesus from the "infidels." The crusades did not bring about the results hoped for by its advocates. What is more, after years of absorbing tremendous human and material costs and constantly having their authority usurped by the leaders of the Church, a number of monarchs decided to reverse the trend.

The struggle between ecclesiastic and lay rulers could be viewed as nothing more than raw power politics. It was much more. It was a clash of ideals. It was a battle between a Church hierarchy that contended it had the authority to order monarchs to protect and advance Christianity's system of beliefs, values, and norms, and monarchs who argued that the Church did not possess the right to dictate how they should prioritize their goals. The conflict between both sets of actors was affected by two other developments.

During the start of the 1400s, merchants in northern Italy began to take advantage of their location to establish commercial networks across Europe. With the growth of commerce came the development of an elite who approached business in a more calculating and pragmatic way than in previous eras. This change helped engender the belief that men should rely more on their own intellect and less on Church doctrine to mold their destinies. In the realm of politics, few were as influential as Machiavelli at crafting the new belief paradigm. His dictums were clear-cut: men rarely engage in good acts unless necessary; rulers act solely for the purpose of serving their own political interests; a leader's self-interests, not morality, must always determine a state's political concerns; power is a major transformer of behavior; the use of force, along with a deep understanding of the art of war, helps brings about political success. Before Machiavelli's political precepts could attain the status of political ideology, however, another important change would first have to materialize.

By the end of the fifteenth century, the Christian church was facing a new set of challenges. It was criticized for disregarding the discrepancies that existed between the principles on which the religion was founded and the way they were practiced by its clergy. The purchasing of indulgences, which was a common practice during that period, ignited the revolt that split the Church. Troubled by these deeds, Martin Luther published several critiques of the Church's doctrine. One of his most damaging contentions was the claim that the Holy Scripture made no distinction between the laity and priests, and that the differentiation invented by the Church had led to the formation of a corrupt system. Those who for some time had been trying to curtail the authority and role of the Church in matters of politics welcomed his opinions. The papal monarchy and its allies responded with their own caustic attacks. This ideological divide within Christianity prompted a series of wars that went on for decades and in the end further undermined the papacy's ability to affect politics.

Worried by the human and material costs their religious wars had spawned, Europe's monarchs agreed in 1648 to grant each other the right to decide which version, or mixture, of Christianity would be practiced in their country. Accordingly, the Westphalia accord strengthened the claim that territorial sovereignty was the key component in world politics, and further weakened the papacy's declaration that even in terrestrial matters the authority of its office was superior to that of monarchs. It also freed monarchs to practice Machiavelli's maxim that their interests always overrode morality. Interactions between states began to be driven by their leaders' ideological conviction that their most important responsibility was to protect their states' sovereignty—that is to say, their own political power.

Meanwhile, Arabs had steadily been losing their grip over the Islamic Empire. Its unwieldy size spawned disunity, which led to the establishment of independent regional entities controlled by military despots. With Islam still operating as their driving ideology, they solidified their authority by moving aggressively against the Byzantine Empire. Their triumphs marked the demise of the Byzantine Empire and the dawn of a different Islamic realm—the Ottoman Empire.

The emphasis so far has been on power competition and the ideological clashes affecting European actors and, to a lesser extent, the Islamic Empire/ Ottoman Empire. Obviously, these actors were not the only ones that shaped the structure of the world system. "What-if" speculations are not always analytically helpful; in this case they are. In their struggles, Christianity and Islam were aided, indirectly and without the knowledge of their advocates, by a third political ideology.

In politics, as in everyday life, the decision to avoid action by someone who can have a major effect on events is of great significance. The world's most powerful empire in the early fifteenth century was not a European or Middle Eastern actor; it was China. With a population twice as large as all of Europe's, a soil that produced all the substances needed by its inhabitants, an administration led by highly qualified bureaucrats, technology greatly admired by foreign visitors, an iron industry vastly superior to Britain's, and an armada that surpassed by a substantial margin the might of any European navy, the empire had the means to dominate, and possibly define the structure of, the world system. Steered by Confucianism, an ideology that objected to the idea of enlarging the empire's material wealth via trade and the conquest of distant territories, China made it possible for other, less powerful, actors on the other side of the globe to dictate the material form the world system would assume and the ideology that would help engender future ones.[7]

History seldom moves along a clearly defined course. While throughout much of Europe Christians confronted one another along a religious divide, in one of its corners a couple of its leaders made it evident that they had no doubts about where they stood. Elated by their successful campaign against the last Moorish stronghold in the Iberian Peninsula, two of Spain's monarchs decided to transform it into an economic powerhouse and a Catholic citadel. Upon learning that their initially tepid support of explorations in distant regions promised sizeable material rewards, their attitude toward the "new world" underwent a momentous change. With the enthusiastic backing of a papacy convinced that by endorsing their actions it might prevent the further loss of its own power and authority, the Spanish monarchs proudly assumed the role of conquerors. They were driven by material greed and the conviction that, as the rulers of a superior civilization, they were duty bound to expose infidels to the greater glories of the Catholic faith.

An empire with the greatest material resources can in a brief period become a feeble actor if its leaders adhere to a rigid system of beliefs, values, and ideas. In the course of history, the presence of such actors has provided others the opportunity to structure the world arena according to their own ideological tenets. Spain's conquest of vast portions of the Americas proved to be significant to the world system mainly because of the political, economic, and social system it imposed on its new subjects for some three centuries. It was a system engendered by an ideology that favored rigid social divides, belittled work and industry, vehemently opposed religious diversity, and resisted change.

Spain's imposition of a largely inert ideology on sizeable segments of the Western Hemisphere, and its eventual decision not to try to colonize most of North America (with the exception of Mexico), provided another group of people, with a different set of values, the chance to conduct a very different type of political, economic, and social experiment. Britain's role in helping transform the world system can best be characterized as a two-step process. It began with the colonization of parts of the Americas. For the early colonizers, the Americas symbolized two types of opportunities, both of which were designed to reaffirm their interpretation of history as a progressive movement. Committed to the idea that one of their central responsibilities was to enlighten non-Christians of the teachings of Jesus, Protestant immigrants from Europe, but particularly from England, viewed America and members of its indigenous civilization as souls who needed to be saved. They thought of America's natives not as inferior beings, but as members of an uneducated society who deserved external assistance in order to realize their potential.

The notion that it was their obligation to convert Native Americans to Christianity, however, did not lie outside the realm of self-interest. It was not uncommon to assume that conversion would engender a successful colonial enterprise. But the link between devoutness and self-interest had a deeper significance. The form of Protestantism introduced by the colonizers to parts of North America advocated the economic ethic of unceasing work, a system of principles that, according to Max Weber, was the most important root from "which modern market-oriented industrial capitalism grew."[8] It was this type of ethic that would eventually make it possible for the citizens of the USA to create a state that valued economic competition, private property, legal equality, limited governmental intervention in the private affairs of the individual, and the separation of state and church. Though they failed to fully live up to their ideals, they adhered to them closely enough to transform the USA into one of the most powerful actors in the world arena in a little over a century.

Before the USA could become the definer of the world system, however, another actor had to set up its ideological foundation. By 1815, despite the fact that Britain was no longer the ruler of parts of North America, it was in an excellent position to promote liberalism and develop free trade without augmenting its territorial possessions. The specific steps taken by Britain to become the world's leading actor in the nineteenth century were delineated earlier. The system of beliefs, values, and ideas that guided its actions are worth repeating here. Britain's policies were built on the notion that it was in its interest to "transfer to distant regions the greatest possible amount both of the civil liberty and the forms of social order to which Great Britain is chiefly indebted for the rank she holds among the civilized nations."[9] It would design policies that encouraged the establishment of "like-minded" cooperative elites in the peripheries. These elites would prove to the world that economic progress was compatible with individual liberty, differential property rights, and political stability.[10] Commerce would promote prosperity; prosperity would spawn the establishment of friendly states; and a number of sympathetic entities would help maintain stability in an international arena inhabited by the exhausted monarchies of continental Europe and the new revolutionary states led by the USA.[11]

Britain's free-trade ideology had, along with an arrogant attitude, a moral and religious tone. Convinced that no other civilization had reached the level of development attained by Britain, its leaders proudly claimed that it was their country's duty to improve the material and moral conditions of others. With a Protestant doctrine that believed in salvation by good works, the British missionaries formulated comprehensive plans designed to evangelize "heathens" globally. "Go to the conquest of all lands. All must be at His length," became their motto.[12] Though missionaries and the leaders of the British Empire often disagreed on values and methods, they accepted and cherished the contention that while attempts to "induce natives to adopt civilization by merely educational instruction [had] failed," the moment they converted to Christianity, they began to exhibit a desire for the "advantages of the civilized life."[13]

To many contemporary readers, the assertion that commerce would engender prosperity may seem self-evident; it was not in the nineteenth century. During the early years of the century, the theory remained untested. Other actors began to subscribe to liberalism only after they had recognized that by adopting it their benefits would be greater than if they continued to assume that it was preferable to remain economically self-sufficient or accepted the continued division of the world economy. Those who initially accepted the new ideology practiced it only so long as Britain had the economic capacity to govern and protect the system. As will be explained later, the implementation of liberalism was temporarily discontinued in 1929, when Britain no longer had the means to lead the world economic system and the USA refused to take its place.[14]

While Britain was trying to propagate a new political economic idea, the countries in the European continent were coping with two other competing ideologies. One was a balance-of-power doctrine designed by a few domineering actors determined to repel challenges to their empires from like entities and nationalist movements. The other was a nationalist ideology advocated by leaders of political communities who sought to create single states from units that shared similar histories, culture, and language, or to free themselves from empires in order to craft their own independent nation-states. It was nationalism that helped Italy and Germany form their own distinct states and distance themselves from the Austrian Empire. It was nationalism, erupting in different corners of the Ottoman and the Austrian Empires, which led to the formation of frail states, steadily eroded the strength of both realms, and generated power vacuums. These vacuums were exploited by other international agents and, in the end, helped spawn the First World War. Thus, balance-of-power and nationalism symbolized, as ideologies, distinctly different interests. The first one represented the interests of powerful European entities determined to protect their own position in the system, prevent any one actor from becoming excessively powerful, and suppress nationalism as a political force. The second ideology, nationalism, stood for the interests of those who believed that peoples with common characteristics, such as ethnic background, history, language, and/or religion, should be able to unite under a nation-state umbrella.

In short, to comprehend the nature of the structure of Europe's nineteenth-century system, the way it changed, and the reason for its collapse, it is imperative to consider its origin, and to look beyond its material aspect. The system emerged for a purpose; it was designed to prevent any one actor from becoming too powerful, maintain a modicum of regional stability, and debilitate the forces of nationalism. In time, it was undermined by the forces of nationalism, which were sometimes guided by elites with mindsets different from those that sought to create the balance-of-power system. They succeeded either by advocating the division of empires into nation-states or by promoting the creation of independent nation-states via the merger of kingdoms that shared a common language and culture.

The period between 1919 and 1939 was a time when the USA refused to behave as its leading figure. Before 1929, Washington was reluctant to take the steps that might have prevented the collapse of the world economic system. In the 1930s it did not work with Great Britain and France to stop Adolf Hitler from bringing back to life Germany's military and economic power in order to redesign the balance-of-power system. With power distribution unable to capture the dynamics of the interwar period, it is appropriate to reintroduce the role of ideology.

The end of the First World War elicited the belief—advocated by a non-European leader—that a world devoid of wars was a realizable goal. Driven by the conviction that the USA was destined to create a different, more peaceful, international environment, Wilson traveled to Europe to propagate the idea that a world system framed by democracies and nourished by market economies must replace the balance-of-power ideology that guided the actions of Europe's leaders.

An ideology will not be effective without forceful and resolute activists. The USA possessed the power to propagate Wilson's ideology, but its people and their subsequent leaders did not share his belief that it was their task to mold the world system according to their tenets. Though democracy did not gain many converts, the idea treasured most by its supporters was that democracies must renounce wars. Ironically, this conviction, along with the absence of a tenacious entity disposed to containing the spread of rival ideologies, made it

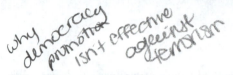
possible for communism, fascism, and Nazism to become powerful counter-ideologies in the world system.

Victory at the end of the Second World War went to the two actors with the greatest material capabilities. Its initiation, however, though instigated by self-interest, was also greatly influenced by ideology. Dreams of grandeur, which were the end result of an ideological conception that combined biological determinism, nationalism, and geopolitics, drove Hitler to initiate a war that Germany could not win, and to devise a war plan that no rational actor would have designed. Japan's leaders, emboldened by a nationalist ideology that dictated that their nation's superior station entitled it to be Asia's empire, ignored reality and made the fateful decision to attack an actor they knew they could not defeat. While the USA and the Soviet Union put aside their ideological differences in order to exit the war triumphantly, they were equally committed to guard, and whenever feasible promote, their distinct ideological conceptions.

It is not uncommon for political scientists to argue that to understand the Cold War it is unnecessary to account for the ideological differences between its two principal protagonists: the Soviet Union and the USA. The idea is partly correct. During the Cold War, the USA and the Soviet Union, as the world system's two most powerful entities, consistently strove to match each other's military capability, create their individual spheres of influence, ensure that members in their own spheres did not break rank, and broaden their separate areas whenever they estimated that the expected benefits would outweigh the expected costs. By focusing on material capabilities alone, however, analysts disregard the USA's repeated efforts to create spheres of influence inhabited by market democracies, or the Soviet Union's constant drive to ensure that its own orb would be occupied solely by communist regimes.[15]

To contend that Moscow and Washington took major steps to advocate their ideologies is not to argue that either refused to establish friendly relationships with agents that did not adhere to their values. Washington had no qualms about establishing cordial relationships with Latin American, African, or Asian dictatorial regimes, and on several occasions even encouraged their formation. Likewise, Moscow was willing to work, for instance, with Middle Eastern states, despite the fact that communism was not the ideology that defined the interests and guided the actions of most of its members. In both instances, however, one of each actor's leading motivations was to ensure that the region it dominated would not be contaminated by its adversary's ideology.

As the world emerged from the Cold War, numerous analysts assumed that ideological struggles had run their course and that Western liberalism was the only surviving model.[16] It was not long before a set of horrific events dispelled such an unfounded illusion. The emergence of market democracy as the undisputed ideology nearly guaranteed that eventually a counter-ideology or counter-ideologies would materialize.

Knowledge about the ideology that guides the actions of the world system's new leader does not necessarily enable analysts to predict which actors will defy its authority and which ideologies will steer their actions. However, information about ideologies that have been obscured by other competing belief systems enable analysts to estimate which challenges are likely to ensue as the overriding ideological struggle loses intensity. As the new world system emerged from the doldrums induced by the Cold War, a number of old ideologies resurfaced and demanded attention. Nationalism and ethnicity, which had been forced underground by the more formidable ideological struggle between the superpowers, regained some of their earlier notoriety. Islam, which as a belief system had not played a very important role in the world's political arena since the demise of the Ottoman Empire, gained repute during the 1979 Iranian revolution. It reenergized itself when the Taliban, having helped defeat Afghanistan's Soviet-backed regime, marched into Kabul and imposed on the entire country its own form of Islamism. And this version became a threat to be reckoned with when al-Qaeda operatives, responding to Osama bin Laden's call for a jihad-like struggle against the West, destroyed thousands of lives and vital symbols of US power in 2001. In a smaller magnitude, populism, with a tinge of Marxism, became the chosen call to arms for a few Latin American actors as a rejoinder to Washington's unyielding demand that they restructure their domestic economies according to its ideological tenets. To bring to life the reemergence of some of these ideologies, it is necessary to retrace an earlier argument.

By the 1880s, Britain had become the world's greatest exporter of industrial products and capital, as well as of financial, commercial, and transport services. It was also during this period that other world actors began to challenge its domination. Industrialization throughout the USA and parts of Europe had reduced Britain's initial advantage, and returns from its domestic and foreign investments had shrunk significantly. As Britain's leaders became cognizant that it risked losing its standing as the world's leading entity, their readiness to rely on nationalism and imperialism to avert the descent intensified. Their message was simple: the English are patriotic people, proud of their nationality and honored to support Britain's imperial policy. To buttress their message, British leaders called on their subjects' sense of virtue. Superior civilizations, they noted, were morally obligated to elevate the life value of "inferior" members of the human race. Britain's economic might was indicative of a God-extended authority to export Christianity and the rule of law to the less fortunate. The messages conveyed by other European actors and the USA differed somewhat in content from the one relayed by Britain, but each one called on the nationalist sentiments of its citizens, their feelings of superiority and entitlement, and, thus, on their sense of responsibility to civilize the "others."

The end the First World War began to turn nationalism on its head. Nationalism had gained some strength in the non-European world before the start of the war; still, its effectiveness as a political tool was limited. In the

Western Hemisphere, the Caribbean Basin countries experienced a surge in direct US military and economic involvement in their domestic affairs, but with the exception of Mexico they were not particularly effective at fencing off the interloper. On the other side of the Atlantic, Africans, despite having been amongst the principal targets of imperialism, had yet to fully assimilate the significance and value of nationalism as an anti-imperialist political instrument. Throughout Asia, particularly in China, India, and Japan, national-ist leaders had tried to use nationalism as a means to create a united front against the foreign powers, but with limited success. The critical exception was Japan, which by the end of the war had managed to generate a strong nationalist emotion and use it as a means to gain domestic support for, and justify, its own imperialist aspirations.

As leaders in Africa, Asia, and Latin America slowly but steadily adopted nationalism as the ideology of choice to counter the forces of imperialism, Islam began to reemerge as an alternative political belief system. Muslims were not of one mind concerning how to use Islam to advance their interests. Some proposed creating a Muslim state designed to bring Muslims together, regardless of the intensity of their religious beliefs. Others advocated the establishment of a stern Islamic political community—one that would rule in the name of Allah and demand strict adherence to Islamic tenets. Despite their differences, Muslims of that period shared a set of common objectives. Their two leading goals were to use Islam as a means to mobilize Muslims in a common cause against Western encroachers, and to rejuvenate their socie-ty's old vigor and purity in order to guarantee its continued moral and phy-sical existence. The intense efforts by numerous political leaders in the Muslim world did not transform Islamism into an ideological powerhouse immediately. Radical Islamism became a commanding political ideology only after Israel became a modern state and had humbled Arab states in a number of wars; the USA became Israel's most fervent supporter; the Islamic revolu-tion in Iran toppled the shah and restructured its political and social system; and Saudi Arabia authorized the USA to station its forces in the land of Muhammad.

Conclusion

Social power entails the mastery of people. When effective, it results in the tight organization and mobilization of large groups of people over a very large region. Realists and Neorealists consider almost exclusively the role of coercion and force as the base of control and domination. However, no agent, regardless of how strong it is, can constantly depend on its material cap-abilities to impose its will. To perpetuate its control, it relies on ideology to instill amongst its subjects its own system of beliefs, values, and ideas. In time, the ideology being disseminated is so internalized by the agent's subjects that they view it as the natural order of things.

The identities and interests of a system's actors, imparted in the form of ideologies, shape the ideology or ideologies of the system. Though the ideology or ideologies assumed by the system are reflections of those projected by some of the system's principal actors, ultimately they take on lives of their own—they begin to exist as separate, if not distinct, systems of beliefs, values, and ideas from those advocated by their originators. The ideologies of the system, in turn, can have multiple effects on its actors. An ideology can help reinvigorate an actor's commitment to the ideology endorsed by the system or to one that stands in opposition to it, and it can generate a new ideology or counter-ideology. The various, and sometimes conflicting, effects on the ideologies of the actors eventually reverberate in the system itself, sometimes in the form of a major transformation.

As a way of bringing ashore the various nets spread throughout this study, it is worthwhile accentuating three arguments. First, an examination of the way the structure of meaning of the international system changed throughout the centuries, of the actors who sought to define it, and of the impact their actions and ideologies had on the system and on other actors, enables analysts to develop a deeper understanding of the international system's present structure. From such study, several arguments can be derived.

To begin with, it reminds us that today's world system might have developed differently had China endeavored to become a world empire in the fifteenth century. Had it chosen that path, in all probability it would have dominated territories subsequently sought by Western actors, and propagated its own unique system of beliefs, values, and ideas. It would be unwise to argue that China's "Confucian ideology" was the sole determinant of its decision to remain a regional empire. But, as explained earlier, in view of the behavior on the part of Spain's monarchs in the early sixteenth century, it would be equally imprudent to contend that China's ideology played no role whatsoever. Spain's material capabilities at the start of that century were demonstrably inferior to China's in the 1430s, and yet the former did what the latter did not want to do: it tried to become a global imperial power.

Spain, because of its early control over a very rich, diverse, and large territory, should have led the world system for an extended period; instead, it lost its dominance rapidly. An analysis of its rigidly hierarchical ideology enables us to understand better its decline in power. Paradoxically, Spain's early success as a transoceanic empire helped inspire another actor, with a distinctly different ideology, to try to become one. Like Spain, Britain ventured into the Americas with the intent of enlarging its power and wealth. But unlike the Spaniards, those who conquered the northern parts of the Americas were guided by a system of beliefs, values, and ideas that prioritized the role of the individual and of political and economic competition. It was not mere coincidence, thus, that in time this disposition helped the USA inherit Britain's world power mantle, and refine the structure of meaning of the world system devised by the latter. Impressed by the benefits Britain had amassed via the promotion of free trade during parts of the nineteenth century, Washington made the doctrine its own. Despite their readiness to borrow aspects of their transatlantic cousins' doctrine, the USA's leaders remained deeply attached to the belief that their civilization was superior to Britain's and, consequently, that it was their obligation to create a world system built on a modified and highly improved ideological foundation. In time, a world system inhabited by democracies committed to the propagation and solidification of a world-market economy would become the USA's defining maxim.

Second, this study reaffirms the contention that the most successful political communities are those that are guided by political ideologies that enable them to adapt to changing circumstances. The USA, despite being the leading designer of the world economic system, seemed in the 1970s and 1980s unable to react fast enough to the predicaments engendered by the increasing competition within the system. Because its economic system was anchored to an ideology that prized competition, eventually it was able to address the new challenges. The Soviet Union's economic system, on the other hand, was built on an ideology that was hierarchical and abhorred competition. As noted in an earlier chapter, the Soviet constitution defined the Soviet economy "as a single public economic complex embracing all sectors of social production, distribution and exchange on the country's territory." This meant that, with very few exceptions, the Soviet constitution prohibited individuals or groups from owning the means of production or from engaging independently in entrepreneurial activities. Encircled by a world economic system that had become more competitive and more efficient, the Soviet economy eventually became the victim of its own ideological inflexibility.

And third, by analyzing the USA's and the Soviet Union's conflicting ideologies it was possible to predict the kind of ideological context the victorious actor would attempt to impose on the world system. No one was surprised by Washington's decision in the mid-1990s to try to create a world system composed of market democracies. Had Moscow emerged victorious, no one would have been astonished if the world system it sought to create had differed radically from the one advocated by Washington. As Condoleezza Rice, President George W. Bush's national security adviser and secretary of state, commented: "The Soviet Union … strove to lead a universal alternative to markets and democracy."[17]

As we look toward the future, it is advisable to keep in mind the various structures of meaning that were forced underground by the ideological struggle between Washington and Moscow during the Cold War. Thoughtful analyses of the ignored systems would have enabled analysts to avert being surprised by the destruction prompted by the re-emergence of radical forms of Islamism, nationalism, and ethnicity in parts of Asia, Africa, and the former communist states during the post-Cold War era. It could be tempting to write off these developments with the contention that their effects on the overall structure of the international system are not likely to be momentous. But lest we forget, many leaders, observing the rise of nationalism in Europe in the early nineteenth century or in parts of the developing world immediately after the end of the First World War, assumed that their powerful states possessed the material means to contain it. What is more, as Washington has attempted in the post-Cold War era to impose on the world system its own structure of meaning, its main challenges have not come from actors with the greatest material capabilities; they have come from entities that, though distinctly weaker, are inspired by ideologies that contest liberalism. It is still too early to predict whether Iran's and al-Qaeda's type of radical Islam or Hugo Chavez's Marxist populist version will have a lasting effect on the structure of the international system. But it would be a perilous mistake to dismiss them as ideologies destined to rapidly disappear inside history's dustbin. Their goal is no different from that aspired to by the world's most powerful entities: to impose on the world system their own structure of meaning. Throughout history, even those with limited resources have altered its course appreciably.

Notes

Introduction

1 Quoted in W. Mommsen, *The Political and Social Theory of Max Weber*, Chicago, Illinois: University of Chicago Press, 1989, p. 134.

2 See R. Merton, *The Sociology of Science*, Chicago, Illinois: University of Chicago Press, 1973, p. 120.

3 As F. Halliday put it, "one cannot explain any society, political system or international relationship without a parallel analysis of values and ideology." F. Halliday, *The Middle East in International Relations*, Cambridge: Cambridge University Press, 2005, p. 32.

4 T. Ball and R. Dagger, *Political Ideologies*, New York: Pearson-Longman, 2003, pp. 4–6.

5 By anarchic ordering principle, Kenneth Waltz and other Neorealists mean the absence of a legitimate and formal government in the international system with the authority to regulate the behavior of its members. See K. Waltz, *Theory of International Politics*, New York: Random House, 1979, p. 75.

6 K. Waltz, "The Anarchic Structure of World Politics," in R. Art and R. Jervis (eds.) *International Politics*, New York: Pearson, Longman, 2007, pp. 387–8.

7 S. Lamy, "Contemporary Mainstream Approaches: Neo-Realism and Neo-Liberalism," in J. Baylis and S. Smith (eds.) *The Globalization of World Politics*, New York: Oxford University Press, 2001, pp. 213–14; and A. Wendt, *Social Theory of International Politics*, New York: Cambridge University Press, 1999, p. 5.

8 By theory, traditionalists generally mean a set of facts, propositions, or principles analyzed in their relation to one another and used to explain phenomena. Critics of the traditional approach, on the other hand, tend to refer to theory as the body of rules, ideas, principles, and techniques that applies to a particular subject. It might be sensible, thus, to refer to the alternative perspectives not as theories but as approaches. I recognize that by forwarding this suggestion many will think that I am explicitly siding with traditionalists, and rejecting the possibility that critics of the traditional approach have developed, or will develop, a set of propositions designed to explain a social phenomenon. As should become evident shortly, such is not my intent.

9 I have relied extensively on the works by C. Reus-Smit and S. Smith for the analysis I present in this section of the introduction. See C. Reus-Smit, "The Constructive Turn: Critical Theory After the Cold War." Working Paper No. 1996/4, Canberra: National Library of Australia, August 1996; and S. Smith, "Reflectivist and Constructivist Approaches to International Theory," in Baylis and Smith (eds.) *The Globalization of World Politics*, Oxford: Oxford University Press, 2001, pp. 224–49.

10 A. Wendt and R. Duvall, "Institutions and International Order," in E. Otto-Czempiel and J. Rosenau (eds.) *Global Changes and Theoretical Challenges: Approaches to World Politics in the 1990s*, Lexington, Massachusetts: Lexington Books, 1989, p. 60. For a detailed analysis of the shortcomings encountered by theorists of international politics whose starting point is power, defined as material capability, and national interest, defined as egotistic desire for power, security, or wealth, see A. Wendt, *Social Theory of International Politics*, New York: Cambridge University Press, 1999, Chapter 3.

11 One ought not to infer from this discussion that all the sources of a state's identity come from the international system's structure of meaning. To fully grasp the nature of a state's identity one must at some point take into account its non-systemic sources of identity—such as its own domestic political culture.

12 I consciously refer to the world system instead of the international system because conceptually the international system has a very short history.

13 M. Weber, *The Methodology of the Social Sciences*, E. Shils and H. Finch (eds.) New York: Free Press, 1949, p. 81.

14 A. Wendt, *Social Theory of International Politics*, p. 42.

15 Because Wendt refers specifically to the international system and not the world system, during my discussion of his analytical framework I will do the same.

16 Wendt acknowledges that it is possible to explain the absence of violence in the region from a neorealist perspective. From such a perspective one could propose that what has suppressed intra-Western rivalries has been the bipolar distribution of capabilities. See Wendt, *Social Theory of International Politics*, p. 279.

17 See Wendt, *Social Theory of International Politics*, p. 314. Wendt does not state that conflict has been curbed further by the development of a collective security culture in the West, but I assume that that is the kind of inference one should be able to derive from his argument.

18 I address this matter in some detail in Chapters 3 and 4.

19 For a discussion of the three types of mandates created by the League of Nations, see Chapter 6.

20 See Wendt, *Social Theory of International Politics*, p. 281.

21 From now on I will refer to the system as a regional or world system.

22 K. Waltz, *Man, the States and War*, New York: Columbia University Press, 1954, pp. 176–7.

23 See F. Adamson, "The Constitutive Power of Political Ideology: Nationalism and the Emergence of Corporate Agency in World Politics," paper presented at 2006 *Annual Meeting of the American Political Science Association*, Philadelphia, Pennsylvania, August 31–September 3, 2006.

24 Adamson's actual statement is: "Before there was an Algerian state, there was an Algerian nationalist movement." See Adamson, "The Constitutive Power of Political Ideology."

25 D. Mclellan, *Ideology*, Minneapolis, Minnesota: University of Minnesota Press, 1989, p. 2.

26 M. Mann, *The Sources of Social Power*, Vol. I, New York: Cambridge University Press, 1986, pp. 6–7.

27 See A. Gramsci, *Selections from the Prison Notebooks*, London: Lawrence and Wishart, 1971.

28 C. Boggs, *Gramsci's Marxism*, London: Pluto Press, 1976, p. 39.

29 M. Mann, *The Sources of Social Power*, Vol. II, New York: Cambridge University Press, 1993, p. 9.

30 Gramsci, *Selections from the Prison Notebooks*, p. 405.

31 Mann, *The Sources of Social Power*, pp. 22–3.

32 Mann, *The Sources of Social Power*, p. 7.

33 See N. Gould-Davies, "Rethinking the Role of Ideology in International Politics During the Cold War," *Journal of Cold War Studies*, 1.1, 1999, 92–4.
34 See Gould-Davies, "Rethinking the Role of Ideology in International Politics During the Cold War," 95–7.
35 M. Rejai, *Comparative Political Ideologies*, New York: St. Martin's Press, 1984, pp. 3–4.
36 M. Rejai (ed.), *Decline of Ideology?* Chicago, Illinois: Aldine Atherton, 1971, p. 5.
37 Rejai (ed.), *Decline of Ideology?* p. 8. See also J. Nogee and R. Donaldson, *Soviet Foreign Policy Since World War II*, New York: Pergamon Press, 1988, pp. 32–3.
38 Rejai, *Comparative Political Ideologies*, p. 5.
39 Quoted in Rejai (ed.), *Decline of Ideology?* p. 35.
40 Ibid., pp. 8–16.
41 Ibid., pp. 15–22.
42 Rejai, *Comparative Political Ideologies*, p. 9.
43 Ibid., p. 11.
44 For a related argument see, Mann, *The Sources of Social Power*, Vol. I, pp. 341–72.
45 T. Burke, *The Major Religions of the World*, Oxford, UK: Blackwell, 1999, p. 2.
46 B. Lewis, *The Middle East*, New York: Simon and Schuster, 1995, p. 53.
47 Attributed to R. Graham. Quoted in R. Hyam, *Britain's Imperial Century, 1815–1914*, New York: Harper and Row, 1976, p. 18.
48 See Mann, *The Sources of Social Power*, Vol. I, Chapter 7.
49 The decision to go so far back in history might generate some concern amongst analysts who have sought to explain the role of ideology in international politics. For most of them, the term is a modern concept, born during the French Revolution of 1789. That claim is correct. As explained by Alan Cassels, the word *idéologie* came into being for the purpose of creating, via the revolution, "an ideal commonwealth founded on Enlightenment precepts of empiricism, human reason and natural law." He acknowledges, however, that ideological thinking before that date was not uncommon. See A. Cassels, *Ideology and International Relations in the Modern World*, London: Routledge, 1996, pp. 1 and 7.
50 D. Goffman *The Ottoman Empire and Early Modern Europe*, Cambridge: Cambridge University Press, 2002, p. 8
51 M. Doyle, *Empires*, Ithaca, New York: Cornell University Press, 1986, p. 107.
52 See C. Kadafar, *Between Two Worlds: The Construction of the Ottoman Empire*, Berkeley, California: University of California Press, 1995, p. 79.
53 Clearly, other European actors besides Spain and England engaged in colonial activities during the period in question. As I explain later on, I focus principally on the two in order to underscore the critical differences in the ideologies that guided their actions towards their colonies.
54 As Doyle explains, empire and imperialism are tightly related concepts. By empire, Doyle means a formal or informal relationship "in which one state controls the effective political sovereignty of another political society." Imperialism, in turn, refers to "the process or policy of establishing or maintaining an empire." See Doyle, *Empires*, p. 45.
55 I. Berlin, *The Crooked Timber of Humanity: Chapters in the History of Ideas*, New York: Vintage Books, 1992, p. 1.
56 Obviously, Italy was also a major advocate of fascism, and its role will be analyzed in Chapter 4. Italy, however, lacked the material capabilities to act as one of the world's leading powers.

1 Political ideology in late antiquity and the Middle Ages

1 Attributed to Muhammad. Quoted in R. Finucane, *Soldiers of the Faith*, New York: St. Martin's Press, 1983, p. 7.

2 Merchants and missionaries of the period believed that there were four "great empires"—the Roman, Sassanid, Ethiopian, and Chinese Empires. By "empire" I mean the control imposed by a political community on peoples who at earlier times lived as members of separate political communities. The controlling political community might or might not have shared cultural similarities with those under its dominion.

3 R. Gilpin, *War and Change in World Politics*, Cambridge: Cambridge University Press, 1983, pp. 111–12.

4 It goes without saying that at some point the further expansion of territory would stop being cost-effective. See Gilpin, *War and Change*, p. 112. Moreover, the costs of creating and protecting the empire varied significantly, depending on whether the expansion was carried out along sea routes or inland. As Peter Brown notes, it was inland "that the heavy cost of empire was most obvious, along the verges of the great land routes." See P. Brown, *The World of Late Antiquity*, London: Harcourt Brace Jovanovich, 1971, pp. 12–13.

5 Quoted in D. Kagan, S. Ozment and F. Turner, *The Western Heritage*, 7th edition, Upper Saddle River, New Jersey: Prentice Hall, 2001, p. 171.

6 The Sassanian Empire replaced the Parthian Empire in 224, when Ardashir Papakan defeated his Parthian overlord, Artabanus. I discuss the nature of the Sassanian Empire later in this chapter.

7 B. Ward-Perkins, *The Fall of Rome and the End of Civilization*, New York: Oxford University Press, 2005, p. 34.

8 M. Grant, *The Collapse and Recovery of the Roman Empire*, New York: Routledge, 1999, p. 3.

9 Kagan, Ozment, and Turner, *The Western Heritage*, pp. 171–3. See also Ward-Perkins, *The Fall of Rome*, p. 41.

10 P. Southern, *The Roman Empire: From Severus to Constantine*, New York: Routledge, 2001, p. 147.

11 Diocletian remained first among not exactly equals.

12 Some contemporary scholars dispute the idea that the ancient Jewish tradition was a culture different from Hellenism. According to Thomas Thompson, the Old Testament is not a history of anyone in particular. It is "a philosophical metaphor of a mankind that has lost its way." See T. Thompson, *The Bible in History*, London: Jonathan Cape, 1999, p. 15.

13 Brown, *The World of Late Antiquity*, pp. 82–4; and K. Armstrong, *A History of God*, New York: Ballantine Books, 1993, p. 105. See also R. Stark, *The Rise of Christianity*, Princeton, New Jersey: Princeton University Press, 1996, p. 147.

14 Kagan, Ozment, and Turner, *The Western Heritage*, p. 169.

15 Armstrong, *A History of God*, p. 105.

16 As already noted, by the time Constantine became emperor, Christianity had already spread widely throughout society. It would be incorrect, thus, to argue that his actions automatically legitimized Christianity. It is valid to contend, however, that his policies helped enhance Christianity's status. See Stark, *The Rise of Christianity*, pp. 10–11.

17 D. Bowder, *The Age of Constantine and Julian*, New York: Harper and Row, 1978, p. 28. See also M. Grant, *Constantine the Great*, New York: Charles Scribner's Sons, 1994, pp. 156–7.

18 Southern, *The Roman Empire: From Severus to Constantine*, pp. 176–7.

19 Bowder, *The Age of Constantine and Julian*, pp. 31–2.

20 Quoted in Grant, *Constantine the Great*, p. 168.

21 Historians are not of one mind regarding whether Constantine became a "true" believer, or promoted himself as Christian solely for political purposes. The issue is not pertinent to the task at hand. However, I concur with scholars who wonder why Constantine would choose to promote Christianity when the power of its

advocates in the early part of the fourth century was not substantial, unless he shared its beliefs.

22 M. Salzman, *The Making of a Christian Aristocracy*, Cambridge, Massachusetts: Harvard University Press, 2002, p. 61.

23 Grant, *Constantine the Great*, p. 106.

24 Salzman, *The Making of a Christian Aristocracy*, p. 205.

25 Unsurprisingly, when comparing the nobility of a pious common man with that of a devout aristocrat, bishops apportioned greater worth to the latter. See Salzman, *The Making of Christian Aristocracy,* pp. 214–15.

26 See C. Mango, *Byzantium: The Empire of New Rome*, New York: Charles Scribner's Sons, 1980, p. 88.

27 B. Lewis, *The Middle East*, New York: Touchstone, 1995, p. 29.

28 For an account of the various wars between the Byzantine and Sassanid Empires, see W. Kaegi, *Byzantium and the Early Islamic Conquests*, Cambridge: Cambridge University Press, 1992, Chapters 1–3.

29 Both quotes appear in Ward-Perkins, *The Fall of Rome*, pp. 40–1.

30 See Herrin, *The Formation of Christendom*, p. 144; Ward-Perkins, *The Fall of Rome*, p. 41; Grant, *Constantine the Great*, p. 223; and Doyle, *Empires*, p. 101.

31 See Gilpin, *War and Change in World Politics*, pp. 113 and 192.

32 Barraclough (ed.), *The Times Atlas of World History*, p. 113.

33 M. Cranston, "Ideology," in *Encyclopedia Britannica*. www.culturaleconomics. atfreeweb.com/Anno/Cranston%20Ideology%20

34 For a brief explanation as to how Christianity became a religion, see S. Cohen, "Legitimization Under Constantine: The Path to Victory." www.pbs.org/wegbh/ pages/frontline/shows/religion/why/legitimization.html

35 For a detailed interpretation of Christianity as a type of ideological power within the Roman Empire, see Mann, *The Sources of Social Power*, Vol. I, pp. 301–40.

36 The Qur'an was compiled after Muhammad's death, between the years 650 and 651.

37 Muhammad did not see himself as the creator of a new religion. His principal claim was that he was attempting to restore the proper application of the principles of the eternal truth. See M. Shaban, *Islamic History, A.D. 600–750*, London: Cambridge University Press, 1971, pp. 14–15.

38 F. Donner, *The Early Islamic Conquests*, Princeton, New Jersey: Princeton University Press, 1981, p. 55.

39 Muhammad did not return to govern Mecca. He stayed in Medina until his death, and it was from there that he started to build the empire.

40 Lewis, *The Middle East*, p. 53.

41 Abu Bakr was viewed not as another prophet, but as the successor to the Prophet of God. See F. Donner, "Muhammad and the Caliphate," in J. Esposito (ed.) *The Oxford History of Islam*, New York: Oxford University Press, 1999, p. 11.

42 For a discussion of the politics of succession following Muhammad's death, see W. Madelung, *The Succession to Muhammad*, Cambridge: Cambridge University Press, 1997.

43 Donner, "Muhammad and the Caliphate," pp. 15–16.

44 For a discussion about the struggle for power that ensued between competing groups following Muhammad's death, see Donner, "Muhammad and the Caliphate," pp. 14–18.

45 Lewis, *The Middle East*, pp. 70–4.

46 Ibid., pp. 75–9. See also Donner, "Muhammad and the Caliphate," p. 22.

47 See Fowden, *Empire to Commonwealth*, p. 153.

48 The capital of the Islamic Empire was moved first from Mecca to Damascus, and then, in 750, to Baghdad.

49 Fowden, *Empire to Commonwealth*, p. 165; see also Lewis, *The Middle East*, pp. 78–81.

50 By "commonwealth," Fowden means "a group of politically discrete but related polities collectively distinguishable from other polities or commonwealths by a shared culture or history." See Fowden, *Empire to Commonwealth*, p. 6. See also A. Watson, *The Evolution of International Society*, London: Routledge, 1992, pp. 112–16.
51 Geary, *The Myth of Nations*, pp. 114–17.
52 F. Cardini, *Europe and Islam*, Oxford: Blackwell Publishers, 2001, pp. 8–11.
53 Barraclough (ed.), *Atlas of World History*, p. 107.
54 T. Knutsen, *A History of International Relations Theory*, Manchester: Manchester University Press, 1992, p. 17.
55 Ibid., p. 15. See also D. North and R. Thomas, *The Rise of the Western World*, Cambridge: Cambridge University Press, 1982, p. 28.
56 Quoted in T. Mastnak, *Crusading Peace*, Berkeley, California: University of California Press, 2002, p. 2.
57 See R. Finucane, *Soldiers of Faith*, New York: St. Martin's Press, 1983, p. 17.
58 Quoted in Mastnak, *Crusading Peace*, p. 5.
59 This process is referred to as the Peace of God—a peace movement that emerged in what today is central France and was carried out in the name of God. See Finucane, *Soldiers of Faith*, p. 17.
60 Mastnak, *Crusading Peace*, pp. 9–10.
61 Ibid., pp. 60–4.
62 Christianity did not originate the holy war tradition.
63 Mastnak, *Crusading Peace*, pp. 62–3.
64 Ibid., pp. 18–20.
65 Tyerman, *The Invention of the Crusades*, p. 15; Finucane, *Soldiers of Faith*, p. 12; and Mastnak, *Crusading Peace*, pp. 96–107.
66 Quoted in Mastnak, *Crusading Peace*, pp. 52–3.
67 During that period no one ever spoke of Muslims as Muslims. They were referred to by the ethnic term "Saracens."
68 Quoted in Mastnak, *Crusading Peace*, pp. 115–20, 124 and 128.
69 Munro, D. C. "Urban and the Crusaders," Translations and Reprints from the *Original Sources of European History*, Vol. 1:2, Philadelphia, Pennsylvania: University of Pennsylvania, 1895, p. 12.
70 Some analysts contend that there were eight crusades; others propose that there were seven. For our purposes the exact number is unimportant. In 1291, some forty-three years after Louis IX, king of France, had launched the last crusade and sought to invade Egypt, the sultan, Khalil, took Acre and put an end to two centuries of the crusaders' presence in the Middle East.
71 C. Maier, *Crusade Propaganda and Ideology*, Cambridge: Cambridge University Press, 2000, p. 67.
72 Tyerman, *The Invention of the Crusades*, p. 1.
73 S. Ehler and J. Morrall (eds.), *Church and States Through the Centuries: A Collection of Historical Documents*, New York: Biblo and Tannen, 1967, pp. 43–4.
74 Quoted in Mastnak, *Crusading Peace*, p. 138.
75 Ibid., p. 151 (note 431).
76 F. Mote, *Imperial China*, Cambridge, Massachusetts: Harvard University Press, 1999, pp. 403–4.
77 Lewis, *The Middle East*, p. 97.
78 M. Doyle, *Empires*, Ithaca, New York: Cornell University Press, 1986, pp. 106–7. Also of deep significance was the claim by Osman's chroniclers, and their subjects and potential subjects, that Osman's bid for political power "was endowed with divine sanction." See C. Kadafar, *Between Two Worlds: The Construction of the Ottoman Empire*, Berkeley, California: University of California Press, 1995, p. 30.
79 Goffman, *The Ottoman Empire and Early Modern Europe*, p. 8.
80 Doyle, *Empire*, p. 107.

81 Goffman, *The Ottoman Empire and the Early Modern World*, p. 12.
82 See Kafadar, *Between Two Worlds*, p. 79.
83 Mote, *Imperial China*, pp. 517–72.
84 According to Louis Levathes, "Confucius thought foreign travel interfered with important familial obligations and believed trade was inherently mean and debasing." In Confucius's words: "The mind of the superior man dwells in righteousness; the mind of the little man dwells on profit." See L. Levathes, *When China Ruled the Seas*, New York: Oxford University Press, 1994, p. 33. See also G. Wang, *The Chinese Overseas*, Cambridge, Massachusetts: Harvard University Press, 2000, p. 21. According to Wang, Zhu Yuanzhang's decision reaffirmed the tradition that the coastal southern Chinese would look inward and northward again.
85 Levathes, *When China Ruled the Seas*, p. 88.
86 By the time Zhu Di became China's new ruler, eunuchs had become highly influential figures in the imperial system. The founder of the Ming Dynasty had established a bureau for eunuchs in Nanjing in 1367. Eager to ensure that the imperial succession process would not be stained by scandal, and in need of people able to carry out difficult tasks within the Chinese courts, imperial leaders became highly dependent on non-Chinese men from bordering areas who had been captured and castrated in their childhood. In time, eunuchs widened their functions and began to assume governing responsibilities. Under Zhu Di's leadership, they established a well-organized bureaucracy that came to be known as the Twenty-four Offices. It was under this system that Admiral Zheng He, a Muslim captured and castrated at the age of ten in Yunnan in 1381, attained his formidable reputation.
87 See Levathes, *When China Ruled the* Seas, pp. 74–85; Mote, *Imperial China*, pp. 614–5; and P. Kennedy, *The Rise and Fall of the Great Powers*, New York: Random House, 1987, pp. 6–7.
88 Mote, *Imperial China*, pp. 613–16. See also J. Fairbank and M. Goldman, *China. A New History*, Cambridge, Massachusetts: The Belknap Press of Harvard University Press, 2006, p. 138.
89 J. Needham, *Science and Civilization in China, Civil Engineering and Nautics*, Vol. IV, Cambridge: Cambridge University Press, 1971, p. 524.
90 Levathes, *When China Ruled the Seas*, p. 164.
91 See Hucker, *The Censorial System of Ming China*, p. 112.
92 See Levathes, *When China Ruled the Seas*, pp. 168–70. Quote appears on p. 169.
93 Ibid., pp. 171–3.
94 Ibid., pp. 174–5.
95 Fowden, *Empire to Commonwealth*, pp. 3 and 98.
96 Fowden posits a slightly different argument. He claims that while Rome became an *aspiring politico-cultural world empire*, the Islamic Empire became antiquity's only *politico-cultural world empire*. By "world empire" Fowden means "control without serious competition of an area large enough to pass for 'the world'." Ibid., p. 6.
97 See Ibid., pp. 139–40.
98 Mann, *The Sources of Social Power*, Vol. I, p. 22.

2 Beginnings and restructuring: The intermingling of religion and politics between the sixteenth and eighteenth centuries in Europe and the Americas

1 The largest population shift is taking place presently in China.
2 L. McAlister, *Spain and Portugal in the New World*, Minneapolis, Minnesota: University of Minnesota Press, 1984, pp. 13–16; and J. Edwards, *The Spain of the Catholic Monarchs, 1474–1520*, Oxford: Blackwell, 2000, pp. 1–4.
3 Edwards, *The Spain of Catholic Monarchs*, p. 194.
4 J. Hillgarth, *The Spanish Kingdoms, 1250–1516*, Vol. II, Oxford: Clarendon Press, 1978, pp. 367–70; see also McAllister, *Spain and Portugal*, pp. 13–16.

5 Quoted in Hillgarth, *The Spanish Kingdoms*, p. 392.
6 Edwards, *The Spain of Catholic Monarchs*, pp. 68–85.
7 Ibid., pp. 228–9.
8 McAlister, *Spain and Portugal*, pp. 58–9.
9 I. Wallerstein, *The Modern World System*, Vol. I, New York: Academic Press, 1974, pp. 48–52.
10 A mile is equal to 1.6 km while a nautical mile is 1.8532 km long. The actual distance was some ten thousand nautical miles.
11 See J. Diamond, *Guns, Germs, and Steel*, New York: W. W. Norton, 1999, pp. 67–81; and A. Taylor, *American Colonies*, New York: Penguin Putnam Inc., 2001, pp. 24–90.
12 Quoted in M. Donelan, "Spain and the Indies," in H. Bull and A. Watson (eds.) *The Expansion of International Society*, Oxford: Clarendon Press, 1984, p. 79. For an analysis of the bulls issued by the Vatican to the kings of Portugal and Spain during the fifteenth century, see A. García-Gallo de Diego, *Las Bulas de Alejandro VI Sobre el Nuevo Mundo Descubierto por Colón*, Madrid: Ministerio de Cultura, Compañía Editorial, 1992.
13 Quoted in McAlister, *Spain and Portugal*, p. 12.
14 Donelan, "Spain and the Indies," p. 81.
15 See McAlister, *Spain and Portugal*, pp. 56–69. The Crown's principal concern was whether it "might legitimately benefit from the fruits of their [indigenous people] labour and from the profits to be had from their land and, more crucially, from what lay beneath their land." For the Crown's contemporaries the most compelling argument was presented by those who proposed that because the indigenous people had not created legitimate civil societies, that is, societies based on property relations, their members could not make claims to rights of ownership; hence, it was legitimate for Spaniards to appropriate the lands. The lands, in other words, were not the lands of the indigenous people, but open spaces that they happened to inhabit. See A. Pagden, *Spanish Imperialism and the Political Imagination*, New Haven, Connecticut: Yale University Press, 1990, p. 15.
16 Quoted in McAlister, *Spain and Portugal*, pp. 108–9.
17 Quoted in A. Pagden, *Lords of All the World: Ideologies of Empire in Spain, Britain, and France, c.1500–c. 1800*, New Haven, Connecticut: Yale University Press, 1995, p. 42. For a discussion of attempts by theologians and political analysts to address this matter, see Pagden, *Spanish Imperialism*, pp. 13–63.
18 The pope's bull generated great controversy within and outside Castile. Neo-Thomist theologians, though they recognized the pope as the spiritual ruler of all Christians, argued that he could not exercise authority in the secular world or over non-Christians. Moreover, French and English attacks on Spanish claims to sovereignty throughout the Americas almost invariably began with a rejection of the validity of the bull. See Pagden, *Lords of all the World*, pp. 47 and 48.
19 Notwithstanding attempts by the conquerors and the Franciscan and Dominican orders to create an independent Church in the Americas, the Crown retained control of the ecclesiastical institutions in Spanish America throughout the colonial period. See Pagden, *Lords of all the World*, p. 59.
20 Hostility within Spain towards the pope's relentless drive to centralize power reached its peak around the start of the fifteenth century. Though attempts to change the ways of the Church had been initiated in the late fourteenth century, it was not until after Ferdinand and Isabelle had married that the Church's authority in Spain started to diminish. In 1474 and 1475 the king and queen sought to restrict and control papal tax collectors and to prevent the pope from appointing anyone to the archbishoprics, bishoprics, or military orders, unless the application came from them. Despite his initial unwillingness to acquiesce to the monarchs' challenge, the pope agreed to compromise in 1482, when Isabella and Ferdinand

requested that a major portion of the taxes collected from the clergy be used to finance the war against the Moors in Granada. See Hillgarth, *The Spanish Kingdoms*, pp. 395–8.

21 See McAlister, *Spain and Portugal*, pp. 78–9, 157–60, 194.
22 McAlister, *Spain and Portugal*, pp. 291 and 293. See also Pagden, *Lords of all the World*, p. 43.
23 McAlister, *Spain and Portugal*, pp. 293–4.
24 T. Knutsen, *A History of International Relations Theory*, New York: Manchester University Press, 1992, p. 27.
25 J. Schumpeter, *A History of Economic Analysis*, Oxford: Oxford University Press, 1954, p. 78.
26 A. Watson, *Evolution of International Society*, London: Routledge, 1992, pp. 152–3; see also Knutsen, *A History of International Relations Theory*, pp. 27–9.
27 See T. Pangle and P. Ahrensdorf, *Justice among Nations*, Lawrence, Kansas: University Press of Kansas, 1999, pp. 132–3.
28 Knutsen, *A History of International Relations Theory*, pp. 33–5.
29 N. Machiavelli, *The Prince and the Discourses,* New York: The Modern Library, 1950, p. 53; see also J. Haslam, *No Virtue Like Necessity: Realist Thought in International Relations Since Machiavelli*, New Haven, Connecticut: Yale University Press, 2002, pp. 28–9.
30 Machiavelli, *The Prince and the Discourses*, p. 65.
31 M. Lerner's "Introduction," to Machiavelli's *The Prince and the Discourses*, p. xxxiv.
32 Quoted in T. Mastnak, *Crusading Peace*, Berkeley, California: University of California Press, 2002, pp. 236–7. Moreover, Pope Boniface VIII had reiterated at the start of the fourteenth century the Church's long-standing belief that the pope possessed superior temporal power.

> We are taught by the words of the Gospel that in this church and in her power there are two swords, a spiritual and a temporal one. Certainly any one who denies that the temporal sword is in the power of Peter has not paid heed to the words of the Lord when he said, 'Put up thy sword into its sheath.' Both then are in the power of the church, the material sword and the spiritual. But the one is exercised for the church, the other by the church, the one by the hand of the priest, the other by the hand of kings and soldiers, though at the will and sufferance of the priest. One sword ought to be under the other and the temporal authority subject to the spiritual power.
>
> Quoted in Mastnak, *Crusading Peace*, p. 229.

33 Though Boniface VIII managed to escape his captors, he died shortly afterward.
34 K. Armstrong, *A History of God*, New York: Ballantine Books, 1993, p. 272.
35 Quoted in W. Manchester, *A World Lit Only By Fire*, Boston, Massachusetts: Little, Brown and Company, 1993, pp. 130–3.
36 See Manchester, *A World Lit Only By Fire*, p. 131.
37 Quoted in Manchester, *A World Lit Only By Fire*, p. 141.
38 M. Luther, "Concerning Christian Liberty," in *The Harvard Classics*, Vol. 36, New York: P. F. Collier and Son, 1910, pp. 353–97.
39 Manchester, *A World Lit Only By Fire*, pp. 175–6.
40 Geoffrey Barraclough (ed.) *The Times Atlas of World History*, London: Times Books, 1986, p. 183.
41 *Cujus regio ejus religio*. Roughly translated it means: "He who reigns, chooses the religion." Calvinist Zwinglians were not extended similar rights.
42 Scholars have divided the war into the: i) Bohemian Phase, 1618–1621; ii) Palatinate Phase, 1621–1624; iii) Danish Phase, 1625–1630; iv) Swedish Phase, 1630–1634; and v) French Phase, 1634–1648.

43 Charles Tilly estimated the battle deaths exceeded two million. See C. Tilly, *Coercion, Capital, and European States, AD 990–1990*, Cambridge, Massachusetts: Basil Blackwell, 1990, p. 165.

44 In Christian Reus-Smit's words, the "Peace of Westphalia resolved the long-standing, hard-fought issue of the rights of monarchs to determine the predominant religion in their domains." C. Reus-Smit, *The Moral Purpose of the State: Culture, Social Identity, and Institutional Rationality in International Relations*, Princeton, New Jersey: Princeton University Press, 1999, p. 116. One of the main differences between the original agreement and the one formulated in 1648 was that the toleration that had been granted to Catholics and Lutherans was now extended to Calvinists.

45 In 1356, the emperor of the Holy Roman Empire and the rulers of its various states agreed that each emperor would be chosen by election, and that seven electoral states, three of which were ruled by leaders of the Church, would participate in the election.

46 See M. Prak, *The Dutch Republic in the Seventeenth Century*. Trans. by Diane Webb. New York: Cambridge University Press, 2005, p. 15; see also Wallerstein, *The Modern World-System*, Vol. I, p. 201.

47 See S. Schama, *The Embarrassment of Riches: An Interpretation of Dutch Culture in the Golden Age*, New York: Alfred A. Knopf, 1987, pp. 38–41.

48 Prak, *The Dutch Republic in the Seventeenth Century*, p. 15.

49 Wallerstein, *The Modern World-System I*, p. 204.

50 Prak, *The Dutch Republic in the Seventeenth Century*, p. 20.

51 P. Geyl, *Debates with Historians*, New York: Meridian, 1958, p. 209.

52 H. Koenigsberger, "The Organization of Revolutionary Parties in France and the Netherlands During the Sixteenth Century," *The Journal of Modern History*, XXVII, 4, December 1955, 350.

53 It was during this period that the Zeeland Chamber of the newly established Dutch East India Company approached Hugo Grotius to write a challenge to Portugal's claim that it had exclusive access to the East Indies. Grotius broke the argument into three parts. In the first section he contended that the right of possession by virtue of first discovery was inapplicable because the territory was not uninhabited. It did not matter that the rulers of the "discovered" land were "partly idolaters, partly Mahometans" given that, as others had noted, grace did not confer dominion. The natives, moreover, were not "out of their wits and insensible but ingenious and sharp-witted." Thus, the Portuguese could not rely on Aristotle's conceptions of natural servitude to divest the natives of their original rights. In the second part Grotius focused on the right of navigation. He emphasized the difference between territorial and maritime ownership and linked each kind, respectively, to things that can be appropriated and to things that remained common to nature. Dominion can be achieved only via the actual attainment of physical possession. Land can be physically controlled, transformed by human labor, and products derived from it used for private purposes. The sea, on the other hand, because it constantly flows and shifts, cannot be possessed. The sea, he wrote, is "in the number of things which are not in merchandise and trading, that is to say, cannot remain proper." It would follow, therefore, that no one, including the Portuguese, could claim the right to control the ocean around and leading to the East Indies. From this argument, Grotius went on to contend that the right of trading, just like the right of navigation, was derived from the law of nations. To Seneca's contention, "the law of nations [extends man the right] to sell that which [he] has bought," he added, no "man [can] take [that right] away." After 1648, the power of the Dutch Republic surged. Backed by the claim that the laws of nations freed its merchants to navigate and trade freely, the Dutch Republic, which for some time had been the center of

Baltic trade, soon became a center of world trade. By the end of the 1650s it had become one of the three main European actors, with France and England completing the trio. I have based my comments on D. Armitage's introduction to H. Grotius, *The Free Sea*, Indianapolis: Liberty Fund, 2004, pp. xv–xvii. The quotes appear on pp. 30, 51, and 49.

54 See Knutsen, *A History of International Relations Theory*, pp. 70–6. The Treaty of Westphalia is a series of treaties. Spain and the Netherlands signed the Treaty of Munster in early 1648, which confirmed the independence of the Netherlands. France, England, and the Holy Roman Empire signed the same treaty in October. Sweden and the Holy Roman Empire signed the Treaty of Osnabruck.

55 Knutsen, *A History of International Relations Theory*, pp. 58–64, 70–6.

56 For a related argument, see S. Krasner, *Sovereignty: Organized Hypocrisy*, Princeton, New Jersey: Princeton University Press, 1999. According to the Stanford Encyclopedia of Philosophy, sovereignty stands for "supreme authority within a territory." It adds that the definition highlights two components. First, the holder of sovereignty must possess authority. The person or entity does not merely wield coercive power, but also possesses "the right to command and correlatively the right to be obeyed." In other words, "the holder of sovereignty derives authority from some mutually acknowledged source of legitimacy," which can be natural law, a divine mandate, hereditary law, a constitution, or international law. Sovereignty, however, is not just a matter of authority, but of *supreme* authority. More to the point, the "holder of sovereignty is superior to all authorities under its purview." See "Sovereignty," in the *Stanford Encyclopedia of Philosophy*, June 18, 2003, www.plato.stanford.edu/entries/sovereignty/

57 For a concise discussion of the evolution of the modern state see, B. Buzan and R. Little, *International Systems in World History*, New York: Oxford University Press, 2000, pp. 246–55.

58 As Reus-Smit reminds us, though the Peace of Westphalia clarified the scope of sovereign authority, it did not properly delineate the geographical extension of sovereign rule. This ambiguity became the principal source of contestation and war after 1648. The Treaties of Utrecht of 1713 helped establish the claim that it was imperative to curtail the reach of dynastic entitlements in order to preserve European peace and security. More specifically, in article six of the *Treaty of Utrecht between Great Britain and France*, the signatories recognized that the security and liberty of Europe required that France and Spain not be ruled by one king. As will be noted later, Napoleon disregarded the treaty in the early 1800s, when he appointed his brother king of Spain. See Reus-Smit, *The Moral Purpose of the State*, pp. 116 and 117.

59 Machiavelli, *The Prince and the Discourses*, p. 150.

60 P. Kennedy, *The Rise and Fall of the Great Powers*, New York: Random House, 1987, p. 33.

61 Quoted in Pagden, *Lords of all the World*, p. 44.

62 M. Oberg, *Dominion and Civility. English Imperialism of Native America, 1585–1685*, Ithaca, New York: Cornell University Press, 1999, p. 13.

63 Ibid., p. 13.

64 Quoted in G. Elton, "An Early Tudor Poor Law," in G. R. Elton, *Studies in Tudor and Stuart Politics and Government*, Vol. II, Cambridge: Cambridge University Press, 1974, pp. 152–3.

65 Quoted in A. Taylor, *American Colonies*, New York: Penguin Putnam, Inc., 2001, p. 160.

66 See C. Hill, *The Century of Revolution, 1603–1714*, Edinburgh: Thomas Nelson and Sons, 1961, p. 80.

67 G. Mosse, "Puritan Political Thought and the Cases of Conscience," in *Church History*, 23.2 June 1954, 109–18.

68 As Manchester notes, Henry VIII "remained a faithful Catholic in every particular except one. He rejected the supremacy of Rome because the pontiff – for political, not religious reasons – resisted what the king regarded as a royal prerogative." See Manchester, *A World Lit By Fire*, p. 206.

69 See Taylor, *American Colonies*, pp. 160–4; see also Hill, *The Century of Revolution*, pp. 80–92.

70 Quoted in Oberg, *Dominion and Civility*, p. 17.

71 Ibid., pp. 17 and 18, 34 and 52. The various quotes appear in the original spelling. To minimize confusion I changed many of the words to contemporary spelling.

72 Taylor, *American Colonies*, pp. 118 and 123.

73 It started in 1622, when a band of Native Americans, angered by the colonists' agricultural practices and their seemingly uncontainable appetite for land in the broad coastal plain around the Chesapeake Bay, launched a well-coordinated attack on March 22. Their assault brought about the destruction of plantations and the death of three hundred and forty-seven men, women, and children. Enraged by the action, the colonists in the area rapidly exploited the opportunity. Virginia's English governor announced that based on the incident the colonists' principal goal would be "the expulsion of the Savages to gain the free range of the country for increase of Cattle, swine ... for it is infinitely better not to have heathen among us, who at best were but thorns in our sides, than to be at peace and league with them." The London Council, though critical of the colonists' failure to anticipate the attack, pressed that they respond with force. "We must advise you to root out from being any longer a people, so cursed a nation, ungrateful to all benefits, and incapable of all goodness," informed London. It also ordered that Native Americans be forced to move "so far from you, as you may not only be out of danger, but out of fear of them, of whose faith and good meaning you can never be secure." Quoted in Taylor, *American Colonies*, p. 135; and Oberg, *Dominion and Civility*, p. 76.

74 Quoted in Oberg, *Dominion and Civility*, p. 83.

75 Diseases brought from Europe by the colonists also helped ravage Native Americans.

76 Taylor, *American Colonies*, p. 258; see also E. Wright, *The Search for Liberty*, Vol. I, Oxford: Blackwell, 1994, pp. 301–2.

77 Taylor, *American Colonies*, pp. 276–86; and Jones, *England and the World*, pp. 115–16.

78 In 1683, the Ottomans, led by Kara Mustafa, sought to take Vienna and squash Habsburg power in central Europe. The attempt failed, and as the forces retreated they were pursued and destroyed by the Habsburgs and the Poles. See J. McCarthy, *The Ottoman Turks*, London: Longman, 1997, pp. 182–3.

79 This change was noticeable in the area of offensive versus defensive strategies. During earlier periods the Ottomans' offensive strategies carried a substantial advantage over the Europeans' defensive ones; in time, the Europeans gained the upper hand by creating tactics capable of shielding their cities. See Donald Quataert, *The Ottoman Empire, 1700–1922*, Cambridge: Cambridge University Press, 2000, pp. 37–8.

80 Goffman, *The Ottoman Empire and Early Modern Europe*, p. 233.

81 K. Karpat, *The Politicization of Islam. Reconstructing Identity, State, Faith, and Community in the Late Ottoman State*, New York: Oxford University Press, 2001, pp. 4–5.

82 See H. Spryut, *The Sovereign State and its Competitors: An Analysis of Systems Change*, Princeton, New Jersey: Princeton University Press, 1994; and Tilly, *Coercion, Capital and European States*, p. 167.

83 Christianity, as a political ideology, regained much of its earlier luster towards the end of the nineteenth century and start of the twentieth century. I discuss the matter in the next two chapters.

84 See Wright, *The Search for Liberty*, p. 209.

85 As Thomas Hobbes argued in *Leviathan*, the interest of the ruler is the interest of the state; because the ruler is sovereign he represents his state as he deals with the leaders of other states. T. Hobbes, *Leviathan*, Harmondsworth: Penguin, 1951.

3 The strengthening of an empire, the materialization of a new one, and the emergence of novel ideologies: 1750–1871

1 See P. Kennedy, *The Rise and Fall of the Great Powers*, New York: Random House, 1987, pp. 86–93; F. Quinn, *The French Overseas Empire*, Westport, Connecticut: Praeger, 2000, pp. 67–8; and G. Barraclough (ed.), *The Times Atlas of World History*, London: Times Book, 1986, pp. 160–3, 190–1, and 196–7.

2 See J. Lynch, *The Hispanic World in Crisis and Change*, Oxford: Blackwell, 1992, pp. 383–92.

3 A. Pagden, *Spanish Imperialism and the Political Imagination*, New Haven, Connecticut: Yale University Press, 1990, p. 8.

4 See Kennedy, *The Rise and Fall of the Great Powers*, pp. 73–5.

5 A. Taylor, *American Colonies*, New York: Penguin Putnam Inc, 2001, pp. 428–33. See also E. Wright, *The Search for Liberty*, Oxford: Blackwell, 1994, pp. 414 and 420; and Kennedy, *The Rise and Fall of the Great Powers*, pp. 107–13.

6 See Taylor, *American Colonies*, p. 439.

7 T. Draper, *A Struggle for Power*, New York: Times Books, 1996, pp. 197–9.

8 P. Thomas, "The Greenville Program, 1763-1765," in Jack P. Greene and J. Pole (eds.) *The Blackwell Encyclopedia of the American Revolution*, Oxford: Blackwell, 1991, pp. 110–11.

9 Quoted in Draper, *A Struggle for Power*, p. 215.

10 Quoted in Taylor, *American Colonies*, p. 439.

11 Quoted in Draper, *A Struggle for Power*, p. 217.

12 Ibid., p. 306.

13 Ibid., p. 415.

14 Ibid., p. 422.

15 France recognized the independence of the rebelling colonies in early 1778, when it signed political and commercial treaties with them and agreed to fight Britain until the colonies gained their independence. Spain joined the war the following year as an ally of France but not of the rebelling colonies; and the Netherlands went to war against Britain in 1780. See W. McDougall, *Promised Land, Crusader States*, Boston, Massachusetts: Houghton Mifflin Company, 1997, p. 5.

16 See McDougall, *Promised Land, Crusader State*, p. 6. As McDougall notes, the first twenty-nine of the eighty-five *Federalist Papers* present arguments for the ratification of the Constitution on foreign policy grounds. See also Wright, *The Search for Liberty*, p. 474.

17 For a summary discussion of the evolution of the idea of balance of power, see H. Butterfield, "Balance of Power," in *Dictionary of the History of Ideas*, Charlottesville, Virginia: The Electronic Text Center at the University of Virginia, May 2003. www.historyofideas.org/

18 Quoted in T. Knutsen, *A History of International Relations Theory*, Manchester, UK: Manchester University Press, 1992, p. 125.

19 W. Doyle, *The Oxford History of the French Revolution*, New York: Oxford University Press, 1990, p. 69.

20 During much of the eighteenth century, the debate regarding the nature of the nation was between those who viewed the monarch as the sole representative of the state and those who claimed that it had to include the aristocracy. Louis XIV, because he considered himself the nation, seldom referred to the nation; and because he ruled without the elite's participation, he paid little attention to the nation. On the other hand, to the question "What is a nation?" Joseph de Maitres

answered: "It is the sovereign and the aristocracy." The French Revolution altered the scope of the concept significantly, but not as extensively as often claimed. The Third Estate did not rename itself the "National Assembly" in order to represent the *populus*. Members of the Third Estate were civil servants, lawyers, financiers, businessmen, and part of the literate class in general. As such, they endeavored to differentiate themselves from the *populus*, a term that historically had carried a derogatory meaning. The import of this distinction became clear when, upon considering whether to call itself *assemblée nationale* or *représentants de peuple Français*, the Third Estate opted for the first name. In other words, the intent of the French Revolution was not to make all men equal but to make the most successful members of the working class more aristocratic.

21 E. Weber, *Europe Since 1715*, New York: W. W. Norton and Company, 1972, p. 118. See also D. Kaiser, *Politics and War – European Conflict from Philip II to Hitler*, Cambridge, Massachusetts: Harvard University Press, 2000, p. 215.

22 The analysis of nationalism has moved along two paths. One group of analysts considers nationalism as reflections of primordial identities. This group's intellectual commitment has been to find evidence of the existence of nationalism throughout history. A second group claims that nationalism is a relatively modern phenomenon that arises out of specific forms of interaction between the leaders of centralized states and elites from non-dominant groups. To the extent that our focus is on nationalism as a political ideology, consideration of the first perspective is of limited significance to this study. See P. Brass, *Ethnicity and Nationalism*, London: Sage Publications, 1991, p. 8.

23 M. Weber, "The Nation," in J. Hutchinson and A. Smith (eds.) *Nationalism: Critical Concepts in Political Science*, Vol. I, New York: Routledge, 2000, pp. 5–7.

24 See J. Kellas, *The Politics of Nationalism and Ethnicity*, New York: St. Martin's Press, 1998, p. 28.

25 B. Anderson, *Imagined Communities*, London: Verso, 1993, p. 4.

26 Knutsen, *A History of International Relations Theory*, pp. 144–5.

27 See H. Kissinger, "The Congress of Vienna: A Reappraisal," in *World Politics*, 8.2, January 1956, 264–80.

28 J. Derry, *Castlereagh*, London: Allen Lane, 1976, p. 158.

29 Weber, *Europe Since 1715*, pp. 142–3.

30 C. Breunig, *The Age of Revolution and Reaction, 1789–1850*, New York: W. W. Norton, 1970, p. 130.

31 For Castlereagh the real issue was not that Spain was striving towards democracy, but that in the process its hold over Latin America would further loosen, thus enabling Britain to fill the power vacuum that had been growing in that region for some time.

32 Quoted in J. Robinson, *Readings in European History*, London: Ginn, pp. 519–20.

33 Ibid., pp. 521–2.

34 Breunig, *The Age of Revolution and Reaction*, pp. 140–1.

35 Jeremy Bentham initially postulated the argument. His argument is quoted in Knutsen, *A History of International Relations Theory*, p. 135.

36 Breunig, *The Age of Revolution and Reaction*, p. 155.

37 H. Hahn, "The Polish Nation in the Revolution of 1846–49," in D. Dowe, H. Gerhard Haupt, D. Langewiesche, and J. Sperber (eds.) *Europe in 1848. Revolution and Reform*, New York: Bergham Books, 2001, pp. 171–3.

38 Weber, *Europe Since 1715*, p. 412.

39 S. Soldani, "Approaching Europe in the Name of the Nation: The Italian Revolution, 1846/49," in Dowe *et al.* (eds.) *Europe in 1848*, pp. 66–9.

40 Quoted in Breunig, *The Age of Revolution and Reaction*, p. 232.

41 P. Lévêque, "The Revolution Crisis of 1848/51 in France," in Dowe *et al.* (eds.) *Europe 1848*, pp. 95–7.

42 A. Briggs and P. Clavin, *Modern Europe, 1789-1989*, London: Routledge, 1997, pp. 86–7.

43 J. Koralka, "Revolution in the Habsburg Monarchy," in Dowe *et al.* (eds.) *Europe in 1848*, p. 146.

44 W. Simpson and M. Jones, *Europe, 1783–1914*, London: Routledge, 2000, pp. 150–1.

45 Simpson and Jones, *Europe 1783–1914*, p. 153.

46 I discuss the challenges engendered by nationalism against the Ottoman Empire in Chapter 5.

47 See R. Hyam, *Britain's Imperial Century, 1815–1914*, London: Harper and Row Publishers, 1976, p. 25; and Kennedy, *The Rise and Fall of the Great Powers*, p. 151.

48 Hyam, *Britain's Imperial Century*, p. 52.

49 Ibid., p. 54.

50 Cain and Hopkins, *British Imperialism*, pp. 205–6.

51 Quoted in Hyam, *Britain's Imperial Century*, p. 30. See also D. Jud, *Empire*, New York: Basic Books, 1997, p. 58; and L. James, *The Rise and Fall of the British Empire*, New York: St. Martin's Press, 1996, p. 171.

52 G. Sabine, *A History of Political Theory*, New York: H. Holton and Company, 1937, p. 656.

53 P. Cain and A. Hopkins, *British Imperialism, 1688–2000*, London: Longman, 2002, p. 110.

54 N. Gash, *Pillars of Government and Other Essays in State and Society, c. 1770–c. 1880*, London: Edward Arnold, 1986, pp. 43–54.

55 Cain and Hopkins, *British Imperialism*, p. 135.

56 A. Peacock and J. Wiseman with J. Veverka, *The Growth of Public Expenditure in the United Kingdom*, Princeton, New Jersey: Princeton University Press, 1961, p. 37.

57 Hyam, *Britain's Imperial Century*, pp. 27–8.

58 R. Gilpin, *U. S. Power and the Multinational Corporation*, New York: Basic Books, 1975, p. 84; see also James, *The Rise and Fall of the British Empire*, pp. 172–3.

59 Gilpin, *War and Change in World Politics*, p. 138.

60 Cain and Hopkins, *British Imperialism*, p. 98.

61 Quoted in Cain and Hopkins, *British Imperialism*, p. 98.

62 Cain and Hopkins, *British Empire*, p. 247.

63 Ibid., p. 272.

64 Ibid., p. 247.

65 Quoted in Hyam, *Britain's Imperial Century*, p. 49.

66 Ibid., p. 51.

67 Ibid., p. 57. See also R. Johnson, *British Imperialism*, New York: Palgrave, 2003, pp. 99–100.

68 See A. Hybel, *Made by the U.S.A. – The International System*, New York: Palgrave, 2001, pp. 21–5.

69 The issue was more complex. I will address it in some detail later on.

70 See Hybel, *Made by the U.S.A.*, p. 24.

71 See S. Ofsdahl, "Nationalism as a Contributing Factor in the American Civil War." Maxwell Air Force Base, Alabama: Air Command and Staff College, Air University, 2000.

72 The major exception was Cuba. Cuba did not attain independence until the late nineteenth century.

73 For a discussion of the differences between harmony, cooperation, and discord, see R. Koehane, *After Hegemony*, Princeton, New Jersey: Princeton University Press, 1984, pp. 51–7.

74 See S. Rokkan, "Dimensions of State Formation and Nation Building: A Possible Paradigm for Research on Variations within Europe," in C. Tilly (ed.) *The Formation of National States in Western Europe*, Princeton, New Jersey: Princeton University Press, 1975, pp. 586–8. As Rokkan notes, the closer the ties of interaction between urban and rural economic elites within a particular territory, the greater the chances for territorial centralizers to consolidate the power of the state.

75 Each former Spanish–American colony endured its own set of problems as it sought to consolidate and legitimize the power of the state. Discussing each country's experience, however, would require writing a separate volume. I have chosen Chile, Peru, and Mexico because together they reflect the most common problems the newly created Spanish–American states encountered.

76 S. Collier, "Chile," in S. Collier, T. Skidmore, and H. Blakemore (eds.) *The Cambridge Encyclopedia of Latin America and the Caribbean*, New York: Cambridge University Press, 1985, p. 284.

77 Quoted in S. Collier, *Ideas and Politics of Chilean Independence, 1808–1833*, Cambridge: Cambridge University Press, 1967, p. 338.

78 Diego Portales forwarded this argument in 1822. Quoted in Collier, *Ideas and Politics of Chilean Independence*, p. 339.

79 For a similar argument, see B. Loveman, *Chile: The Legacy of Hispanic Capitalism*, New York: Oxford University Press, 1988, pp. 124–6.

80 F. Gil, *The Political System of Chile*, Boston, Massachusetts: Houghton Mifflin Company, 1966, p. 86.

81 Loveman, *Chile: The Legacy of Hispanic Capitalism*, p. 124.

82 J. Dominguez, *Insurrection or Loyalty*, Cambridge, Massachusetts: Harvard University Press, 1980, p. 33.

83 According to Robert Dahl, "[t]he stronger and more distinctive a subculture, the more its members identify and interact with one another, and the less they identify and interact with nonmembers." From this it can be inferred that an entity seeking to gain state status over a territory inhabited by a population marked with sub-cultural pluralism is less likely to fulfill its goal than one that endeavors to achieve the same end over a territory occupied by a population that is culturally homogeneous. See R. Dahl, *Dilemmas of Pluralist Democracy*, New Haven, Connecticut: Yale University Press, 1989, p. 255.

84 For a similar conclusion, see F. Cardoso and E. Faletto, *Dependency and Development in Latin America*, Berkeley, California: University of California Press, 1979, p. 54. See also T. Halperin Donghi, *Historia Contemporaria de America Latina*, Madrid: Alianza Editorial, 1975, p. 205.

85 Collier, "Chile," p. 293. The Chilean peso remained relatively constant for that period and was worth slightly less than one American dollar.

86 Collier, "Chile," pp. 300–3.

87 For a related argument, see C. Forment, "Selfhood and Nationhood in Latin America: From Colonial Subject to Democratic Citizen," in J. Esherick, H. Kayali, and E. Van Young (eds.) *Empire to Nation*, Lanham, Maryland: Rowman and Littlefield Publishers, Inc., 2006, pp. 106–33.

88 F. Pike, *The Modern History of Peru*, New York: Frederick A. Praeger, 1967, p. 24.

89 Dominguez, *Insurrection or Loyalty*, p. 129.

90 The Spanish laws of 1542 ended the slavery of indigenous people in Spanish-America, except in very special cases. In time, however, the labor supply decreased and the Spanish crown was pressed to find a new instrument that would facilitate access to cheap labor. Spaniards in Peru sought to address the problem with a system called *mita*. Under this system, which had been put in place by the Incas and then adopted by the conquistadors, the Spaniards demanded from each village a quota of workers that would serve on rotation. See

L. McAlister, *Spain and Portugal in the New World*, Minneapolis, Minnesota: The University of Minneapolis Press, 1987, p. 211. It is worth noting that the production of sugar, cotton, and cacao was significantly more dependent on slave labor than was the production of wheat. It is not a coincidence that during the colonial period slaves constituted the basic labor force in Peru's coastal force. J. Cotler, *Clases, Estado y Nación en el Perú*, Lima: Instituto de Estudios Peruanos, 1986, p. 30.

91 P. Gootenberg, *Between Silver and Guano*, Princeton, New Jersey: Princeton University Press, 1989, p. 6.

92 Ibid., p. 277.

93 P. Gootenberg, "North-South: Trade Policy, Regionalism and Caudillismo in Post Independence Peru," in *Journal of Latin American* Studies, XXIII, 2, May 1991, 295.

94 The inability of the north and the south to reach a stable compromise is reflected in the fact that between 1826 and 1836 Peru enacted six constitutions.

95 Gootenberg, "North-South: Trade Policy, Regionalism and Caudillismo," p. 305.

96 Ibid., p. 241.

97 See Cotler, *Clases, Estado y Nación*, pp. 95–6; and H. Bonilla, "Peru and Bolivia," in L. Bethell (ed.) *Spanish America After Independence, c. 1820 – c. 1870*, Cambridge: Cambridge University Press, 1987, pp. 253–4.

98 Bonilla, "Peru and Bolivia," p. 254.

99 J. Levine, *The Export Economies. Their Patterns of Development in Historical Perspective*, Cambridge, Massachusetts: Harvard University Press, 1960, p. 81. See also Cotler, *Clases, Estado y Nacion*, pp. 95–7.

100 Cotler, *Clases, Estado y Nacion*, p. 95.

101 Ibid., p. 99.

102 Pike, *The Modern History of Peru*, pp. 106–9.

103 See M. Centeno, "Symbols of State Nationalism in Latin America," *European Review of Latin American and Caribbean Studies*, 66, 1999, 75–105.

104 Native Americans were above Blacks but were treated legally as minors, paid tribute, "and were forced to supply their labor for private and public gain." Dominguez, *Insurrection or Loyalty*, p. 40.

105 Ibid., p. 34.

106 Ibid., p. 37.

107 T. Anna, *The Mexican Empire of Iturbide*, Lincoln, Nebraska: University of Nebraska, 1990, p. 4.

108 Ibid., p. 4.

109 Ibid., p. 8.

110 Although independence made native Mexicans legally free and equal, it did not alter social mores. Mexicans habitually discussed the social structures in terms of blood lines, with Blacks at the bottom, followed by native Mexicans, then by Mestizos, and finally, at the top, by Whites. See S. Green, *The Mexican Republic: The First Decade, 1823-1832*, Pittsburgh, Pennsylvania: Pittsburgh University Press, 1987, p. 53.

111 For a discussion of how the boundaries for the various provinces were carved, see Green, *The Mexican Republic*, pp. 45–7.

112 Green, *The Mexican Republic*, p. 53.

113 R. Sinkin, *The Mexican Reform, 1855–1876. A Study of Liberal Nation-Building*, Austin, Texas: University of Texas Press, 1979, p. 23.

114 Ibid., p. 25.

115 Ibid., pp. 25–7.

116 D. Munro, *The Latin American Republics*, New York: Appleton-Century, Inc, 1960, p. 363.

117 Ibid., p. 364.

118 Quoted in Sinkin, *The Mexican Reform*, p. 84.
119 Sinkin, *The Mexican Reform*, p. 81.
120 Ibid., p. 90.
121 Quoted in McDougall, *Promised Land, Crusader State*, pp. 76–7.
122 J. Crow, *The Epic of Latin America*, Berkeley, California: University of California Press, 1980, p. 575.
123 "Memorial to the Citizens of New Granada by a Citizen of Caracas," December 15, 1812, in V. Lecuna and H. A. Bierck, Jr. (eds.) *Selected Writings of Bolívar*, Vol. I, New York: The Colonial Press, 1951.
124 See Butterfield, "The Balance of Power," in H. Butterfield and M. Wight (eds.) *Diplomatic Investigations*, Cambridge, Massachusetts: Harvard University Press, 1966, p. 145.
125 As noted, during its early days, the balance-of-power doctrine had, as an ideology, a very narrow social base—the leaders of the Europe's major powers. But like most ideologies, this social base eventually widened. Today, in the USA, it is an ideology that has transcended its initial boundaries and is widely accepted by most of its citizens.

4 A world system destabilized by five ideologies: 1871–1914

1 D. Quataert, *The Ottoman Empire: 1700–1922*, New York: Cambridge University Press, 2005, pp. 55–7.
2 Ibid., pp. 55–7.
3 J. McCarthy, *The Ottoman Turks*, London: Longman, 1997, p. 285.
4 Ibid., pp. 295–7.
5 Ibid., pp. 299–300.
6 Quoted in L. Lafore, *The Long Fuse*, Philadelphia, Pennsylvania: Lippincott, 1965, p. 178.
7 Nationalism had a similar impact on the British Empire and the French Empire after the end of the Second World War.
8 For a discussion of Eric Hobsbawn's analysis of nineteenth-century European nationalist movements, see A. Smith, *Nationalism and Modernism*, London: Routledge, 1998, p. 121.
9 For an analysis of attempts on the part of the Ottoman Empire's rulers to use Islamism as a means to reconstruct the state and create a community-type identity during the latter part of the nineteenth century and early years of the twentieth century, see K. Karpat, *The Politicization of Islam. Reconstructing Identity, State, Faith, and the Community in the Late Ottoman States*, New York: Oxford University Press, 2001, pp. 308–27.
10 E. Hobsbawm, *The Age of Empire, 1875–1914*, New York: Vintage Books, 1989, p. 62. As noted by Louise Young, imperialism involves formal or informal, and direct or indirect, mechanisms of domination. See L. Young, *Japan's Total Empire*, Berkeley, California: University of California Press, 1998, p. 11.
11 E. Kedourie (ed.) *Nationalism in Asia and Africa*, London: Weidenfeld and Nicolson, 1971, p. 27.
12 Hobsbawm, *The Age of Empire*, p. 78.
13 A. Smith, *The Ethnic Origin of Nations*, New York: Blackwell, 1987, p. 131. See also, C. Tilly (ed.) *The Formation of National States in Western Europe*, Princeton, New Jersey: Princeton University Press, 1975, Introduction; and I. Wallerstein, *The Modern World System*, Vol. I, New York: Academic Press, 1974, Chapter 3.
14 Smith, *The Ethnic Origin of Nations*, 132. See also Tilly (ed.) *The Formation of National States in Western Europe*, Introduction; and M. Howard, *War in European History*, London: Oxford University Press, 1976, Chapter 6.

15 Smith, *The Ethnic Origins of Nations*, pp. 133–4.
16 See H. Gollwitzer, *Europe in the Age of Imperialism, 1880–1914*, London: Thames and Hudson, 1969, p. 24. The quoted passage appears on the same page.
17 Ibid., p. 64.
18 W. Simpson and M. Jones, *Europe, 1783–1914*, New York: Routledge, 2000, p. 235.
19 P. Kennedy, *The Rise and Fall of the Great Powers*, New York: Random House, 1987, p. 155.
20 Hobsbawm, *The Age of Empire*, p. 39.
21 J. Lowe, *The Great Powers, Imperialism and the German Problem*, New York: Routledge, 1994, pp. 77–8.
22 W. Smith, *European Imperialism in the Nineteenth and Twentieth Centuries*, Chicago, Illinois: Nelson-Hall, 1982, p. 87.
23 See M. Doyle, *Empires*, Ithaca, New York: Cornell University Press, 1986, p. 262.
24 Quoted in D. Judd, *Empire*, New York: Basic Books, 1997, p. 121.
25 Quoted in Gollwitzer, *Europe in the Age of Imperialism*, p. 136.
26 F. Gilbert, *The End of the European Era, 1890 to the Present*, New York: W. W. Norton, 1979, p. 40.
27 L. James, *The Rise and Fall of the British Empire*, New York: St. Martin's Press, 1996, p. 26.
28 Gollwitzer, *Europe in the Age of Imperialism*, p. 41.
29 See A. Cassels, *Ideology and International Relations in the Modern World*, London: Routledge, 1996, p. 98.
30 Ibid., p. 98; Hobsbawm, *The Age of Empire*, pp. 160–1; and Gilbert, *The End of the European Era*, p. 46.
31 Quoted in Cassels, *Ideology and International Relations in the Modern World*, p. 105.
32 James, *The Rise and Fall of the British Empire*, p. 207.
33 Simpson and Jones, *Europe*, p. 237. See also Gilbert, *The End of the European Era*, p. 40.
34 Smith, *European Imperialism in the Nineteenth and Twentieth Centuries*, p. 86.
35 James, *The Rise and Fall of the British Empire*, p. 206.
36 Quoted in Cassels, *Ideology and International Relations in the Modern World*, p. 104.
37 The quotes appear in A. Hybel, *Made by the U.S.A. – The International System*, New York: Palgrave, 2001, pp. 39–40.
38 Quoted in W. LaFeber, *The American Age: United States Foreign Policy at Home and Abroad Since 1750*, New York: W. W. Norton, 1989, p. 164.
39 The provisions, which were drawn by President McKinnley and his advisers, were submitted to Congress by Senator Oliver Platt and came to be known as the Platt Amendment. Reprinted in T. Paterson (ed.), *Major Problems in American Foreign Policy: To 1914*, vol. I, Lexington, Massachusetts: D. C. Heath and Company, 1989, pp. 455–6. See also LaFeber, *The American Age*, p. 197.
40 In 1934, the United States Congress passed the Tydings-McDuffie Act. The act gave way to the creation of a Philippine Commonwealth for a ten-year period, at which time the Philippines would become an independent and sovereign state.
41 Quoted in F. Hindman Golay, *Face of Empire. United States-Philippine Relations, 1896-1946*, Manila: Ateneo de Manila University Press, 1997, p. 64.
42 S. Karnow, *In Our Images. America's Empire in the Philippines*, New York: Ballantine Books, 1989, p. 128.
43 Quoted in W. Zimmermann, *First Great Triumph*, New York: Farrar, Strauss and Girouz, 2002, p. 33.
44 Karnow, *In Our Images*, p. 109.
45 Quoted in Zimmermann, *First Great Triumph*, p. 239.

46 Quoted in Golay, *Face of Empire*, pp. 34–5.
47 Quoted in R. Smith, "Wilson's Pursuit of Order," in Paterson (ed.) *Major Problems in American Foreign Policy*, p. 516.
48 Smith, *European Imperialism*, pp. 103–7.
49 Gilbert, *The End of the European Era*, pp. 82–4.
50 Cassels, *Ideology and International Relations in the Modern World*, p. 95.
51 Quoted in Gollwitzer, *Europe in the Age of Imperialism*, pp. 139–40.
52 F. Quinn, *The French Overseas Empire*, Westport, Connecticut: Praeger, 2000, p. 108.
53 J. Keiger, *France and the World Since the 1870s*, London: Arnold, 2001, p. 202; and Quinn, *The French Overseas Empire*, p. 110.
54 Keiger, *France and the World Since the 1870s*, p. 201.
55 Quinn, *The French Overseas Empire*, p. 110.
56 See Keiger, *France and the World Since the 1870s*, pp. 202–3.
57 France's population did not undergo a substantial increase during the last decades of the nineteenth century. Moreover, very few French were interested in moving to one of the colonies in order to improve their standard of living.
58 See Hobsbawm, *The Age of Empire*, p. 59.
59 See Young, *Japan's Total Empire*, p. 23.
60 Hobsbawm, *The Age of Empire*, p. 59.
61 H. Suganami, "Japan's Entry Into International Society," in H. Bull and A. Watson (eds.) *The Expansion of International Society*, Oxford: Clarendon Press, 1984, p. 185.
62 See C. Tsuzuki, *The Pursuit of Power in Modern Japan, 1825–1995*, New York: Oxford University Press, 2000, pp. 19–21.
63 See S. Klein, *Rethinking Japan's Identity and International Role*, New York: Routledge, 2002, p. 42. The quote appears on the same page.
64 A. Dudden, *The American Pacific*, New York: Oxford University Press, 1992, pp. 18–19.
65 Kennedy, *The Rise and Fall of the Great Powers*, p. 207. See also Klein, *Rethinking Japan's Identity and International Role*, pp. 46–52.
66 Gluck explains that from "the 1880s through the first fifteen years of the twentieth century, Japanese sought first to conceive and then to inculcate an ideology suitable for modern Japan." C. Gluck, *Japan's Modern Myths. Ideology in the Late Meiji Period*, Princeton, New Jersey: Princeton University Press, 1985, p. 3.
67 Tsuzuki, *The Pursuit of Power in Modern Japan*, pp. 114–15. See also Klein, *Rethinking Japan's Identity and International Role*, p. 55.
68 Quoted in Gluck, *Japan's Modern Myths*, p. 130. My italics.
69 Klien, *Rethinking Japan's Identity and International Role*, p. 57.
70 Ibid., p. 57. See also Tsuzuki, *The Pursuit of Power in Modern Japan*, p. 116.
71 Dudden, *The American Pacific*, pp. 142–3.
72 Quoted in Klein, *Rethinking Japan's Identity and International Role*, p. 58.
73 Young, *Japan's Total Empire*, p. 96.
74 Gluck, *Japan's Modern Myths*, p. 135.
75 Klein, *Rethinking Japan's Identity and International Role*, p. 58.
76 Gluck, *Japan's Modern Myths*, p. 136.
77 Quoted in Dudden, *The American Pacific*, p. 143.
78 Tsuzuki, *The Pursuit of Power in Modern Japan*, pp. 130–1.
79 Quoted in Kennedy, *The Rise and Fall of the Great Powers*, p. 208.
80 Japan also agreed to remain neutral if Britain were to engage in war with another party. Both parties, moreover, consented to assist the other party if the original aggressor were to be joined by another party. See Tsutzuki, *The Pursuit of Power in Modern Japan*, pp. 168–9.
81 Ibid., pp. 169–75.
82 Kennedy, *The Rise and Fall of the Great Powers*, p. 209.

83 S. Adshead, *China in World History*, New York: St. Martin's Press, 1988, p. 243–4. See also G. Gong, "China's Entry Into International Society," in Bull and Watson (eds.) *The Expansion of International Society*, pp. 171–2.

84 Adshead, *China in World History*, pp. 249–51.

85 Ibid.

86 Gong, "China's Entry Into International Society," pp. 175–6.

87 P. Duara, *Rescuing History from the Nation*, Chicago, Illinois: The University of Chicago Press, 1995, pp. 118–22.

88 Quoted in Duara, *Rescuing History from the Nation*, p. 123.

89 As Lung-Kee Sun points out, China's evolutionary scheme resembled Western social thinking, except that it "shifted the white man's burden onto the shoulders of Confucius." See Lung-Kee Sun, *The Chinese National Character*, London: M. E. Sharpe, 2002, pp. 5–7.

90 The attacks are commonly referred to as the Boxer Uprising.

91 G. Barraclough (ed.) *The Times Atlas of World History*, London: Times Books, 1986, pp. 232–3.

92 Sun, *The Chinese National Character*, pp. 9–21.

93 See Duara, *Rescuing History from the Nation*, pp. 179–81. The quote appears on p. 181.

94 H. Schiffrin, *Reluctant Revolutionary*, Boston, Massachusetts: Little, Brown, and Company, 1980, p. 161.

95 Gong, "China's Entry Into International Society," p. 177.

96 Barraclough (ed.) *The Times Atlas of World History*, p. 262.

97 G. Xu, *China and the Great War*, New York: Cambridge University Press, 2005, p. 42.

98 J. Fitzgerald, *Awakening China*, Stanford, California: Stanford University Press, 1996, p. 9.

99 Quoted in Fitzgerald, *Awakening China*, p. 10. Sun also noted that the main reason China had fallen back was because of failure on the part of the "Chinese to cultivate personal virtue."

100 Quoted in J. Eserick, "How the Qing Dynasty Became China," in J. Eserick, H. Kayali, and E. Van Young (eds.) *Empire to Nation*, Lanham, Maryland: Rowman and Littlefield Publishers, 2006, p. 246.

101 Sun died in 1924.

102 C. Clendenen, *Blood on the Border: The United States and the Mexican Irregulares*, New York: The Macmillan Company, 1969, pp. 116–18.

103 Diaz ruled between 1876 and 1880, and then again from 1884 until 1911.

104 A. Knight, *The Mexican Revolution*, Vol. I, Lincoln, Nebraska: University of Nebraska Press, 1986, p. 23.

105 See F. Katz, Friedrich, "The Liberal Republic and the Porfiriato," in L. Bethell (ed.) *Mexico Since Independence*, Cambridge: Cambridge University Press, 1991, pp. 81–8; and Knight, *The Mexican Revolution*, pp. 15–36.

106 One hacienda was larger than Belgium and the Netherlands combined. See C. Fuentes, *The Buried Mirror*, Boston, Massachusetts: Houghton Mifflin Company, 1992, pp. 299–300. See also S. Krasner, *Defending the National Interest*, Princeton, New Jersey: Princeton University Press, 1978, p. 158.

107 Knight, *The Mexican Revolution*, pp. 55–77.

108 J. Brown, "The Structure of the Foreign-Owned Petroleum Industry in Mexico, 1880–1938," in J. Brown and A Knight (eds.) *The Mexican Petroleum Industry in the Twentieth Century*, Austin, Texas: University of Texas Press, 1992, p. 14.

109 A. Knight, "The Politics of Expropriation," in Brown and Knight (eds.) *The Mexican Petroleum Industry in the Twentieth Century*, p. 90.

110 Krasner, *Defending the National Interest*, pp. 160–78.

111 D. Levy and K. Bruhn, "Mexico: Sustained Civilian Rule and the Question of Democracy," in L. Diamond, J. Hartlyn, J. Linz, and S. Lipset (eds.) *Democracy*

in Developing Countries – Latin America, Boulder, Colorado: Lynn Reinner Publishers, 1999, pp. 526–7.

112 Krasner, *Defending the National Interest*, pp. 180–1.

113 Quoted in Knight, "The Politics of Expropriation," p. 98.

114 Ibid., p. 102.

115 Ibid., pp. 102, and 107–8.

116 James, *The Rise and Fall of the British Empire*, pp. 25–6.

117 Ibid., pp. 123; and Judd, *Empire – The British Imperial Experience from 1765 to the Present*, p. 26. The East India Company gained control of Bengal in 1757.

118 R. Johnson, *British Imperialism*, New York: Palgrave, 2003, pp. 24–7.

119 Ibid., p. 36.

120 R. Hyam, *Britain's Imperial Century, 1815–1914*, New York: Harper and Row, 1976, p. 221.

121 Hindu and Muslim soldiers believed cartridges had been greased with cow and hog fat. For Hindus the cow is a sacred animal, while Muslims believe that contact with an unclean pig will defile them.

122 Quoted in Hyam, *Britain's Imperial Century*, p. 225.

123 Ibid., p. 226.

124 Judd, *Empire*, pp. 74–6.

125 Ibid., p. 77.

126 Johnson, *British Imperialism*, p. 133.

127 Cain and Hopkins, *British Imperialism*, p. 153; and James, *The Rise and Fall of the British Empire*, p. 219.

128 Quoted in S. Choudhary, *Growth of Nationalism in India, 1857–1918*, Vol. 1, New Delhi: Trimurty Publications, 1973, pp. 4–5.

129 James, *The Rise and Fall of the British Empire*, pp. 412–13. I address the Hindu–Muslim problem at the end of this section.

130 Ibid., pp. 230 and 414.

131 Quoted in Choudhary, *Growth of Nationalism in India*, Vol. I, p. 148.

132 Ibid., p. 150.

133 Ibid., p. 151.

134 Ibid., p. 154.

135 James, *The Rise and Fall of the British Empire*, pp. 236 and 239.

136 Judd, *Empire*, p. 228.

137 Johnson, *British Imperialism*, 135–6; see also B. Tomlinson, *The Indian National Congress and the Raj, 1929-1942*, London: The Macmillan Press, 1976, p. 10.

138 James, *The Rise and Fall of the British Empire*, pp. 416–17; and Judd, *Empire*, p. 260.

139 Judd, *Empire*, pp. 270–2.

140 Muslims and Hindus tolerated one another and cooperated extensively under the rule of Akbar, the third Moghul emperor. Akbar founded in 1575 the House of Worship, a place where scholars from all religions could meet to discuss God. To show his respect of Hindus, Akbar became a vegetarian, gave up hunting, and prohibited the sacrifice of animals on his birthday or in Hindu Holy places. See K. Armstrong, *A History of God*, New York: Ballantine Books, 1993, pp. 262–3.

141 Ibid., p. 263.

142 It is estimated that some four hundred to five hundred died as a result of the riot.

143 Quoted in Quinn, *The French Overseas Empire*, p. 125.

144 Decades later, the French also moved against Tunisia and Morocco. See Smith, *European Imperialism in the Nineteenth and Twentieth Centuries*, pp. 44–5; Quinn, *The French Overseas Empire*, pp. 107–8 and 121–2; and B. Stora, *Algeria, 1830–2000*, Ithaca, New York: Cornell University Press, 2001, pp. 3–4.

145 Algeria can be divided in three: the coastal region, the high plains of the interior, and the Sahara. The bulk of the people lived in the fertile area, where the plain

meets the Mediterranean. See D. Prochaska, *Making Algeria French,* Cambridge: Cambridge University Press, 1990, pp. 32 and 34.

146 My description in this paragraph is derived from Raphael Danzinger's *Abd Al-Qadir and the Algerians*, New York: Holmes and Meier Publishers, 1977, pp. 3–15.

147 *Sufism* is defined by Webster as "ascetic Islamic of which the goal is communion with the deity through contemplation and ecstasy." Quoted in Danzinger, *Abd Al-Qadir and the Algerians*, p. 10.

148 Ibid., pp. 15–26.

149 See J. Entelis, *Algeria: The Revolution Institutionalized*, Boulder, Colorado: Westview Press, 1986, p. 26; and Quinn, *The French Overseas Empire*, pp. 122–3.

150 M. Willis, *The Islamist Challenge in Algeria*, New York: New York University Press, 1997, p. 3.

151 Quoted in P. Naylor, *France and Algeria*, Gainesville, Florida: University Press of Florida, 2000, p. 13.

152 Quoted in J. Pitts (ed. and trans.) *Alexis De Tocqueville – Writings on Empire and Slavery*, Baltimore, Maryland: Johns Hopkins University Press, 2001, p. 59.

153 Ibid., pp. 61 and 63.

154 The colonists were divided into two groups: *grands colons* and *petits blancs.* The first group was made up of wealthy businessmen and prosperous landowners; the second group came from a modest background and occupied lower-level positions. Both groups, however, shared one sentiment: intense hostility towards the indigenous Muslims. See Entelis, *Algeria: The Revolution Institutionalized*, p. 27.

155 Quoted in Quinn, *The French Overseas Empire*, pp. 124–5.

156 Ibid., p. 125.

157 Willis, *The Islamist Challenge in Algeria*, pp. 5–6.

158 Quoted in Stora, *Algeria, 1830–2000*, p. 5.

159 Quoted in Quinn, *The French Overseas Empire*, p. 126.

160 See Entelis, *Algeria: The Revolution Institutionalized*, pp. 32–3.

161 See Naylor, *France and Algeria*, p. 16.

162 See Willis, *The Islamist Challenge in Algeria*, pp. 7–8; and Entelis, *Algeria: The Revolution Institutionalized*, p. 33.

163 Quinn, *The French Overseas Empire*, p. 195.

164 See Entelis, *Algeria: The Revolution Institutionalized*, pp. 34–48; Stora, *Algeria, 1830–2000*, pp. 15–19; and Willis, *The Islamist Challenge in Algeria*, pp. 13–22.

165 See Entelis, *Algeria: The Revolution Institutionalized*, pp. 38–9; Stora, *Algeria, 1830–2000*, pp. 18–19; and Willis, *The Islamist Challenge in Algeria*, pp. 16–19.

166 According to Smith, though it is appropriate to contend that the diffusion of Western ideas through restless indigenous intellectuals helped generate and develop nationalism in a place such as India, one ought not to disregard the important role played by India's pre-colonial ethnic communities and politics. I concur with Smith's observation, but I also think that it is imperative to keep in mind that consideration of such additional factors does not help explain what made it possible for the competing domestic groups to forge a common anti-colonial nationalist front. See Smith, *Nationalism and Modernism*, p. 108.

167 See A. Watson, *The Evolution of International Society*, London: Routledge, 1992, pp. 265–87.

168 Gong, "China's Entry Into International Society," p. 179.

5 A world still burdened by multiple conflicting ideologies: 1919–1990

1 Article Fourteen of Wilson's "Fourteen Points" peace program.

2 Quoted in E. Carr, *The Twenty Years' Crisis, 1919–1939*, New York: Harper and Row, 1964, p. 33.

3 See G. Ikenberry, "America's Liberal Grand Strategy: Democracy and National Security in the Post-War Era," in G. Ikenberry (ed.) *American Foreign Policy*, New York: Longman, 2002, p. 284.

4 See G. Sartori, *The Theory of Democracy Revisited*, Vol. II, Chatham, New Jersey: Chatham House, 1987, p. 289.

5 Ibid., pp. 337–45. See also R. Dahl, *Democracy and Its Critics*, New Haven, Connecticut: Yale University Press, 1989, pp. 83–106.

6 A. de Tocqueville, *Democracy in America*, Vol. II, Chapter XIV (translated, revised and corrected, 1899). www.xroads.virginia.edu/~HYPER/DETOC/colophon.html

7 I am not assuming that the reverse is always the case.

8 See C. Lindblom, *Politics and Markets*, New York: Basic Books, 1977, p. 162.

9 L. Gardner, *Safe for Democracy: The Anglo-American Response to Revolution, 1919–1923*, New York: Oxford University Press, 1984, pp. 258–60.

10 The human and material costs absorbed by France during the First World War were far greater than Germany's and Britain's. See A. Hybel, *Made by the U.S.A.— The International System*, New York: Palgrave, 2001, p. 53.

11 J. Nogee and R. Donaldson, *Soviet Foreign Policy Since World War II*, New York: Pergamon Press, 1988, p. 15.

12 Quoted in N. Riasanovsky, *A History of Russia*, New York: Oxford University Press, 2000, p. 467.

13 Riasanovsky, *A History of Russia*, pp. 380–2.

14 Ibid., pp. 447–50.

15 Ibid., pp. 467–8.

16 Nogee and Donaldson, *Soviet Foreign Policy Since World War II*, p. 18.

17 N. Robinson, *A Critical History of Soviet Ideology*, Brookfield, Vermont: Edgar Elgar Publishing Company, 1995, p. 467.

18 Quoted in W. Taubman, *Stalin's American Foreign Policy: From Entente to Détente to Cold War*, New York: W. W. Norton, 1982, p. 13.

19 Point six of his Fourteen Points peace plan.

20 Quoted in Taubman, *Stalin's American Foreign Policy*, p. 13.

21 See R. English, *Russia and the Idea of the West*, New York: Columbia University Press, 2000, p. 33.

22 N. Khrushchev, *Khrushchev Remembers*, Boston, Massachusetts: Little, Brown, 1970, p. 17.

23 English, *Russia and the Idea of the West*, p. 35.

24 Quoted in English, *Russia and the Idea of the West*, p. 35.

25 See Riasanovsky, *A History of Russia*, pp. 489–90.

26 J. Stalin, "Political Report of the Central Committee to the Sixteenth Congress of the CPSU (B)," June 27, 1930, in his *Works*, Vol. 12, Moscow: Foreign Languages Publication House, 1955, pp. 242–385.

27 Statement by Stalin in 1928 while speaking to visiting American labor leaders. Quoted by G. Kennan in "February 26, 1946 telegram," in D. Merrill (ed.) *Documentary History of the Truman Presidency*, Vol. 7, Bethesda, Maryland: University Publications of America, 1976, p. 71.

28 Stalin, "Political Report of the Central Committee to the Sixteenth Congress," pp. 242–385.

29 Quoted in Taubman, *Stalin's American Foreign Policy*, p. 21.

30 See Hybel, *Made by the U.S.A.*, p. 88. See also T. Ball and R. Dagger, *Political Ideologies and the Democratic Ideal*, New York: Pearson, Longman, 2004, p. 182.

31 Quoted in Ball and Dagger, *Political Ideologies*, p. 183

32 Ball and Dagger, *Political Ideologies*, pp. 174–5.

33 Ibid., pp. 175–6.

34 B. Mussolini, "The Doctrines of Fascism," in J. Somerville and R. Santoni (eds.) *Social and Political Philosophy*, Garden City, New York: Doubleday, 1963, p. 44.

35 B. Mussolini, *The Political and Social Doctrine of Fascism*, London: Hogarth Press, 1933, p. 3.
36 Ball and Dagger, *Political Ideologies*, p. 185.
37 See Carr, *The Twenty Years' Crisis, 1919–1939*, p. 140.
38 R. Visser, "Fascist Doctrine and the Cult of the Romanita," *Journal of Contemporary History*, 27, 1992, 5–22.
39 Quoted in A. Briggs and P. Clavin, *Modern Europe, 1789–1989*, London: Longman, 1997, p. 329.
40 See A. Cassels, *Ideology and International Relations in the Modern World*, New York: Routledge, 1996, pp. 160–1; Briggs and Clavin, *Modern Europe, 1789–1989*, p. 329; and W. Keylor, *The Twentieth Century World – An International History*, New York: Oxford University Press, 1996, pp. 151 and 158.
41 See A. J. Gregor, *Italian Fascism and Developmental Dictatorship*, Princeton, New Jersey: Princeton University Press, 1979, pp. 138–9.
42 Cassels, *Ideology and International Relations in the Modern World*, pp. 160–1; and Keylor, *The Twentieth Century World*, p. 158. Mussolini's decision to intervene in Spain's civil war also had a strategic and ideological foundation. See D. Kaiser, *Politics and War – European Conflict from Philip II to Hitler*, Cambridge, Massachusetts: Harvard University Press, 2000, p. 366.
43 Quoted in B. Stegemann, "Politics and Warfare in the First Phase of the German Offensive," in K. Maier, H. Rohde, B. Stegemann, and H. Umbreit (eds.) *Germany and the Second World War*, Oxford: Clarendon Press, 1991, p. 7.
44 Quoted in G. Mosse, *Toward the Final Solution*, New York: Howard Fertig, 1978, p. 52.
45 A. Hitler, "Mein Kampf," in T. Ball and R. Dagger (eds.) *Ideals and Ideologies*, New York: Pearson Education, 2004, pp. 320–1.
46 A. Hitler, *Mein Kampf*, New York: Reynal and Hitchcock, 1939, p. 434.
47 Hitler, "Mein Kampf," in Ball and Dagger (eds.) *Ideas and Ideologies*, pp. 328 and 329.
48 Ibid., p. 334.
49 Quoted in Hybel, *Made by the U.S.A. – The International System*, p. 93.
50 Keylor, *The Twentieth Century World*, p. 139.
51 Hitler, *Mein Kampf*, pp. 169–78.
52 Ibid., p. 180. Regarding the difficulties Germany would have faced if it had sought to attain new colonies, see G. Weinberg, *The Foreign Policy of Hitler's Germany*, Chicago, Illinois: The University of Chicago Press, 1980, p. 36. Hitler's fear that colonization of distant lands could undermine the Aryan race is best captured in his interpretation of France's own colonial experience. As he stated, France:

> racially is making such progress in negrofying herself that one can really speak of the establishment of an African State on European soil ... Let the development of France continue three centuries more in the present manner, and the last remnants of Frankish blood will have succumbed in the developing European-African mulatto state. A mighty self-contained area of settlement from the Rhine to the Congo filled with an inferior race developing out of continual hybridization.

> Ibid., pp. 937–8.

53 Quoted in Cassels, *Ideology and International Relations in the Modern World*, p. 163.
54 See Weinberg, *The Foreign Policy of Hitler's Germany*, pp. 12–13.
55 According to Hitler, Jews relied on communism to win the political battle in Russia.
56 M. Messerschmidt, "Foreign Policy and Preparation for War," in *Germany and the Second World War*, Vol. I, New York: Oxford University Press, 1990, p. 551.

57 Hitler, *Mein Kampf*, pp. 960–1.
58 See Keylor, *The Twentieth Century World*, p. 139; and Cassels, *Ideology and International Relations in the Modern World*, pp. 162–3.
59 Weinberg, *The Foreign Policy of Hitler's Germany*, pp. 36–41. A question often posed by analysts is whether Hitler had in mind absolute world dominion. Thus far, no one has been able to come up with a reasonable answer. In a sense, the question is irrelevant, if for no other reason than Hitler failed to fulfill his more limited goals. It suffices to keep in mind three things. First, at minimum he was determined to increase Germany's continental power, and its extension entailed gaining control over Eastern Europe and parts of the Soviet Union. Second, part of his rationale for expanding Germany's power was linked to his belief that the country's future was dependent on its ability to both protect and enhance the quality of the Aryan race. And third, his foreign policy was informed by ideology and by his deep belief in its correctness. Germans, he was convinced, would obey him if he fashioned "towering great ideas," and showed "absolute belief in them" and a "fanatical courage to fight for them." Quoted in Cassels, *Ideology and International Relations in the Modern World*, p. 166.
60 Hitler, *Mein Kampf*, pp. 283 and 286.
61 Portions of this section appear in Hybel, *Made by the U.S.A. – The International System*, pp. 93–6.
62 J. Fest, *Hitler*, New York: Harcourt Brace Jovanovich, 1974, p. 489.
63 Quoted in Fest, *Hitler*, pp. 548, 595, and 642–3.
64 Fest, *Hitler*, p. 656.
65 See C. Tsuzuki, *The Pursuit of Power in Modern Japan, 1825-1995*, Oxford: Oxford University Press, 2000, p. 243. A comment about the use of Japanese names is appropriate at this stage. In Japan, a family name or surname always precedes a given name. I follow the same style in the main body and in notes when referring to a statement or an act by a Japanese person. However, because notes refer to authors from a wide range of nations, I rely on the Western style by presenting given names of Japanese authors first, followed by their family name or surname.
66 The agreement, often referred to as the Lansing-Ishii Agreement, was reached in November 1917. See Keylor, *The Twentieth Century World*, pp. 220–1.
67 Tsuzuki, *The Pursuit of Power in Modern Japan, 1825–1995*, pp. 212–13 and 219–20; see also W. Fletcher III, *The Search for a New Order – Intellectuals and Fascism in Prewar Japan*, Chapel Hill, North Carolina: The University of North Carolina Press, 1982, p. 10.
68 Between 1929 and 1931 Japanese exports to China dropped by half, and unemployment swelled to nine percent. Tokyo responded by combining low interest rate and financial aid for rural reconstruction, and trying to meet the needs and demands of both the military and business leaders. Still, though Japan, like most other entities in the world system, experienced business bankruptcies and rural and industrial discord during the depression, according to international standards its economy grew fast. See Tsuzuki, *The Pursuit of Power in Modern Japan, 1825–1995*, p. 223.
69 The chief of Japan's Naval General Staff was so disappointed with the outcome of the negotiations that he resigned. As Nish notes: "The London treaty poisoned the delicate civil-military relationship that had existed in the past." I. Nish, *Japanese Foreign Policy in the Interwar Period*, Westport, Connecticut: Praeger, 2002, pp. 66–70. See also Tsuzuki, *The Pursuit of Power in Modern Japan, 1825–1995*, p. 257.
70 See Nish, *Japanese Foreign Policy in the Interwar Period*, pp. 51 and 76; and Tsuzuki, *The Pursuit of Power in Modern Japan, 1825–1995*, p. 259. For an analysis on how Japan's mass media depicted developments in Manchuria prior to

and after the September 18, 1931 clash, see L. Young, *Japan's Total Empire*, Berkeley, California: University of California Press, 1998, pp. 55–114.

71 Quoted in Y. Maxon, *Control of Japanese Foreign Policy*, Westport, Connecticut: Greenwood Press, 1973, p. 94.

72 Quoted in Tsuzuki, *The Pursuit of Power in Modern Japan, 1825-1995*, p. 223. The takeover was initiated by a group of Japanese army officers in Manchuria who staged a bomb attack on the track of a Japanese-owned railway and accused Chinese soldiers of orchestrating the incident.

73 See Tsuzuki, *The Pursuit of Power in Modern Japan, 1825–1995*, p. 255; and Nish, *Japanese Foreign Policy in the Interwar Period*, pp. 107–8. The term "effete leadership" appears in Nish's *Japanese Foreign Policy*.

74 Both quotes appear in Tsuzuki, *The Pursuit of Power in Modern Japan, 1825–1995*, p. 251.

75 W. Beasley, *Japanese Imperialism, 1894–1945*, New York: Oxford University Press, 1987, p. 178; K. Hayashi, "Germany and Japan in the Interwar Period," in J. Morley (ed.) *Dilemmas of Growth in Prewar Japan*, Princeton, New Jersey: Princeton University Press, 1971, pp. 474–5; and Tsuzuki, *The Pursuit of Power in Modern Japan, 1825-1995*, p. 252.

76 Quoted in Beasley, *Japanese Imperialism, 1894–1945*, p. 178.

77 Quoted in Tsuzuki, *The Pursuit of Power in Modern Japan, 1825-1995*, p. 253.

78 Quoted in Beasley, *Japanese Imperialism, 1894–1945*, p. 178. Kita's contention that Japan had to expand its territory in order to accommodate its rapidly growing population differed little from that posited by Japanese Realists. Yoshida Shigeru, one of Japan's most prominent Realists prior to and after the Second World War, feared that Japan would not survive unless it launched a policy of expansion in the Asian continent. See J. Dower, *Empire and Aftermath*, Cambridge, Massachusetts: Harvard University Press, 1979, pp. 5–6.

79 Beasley, *Japanese Imperialism, 1894–1945*, pp. 181–2.

80 See Beasley, *Japanese Imperialism, 1894–1945*, p. 204; and Maxon, *Control of Japanese Foreign Policy*, p. 117.

81 See P. Kennedy, *The Rise and Fall of the Great Powers*, New York: Random House, 1987, p. 300.

82 Quote in Beasley, *Japanese Imperialism, 1894–1945*, p. 204.

83 Quoted in R. Mitchell, *Thought Control in Prewar Japan*, Ithaca, New York: Cornell University Press, 1976, p. 164.

84 See Young, *Japan's Total Empire*, p. 364; and Mitchell, *Thought Control in Prewar Japan*, p. 162.

85 See J. Dower, *War Without Mercy: Race and Power in the Pacific*, New York: Pantheon Books, 1993, p. 264; and Young, *Japan's Total Empire*, p. 366.

86 Quoted in Dower, *War Without Mercy*, p. 264.

87 See Dower, *War Without Mercy*, p. 266.

88 Quoted in Young, *Japan's Total Empire*, p. 366. The idea that Japan had to lead the Orient, and that it should do so via the establishment of an economic environment that rejected the evils of capitalism, class struggle, and the bureaucratization of Japanese life, had substantial support among intellectuals. To create an efficient, cooperative, economic system, some argued, Japan had to develop a plan "based on the whole and control of individual freedom ... [i]n contrast to individualism, which considers the individual first and society second, corporatism considers society first and the individual second." See W. Fletcher III, *The Search for a New Order – Intellectuals and Fascism in Prewar Japan*, Chapel Hill, North Carolina: The University of North Carolina Press, 1982, pp. 112–13. The quotes appear on p. 113.

89 See Mitchell, *Thought Control in Prewar Japan*, p. 161.

90 See Mitchell, *Thought Control in Prewar Japan*, pp. 166–70.

91 See Beasley, *Japanese Imperialism, 1894–1945*, pp. 220–4; and Hybel, *Made by the U.S.A. – The International System*, p. 86.

92 Quoted in Beasley, *Japanese Imperialism, 1894–1945*, p. 226.

93 See Hybel, *Made by the U.S.A. – The International System*, p. 86; and Beasley, *Japanese Imperialism, 1894–1945*, pp. 229–30.

94 Tsuzuki, *The Pursuit of Power in Modern Japan, 1825–1995*, p. 290.

95 See Beasley, *Japanese Imperialism, 1894–1945*, pp. 229–31; and Hybel, *Made by the U.S.A. – The International System*, p. 86. In 1937, Japan imported seventy-four percent of its petroleum and crude oil from the USA. See Tsuzuki, *The Pursuit of Power in Modern Japan, 1825–1995*, p. 294.

96 Quoted in Hybel, *Made by the U.S.A. – The International System*, pp. 86–7.

97 Tsuzuki, *The Pursuit of Power in Modern Japan, 1825–1995*, p. 297.

98 For a discussion of the concerns voiced by Japan's navy regarding war with the USA, see A. Hybel, *The Logic of Surprise in International Conflict*, Lexington, Massachusetts: D. C. Heath and Company, 1986, pp. 33–6.

99 See Hybel, *Made by the U.S.A. – The International System*, pp. 111–12, and 293 (note 5).

100 Quoted in D. Yergin, *Shattered Peace*, Boston, Massachusetts: Houghton Mifflin Company, 1978, p. 119.

101 E. Willett, "Dialectic Materialism and Russian Objectives," in Merrill (ed.) *Documentary History of the Truman Presidency*, Vol. 7, p. 12.

102 Ibid., pp. 32–43.

103 George Kennan, "February 26, 1946 telegram," in Merrill, D. (ed.) *Documentary History of the Truman Presidency*, p. 71.

104 Ibid., pp. 87–8.

105 Ibid., pp. 90–1.

106 M. Birch and T. Biersteker, "The World Bank," in T. Biersteker (ed.) *Dealing with Debt*, Boulder, Colorado: Westview Press, 1993, pp. 37–8.

107 See R. Suny, *The Soviet Experiment*, New York: Oxford University Press, 1998, p. 354.

108 Keylor, *The Twentieth Century*, pp. 262–3.

109 Quoted in Suny, *The Soviet Experiment*, p. 354.

110 See Suny, *The Soviet Experiment*, pp. 352–3. As Suny notes, the Soviet ambassador in Washington had also sent his own "long telegram" to Moscow in which he states that the USA was striving for "world dominance."

111 J. Stalin, *Economic Problems of Socialism in the USSR*, Beijing: Foreign Languages Press, 1972, pp. 33–4.

112 "A Report to the President Pursuant to the President's Directive of January 31, 1950," in Merrill D. (ed.) *Documentary History of the Truman Presidency*, Vol. 7, p. 333.

113 Ibid., pp. 386–9.

114 For Henry Kissinger's analysis of the effect of Marxist–Leninist ideology on Soviet behavior, see his December 1, 1951 "Soviet Strategy–Possible U.S. Countermeasures," in Merrill D. (ed.) *Documentary History of the Truman Presidency*, Vol. 7, pp. 729–54.

115 Quoted in Suny, *The Soviet Experiment*, p. 401.

116 For an analysis of the role of anti-communist ideology in Washington's foreign policy-making process towards Latin America, see A. Hybel, *How Leaders Reason: U.S. Intervention in the Caribbean Basin and Latin America*, Oxford: Basil Blackwell, 1990.

117 Quoted in Nogee and Donaldson, *Soviet Foreign Policy*, p. 165.

118 Quoted in Cassels, *Ideology and International Relations in the Modern World*, p. 222.

119 H. Kissinger, *White House Years*, Boston, Massachusetts: Little, Brown and Company, 1979, pp. 56–7.

120 Quoted in J. Gaddis, *Strategies of Containment*, Oxford: Oxford University Press, 1982, p. 261.

121 See Hybel, *Made by the U.S.A. – The International System*, pp. 200–14.

122 Quoted in M. Hunt, *Ideology and U.S. Foreign Policy*, New Haven, Connecticut: Yale University Press, 1987, p. 186.

123 Hunt, *Ideology and U.S. Foreign Policy*, p. 186.

124 "President Ronald Reagan Denounces the Soviet Union, 1981." Press-conference comments from January 29, 1981 are published in T. Paterson and D. Merrill (eds.) *Major Problems in American Foreign Relations Since 1914*, Vol. II, Lexington, Massachusetts: D. C. Heath and Company, 1995, p. 709.

125 Quoted in J. Scott, *Deciding to Intervene: The Reagan Doctrine and American Foreign Policy*, Durham, North Carolina: Duke University Press, 1996, p. 17.

126 Ronald Reagan's Speech to the House of Commons, June 8, 1982. www.historyplace.com/speeches/reagan-parliament.htm

127 Hybel, *Made by the U.S.A. – The International System*, p. 223.

128 Quoted in Scott, *Deciding to Intervene*, p. 21.

129 See Hybel, *Made by the U.S.A.*, pp. 224–5; and Nogee and Donaldson, *Soviet Foreign Policy*, pp. 318 and 338–9.

130 I discuss the Soviet Union's economic problems in the next section.

131 See Hybel, *Made by the USA, p. 176.*

132 Quoted in Hybel, *Made by the USA*, p. 158.

133 See B. Spring, "President Reagan's Strategic Defense Initiative Proposal 25 Years Later: A Better Path Chosen," in *The Heritage Foundation*, www.heritage.org/Research/BallisticMissileDefense/wm1841.cfm, March 10, 2008

134 Kennedy, *The Rise and Fall of the Great Powers*, pp. 332 and 355. The quote appears on p. 347.

135 J. Mearsheimer, *The Tragedy of Great Power Politics*, New York: W. W. Norton, 2001, pp. 39–40.

136 See Cassels, *Ideology and International Relations in the Modern World*, pp. 204–5.

137 See Mearsheimer, *The Tragedy of Great Power Politics*, p. 223.

138 Quoted in Mearsheimer, *The Tragedy of Great Power Politics*, p. 224. S. Sagan's piece, "The Origins of the Pacific War," appears in R. Rotberg and T. Rabb (eds.) *The Origin and Prevention of Major Wars*, Cambridge: Cambridge University Press, 1989.

139 Quoted in C. Hosoya, "Retrogression in Japan's Foreign Policy Decision-Making Process," in J. Morley (ed.) *Dilemmas of Growth in Prewar Japan*, Princeton, New Jersey: Princeton University Press, 1971, p. 93. The Kiyomizu Temple is a fairly tall pagoda with an eleven-faced statue of Kannon, the goddess of mercy. It is highly unlikely that Tojo chose randomly the Kiyomizu Temple to make his point. By referring to a temple that shelters the goddess of mercy, he seemed to be acknowledging that the war against the USA was going to be dreadfully costly and that he hoped Kannon would be merciful with them and the Japanese people.

140 Hosoya, "Retrogression in Japan's Foreign Policy Decision-Making," p. 93.

141 Portions of this section are derived from Hybel, *Made by the U.S.A., pp. 226–7. For a discussion of the Soviet economic system, see J. Reshetar*, The Soviet Polity: Government and Politics in the USSR, *New York: Harper and Row, 1989, p. 224.*

142 Ibid., p. 225.

143 See G. Smith, *Soviet Politics: Struggling with Change*, New York: St. Martin's Press, 1992, p. 34.

144 English, *Russia and the Idea of the West*, pp. 118–19.

145 Smith, *Soviet Politics: Struggling with Change*, pp. 62–4.

146 C. Blacker, *Hostage to Revolution*, New York: Council of Foreign Relations Press, 1993, p. 61.

147 Quoted in Nogee and Donaldson, *Soviet Foreign Policy*, p. 336.

148 Smith, *Soviet Politics: Struggling with Change*, pp. 310–33. See also J. Checkel, *Ideas and International Political Changes: Soviet/Russian Behavior and the End of the Cold War*, New Haven, Connecticut: Yale University Press, 1997, pp. 24–7.

149 Quoted in Cassels, *Ideology and International Relations in the Modern World*, p. 225.

150 Quoted in Nogee and Donaldson, *Soviet Foreign Policy*, p. 337.

151 Suny, *The Soviet Experiment: Russia, the USSR, and the Successor States*, p. 484.

6 The resurgence of forgotten ideologies

1 Stated by Max Weber and quoted in W. Mommsen, *The Political and Social Theory of Max Weber*, Chicago, Illinois: The University of Chicago Press, 1989, p. 140.

2 A. Lake, speech entitled "From Containment to Enlargement" and delivered at the Johns Hopkins School of Advanced International Studies, September 21, 1993.

3 See D. Yergin and J. Stanislaw, *The Commanding Heights*, New York: Simon and Schuster, 1998, p. 158.

4 See R. Wade, "The Fight Over Capital Flows," *Foreign Policy*, 113, 1998–99, 48–53. As Wade also notes, though most of the affected Asian countries complied initially, by the second half of 1998, as domestic turmoil began to mount, they began to adopt measures that countered those demanded by the USA and the IMF.

5 J. Garten, "Is America Abandoning Multilateral Trade," *Foreign Affairs*, 74.6, 1995, 53–7.

6 Quoted in B. Jentleson, *American Foreign Policy*, New York: W. W. Norton, 2004, p. 308.

7 C. Rice, "Promoting the National Interest," *Foreign Affairs*, 79.1, 2000, 45–62.

8 W. Keylor, *The Twentieth Century World – An International History*, New York: Oxford University Press, 1996, p. 74; and G. Barraclough (ed.) *Atlas of World History*, Ann Arbor, Michigan: Borders Press and HarperCollins, 2001, p. 264.

9 See www.britannica.com/EBchecked/ topic/120113/Class-A-mandate; www.brit-annica.com/EBchecked/ topic/120118/Class-B-mandate; original.britannica.com/eb/topic-120120/Class-C-mandate

10 See United Nations Resolution 1514 approved by the General Assembly on December 14, 1960.

11 South Africa illegally incorporated Namibia in 1979. Namibia became an independent state in 1990. Zimbabwe established Black majority rule in 1980. And South Africa moved in the same direction during the first half of the 1990s.

12 The questions are proposed by T. Falola in *Nationalism and African Intellectuals*, Rochester, New York: The University of Rochester Press, 2001, pp. 15, and 19–20.

13 Quoted in Falola, *Nationalism and African Intellectuals*, p. 144.

14 Ibid., see also W. E. B. Du Bois, "The Pan-African Movement," in E. Kedourie (ed.) *Nationalism in Asia and Africa*, New York: The New American Library, 1970, p. 372.

15 Quoted in Du Bois, "The Pan-African Movement," p. 373.

16 See Du Bois, "The Pan-African Movement," p. 376.

17 See Kedourie (ed.) *Nationalism in Asia and Africa*, pp. 25–8; and A. Smith, *Nationalism and Modernism*, London: Routledge, 1998, pp. 99–100.

18 Falola, *Nationalism and African Intellectuals*, p. 28.

19 See Falola, *Nationalism and African Intellectuals*, pp. 32–3. It goes without saying that significant differences existed not just between the two groups just identified, but also within each group.

20 Ibid., p. 28.

21 Ibid., p. 154.

244   *Notes*

22 Ibid., p. 155.
23 See J. Iliffe, *Africans: The History of a Continent*, Cambridge: The University of Cambridge Press, 1995, p. 246.
24 Quoted in Iliffe, *Africans: The History of a Continent*, p. 246.
25 SIPRI Yearbook, 1999, *Armaments, Disarmament, and International Security*, New York: Oxford University Press, 1999, p. 20.
26 Wars between states were noticeably less common and ensued primarily during the early years after independence.
27 The majority of Tutsis were poor peasants, but because the colonialists had seen a disproportionate number being part of the ruling elite, they decided that the Tutsis were racially superior and, thus, should make up the entire ruling elite.
28 Quotes appear in J. P. Chretien, *The Great Lakes of Africa – Two Thousand Years of History*, New York: Zone Books, 2003, pp. 72–3.
29 Ibid., p. 256.
30 The Belgian Catholic Church also favored the Tutsis.
31 For a discussion of the differences and tensions between civic nationalism and ethno-cultural nationalism, see D. Brown, *Contemporary Nationalism*, London: Routledge, 2000, pp. 125–8.
32 See Chretien, *The Great Lakes of Africa – Two Thousand Years of History*, pp. 304–5.
33 See Brown, *Contemporary Nationalism*, p. 162. Brown suggests the Tutsis had favored all along a form of civic nationalism, one designed to create a "kinship community of equal citizens" in Rwanda, regardless of their ethno-cultural backgrounds. This contention may be applicable for the period after 1994, but not prior to that time. Though the Tutsis did view themselves and the Hutus as Rwandans, as part of the same community, they did not view the Hutus as equals.
34 See I. Kabongo, "The Catastrophe of Belgian Decolonization," in P. Gifford and W. R. Lewis (eds.) *Decolonization and African Independence*, New Haven, Connecticut: Yale University Press, 1988, pp. 384–6.
35 Ibid., pp. 386–8.
36 See J. F. Ade Ayayi and A. E. Ekoko, "Transfer Power in Nigeria: Its Origins and Consequences," in P. Gifford and W. M. R. Lewis (eds.) *Decolonization and African Independence*, pp. 246–7.
37 Quoted in Ayayi and Ekoko, "Transfer Power in Nigeria: Its Origins and Consequences," p. 250.
38 See R. Oliver and A. Atmore, *Africa Since 1800*, Cambridge: Cambridge University Press, 1994, pp. 221 and 271; see also Iliffe, *Africans*, p. 265.
39 Quoted in Ayayi and Ekoko, "Transfer Power in Nigeria: Its Origins and Consequences," pp. 256–7.
40 Ibid., p. 257.
41 For a heartbreaking depiction of the trauma experienced by Biafrans during the civil war, read C. N. Adichie's novel, *Half of Yellow Sun*, London: Harper Perennial, 2006.
42 See Iliffe, *Africans*, p. 258; see also Oliver and Atmore, *Africa Since 1800*, pp. 270–1.
43 Quoted in Ayayi and Ekoko, "Transfer Power in Nigeria: Its Origins and Consequences," p. 266.
44 Ayayi and Ekoko, "Transfer Power in Nigeria: Its Origins and Consequences," p. 267.
45 A. Boahen, "Ghana since Independence," in P. Gifford and W. M. R. Louis (eds.) *Decolonization and African Independence*, p. 203.
46 Quoted in Oliver and Atmore, *Africa Since 1800*, p. 218.
47 See Oliver and Atmore, *Africa Since 1800*, pp. 219–20.
48 See Falola, *Nationalism and African Intellectuals*, p. 128.

49 See Adu Boahen, "Ghana since Independence," pp. 204–5.

50 See Oliver and Atmore, *Africa Since 1800*, pp. 267–8.

51 Ibid., pp. 268–9.

52 See A. Lowenthal, "The United States and Latin American Democracy: Learning from History," in A. Lowenthal (ed.) *Exporting Democracy – The United States and Latin America: Case Studies*, Baltimore, Maryland: Johns Hopkins University Press, 1991, p. 262.

53 See E. Helleiner, *States and the Reemergence of Global Finance*, Ithaca, New York: Cornell University Press, 1994, pp. 15–16.

54 J. Stiglitz and A. Charlton posit an argument that is quite similar to the argument being made by Latin American leaders who have challenged the "Washington consensus." See J. Stiglitz and A. Charlton, *Fair Trade for All*, New York: Cambridge University Press, 2005. For a review of the book, see Robert B. Reich, "The Poor Get Poorer," in *The New York Times Book Review*, April 2, 2006. www.nytimes.com/2006/04/02/books/review/02re

55 The Declaration was not announced until November 9, 1917. See D. Fromkin, *A Peace to End All Peace: Creating the Modern Middle East, 1914–22*, New York: H. Holt, 1989, pp. 276–7; and F. Cardini, *Europe and Islam*, Oxford: Blackwell, 2001, p. 209.

56 Fromkin, *A Peace to End All Peace*, pp. 297–301.

57 Palestine's population at the start of 1918 was seven hundred and forty-eight thousand, of whom six hundred and nineteen thousand were Muslim, seventy thousand were Christian, and fifty-nine thousand were Jewish.

58 France took over Syria and Lebanon, while Britain assumed control over Palestine, Iraq and Transjordan.

59 Quoted in James, *The Rise and Fall of the British Empire*, New York: St. Martin's Press, 1996, p. 366.

60 Ibid., p. 371.

61 F. Halliday, *The Middle East in International Relations*, New York: Cambridge University Press, 2005, p. 91.

62 Ibid., p. 200.

63 According to Vincent J. Cornell, when "speaking about Islamic law, informed Muslims use the term shariah to connote the sacred law as a global concept or ideal, while fiqh is used to connote the ongoing interpretation of the law through the schools (four Sunni and one Shiite) of juridical practice." See V. Cornell, "Fruit of the Tree of Knowledge," in J. Esposito (ed.) *The Oxford History of Islam*, New York: Oxford University Press, 1999, p. 91.

64 J. Esposito, "Contemporary Islam: Reformation or Revolution?" in Esposito (ed.) *The Oxford History of Islam*, p. 652.

65 See S. V. R. Nasr, "European Colonialism and the Emergence of Modern Muslim States," in J. Esposito (ed.) *The Oxford History of Islam*, pp. 560–1.

66 B. Tibi, *The Challenge of Fundamentalism*, Berkeley, California: University of California Press, 1997, pp. 7–8. In Gilles Kepel's words, the "first Islamist onslaught was against nationalism, and its aim was to substitute one vision of world community for another." See G. Kepel, *Jihad – The Trail of Political Islam*, Cambridge, Massachusetts: The Belknap Press of Harvard University Press, 2002, p. 24.

67 Kepel, *Jihad – The Trail of Political Islam*, p. 24.

68 See S. Alaqui, "Muslim Opposition Thinkers in the Nineteenth Century," in C. Butterworth and I. Zartman (eds.) *Between the State and Islam*, New York: Cambridge University Press, 2001, pp. 95–6. Quotes appear on the same pages. See also J. Landau, *The Politics of Pan-Islam*, Oxford: Clarendon Press, 1990, pp. 14–21.

69 See L. C. Brown, *Religion and State*, New York: Columbia University Press, 2000, pp. 32 and 96.

70 See Brown, *Religion and State*, pp. 144–5.
71 Ibid., p. 223.
72 Quoted in Landau, *The Politics of Pan-Islam*, p. 224. The significance of the claim that all Muslims are part of the same nation cannot be overemphasized. An al-Qaeda representative voiced a similar contention in March 2007 when he warned Spain that its involvement in the war in Afghanistan endangered Spaniards in their own country. "The Islamic states are the same nation, and the Spanish Government, by sending troops to Afghanistan once again endangers its country." Quoted in the Spanish newspaper, *El Pais*, under the heading: "Al Qaeda Threatens Spain for Sending Troops to Afghanistan," March 13, 2007, 21 (my translation).
73 See Kepel, *Jihad – The Trail of Political Islam*, p. 28.
74 See Brown, *Religion and State*, p. 156.
75 Ibid., p. 159.
76 See Landau, *The Politics of Pan-Islam*, p. 227.
77 Kepel, *Jihad – The Trail of Political Islam*, pp. 34–5.
78 Esposito, "Contemporary Islam: Reformation or Revolution?" pp. 655–6.
79 E. Abrahamian, *Iran Between Two Revolutions*, Princeton, New Jersey: Princeton University Press, 1982, p. 531.
80 Quoted in Brown, *Religion and State*, p. 164.
81 Ibid., p. 165.
82 See Brown, *Religion and State*, pp. 165–9. See also Halliday, *The Middle East in International Relations*, p. 104.
83 The Khomeini regime referred to the Soviet Union as the "little Satan." See Halliday, *The Middle East in International Relations*, p. 105.
84 J. Mearsheimer and S. Walt, "The Israel Lobby," in *London Review of Books*, Vol. 28, No. 6, March 23, 2006. www.lrb.co.uk/v28/n06/mear01_.html
85 Quoted in Mearsheimer and Walt, "The Israel Lobby."
86 Quoted in Anonymous, *Imperial Hubris*, Washington, D.C.: Brassey's, Inc., 2004, p. 227.
87 F. Gerges, *The Far Enemy. Why Jihad Went Global*, New York: Cambridge University Press, 2005, p. 82.
88 Quoted in Gerges, *The Far Enemy*, p. 84.
89 Ibid., p. 85.
90 See *The 9/11 Commission Report*, New York: W. W. Norton, 2004, p. 61.
91 See Gerges, *The Far Enemy*, p. 146.
92 Ibid., p. 148.
93 Quoted in Gergen, *The Far Enemy*, p. 149.
94 Quoted in Anonymous, *Imperial Hubris*, p. 140. See also Gerges, *The Far Enemy*, p. 150.
95 See J. Mearsheimer, "Why We Will Soon Miss the Cold War," in *The Atlantic*, Vol. 266, No. 2, August 1990, pp. 35–50.
96 Ibid., 35–8.
97 See A. Wendt, *Social Theory of International Politics*, New York: Cambridge University Press, 1999, p. 299.

7 The dialectical nature of political ideologies in the world system

1 During a press interview in Spain, the Mexican writer Carlos Fuentes stated: "Literature teaches to know in order to doubt and to know in order to continue doubting." I took the liberty to alter slightly his comment, for in a sense written history is a form of literature. See J. Rojo, "Fuentes, la voz americana de La Mancha," in *El Pais*, June 12, 2007, 44.
2 See, for instance, R. Keohane, *After Hegemony*, Princeton, New Jersey: Princeton University Press, 1984, pp. 125–7.

3 See J. Ferejohn, "Structure and Ideology," in J. Goldstein and R. Keohane (eds.) *Ideas and Foreign Policy: Beliefs, Institutions, and Political Change*, Ithaca, New York: Cornell University Press, 1993, pp. 208–9.

4 A. Wendt, *Social Theory of International Politics*, Cambridge: Cambridge University Press, 1999, p. 371.

5 Or as noted by Fred Halliday, "one cannot explain any society, political system or international relationship" without a parallel analysis of values and ideology. See F. Halliday, *The Middle East in International Relations*, Cambridge: Cambridge University Press, 2005, p. 32.

6 See N. Gould-Davies, "Rethinking the Role of Ideology in International Politics During the Cold War," in *Journal of Cold War Studies*, 1.1, 1999, 90–109.

7 As I explained in Chapter 1, though the emperor's Confucian advisors repeatedly questioned China's drive to sail to distant lands and vehemently opposed engaging in trade with foreign entities, a weakened domestic economy and the threat posed by the Mongolian forces might have also helped convince the emperor that it would be best to bring to an end long-distance sea voyages.

8 W. Mommsen, *The Political and Social Theory of Max Weber*, Chicago, Illinois: University of Chicago Press, 1989, p. 149.

9 Quoted in P. Cain and A. Hopkins, *English Imperialism, 1688–2000*, Harlow: England, 2002, p. 98.

10 Cain and Hopkins, *British Imperialism*, p. 98.

11 Ibid., p. 247.

12 Quoted in R. Hyam, *Britain's Imperial Century, 1815–1914*, New York: Harper and Row, 1976, p. 51.

13 Ibid., p. 57. See also R. Johnson, *British Imperialism*, New York: Palgrave, 2003, pp. 99–100.

14 See C. Kindlerberger, *The World in Depression 1929–1939*, Berkeley, California: University of California Press, 1973, p. 293.

15 Kenneth Waltz would contend that by trying to explain the types of political allies the Soviet Union and the USA tried to enlist, I obscure the boundary that exists between international politics and foreign policy. Though that aspect of his challenge would be correct, one cannot help questioning the utility of a theory that explains as little as his does. See K. Waltz, *Theory of International Politics*, New York: Random House, 1979, pp. 121–2.

16 According to Larry Diamond, the "end of the Cold War and the collapse of communism have discredited all models other than liberal democracy." Quoted in K. Waltz, "Globalization and Governance," in R. Art and R. Jervis (eds.) *International Politics*, New York: Pearson, Longman, 2007, p. 337.

17 C. Rice, "Promoting the National Interest," in *Foreign Affairs,* 79.1, 2000, 45.

Bibliography

(1999) *Stockholm International Peace Research Institute Yearbook, Armament, Disarmament and International Security*, Stockholm: SIPRI.

(2004) *The 9/11 Commission Report*, New York: W. W. Norton.

Abrahamian, E. (1982) *Iran Between Two Revolutions*, Princeton, New Jersey: Princeton University Press.

Achen, C. and Snidal, D. (1989) "Rational Deterrence Theory and Comparative Case Studies," *World Politics* 41, no. 2.

Adamson, F. (2006) "The Constitutive Power of Political Ideology: Nationalism and the Emergence of Corporate Agency in World Politics," *Annual Meeting of the American Political Science Association*, Philadelphia, Pennsylvania, August 31–September 3.

Adshead, S. (1988) *China in World History*, New York: St. Martin's Press.

Adu Boahen, Adu (1998) "Ghana Since Independence," in P. Gifford and W. Lewis (eds.) *Decolonization and African Independence*, New Haven, Connecticut: Yale University Press.

Alaqui, S. (2001) "Muslim Opposition Thinkers in the Nineteenth Century," in C. Butterworth and I. Zartman, (eds.) *Between the State and Islam*, New York: Cambridge University Press.

—(2007) "Al Qaeda Threatens Spain for Sending Troops to Afghanistan," *El País*, March 13.

Anderson, B. (1993) *Imagined Communities*, London: Verso.

Anna, T. (1990) *The Mexican Empire of Iturbide*, Lincoln, Nebraska: University of Nebraska.

Anonymous (2004) *Imperial Hubris*, Washington, D.C.: Brassey's, Inc.

Armstrong, K. (1993) *A History of God*, New York: Ballantine Books.

Ayayi, J. and Ekoko, A. (1998) "Transfer Power in Nigeria: Its Origins and Consequences," in P. Gifford and W. Lewis (eds.) *Decolonization and African Independence*, New Haven, Connecticut: Yale University Press.

Ball, T. and Dagger, R. (2004) *Political Ideologies and the Democratic Ideal*, New York: Pearson, Longman.

Barraclough, G. (ed.) (1986) *The Times Atlas of World History*, London: Times Books Limited.

— (ed.) (2001) *Atlas of World History*, Ann Arbor, Michigan: Borders Press and HarperCollins.

Beasley, W. (1987) *Japanese Imperialism, 1894–1945*, New York: Oxford University Press.

Bell, D. (1976) "The End of Ideology," in M. Rejai (ed.) *Decline of Ideology?* Chicago, Illinois: Aldine.

Berlin, I. (1992) *The Crooked Timber of Humanity: Chapters in the History of Ideas*, New York: Vintage Books.

Birch, M. and Biersteker, T. (1993) "The World Bank," in T. Biersteker (ed.) *Dealing with Debt*. Boulder, Colorado: Westview Press.

Blacker, C. (1993) *Hostage to Revolution*, New York: Council of Foreign Relations Press.

Bloch, M. (1961) *Feudal Society*, Chicago, Illinois: Chicago University Press.

Boggs, C. (1976) *Gramsci's Marxism*, London: Pluto Press.

Bolivar, S. (1812) "Memorial to the Citizens of New Granada by a Citizen of Caracas – December 15, 1812," in V. Lecuna and H. Bierck, Jr. (eds.) (1951) *Selected Writings of Bolívar*, Vol. I, New York: The Colonial Press.

Bonilla, Heraclio (1987) "Peru and Bolivia," in L. Bethell (ed.) *Spanish America After Independence, c.1820–c.1870*, Cambridge: Cambridge University Press.

Bowder, D. (1978) *The Age of Constantine and Julian*, New York: Harper and Row.

Brass, P. (1991) *Ethnicity and Nationalism*, London: Sage Publications.

Breunig, C. (1970) *The Age of Revolution and Reaction, 1789–1850*, New York: W. W. Norton and Company.

Briggs, A. and Clavin, P. (1997) *Modern Europe, 1789–1989*, London: Routledge.

Brown, D. (2000) *Contemporary Nationalism*, London: Routledge.

Brown, J. (1992) "The Structure of the Foreign-Owned Petroleum Industry in Mexico, 1880–1938," in J. Brown and A. Knight (eds.) *The Mexican Petroleum Industry in the Twentieth Century*, Austin, Texas: University of Texas Press.

Brown, L. (2000) *Religion and State*, New York: Columbia University Press.

Brown, Peter (1971) *The World of Late Antiquity*, London: Harcourt Brace Jovanovich Inc., 1971.

Bull, H. (1977) *The Anarchical Society. A Study in Order in World Politics*, London: Macmillan.

Burke, T. (1999) *The Major Religions of the World*, Oxford, UK: Blackwell.

Butterfield, H. (May 2003) "The Balance of Power," in H. Butterfield and M. Wight (eds.) *Diplomatic Investigations*, Cambridge, Massachusetts: Harvard University Press, 1966, p. 145.

Buzan, B. and Little, R. (2000) *International Systems in World History*, New York: Oxford University Press.

Cain, P. and Hopkins A. (2002) *English Imperialism, 1688–2000*, Harlow, England: Longman.

Cardini, F. (2001) *Europe and Islam*, Oxford: Blackwell.

Cardoso, F. and Faletto, E. (1979) *Dependency and Development in Latin America*, Berkeley, California: University of California Press.

Carr, E. (1964) *The Twenty Years' Crisis, 1919–1939*, New York: Harper and Row.

Carver, T. (2004) "Ideology: The Career of a Concept," in T. Ball and R. Dagger (eds.) *Ideals and Ideologies*, New York: Pearson.

Cassels, A. (1996) *Ideology and International Relations in the Modern World*, London: Routledge.

Centeno, M. (1999) "Symbols of State Nationalism in Latin America," in *European Review of Latin American and Caribbean Studies*, 66.

Checkel, J. (1997) *Ideas and International Political Changes: Soviet/Russian Behavior and the End of the Cold War*, New Haven, Connecticut: Yale University Press.

Choudhary, S. (1973) *Growth of Nationalism in India, 1857–1918*, Vol. 1, New Delhi: Trimurty Publications.

Chretien, J. P. (2003) *The Great Lakes of Africa – Two Thousand Years of History*, New York: Zone Books.

Clendenen, C. (1969) *Blood on the Border: The United States and the Mexican Irregulares*, New York: The Macmillan Company.

Collier, S. (1967) *Ideas and Politics of Chilean Independence, 1808–1833*, Cambridge: Cambridge University Press.

— (1985) "Chile," in S. Collier, T. Skidmore, and H. Blakemore (eds.) *The Cambridge Encyclopedia of Latin America and the Caribbean*, New York: Cambridge University Press.

Cornell, V. (1999) "Fruit of the Tree of Knowledge," in J. Esposito (ed.) *The Oxford History of Islam*, New York: Oxford University Press.

Cotler, J. (1986) *Clases, Estado y Nacion en Peru*, Lima: Instituto de Estudios Peruanos.

Craig, G. and George, A. (1983) *Force and Statecraft: Diplomatic Problems of Our Times*, New York: Oxford University Press.

Cranston, Maurice (2003) "Ideology," *Encyclopedia Britannica*. www.culturaleconomics.atfreeweb.com/Anno/Cranston%20Ideology%20EB%202003.htm

Crow, J. (1980) *The Epic of Latin America*, Berkeley, California: University of California Press.

Dahl, R. (1989a) *Democracy and Its Critics*, New Haven, Connecticut: Yale University Press.

— (1989b) *Dilemmas of Pluralist Democracy*, New Haven, Connecticut: Yale University Press.

Danzinger, R. (1977) *Abd Al-Qadir and the Algerians*, New York: Holmes and Meier Publishers.

Derry, J. (1976) *Castlereagh*, London: Allen Lane.

Diamond, J. (1999) *Guns, Germs, and Steel*, New York: W. W. Norton.

Dominguez, J. (1980) *Insurrection or Loyalty*, Cambridge, Massachusetts: Harvard University Press.

Donelan, M. (1984) "Spain and the Indies," in H. Bull and A. Watson (eds.) *The Expansion of International Society*, Oxford: Clarendon Press.

Donner, F. (1981) *The Early Islamic Conquests*, Princeton, New Jersey: Princeton University Press.

— (1999) "Muhammad and the Caliphate," in J. Esposito (ed.) *The Oxford History of Islam*, New York: Oxford University Press.

Dower, J. (1979) *Empire and Aftermath*, Cambridge, Massachusetts: Harvard University Press.

— (1993) *War Without Mercy: Race and Power in the Pacific*, New York: Pantheon Books.

Doyle, M. (1986) *Empires*, Ithaca, New York: Cornell University Press.

Doyle, W. (1990) *The Oxford History of the French Revolution*, New York: Oxford University Press.

Draper, T. (1996) *A Struggle for Power*, New York: Times Books.

Drucker, H. (1974) *The Political Uses of Ideology*, New York: Harper and Row Publishers.

Duara, P. (1995) *Rescuing History from the Nation*, Chicago, Illinois: The University of Chicago Press.

Du Bois, W. (1970) "The Pan-African Movement," in E. Kedourie (ed.) *Nationalism in Asia and Africa*, New York: The New American Library.

Dudden, A. P. (1992) *The American Pacific*, New York: Oxford University Press.

Eatwell, R. and Wright, A. (eds.) (1993) *Contemporary Political Ideologies*, San Francisco, California: Westview Press.

Edwards, J. (2000) *The Spain of the Catholic Monarchs. 1474–1520*, Oxford: Blackwell.

Ehler, S. and Morrall, J. (eds.) (1967) *Church and States Through the Centuries: A Collection of Historical Documents*, New York: Biblo and Tannen.

Elbadawi, I. and Sambani, N. (2000) "Why Are There So Many Civil Wars in Africa. Understanding and Preventing Violent Conflict," in *Journal of African Economies*, 9, 244–69.

Elton, G. (1974) "An Early Tudor Poor Law," in G. Elton (ed.) *Studies in Tudor and Stuart Politics and Government*, Vol. II, Cambridge: Cambridge University Press.

English, R. (2000) *Russia and the Idea of the West*, New York: Columbia University Press.

Entelis, J. (1986) *Algeria: The Revolution Institutionalized*, Boulder, Colorado: Westview Press.

Erikson, E. (1969) *Gandhi's Truth*, New York: W. W. Norton and Company.

Eserick, J. (2006) "How the Qing Dynasty Became China," in J. Eserick, H. Kayali, and E. Van Young (eds.) *Empire to Nation*, Lanham, Maryland: Rowman and Littlefield Publishers.

Esposito, J. (1999) "Contemporary Islam: Reformation or Revolution?" in J. Esposito (ed.) *The Oxford History of Islam*, New York: Oxford University Press.

Fairbank, J. and Goldman, M. (2006) *China: A New History*, Cambridge, Massachusetts: The Belknap Press of Harvard University Press.

Falola, T. (2001) *Nationalism and African Intellectuals*, Rochester, New York: University of Rochester Press.

Ferejohn, J. (1993) "Structure and Ideology," in J. Goldstein and R. Keohane (eds.) *Ideas and Foreign Policy: Beliefs, Institutions, and Political Change*, Ithaca, New York: Cornell University Press, 1993.

Fest, J. (1974) *Hitler*, New York: Harcourt Brace Jovanovich.

Finucane, R. (1983) *Soldiers of the Faith*, New York: St. Martin's Press.

Fitzgerald, J. (1996) *Awakening China*, Stanford, California: Stanford University Press.

Fletcher III, W. (1982) *The Search for a New Order – Intellectuals and Fascism in Prewar Japan*, Chapel Hill, North Carolina: The University of North Carolina Press.

Fowden, G. (1993) *Empire to Commonwealth*, Princeton, New Jersey: Princeton University Press.

Froment, C. (2006) "Selfhood and Nationhood in Latin America: From Colonial Subjects to Democratic Citizens," in J. Esherick, H. Kayali, and E. Van Yound (eds.) *Empire to Nation*, Lanham, Maryland: Rowman and Littlefield Publishers.

Fromkin, D. (1998) *A Peace to End All Peace*, New York: Henry Holt and Company.

Fuentes, C. (1992) *The Buried Mirror*, Boston, Massachusetts: Houghton Mifflin Company.

Gaddis, J. (1982) *Strategies of Containment*, Oxford: Oxford University Press.

García-Gallo de Diego, A. (1992) *Las Bulas de Alejandro VI Sobre el Nuevo Mundo Descubierto por Colón*, Madrid: Ministerio de Cultura, Compañía Editorial.

Gardner, L. (1984) *Safe for Democracy: The Anglo-American Response to Revolution, 1919–1923*, New York: Oxford University Press.

Garten, J. (1995) "Is America Abandoning Multilateral Trade," *Foreign Affairs* 74.6, 50–62.

Gash, N. (1986) *Pillars of Government and Other Essays in State and Society, c. 1770– c.1880*, London: Edward Arnold.

Geary, P. (2002) *The Myth of Nations: The Medieval Origins of Europe*, Princeton, New Jersey: Princeton University Press.

Gerges, F. (2005) *The Far Enemy. Why Jihad Went Global*, New York: Cambridge University Press.

Geyl, P. (1958) *Debates with Historians*, New York: Meridian.

Gibbon, E. (1990) *The Decline and Fall of the Roman Empire*, Chicago, Illinois: Encyclopedia Britannica.

Gil, F. (1966) *The Political System of Chile*, Boston, Massachusetts: Houghton Mifflin Company.

Gilbert, F. (1979) *The End of the European Era, 1890 to the Present*, New York: W. W. Norton.

Gilpin, R. (1977) *U.S. Power and the Multinational Corporation*, New York: Basic Books.

— (1983) *War and Change in World Politics*, Cambridge: Cambridge University Press.

— (1987) *The Political Economy of International Relations*, Princeton, New Jersey: Princeton University Press.

Gluck, C. (1985) *Japan's Modern Myths. Ideology in the Late Meiji Period*, Princeton, New Jersey: Princeton University Press.

Goffman, D. (2002) *The Ottoman Empire and Early Modern Europe*, Cambridge: Cambridge University Press.

Golay, F. (1997) *Face of Empire. United States–Philippine Relations, 1896–1946*, Manila: Ateneo de Manila University Press.

Gollwitzer, H. (1969) *Europe in the Age of Imperialism, 1880–1914*, London: Thames and Hudson.

Gong, G. (1984) "China's Entry Into International Society," in H. Bull and A. Watson (eds.) *The Expansion of International Society*, Oxford: Clarendon Press.

Gootenberg, P. (1989) *Between Silver and Guano*, Princeton, New Jersey: Princeton University Press.

— (1991) "North–South: Trade Policy, Regionalism and Caudillismo in Post Inde- pendence Peru," in *Journal of Latin American Studies*, XXIII.2, 273–308.

Gould-Davies, N. (1999) "Rethinking the Role of Ideology in International Politics During the Cold War," *Journal of Cold War Studies*, 1.1, 90–109.

Graff, D. (2002) *Medieval Chinese Warfare, 300–900*, London: Routledge.

Grant, M. (1994) *Constantine the Great*, New York: Charles Scribner's Sons.

— (1999) *The Collapse and Recovery of the Roman Empire*, New York: Routledge.

Green, S. (1987) *The Mexican Republic: The First Decade, 1823–1832*, Pittsburgh, Pennsylvania: Pittsburgh University Press.

Greenfeld, L. (2000) "Nationalism Five Roads to Modernity," in J. Hutchinson and A. Smith (eds.) *Nationalism: Critical Concepts in Political Science*, Vol. I, New York: Routledge.

Gregor, A. (1979) *Italian Fascism and Developmental Dictatorship*, Princeton, New Jersey: Princeton University Press.

Gregory, P. and Ruffin, R. (1989) *Basic Microeconomics*, Glenview, Illinois: Scott, Foresman and Company.

Grotius, H. (1853) *De Jure Belli ac Pacis, (On the Law of War and Peace)*, Vol. I, Cambridge: Cambridge University Press.

— (2004) *The Free Sea*, Indianapolis, Indiana: Liberty Fund.

Haas, E. (1979) "Human Rights: To Act or Not to Act?" in K. Oye, D. Rothchild, and R. Lieber (eds.) *Eagle Entangled. U.S. Foreign Policy in a Complex World*, New York: Longman.

Hahn, H. (2001) "The Polish Nation in the Revolution of 1846–49," in D. Dowe, H. Haupt, D. Langewiesche, J. Sperber, and D. Higgins (eds.) *Europe in 1848*, New York: Bergham Books.

Halliday, F. (2005) *The Middle East in International Relations*, Cambridge: Cambridge University Press, 2005.

Halperin Donghi, T. (1975) *Historia Contemporaria de America Latina*, Madrid: Alianza Editorial.

Haslam, J. (2002) *No Virtue Like Necessity: Realist Thought in International Relations Since Machiavelli*, New Haven, Connecticut: Yale University Press.

Hayashi, K. (1971) "Germany and Japan in the Interwar Period," in J. Morley (ed.) *Dilemmas of Growth in Prewar Japan*, Princeton, New Jersey: Princeton University Press.

Helleiner, E. (1994) *States and the Reemergence of Global Finance*, Ithaca, New York: Cornell University Press.

Herrin, J. (1987) *The Formation of Christendom*, Princeton, New Jersey: Princeton University Press.

Hill, C. (1961) *The Century of Revolution, 1603–1714*, Edinburgh: Thomas Nelson and Sons.

Hillgarth, J. (1978) *The Spanish Kingdoms, 1250–1516*, Vol. II, Oxford: Clarendon Press.

Hitler, A. (1939) *Mein Kampf*, New York: Reynal and Hitchcock.

— (2004) "Mein Kampf," in T. Ball and R. Dagger (eds.) (2004) *Political Ideologies and the Democratic Ideal*, New York: Pearson, Longman.

Hobbes, T. (1951) *Leviathan*, Harmondsworth: Penguin.

Hobsbawm, E. (1989) *The Age of Empire, 1875–1914*, New York: Vintage Books.

— (1994) *The Age of Extremes: A History of the World, 1914–1991*, New York: Pantheon.

Hoffman, S. (1977–78) "The Hell of Good Intentions," *Foreign Policy*, 29, 3–26.

Hosoya, C. (1971) "Retrogression in Japan's Foreign Policy Decision-Making Process," in J. Morley (ed.) *Dilemmas of Growth in Prewar Japan*, Princeton, New Jersey: Princeton University Press.

Howard, M. (1976) *War in European History*, London: Oxford University Press.

Hucker, C. (1966) *The Censorial System of Ming China*, Stanford, California: Stanford University Press.

Hunt, M. (1987) *Ideology and U.S. Foreign Policy*, New Haven, Connecticut: Yale University Press.

Huntington, S. (1996) *The Clash of Civilizations and the Remaking of World Order*, New York: Simon and Schuster.

Hyam, Ronald (1976) *Britain's Imperial Century, 1815-1914*, New York: Harper and Row.

Hybel, A. (1986) *The Logic of Surprise in International Conflict*, Lexington, Massachusetts: D.C. Heath.

Hybel, A. (1990) *How Leaders Reason: U.S. Intervention in the Caribbean Basin and Latin America*, Oxford: Basil Blackwell.

— (1993) *Power Over Rationality*, Albany, New York: State University of New York Press.

— (2001) *Made by the U.S.A. – The International System*, New York: Palgrave.

Hybel, A. and Kaufman, J. (2006) *The Bush Administrations and Saddam Hussein: Deciding on Conflict*, New York: Palgrave.

Ikenberry, G. (2002) "America's Liberal Grand Strategy: Democracy and National Security in the Post-War Era," in G. Ikenberry (ed.) *American Foreign Policy*, New York: Longman.

Iliffe, J. (1994) *Africans: The History of a Continent*, Cambridge: The University of Cambridge Press.

James, L. (1996) *The Rise and Fall of the British Empire*, New York: St. Martin's Press.

Jentleson, B. (2004) *American Foreign Policy*, New York: W. W. Norton.

Johnson, R. (2003) *British Imperialism*, New York: Palgrave.

Johnston, A. (1995) *Cultural Realism: Strategic Culture and Grand Strategy in Chinese History*, Princeton, New Jersey: Princeton University Press.

Jones, J. (1980) *England and the World (1649–1815)*, Sussex: The Harvester Press.

Judd, D. (1997) *Empire*, New York: Basic Books.

Kabongo, I. (1988) "The Catastrophe of Belgian Decolonization," in P. Gifford and W. Lewis (eds.) *Decolonization and African Independence*, New Haven, Connecticut: Yale University Press.

Kaegi, W. (1992) *Byzantium and the Early Islamic Conquests*, Cambridge: Cambridge University Press.

Kafadar, C. (1995) *Between Two Worlds: The Construction of the Ottoman Empire*, Berkeley, California: University of California Press.

Kagan, D., Ozment, S. and Turner, F. (2001) *The Western Heritage*, 7th edition, Upper Saddle River, New Jersey: Prentice Hall.

Kaiser, D. (2000) *Politics and War – European Conflict from Philip II to Hitler*, Cambridge, Massachusetts: Harvard University Press.

Karnow, S. (1989) *In Our Images. America's Empire in the Philippines*, New York: Ballantine Books.

Karpat, K. (2001) *The Politicization of Islam. Reconstructing Identity, State, Faith, and Community in the Late Ottoman State*, New York: Oxford University Press.

Katz, F. (1991) "The Liberal Republic and the Porfiriato," in L. Bethell (ed.) *Mexico Since Independence*, Cambridge: Cambridge University Press.

Kedourie, E. (ed.) (1971) *Nationalism in Asia and Africa*, London: Weidenfeld.

Keiger, J. (2001) *France and the World Since 1870*, London: Arnold.

Kellas, J. (1998) *The Politics of Nationalism and Ethnicity*, New York: St. Martin's Press.

Kennan, G. "February 26, 1946 telegram," in D. Merrill (ed.) *Documentary History of the Truman Presidency*, Vol. 7, Bethesda, Maryland: University Publications of America.

Kennedy, P. (1987) *The Rise and Fall of the Great Powers*, New York: Random House.

Keohane, R. (1984) *After Hegemony*, Princeton, New Jersey: Princeton University Press, 1984.

Kepel, G. (2002) *Jihad – The Trail of Political Islam*, Cambridge, Massachusetts: The Belknap Press of Harvard University Press.

Keylor, W. R. (1996) *The Twentieth Century World – An International History*, New York: Oxford University Press.

Khrushchev, N. (1970) *Khrushchev Remembers*, Boston, Massachusetts: Little, Brown and Company.

Kindleberger, C. (1973) *The World in Depression 1929–1939*, Berkeley, California: University of California Press.

Kissinger, H. (1956) "The Congress of Vienna: A Reappraisal," in *World Politics*, 8.2, 264–80.

— (1979) *White House Years*, Boston, Massachusetts: Little, Brown and Company.

— (2001) "Soviet Strategy–Possible U.S. Countermeasures," in D. Merrill (ed.) *Documentary History of the Truman Presidency*, Vol. 7, Bethesda, Maryland: University Publications of America.

Klein, S. (2002) *Rethinking Japan's Identity and International Role*, New York: Routledge.

Knight, A. (1986) *The Mexican Revolution*, Vol. I, Lincoln, Nebraska: University of Nebraska Press.

— (1992) "The Politics of Expropriation," in J. Brown and A. Knight (eds.) *The Mexican Petroleum Industry in the Twentieth Century*, Austin, Texas: University of Texas Press.

Knutsen, T. (1992) *A History of International Relations Theory*, Manchester: Manchester University Press.

Koenigsberger, H. (1955) "The Organization of Revolutionary Parties in France and the Netherlands During the Sixteenth Century," *The Journal of Modern History*, XXVII.4, 335–51.

Koralka, J. (2001) "Revolution in the Habsburg Monarchy," in D. Dowe, H. Haupt, D. Langewiesche, J. Sperber, and D. Higgins (eds.) *Europe in 1848*, New York: Bergham Books.

Krasner, S. (1978) *Defending the National Interest*, Princeton, New Jersey: Princeton University Press.

— (1999) *Sovereignty: Organized Hypocrisy*, Princeton, New Jersey: Princeton University Press.

LaFeber, W. (1989) *The American Age: United States Foreign Policy at Home and Abroad Since 1750*, New York: W. W. Norton.

Lafore, Laurence (1965) *The Long Fuse*, Philadelphia, Pennsylvania: Lippincott.

Lake, A. (1993) "From Containment to Enlargement," Washington, DC: School of Advanced International Studies, Johns Hopkins University, September 21.

Lamy, S. (2001) "Contemporary Mainstream Approaches: Neo-Realism and Neo-Liberalism," in J. Baylis and S. Smith (eds.) *The Globalization of World Politics*, New York: Oxford University Press.

Landau, J. (1990) *The Politics of Pan-Islam*, Oxford: Clarendon Press.

Levathes, L. (2000) *When China Ruled the Seas*, New York: Oxford University Press.

Lévêque, P. (2001) "The Revolution Crisis of 1848/51 in France," in D. Dowe, H. Haupt, D. Langewiesche, J. Sperber, and D. Higgins (eds.) *Europe in 1848*, New York: Bergham Books.

Levine, J. (1960) *The Export Economies. Their Pattern of Development in Historical Perspective*, Cambridge, Massachusetts: Harvard University Press.

Levy, D. and Bruhn, K. (1999) "Mexico: Sustained Civilian Rule and the Question of Democracy," in L. Diamond, J. Hartlyn, J. Linz, and S. Lipset (eds.) *Democracy in Developing Countries – Latin America*, Boulder, Colorado: Lynn Reinner Publishers.

Lewis, B. (1995) *The Middle East*, New York: Touchstone.

Lindblom, C. (1977) *Politics and Markets*, New York: Basic Books.

Lipset, S. (1976) "The End of Ideology?" in M. Rejai (ed.) *Decline of Ideology?* Chicago, Illinois: Aldine.

Loveman, B. (1988) *Chile: The Legacy of Hispanic Capitalism*, New York: Oxford University Press.

Lowe, J. (1994) *The Great Powers, Imperialism and the German Problem*, New York: Routledge.

Lowenthal, A. (1991) "The United States and Latin American Democracy: Learning from History," in A. Lowenthal (ed.) *Exporting Democracy – The United States and Latin America: Case Studies*, Baltimore, Maryland: The Johns Hopkins University Press.

Luther, M. (1910) "Concerning Christian Liberty," in *The Harvard Classics*, Vol. 36, New York: P. F. Collier and Son.

Lynch, J. (1992) *The Hispanic World in Crisis and Change*, Oxford: Blackwell.

Machiavelli, Niccolo (1950) *The Prince and the Discourses*, New York: The Modern Library.

MacLachlan, C. and Rodriguez, J. (1990) *The Forging of the Cosmic Race*, Berkeley, California: University of California Press.

MacMullan, Ramsay (1984) *Christianizing the Roman Empire (A.D. 100–400)*, New Haven, Connecticut: Yale University Press.

Madelung, W. (1997) *The Succession to Muhammad*, Cambridge: Cambridge University Press.

Maier, C. (2000) *Crusade Propaganda and Ideology*, Cambridge: Cambridge University Press.

Manchester, W. (1993) *A World Lit Only By Fire*, Boston, Massachusetts: Little, Brown and Company.

Mango, C. (1980) *Byzantium: The Empire of New Rome*, New York: Charles Scribner's Sons.

Mann, M. (1986) *The Sources of Social Power*, Vols. I and II, New York: Cambridge University Press.

Marantz, P. (1989) "Gorbachev's 'New Thinking' about East–West Relations," in C. Jacobson (ed.) *Soviet Foreign Policy*, London: The Macmillan Press Ltd.

Martin, J. (1998) *Gramsci's Political Analysis*, New York: St. Martin's Press.

Marx, K. (1950) *The Communist Manifesto*, Chicago, Illinois: H. Regnery.

Mastnak, T. (2002) *Crusading Peace*, Berkeley, California: University of California Press.

Maxon, Y. (1973) *Control of Japanese Foreign Policy*, Westport, Connecticut: Greenwood Press.

McAlister, L. (1984) *Spain and Portugal in the New World*, Minneapolis, Minnesota: University of Minnesota Press.

McCarthy, J. (1997) *The Ottoman Turks*, London: Longman.

McDougall, W. (1997) *Promised Land, Crusader States*, Boston, Massachusetts: Houghton Mifflin Company.

McLellan, D. (1986) *Ideology*, Minneapolis, Minnesota: University of Minnesota Press.

Mearsheimer, J. (1990) "Why We Will Soon Miss the Cold War," in *The Atlantic*, 266.2, 35–50.

— (2001) *The Tragedy of Great Power Politics*, New York: W. W. Norton.

Mearsheimer, J. and Walt, S. (2006) "The Israel Lobby," in *London Review of Books*, 28.6, March 23.

Merrill, D. (ed.) (2001) "A Report to the President Pursuant to the President's Directive of January 31, 1950," in *Documentary History of the Truman Presidency*, Vol. 7, Bethesda, Maryland: University Publications of America.

Merton, R. (1973) *The Sociology of Science*, Chicago, Illinois: University of Chicago Press.

Messerschmidt, M. (1990) "Foreign Policy and Preparation for War," in *Germany and the Second World War*, Vol. 1, New York: Oxford University Press.

Mitchell, R. (1976) *Thought Control in Prewar Japan*, Ithaca, New York: Cornell University Press.

Mommsen, W. (1989) *The Political and Social Theory of Max Weber*, Chicago, Illinois: University of Chicago Press.

Morgenthau, H. (1985) *Politics among Nations: The Struggle for Power and Peace*. Revised by Kenneth W. Thompson, New York: Alfred Knopf.

— (2007) "Six Principles of Political Realism," in R. Art and R. Jervis (eds.) *International Politics*, 7th edition, New York: Pearson, Longman.

Mosse, G. (1954) "Puritan Political Thought and the Cases of Conscience," in *Church History*, 23.2, 109–18.

— (1978) *Toward the Final Solution*, New York: Howard Fertig.

Mote, F. (1999) *Imperial China, 900–1800*, Cambridge, Massachusetts: Harvard University Press.

Munro, D. C. (1895) "Urban and the Crusaders," Translations and Reprints from the Original Sources of European History, Vol. 1:2, Philadelphia, Pennsylvania: University of Pennsylvania, pp. 5–19.

Munro, D. G. (1960) *The Latin American Republics*, New York: Appleton-Century, Inc.

Mussolini, B. (1933) *The Political and Social Doctrine of Fascism*, London: Hogarth Press.

— (1963) "The Doctrines of Fascism," in J. Somerville and R. Santoni (eds.) *Social and Political Philosophy*, Garden City, New York: Doubleday.

Nasr, S. (1999) "European Colonialism and the Emergence of Modern Muslim States," in J. Esposito (ed.) *The Oxford History of Islam*, New York: Oxford University Press.

Naylor, P. (2000) *France and Algeria*, Gainesville, Florida: University Press of Florida.

Needham, J. (1971) *Science and Civilization in China*, Vol. IV, Cambridge: Cambridge University Press.

Nish, I. (2002) *Japanese Foreign Policy in the Interwar Period*, Westport, Connecticut: Praeger.

Nogee, J. and Donaldson, R. (1988) *Soviet Foreign Policy Since World War II*, New York: Pergamon Press.

North, D. and Thomas, R. (1982) *The Rise of the Western World*, Cambridge: Cambridge University Press.

Oberg, M. L. (1999) *Dominion and Civility: English Imperialism and Native Americans, 1585–1685*, Ithaca, New York: Cornell University Press.

Ofsdahl, S. (2000) "Nationalism as a Contributing Factor in the American Civil War," Maxwell Air Force Base, Alabama: Air Command and Staff College, Air University.

Oliver, R. and Atmore, A. (1994) *Africa Since 1800*, Cambridge: Cambridge University Press.

Pagden, A. (1990) *Spanish Imperialism and the Political Imagination*, New Haven, Connecticut: Yale University Press.

— (1995) *Lords of All the World: Ideologies of Empire in Spain, Britain, and France, c. 1500–c. 1800*, New Haven, Connecticut: Yale University Press.

Pangle, T. and Ahrensdorf, P. (1999) *Justice Among Nations*, Lawrence, Kansas: University Press of Kansas.

Paterson, T. (ed.) (1989) *Major Problems in American Foreign Policy: To 1914*, Vol. I, Lexington, Massachusetts: D. C. Heath and Company.

Paterson, T. and Merrill, D. (eds.) (1995a) *Major Problems in American Foreign Relations Since 1914*: Vol. I, Lexington, Massachusetts: D. C. Heath and Company.
— (1995b) "President Ronald Reagan Denounces the Soviet Union, 1981," in *Major Problems in American Foreign Relations Since 1914*, Vol. I, Lexington, Massachusetts: D. C. Heath and Company.
Peacock, A. and Wiseman, J. with Veverka, J. (1961) *The Growth of Public Expenditure in the United Kingdom*, Princeton, New Jersey: Princeton University Press.
Pelikan, J. (1987) *The Excellent Empire: The Fall of Rome and the Triumph of the Church*, New York: Harper and Row, Publishers.
Perkins, E. (1980) *The Economy of Colonial America*, New York: Columbia University Press.
Philpott, D. (2003) "Sovereignty," in *Stanford Encyclopedia of Philosophy*. www.plato. stanford.edu/entries/sovereignty
Pierce, R. (1976) "Ideological Thought in France," in M. Rejai (ed.) *Decline of Ideology?* Chicago, Illinois: Aldine.
Pike, F. (1967) *The Modern History of Peru*, New York: Frederick A. Praeger.
Pitts, J. (ed. and trans.) (2001) *Alexis De Tocqueville—Writings on Empire and Slavery*, Baltimore, Maryland: Johns Hopkins University Press.
Prak, M. (2005) *The Dutch Republic in the Seventeenth Century*. Trans. by Diane Webb, New York: Cambridge University Press.
Prochaska, D. (1990) *Making Algeria French*, Cambridge: Cambridge University Press.
Quataert, D. (2000) *The Ottoman Empire, 1700–1922*, Cambridge: Cambridge University Press.
Quinn, F. (2000) *The French Overseas Empire*, Westport, Connecticut: Praeger.
Reich, R. (2006) "The Poor Get Poorer," in *The New York Times Book Review*, April 2. www.nytimes.com/2006/04/02books/review/02re
Rejai, M. (ed.) (1971) *Decline of Ideology?* Chicago, Illinois: Aldine Atherton.
— (1984) *Comparative Political Ideologies*, New York: St. Martin's Press.
Reshetar, J. (1989) *The Soviet Polity: Government and Politics in the USSR*, New York: Harper and Row.
Reus-Smit, C. (1996) "The Constructive Turn: Critical Theory After the Cold War," Working Paper No. 4, Canberra: National Library of Australia.
Riasanovsky, N. (2000) *A History of Russia*, New York: Oxford University Press.
Rice, C. (2000) "Promoting the National Interest," *Foreign Affairs*, 79.1, 45–62.
Robinson, J. (1904) *Readings in European History*, London: Ginn.
Robinson, N. (1995) *A Critical History of Soviet Ideology*, Brookfield, Vermont: Edgar Elgar Publishing Company.
Rokkan, S. (1975) "Dimensions of State Formation and Nation Building: A Possible Paradigm for Research on Variations Within Europe," in C. Tilly (ed.) *The Formation of National States in Western Europe*, Princeton, New Jersey: Princeton University Press.
Rude, G. (1980) *Ideology and Popular Protest*, New York: Pantheon Books.
Sabine, G. (1950) *A History of Political Theory*, New York: Holt.
Sagan, S. (1989) "The Origins of the Pacific War," in R. Rotberg and T. Rabb (eds.) *The Origin and Prevention of Major Wars*, Cambridge: Cambridge University Press.
Salzman, M. (2002) *The Making of a Christian Aristocracy*, Cambridge, Massachusetts: Harvard University Press.
Sartori, G. (1987) *The Theory of Democracy Revisited*, Vol. II, Chatham, New Jersey: Chatham House.

Schama, S. (1987) *The Embarrassment of Riches: An Interpretation of Dutch Culture in the Golden Age*, New York: Alfred A. Knopf.

Schiffrin, H. (1980) *Reluctant Revolutionary*, Boston, Massachusetts: Little, Brown, and Company.

Schumpeter, J. (1954) *A History of Economic Analysis*, Oxford: Oxford University Press.

Scott, J. (1996) *Deciding to Intervene: The Reagan Doctrine and American Foreign Policy*, Durham, North Carolina: Duke University Press.

Seliger, M. (1976) *Ideology and Politics*, New York: The Free Press.

Shaban, M. (1971) *Islamic History, A.D. 600–750*, London: Cambridge University Press.

Simpson, W. and Jones, M. (2000) *Europe, 1783–1914*, London: Routledge.

Sinkin, R. (1979) *The Mexican Reform, 1855–1876. A Study of Liberal Nation-Building*, Austin, Texas: University of Texas Press.

Skinner, K., Anderson, A. and Anderson, M. (eds.) (2003) *Reagan: A Life in Letters*, New York: The Free Press.

Smith, A. (1987) *The Ethnic Origin of Nations*, New York: Blackwell.

— (1998) *Nationalism and Modernism*, London: Routledge.

Smith, G. (1992) *Soviet Politics: Struggling with Change*, New York: St. Martin's Press.

Smith, R. (1989) "Wilson's Pursuit of Order," in T. Paterson (ed.) (1989) *Major Problems in American Foreign Policy: To 1914*, Vol. I, Lexington, Massachusetts: D. C. Heath and Company.

Smith, S. (2001) "Reflectivist and Constructivist Approaches to International Theory," in J. Baylis and S. Smith (eds.) *The Globalization of World Politics*, Oxford: Oxford University Press.

Smith, W. (1982) *European Imperialism in the Nineteenth and Twentieth Centuries*, Chicago, Illinois: Nelson-Hall.

Soldani, S. (2001) "Approaching Europe in the Name of the Nation: The Italian Revolution, 1846/49," in D. Dowe, H. Haupt, D. Langewiesche, J. Sperber, and D. Higgins (eds.) *Europe in 1848*, New York: Bergham Books.

Southern, P. (2001) *The Roman Empire: From Severus to Constantine*, New York: Routledge.

Spryut, H. (1994) *The Sovereign States and Its Competitors: An Analysis of Systems Change*, Princeton, New Jersey: Princeton University Press.

Stalin, J. (1930) "Political Report of the Central Committee to the Sixteenth Congress of the CPSU (B)," June 27, in J. Stalin (1950), *Works*, Vol. 12, Moscow: Foreign Languages Publication House.

— (1972) *Economic Problems of Socialism in the USSR*, Beijing: Foreign Languages Press.

Stark, R. (1996) *The Rise of Christianity*, Princeton, New Jersey: Princeton University Press.

Stegemann, B. (1991) "Politics and Warfare in the First Phase of the German Offensive," in K. Maier, H. Rohde, B. Stegemann, and H. Umbreit (eds.) *Germany and the Second World War*, Oxford: Clarendon Press.

Stiglitz, J. and Charlton, A. (2005) *Fair Trade for All*, New York: Cambridge University Press.

Stora, B. (2001) *Algeria, 1830–2000*, Ithaca, New York: Cornell University Press.

Suganami, H. (1984) "Japan's Entry Into International Society," in H. Bull and A. Watson (eds.) *The Expansion of International Society*, Oxford: Clarendon Press.

Sun, L. K. (2002) *The Chinese National Character*, London: M. E. Sharpe.

Suny, R. (1998) *The Soviet Experiment*, New York: Oxford University Press.

Taubman, W. (1982) *Stalin's American Foreign Policy: From Entente to Détente to Cold War*, New York: W. W. Norton.

Taylor, A. (2001) *American Colonies*, New York: Penguin Putnam Inc

Thomas, P. (1991) "The Greenville Program, 1763–1765," in J. Greene and J. Pole (eds.) *The Blackwell Encyclopedia of the American Revolution*, Oxford: Blackwell.

Thompson, T. (1999) *The Bible in History*, London: Jonathan.

Tibi, B. (1997) *The Challenge of Fundamentalism*, Berkeley, California: University of California Press.

Tilly, C. (ed.) (1975) *The Formation of National States in Western Europe*, Princeton, New Jersey: Princeton University Press.

— (1990) *Coercion, Capital and European States, AD 990–1990*, Cambridge, Massachusetts: Basil Blackwell.

Tomlinson, B. (1976) *The Indian National Congress and the Raj, 1929–1942*, London: Macmillan Press.

Tsuzuki, C. (2000) *The Pursuit of Power in Modern Japan, 1825–1995*, New York: Oxford University Press.

Tyerman, C. (1998) *The Invention of the Crusades*, Toronto: University of Toronto Press.

United Nations (1960) "United Nations Resolution 1514, General Assembly: Declaration on the Granting of Independence to Colonial Countries and Peoples," December 14. www.un.org/documents/ga/res/15/ares15.htm

Visser, R. (1992) "Fascist Doctrine and the Cult of the Romanita," *Journal of Contemporary History*, 27.

Wade, R. (1998–1999) "The Fight Over Capital Flows," *Foreign Policy*. 113, Winter.

Wallerstein, I. (1974) *The Modern World System I*, New York: Academic Press.

Waltz, K. (1954) *Man, the States and War*, New York: Columbia University Press.

— (1979) *Theory of International Politics*, New York: Random House.

— (2007a) "The Anarchic Structure of World Politics," in R. Art and R. Jervis (eds.) *International Politics*, New York: Pearson, Longman.

— (2007b) "Nuclear Stability in South Asia," in R. Art and R. Jervis (eds.) *International Politics*, New York: Pearson, Longman.

— (2007c) "Globalization and Governance," in R. Art and R. Jervis (eds.) *International Politics*, New York: Pearson, Longman.

Wang G. (2000) *The Chinese Overseas*, Cambridge, Massachusetts: Harvard University Press.

Ward-Perkins, B. (2005) *The Fall of Rome and the End of Civilization*, New York: Oxford University Press.

Watson, A. (1992) *The Evolution of International Society*, London: Routledge.

Weber, E. (1972) *Europe Since 1715*, New York: W. W. Norton and Company.

Weber, M. (1958) *The Protestant Ethic and the Spirit of Capitalism*, New York: Charles Scribner's Sons.

— (2000) "The Nation," in J. Hutchinson and A. Smith (eds.) *Nationalism: Critical Concepts in Political Science*, Vol. I, New York: Routledge.

Weinberg, G. (1980) *The Foreign Policy of Hitler's Germany*, Chicago, Illinois: The University of Chicago Press.

Wendt, A. (2006) *Social Theory of International Politics*, Cambridge: Cambridge University Press.

Wendt, A. and Duvall, R. (1989) "Institutions and International Order," in E. Otto-Czempiel and J. Rosenau (eds.) *Global Changes and Theoretical Challenges: Approaches to World Politics in the 1990s*, Lexington, Massachusetts: Lexington Books.

Whitby, M. (2003) *Rome at War: AD 293–696*, New York: Routledge.

Wiarda, H. (1989) "The Dominican Republic: Mirror Legacies of Democracy and Authoritarianism," in L. Diamond, J. Hartlyn, J. Linz, and S. Lipset (eds.) *Democracy in Developing Countries – Latin America*, Boulder, Colorado: Lynn Reinner Publishers.

Willett, E. (1996) "Dialectic Materialism and Russian Objectives," in D. Merrill (ed.) *Documentary History of the Truman Presidency*, Vol. 7, Bethesda, Maryland: University Publications of America.

Willis, M. (1997) *The Islamist Challenge in Algeria*, New York: New York University Press.

Wills, J. (1994) *Mountains of Fame*, Princeton, New Jersey: Princeton University Press.

Wright, E. (1994) *The Search for Liberty*, Vol. I, Oxford: Blackwell.

Xu, G. (2005) *China and the Great War*, New York: Cambridge University Press.

Yergin, D. (1978) *Shattered Peace*, Boston, Massachusetts: Houghton Mifflin Company.

Yergin, D. and Stanislaw, J. (1998) *The Commanding Heights*, New York: Simon and Schuster.

Young, L. (1998) *Japan's Total Empire*, Berkeley, California: University of California Press.

Zagare, F. (1990) "Rationality and Deterrence," *World Politics*, 42.2, 38–60.

Zernatto, G. (2000) "Nation: the History of a Word," in J. Hutchinson and A. Smith (eds.) *Nationalism: Critical Concepts in Political Science*, Vol. I, New York: Routledge.

Zimmermann, W. (2002) *First Great Triumph*, New York: Farrar, Strauss and Girouz.

Index

and relationship with France, 142, 146
and relationship with the Soviet
Union, 142, 144, 145, 146
and relationship with the USA, 146
and struggle against Jews, 142, 143,
144, 145, 146
on task of program-maker, 145
and Treaty of Versailles, 145
Holy Roman Empire, 35, 47, 49, 53, 54,
56, 64, 65
holy war, 32, 33, 36

ideology, 1, 11, 12, 14, 15, 16, 19, 20, 50,
64, 76, 94, 131, 158, 161, 171, 199,
199, 202, 205, 206, 207, 208, 210–13
and elite, 12
and interaction with politics, 15–16
and its degree of openness and
flexibility, 12, 168
and mass mobilization, 12, 13
and its programmatic dimensions, 12,
13, 93
as an action, 12, 13
as a bridge between foreign policy and
the structure of the world system,
201
as an emotion, 12, 13, 93
as a myth, 12, 13
as a normative function 12, 13, 93
conceptualization of, 11, 13
ideological
conviction, 57
disparity, 40, 155, 208
hegemony, 1, 9, 170
power, 10, 41
religion, 65
transformation, 48
imperialism (*see also* under names of
countries or empires), 6, 18, 63, 99,
100,106, 131, 209, 210
and nationalism, 100, 102, 106, 131,
210
India, 118, 210
and East India Company, 118, 119,
124
and 1857 mutiny, 119, 123
and friction between Hindus and
Muslims, 123, 124
and First World War, 120, 122
and Government of India Act, 122,
123
and National Congress, 120, 123, 124
and Lord Curzon, 121
and Mohandas Ghandi, 121–24

and Montagu-Chelmsford
Declaration, 122
and Muslim League, 121, 124
and Muslims, 121, 123, 124
and nationalism, 119, 120, 123, 124,
130
and race, 120,
and relationship with Britain, 118–24,
130
and religion, 120
and Rowlatt Acts, 122–23
inquisition, 45
Isabella (Queen of Spain), 40, 45, 46, 47
Islam, 14, 16, 17, 18, 20, 28, 33, 36, 41,
42, 43, 45, 210
as political ideology, 28, 36, 43, 63, 64,
98, 201
Islamic Empire, 14, 16, 29, 30, 35, 42, 43,
44, 202, 203, 204
Islamic radicalism, 19, 190–98, 210, 212
and Abu A'la al-Maududi, 194
and Afghan war, 196
and al-Qaeda, 196, 197, 209, 213
and Ayatullah Ruhallah Khomeini,
194–95
and Balfour Declaration, 190
and Britain, 190, 191, 193, 194
and creation of Jewish state, 190, 196
and France, 190, 191
and Gamal Abdel Nasser, 193
and Hassan al-Banna, 193
and Iranian revolution, 194, 195
and Jamal al-Din al-Afghani, 192–93
and Muhammad Abduh, 193
and Muslim Brethren, 193
and Mustafa Kemal Ataturk, 191, 196
and nationalism, 191, 192
and Osama bin Laden, 197, 198, 209
and Ottoman Empire, 190, 191
and Pan-Arabism, 193
and Saddam Hussein, 197
and Sayyid Qutb, 193–94
and Sykes-Picot Agreement, 190
and Soviet Union, 196
and USA, 195, 196
Italy, 7, 26,
and nationalism, 131, 206

Japan, 6, 7, 18, 46, 98, 131, 208, 210
and adoption of Western political
practices, 147
and *An Investigation of Global Policy
with the Yamato Race as Nucleus,*
152

ROUTLEDGE
INTERNATIONAL
HANDBOOKS

Routledge International Handbooks is an outstanding, award-winning series that provides cutting-edge overviews of classic research, current research and future trends in Social Science, Humanities and STM.

Each *Handbook*:

- is introduced and contextualised by leading figures in the field
- features specially commissioned original essays
- draws upon an international team of expert contributors
- provides a comprehensive overview of a sub-discipline.

Routledge International Handbooks aim to address new developments in the sphere, while at the same time providing an authoritative guide to theory and method, the key sub-disciplines and the primary debates of today.

If you would like more information on our on-going *Handbooks* publishing programme, please contact us.

Tel: +44 (0)20 701 76566
Email: reference@routledge.com

www.routledge.com/reference

Biomechanics and H
Movement Science
Edited by Youlan Hong and Roger E

The Routledge Compani
Nonprofit Marketing
Edited by Adrian Sargeant and Wa

The Routledge Compani
Fair Value and Financial Re
Edited by Peter Walton

Routledge Handbc
Globalization Stu
Edited by Bryan S. Turner

International
Handbook of